Antitrust and
Regulation

Antitrust and Regulation:
Essays in Memory of
John J. McGowan

edited by Franklin M. Fisher

The MIT Press
Cambridge, Massachusetts
London, England

This book was set in Apollo by Asco Trade Typesetting Ltd., Hong Kong and printed and bound by Halliday Lithograph in the United States of America

Library of Congress Cataloging in Publication Data

Main entry under title:

Antitrust and regulation.

Bibliography: p.
Includes index.
Contents: Mergers for power or progress? / John J. McGowan—Competition and antitrust in the petroleum industry / George A. Hay and Robert J. Reynolds—Anticompetitive mergers / William J. Kolasky, Jr., Phillip A. Proger, and Roy T. Englert, Jr.—[etc.]
1. Antitrust law—United States—Addresses, essays, lectures.   2. McGowan, John J.—Addresses, essays, lectures.   I. McGowan, John J.   II. Fisher, Franklin M.

KF1649.A2A415   1985   343.73′072   84-25063
ISBN 0-262-06093-0   347.30372

Contents

Introduction   vii
Franklin M. Fisher

1   Mergers for Power or Progress?   1
John J. McGowan

2   Competition and Antitrust in the Petroleum Industry: An
Application of the Merger Guidelines   15
George A. Hay and Robert J. Reynolds

3   Anticompetitive Mergers: Prevention and Cure   49
William J. Kolasky, Jr., Phillip A. Proger, and Roy T. Englert, Jr.

4   Market Definition and the SIC Approach   85
James W. McKie

5   Profitability and Market Share   101
M. A. Adelman and Bruce E. Stangle

6   Nonprice Anticompetitive Behavior by Dominant Firms
toward the Producers of Complementary Products   115
J. A. Ordover, A. O. Sykes, and R. D. Willig

7   Market Conduct under Section 2: When Is It
Anticompetitive?   131
Robin C. Landis and Ronald S. Rolfe

8   Can Exclusive Franchises Be Bad?   153
Franklin M. Fisher

9   Mixing Regulatory and Antitrust Policies in the Electric
    Power Industry: The Price Squeeze and Retail Market
    Competition   173
    Paul L. Joskow

10 Policymakers' Preferences for Alternative Allocations of the
    Broadcast Spectrum   241
    Forrest Nelson and Roger Noll

11 The Financial Interest and Syndication Rules in Network
    Television: Regulatory Fantasy and Reality   263
    Franklin M. Fisher

12 Borrowing from Peter to Pay Paul: More on Departures of
    Price from Marginal Cost   299
    Almarin Phillips and Gary L. Roberts

    List of Contributors   309
    Index   311

Introduction

Franklin M. Fisher

John J. McGowan was born in Ottawa in 1936. He received his undergraduate degree from the University of Toronto in 1958. That degree was in chemical engineering, but after a short time in that profession, John found his true vocation, industrial organization economics. He attended graduate school in economics at Yale University and received his master's and doctor of philosophy degrees from that institution.

After receiving his doctorate in 1965, John became a member of the faculty at Yale, where he remained until 1973, specializing in industrial organization and in antitrust and regulation policy. His first published work, "The Effect of Alternative Antimerger Policies on the Size Distribution of Firms," [1] concerned a subject, mergers, to which he was to return periodically throughout his career, ending with his work on merger guidelines as represented by the first chapter in this volume.

Another lifelong interest, the economics of television, also appeared early in John's Yale career. Several publications resulted, culminating in the publication in 1973 of the book *Economic Aspects of Television Regulation*, which he wrote with Roger Noll and Merton J. Peck.[2] The book received the first National Book Award of the National Association of Educational Broadcasters.

While the Noll-Peck-McGowan book was the most important of John's collaborative efforts during his Yale period, it was far from being the only one. While he sometimes worked and published alone, collaboration was a mode of research that came easily to John and, as those who worked with him can attest, he was a great colleague. His principal collaborator while at Yale was Merton J. Peck, but, in addition to Roger Noll, he also worked with George Hay and Henry C. Wallich. After leaving Yale, he collaborated with David S. Evans, Joen E. Greenwood, and me.

John left Yale in 1973 and joined the staff of Charles River Associates

(CRA), a Boston-based consulting and research firm. At CRA, he quickly became Vice President and a member of the Board of Directors. He directed many industry studies connected with litigation support and assisted counsel in preparing major antitrust cases and regulatory proceedings. John was particularly active in the antitrust litigation involving the television networks and in the various IBM antitrust cases. While much of his work during this period was necessarily confidential, he continued to publish. The most important publication during this time was the book arising from the IBM case, *Folded, Spindled, and Mutilated: Economic Analysis and U.S. v. IBM*, which he wrote with Joen Greenwood and me.[3]

Unfortunately, *Folded, Spindled, and Mutilated* was a posthumous publication, for John died in April 1982. He remained at CRA until that time, remarkably continuing a full round of professional activities until the very end, despite the three-year length of his terminal illness. He is survived by his wife Adrienne, his sons John Jr. and Michael, and his daughter Siobhan.

As his career suggests, John McGowan's interest in economics was both academic (in the best sense) and practical. He both published widely and gave detailed practical counsel to private and governmental clients. He had the rare ability to bridge the disciplinary gap that often separates economists and lawyers, and in his last year he served as a member of the task force of lawyers and economists which revised the merger guidelines of the Department of Justice.

John used and appreciated the tools and results of economic analysis but never lost sight of the fact that application of those tools in real situations requires both a detailed knowledge of the facts and a serious understanding of how the analytical results are achieved. He had little use for economists who draw sweeping conclusions from a superficial understanding and application of their discipline.

A tough-minded professional economist, John was far from being a hard man in his personal relations. His teachers, his students, and his colleagues and collaborators remember him with affection as well as respect. His influence was widespread, and the invitation to contribute to a memorial volume was received either with enthusiastic acceptance or with genuine regret when participation proved impractical.

The chapters in this volume reflect John McGowan's lively interest in applied industrial organization, in particular his interest in combining economic and legal analysis to inform public policy. They range from fairly general analyses to studies that focus on specific industries.

The first section of the book is concerned with the antitrust treatment of mergers, specifically, the merger guidelines adopted by the Antitrust Division of the Justice Department in 1982 on the recommendation of the task force of which John was a member. Indeed, the first chapter is a lightly edited part of John's own contribution to the work of the task force; it was a background paper and, like the other works in this volume, has not been published previously.

The existence of merger guidelines should, in principle, be a useful way of increasing certainty and reducing litigation. Whether that is so depends on the ease and certainty with which the guidelines can be applied in practice and how the Justice Department and the prospective merger partners interact. The two other chapters that deal with mergers examine these issues from different points of view. George A. Hay and Robert J. Reynolds offer an economic analysis of the application of the merger guidelines to an actual merger proposal, the proposed 1982 acquisition of Cities Service Corporation, then the nineteenth largest oil company in the United States, by Gulf Oil Corporation, at that time the sixth largest and more recently the object itself of an acquisition by Standard of California. The second chapter, by William J. Kolasky, Jr., Phillip A. Proger, and Roy T. Englert, Jr., studies the way in which the premerger notification provisions of the Hart–Scott–Rodino Antitrust Improvements Act have affected the behavior of potential merger parties and the antitrust authorities.

The next two chapters deal with issues that seem simple in theory but are far from being so in practice. In a sense, both the questions of defining a "market" and the relation between profitability and market share arise because of the understandable but naive desire to identify monopoly power through simple indicators, either market share or profits. The view that this can be done was not one for which John McGowan had much sympathy.[4] He well understood that the world is not that simple and that the analysis of monopoly power requires a full-scale investigation of the facts, particularly of those constraints which the existence of actual and potential competitors and their products place on the ability of a given firm or group of firms to depart from competitive behavior. In his chapter, James W. McKie considers the usefulness of the Standard Industrial Classification as a guide to the constraints placed on a set of firms by supply substitutability, hence, as a guide to sensible market definition. In chapter 5, Morris A. Adelman and Bruce E. Stangle provide a neat empirical demonstration of the proposition that, even putting aside measurement problems, relations between market share and profitability are not a simple matter of one-way causation.

The chapters considered thus far are largely concerned with market structure; the next group are primarily concerned with market conduct. In one way or another, all relate to the issue of what sort of behavior on the part of a dominant firm should be regarded as anticompetitive. J. A. Ordover, A. O. Sykes, and R. D. Willig examine the economics of this question with regard to the actions of a dominant firm toward producers of complementary products; this was an important issue in the IBM case John McGowan was involved in for so long, as was the general issue of what constitutes anticompetitive behavior.[5] That case, a single-firm monopoly case brought under Section 2 of the Sherman Act, involved the *Alcoa*[6] doctrine that a firm with monopoly power can violate Section 2 by deliberately acquiring or maintaining that power even if the firm commits no act illegal in itself. In chapter 7 Robin C. Landis and Ronald S. Rolfe examine the crucial question of what sort of acts such a violation logically requires if the antitrust laws are to protect competition rather than competitors; they propose the test to be used.

In my chapter on exclusive franchises, I ask a much narrower question: whether, given that a manufacturing firm has a legal monopoly, there exist any cases in which that firm will wish to set up an exclusive dealer for anticompetitive reasons rather than those of efficiency. Contrary to much current doctrine, it is shown that such cases do indeed exist.

The final chapter in this group also considers vertical actions on the part of a dominant firm, but it does so in the context of a particular industry rather than merely in theory. Paul L. Joskow analyzes the interaction of antitrust and regulation in the context of the electric power industry. He specifically examines the question whether antitrust concern about "price squeezes" is justified in such a context and concludes that it is not. In doing so, he draws on a rich factual context. Joskow's essay serves as a bridge to the last group of chapters, those on regulation.

Two of those chapters concern the regulation of television, and the third has implications for the regulation of telecommunications, both subjects of considerable interest to John McGowan. In their chapter, Forrest Nelson and Roger Noll consider whether the decisions allocating channels in the broadcast spectrum exhibit consistency with an articulatable decision rule. In examining this question they took the unusual step of performing an experiment, using six members of the Federal Communications Commission and nine members of the congressional committee that oversees it. Nelson and Noll conclude that the preferences involved *do* admit of consistent collective decisions, although congressional and commission preference patterns are by no means identical.

My own chapter in this group is concerned with the economics of the Financial Interest and Syndication Rules, rules imposed on the major television networks by the FCC in the early 1970s and reinforced by the consent decrees that settled the network antitrust cases brought by the Antitrust Division. This was a matter on which John McGowan and I worked together for nearly a decade. John shared the view that neither the rules nor the antitrust cases made any economic sense whatever, a view that at least some policymakers have come to understand.

In the final chapter, Almarin Phillips and Gary L. Roberts consider not how regulation has gone astray in fact but how it should operate in theory. They analyze the optimal pricing of demand-interrelated goods and establish that, contrary to simple doctrine, such pricing may require some rates to be set below marginal cost.

All of the chapters in this book went through an extensive refereeing process under my general supervision. That process was not always easy; some papers had to be heavily revised, and a few were rejected with regret. I am grateful to the many authors who acted as referees and to Alvin Klevorick, Robert Larner, Richard Levin, Richard Mancke, Charles Manski, Stephen Martin, Merton J. Peck, and Richard Schmalensee, all of whom also served in that capacity. Special thanks also go to Robert Bolick, who provided tireless encouragement, administrative support, and invaluable advice, as he also did for *Folded, Spindled, and Mutilated*. Finally, I thank Michael Klass for suggesting this book in the first place. I hope it is a book John McGowan would have been interested in reading. If it is, then others interested in antitrust and regulation will find it worthwhile.

Notes

1. John J. McGowan, "The Effect of Alternative Antimerger Policies on the Size Distribution of Firms," *Yale Economic Essays*, 5, no. 2 (Fall 1965), pp. 423–474.

2. Roger Noll, Merton J. Peck, and John J. McGowan, *Economic Aspects of Television Regulation* (Washington: The Brookings Institution, 1973).

3. Franklin M. Fisher, John J. McGowan, and Joen E. Greenwood, *Folded, Spindled, and Mutilated: Economic Analysis and U.S. v. IBM* (Cambridge: The MIT Press, 1983).

4. See, for example, Fisher, McGowan, and Greenwood, *Folded, Spindled, and Mutilated*, esp. chaps. 3, 4, and 7, and Franklin M. Fisher and John J. McGowan, "On the Misuse of Accounting Rates of Return to Infer Monopoly Profits," *American Economic Review* 73 (March 1983), pp. 82–97.

5. *United States v. International Business Machines Corporation*, Docket number 69 Civ. (DNE) Southern District of New York. The same issue arose in the private suits brought against IBM; see Fisher, McGowan, and Greenwood, *Folded, Spindled, and Mutilated*, chap. 8, esp. pp. 310–339.

6. *United States v. Aluminum Co. of America*, 148 F.2d 416 (2d Cir. 1945).

Antitrust and Regulation

1

Mergers for Power or Progress?

John J. McGowan

The 1968 Merger Guidelines of the Department of Justice embody four main economic principles[1]: first, that the number and size distribution of firms selling in a market are important determinants of competitiveness and, indeed, that rather small increases in market share (as little as one percentage point in some cases) may substantially reduce competition; second, that vertical integration may reduce competition by raising entry barriers; third, that conglomerate acquisitions can reduce competition by eliminating potential entrants, providing opportunities for reciprocity, or entrenching dominant positions; and fourth, that efficiency can be enhanced just as well by internal growth as by mergers and acquisitions. This chapter provides a brief overview of relevant economic arguments and empirical research and offers tentative suggestions as to their implications for merger policy.

Concentration, Market Shares, and Competition

Antitrust lawyers must by now feel well acquainted with the structure, conduct, and performance paradigm used by many economists to analyze competition. In its broadest form the paradigm holds that market performance results from the interaction of market structure (the number and size distribution of firms, entry conditions, demand and cost conditions, among others) and conduct (pricing and product behavior).[2] Briefly, the underlying theoretical justification is that such factors as demand, cost, and entry conditions determine the prospective returns from collusive behavior among market participants, whereas the number and size distribution of firms determine the cost and likely success of undertaking and maintaining collusive strategies. Thus structure determines performance, at least in a probabilistic sense.[3]

Attempts to test the empirical validity of the paradigm led to the hypothesis of a profits-concentration relationship. Among the first efforts at empirical verification and estimation were those of Bain, Stigler, and Mann.[4] By the time the Guidelines were announced, several other studies, most of them tending to confirm an association of rising industry concentration with rising industry profit rates, had been published.[5] Indeed, by early 1969 the White House Task Force on Antitrust Policy asserted:

Studies found a close association between high levels of concentration and persistently high rates of return on capital, particularly in those industries in which the four largest firms account for more than 60 percent of sales. . . . It is the persistence of high profits over extended time periods and over whole industries rather than individual firms that suggests artificial restraints on output and the absence of fully effective competition.[6]

The asserted persistence of the profits-concentration relationship was challenged by Brozen. Unable to replicate successfully the findings of Bain, Mann, and Stigler, he concluded that the relationship, if any, was transitory.[7] Numerous later studies, however, almost uniformly found some support for the relationship, though the strength of the association apparently varies over time for reasons that are not yet well understood. There is, then, general agreement that a positive relationship between profit rates and concentration exists, although the exact form of the relationship, its meaning and relevance for antitrust, are still widely debated.

Most studies of the profits-concentration relationship postulate a linear relationship between some measure of industry profit rate (usually profits as a percentage of total assets or stockholders' equity) and the four-firm concentration ratio, as well as such other explanatory variables as industry growth rate. Most studies find that each percentage-point increase in concentration tends to raise the industry profit rate by one-tenth of a percentage point or less. The implications for merger policy are twofold: (1) horizontal mergers that do not increase the four-firm concentration ratio have no effect on profit rates and hence perhaps no effect on competition; and (2) every merger that leads to an increase in the four-firm concentration ratio increases industry profits and hence reduces competition.

Still other studies hypothesize a nonlinear relationship of profits to concentration and find either no relationship when concentration is below a critical level (generally between 45 and 60 percent) or that increasing concentration has a lesser effect below the critical concentration level than above it.[8] Such studies imply that mergers may have little or no effect when concentration is below the critical level or when they do not increase the excess of the four-firm concentration ratio above its critical Level. A recent study of this kind by Kwoka suggests that mergers would not increase the industry profit rate unless they increased the share of the two largest firms and may actually reduce profits if they increase the market share of the third largest firm.[9]

In addition to differences in the form and parameters of the profits-concentration relationship, the meaning of the relationship has become much less clear. As noted above, most researchers in the field believed, at least initially, that a positive profits-concentration relationship supported the inference that increasing concentration led to increased collusive activity or market power. H. Demsetz was the first to seriously question this inference,[10] pointing out that successful collusion by some firms in a market should raise prices and profits for all participants in the market. Thus, the profit rates of small firms should be correlated with concentration if collusion were the explanation for the positive association between industry profit rates and concentration. Demsetz, however, found no relationship between concentration and small-firm profit rates; thus he rejected collusion as the explanation of the profits-concentration relationship. Instead, he hypothesized that the relationship was due to the superior efficiency of leading firms in concentrated industries, as opposed to leading firms in less concentrated industries. This, Demsetz argued, was likely to be so because concentration could persist only if the leading firms were better than their smaller competitors at producing and marketing products and should result in the positive correlation between the differential profit rate of large firms over small firms and the level of concentration that he found.

Recent research promises to further cloud interpretation of the profits-concentration relationship. Using statistical simulation experiments, David Ravenscraft has shown that studies typical of those done are likely to confound the price and efficiency effects of concentration, to overstate the effect of concentration on market power, and to find critical concentration ratios where there are none.[11] In addition, Franklin Fisher and John McGowan, building on original insights of Ezra Solomon and Thomas R. Stauffer, have shown that accounting measures of profits, such as return on assets or stock-holders' equity, do not give even approximate measures of the economic rate of return in practical applications.[12] Because it is the economic rate of return that is equalized among firms in competitive markets and elevated in non-competitive markets, Fisher and McGowan argue that the profits-concentration relationship as estimated in all the studies described above may not have implications for either a relationship between market structure and market power or a relationship between market structure and efficiency.

We are apparently left with no better empirical foundation for the structure-conduct-performance paradigm than we had when the Guidelines were originally adopted. There still seems to be a reasonable theoretical underpinning for the relationship, particularly when market structure is taken to encompass entry, cost, and demand conditions. The accumulated research of more than a decade, however, seems only to have demonstrated the grave difficulties that empirical verification of the theory faces, while providing little confidence in the strength, magnitude, or cause of the observed association between profit rates and concentration.

Vertical Integration

The extent of vertical integration between stages of production and distribution is an element of market structure whose effect on competition is neither well understood nor accurately measured. It is generally agreed that a monopolist at one stage of production could, through vertical integration, extend his monopoly to other stages of production; but it is far from obvious why he would do so, since he could achieve the fruits of that action merely by setting the price of the already monopolized product. The advantages of vertical integration to a monopolist are clearer when customers can be grouped according to the elasticity of their demand for his product. Maximizing the fruits of monopoly in this case requires setting relatively high prices for customers with inelastic demands and relatively low prices for customers with more elastic demands. Such price differentiation, however, can be successful only if arbitrage (low-price customers reselling to high-price customers) can be suppressed. Vertical integration into the industry of the customers with more elastic demands is one way a monopolist might suppress arbitrage and facilitate price differentiation; but such a strategy, to be effective, requires monopoly at one stage of production and complete vertical integration of the set of customers with highly elastic demands for the monopolized product. Partial integration, with or without preexisting monopoly, has no clear effect on competition.

Another hypothetical effect of vertical integration is an increase in barriers to entry. According to this line of reasoning, vertical integration makes it difficult or impossible to enter a single stage of production and/or distribution, thus requiring integrated entry into both stages, with consequent higher capital requirements and increased entry barriers. Even granting for the moment that vertical integration requires integrated entry, it is by no means clear that an increase in entry barriers occurs. To be sure, integrated entry may require more capital, but whether that raises the entry barriers depends on whether capital requirements are a barrier to entry—a proposition about which economists hold widely different opinions and on which empirical evidence is almost nonexistent. A variant on this analysis of the effects of an integrated-entry requirement finds the possibility of higher entry barriers in the increased transaction and information costs which integrated entry might require.[13]

On even shakier foundation than the notion that integrated entry raises entry barriers is the proposition that vertical integration requires integrated entry. Clearly, if all incumbents are vertically integrated, it may seem that integrated entry is the only feasible alternative, and if the capital requirements or transactions and information costs of integrated entry impose costs on would-be entrants that have not been borne by incumbents, then vertical integration may be said to increase barriers to entry. So long as there are significant transactions in which seller, buyer, or both are not integrated, however, nonintegrated entry seems a feasible alternative, so that some vertical integration will not have raised entry barriers.

A final attempt to discern an anticompetitive effect from vertical integration is the foreclosure argument.[14] By acquiring customers, so the argument goes, one firm can foreclose its competitors from outlets for their products or from their sources of supply, thus using vertical acquisitions to monopolize one or both stages of production or distribution. The most incisive response to the foreclosure argument in this form is that it requires both horizontal integration and vertical integration and therefore provides no separate basis for concern with vertical mergers and acquisitions. A slightly different form of the argument hypothesizes that actual or potential foreclosure arising from one large or several small vertical acquisitions may trigger defensive vertical acquisitions by other suppliers and customers seeking to ensure their outlets or sources of supply.[15] Thus initial foreclosure and the response to it may lead to extensive vertical integration, leading in turn to the possibility that nonintegrated entry may become uneconomic and that entry barriers may be raised. But all of this, as noted above, rests on gross speculation and flimsy evidence about capital requirements as barriers to entry.

None of the preceding discussion represents new theoretical or empirical knowledge. A similar summary would have adequately and accurately characterized the state of knowledge about the competitive consequences of vertical integration and vertical acquisitions when the Guidelines were adopted. Indeed, shortly thereafter, President Nixon's Task Force on Productivity and Competition stated: "Our task force is of one mind on the undesirability of an extensive and vigorous policy against vertical mergers: Vertical integration has not been shown to be presumptively noncompetitive and the guidelines err in so treating it."[16]

Recent economic analysis of vertical integration has focused on it as a means of reducing uncertainty, reducing transactions costs, and providing a superior alternative to contracts as insurance against exploitation by customers or suppliers.[17] These analyses strengthen the position that vertical integration is likely to enhance rather than diminish allocative efficiency.

Potential Entry, Reciprocity, and Entrenchment

The importance of entry conditions and potential entry to market behavior became prominent during the late 1950s and early 1960s, primarily as a result of the work of Joe S. Bain and Paolo Sylos-Labini.[18] The basic point is simple and well recognized: The exercise of market power by incumbent firms is constrained by the ability of new firms to enter their market. The price or profit rate in a market cannot rise above the point at which new entry becomes profitable, because further increases will attract new entrants who compete prices and profits down until additional entry is no longer profitable. During the last fifteen to twenty years the theory has been refined somewhat, particularly in order to cast it in a dynamic framework and explore its implications in cases where incumbents follow strategies that seem to raise the level of price and profit required to induce entry.[19]

It is usual in formal models of the interaction of entry conditions and incumbents' behavior to define the difficulty of entry or the height of the entry barrier in terms of a single price above which entry will occur. Nevertheless, it is undoubtedly more realistic to think of the probability of one or more firms entering (alternatively, the number of likely entrants) as increasing with the price or price-cost margin charged by incumbents. This naturally leads to the idea of some firms being better situated to enter than others and to the possibility that higher prices and profits may be attainable by eliminating the best- or better-situated potential entrants. The Guidelines focus on conglomerate acquisitions as one way to eliminate potential entrants and make such acquisitions challengeable on that basis. They might, however, have included vertical acquisitions as perhaps even more likely to eliminate potential entrants.

There is little disagreement among economists on the theoretical proposition that the presence or absence of potential entry may influence actual competition, particularly when entry barriers are substantial and market conditions are otherwise propitious for collusive behavior. Disagreements arise in the practical application of the theory when the importance of potential entry must be assessed, the set of potential entrants identified and enumerated, and the effects of the elimination of one or more of them on actual competition gauged. The Guidelines as originally promulgated leapt over these difficulties by focusing on acquisitions and mergers among potential entrants and incumbents with large market shares or among the leading firms in markets. Thus the Guidelines implicitly assume that collusive behavior and barriers to entry can be inferred from high market shares and concentration ratios, a proposition whose empirical validity is open to serious doubt. The Guidelines also appear to assume, with no foundation whatsoever, that the elimination of any potential entrant, no matter how many are left or how well situated they are, will adversely affect competition.

Economists who see a danger in reciprocal dealing see it as (1) inefficient (for example, buying at inflated prices in exchange for an implicit agreement for the seller to do likewise), (2) extending market power, or (3) a form of nonprice competition that may tend to make entry more difficult and to increase concentration.[20] While all of these are possibilities, items 1 and 2 are argued to be irrational or minimal in their effects on competition. The importance of item 3 can be questioned on the same grounds as the foreclosure phenomenon associated with vertical integration. Others argue that reciprocity may in fact promote competition by facilitating cheating on regulatorily or colusively set prices.[21]

The concern with entrenchment in the Guidelines seems founded on the notions that (1) absolutely large firms have a "deep pocket" that is likely to be used for nefarious purposes; (2) firms may be able to induce customers to buy from them on the basis of threats, expressed or implied, to withhold other goods or services from them (another monopoly extension argument); and (3) diversified firms may be able to achieve economies of scale or scope in advertising, research, or other activities that facilitate product differentiation. Fear of the deep pocket is perennial, but both economic theory and empirical studies indicate that use of the deep pocket is at worst rare, especially when that use means incurring losses to drive competitors out of business.[22]

Extension of monopoly through the mechanism described in item 2 in the preceding paragraph rests on the same theoretical formulations as the anticompetitive consequences of tying, full-line forcing, or block booking and is subject to the same shortcomings. Briefly, the theory of these practices shows that they are rational ways to exercise monopoly power only where the products are complementary or when they facilitate price discrimination. These practices, while increasing monopoly profits, *may* result in more efficient allocation of resources.

Finally, diversification, even if it enables firms to differentiate their products more effectively, is not demonstrably anticompetitive. Presumably, the authors of the Guidelines believed that increasing product differentiation increases barriers to entry and that increasing product differentiation is (sometimes? always?) undesirable. The first consideration is invalid as a general economic proposition, however, and the second cannot be proved within the strictures of modern welfare economics, requiring, as it does, external judgments about consumers' preferences.

Mergers and Efficiency

The Justice Department's reluctance to concern itself with efficiency-enhancing arguments to justify otherwise objectionable mergers rested on three beliefs, all with some merit. First was the belief that most horizontal mergers that the Guidelines would catch were unlikely to generate substantial additions to efficiency. This was presumably founded on studies by economists showing that the minimum efficient scale of plant was small relative to market size in most American manufacturing industries and rarely, if ever, large enough to account for concentration levels already in existence. Coupled with the absence of evidence of substantial multiplant economies, this might have justified the belief that a hard-nosed policy toward horizontal mergers was essentially costless in terms of foregone efficiency.

Second, restricting mergers did not itself restrict firms from growing within their markets, integrating forward or backward, or diversifying into other markets. Presumably, if growth, integration, or diversification increased efficiency, firms would achieve such efficiencies through other means or through mergers and acquisitions that did not offend the Guidelines. This belief provided further justification for a hard line on horizontal mergers and probably seemed appropriate for other mergers in view of the lack of clear evidence that vertical and conglomerate mergers enhance the efficiency of surviving firms.

The final justification for eschewing judgments about efficiency enhancement was that it is extremely difficult, if not impossible, for the Justice Department or the courts to assess the reliability of the relevant arguments and evidence. This argument is undoubtedly as valid as it ever was, but the first two deserve further consideration.

In an important article, Oliver E. Williamson demonstrated that substantial increases in market power (as measured by increase in price) can be offset by comparatively small increases in efficiency (reductions in unit costs).[23] In addition, several case studies and sample surveys have shown that some mergers, especially horizontal ones, do increase efficiency by facilitating better production planning, adjustment to changing technology, and more effective utilization of central staff resources.[24] The evidence also suggests that increases in efficiency would have come about more slowly, if at all, without the mergers. Finally, Leonard W. Weiss reported that the extent of suboptimal capacity in industries decreased with rising concentration and suggested, therefore, that horizontal mergers contributed to efficiency.[25]

These empirical studies indicate that, even though increases in efficiency or adaptations to changing market conditions can occur through internal growth, mergers and acquisitions may be a speedier and less costly means. Taken together with Williamson's demonstration that allocative efficiency is more sensitive to cost reductions than to increases in market power, these findings warrant reconsideration of the Guidelines' assumption that a restrictive merger policy is unlikely to incur significant costs in foregone efficiency.

Implications for Merger Policy

It is sometimes said, usually by economists, that the ideal merger policy would prevent all mergers with negative net effects on allocative efficiency and permit all others. Such an objective is not only unachievable but also meaningless in a world of necessarily limited, costly, ambiguous information. Any policy, even a case-by-case rule-of-reason approach, would result in errors, allowing mergers with net negative allocative effects and prohibiting mergers that would have been beneficial. Thus, a wise merger policy recognizes that mistakes are inevitable and that information is costly and balances the expected costs of administration with the expected net allocative effects from following the policy. Our knowledge of the effects of mergers on market power and efficiency was not sufficient in 1968 and is not sufficient now to determine an optimal merger policy or even one that has a high degree of likelihood of achieving some specified level of benefit. Consequently there remains plenty of room for both judgment and disagreement about appropriate merger policy.

The original Guidelines embodied the judgment that most mergers, especially those involving firms with large market shares or with leading positions in concentrated industries, had a high likelihood of creating, increasing, or extending market power and almost no likelihood of enhancing efficiency that could not and would not be otherwise achieved. Accepting those judgments, a restrictive policy toward mergers prevents mergers with almost any chance of adversely affecting competition and runs little risk of prohibiting beneficial mergers, since the latter are judged rare if not nonexistent. New evidence on the possible efficiency benefits of mergers and on the profits-concentration relationship raises doubts about the economic foundations of the existing Guidelines and reduces confidence in their wisdom. An obvious modification would alter the stance of the Guidelines toward efficiency arguments. The problem, however, is how to do so without creating an administrative and judicial morass.

One approach is to presume that most mergers are either beneficial or innocuous and challenge only those that clearly promise to be anticompetitive. A number of modifications to the Guidelines would move in this direction. One would be to focus the Guidelines solely on horizontal mergers, but the findings discussed above seem to indicate that horizontal mergers may be the ones with the greatest chance of bringing cost reductions. Thus a relaxing of the strictures against horizontal mergers, perhaps by raising the market-share criteria, seems appropriate. A less dramatic change might be to increase the market-share criteria for horizontal mergers, while retaining some strictures against vertical and conglomerate acquisitions.

If that is to be done, there is economic justification for limiting concern about vertical acquisitions to those in which the acquiring firm already has substantial market power in its vertically related market. In practice in markets where significant barriers to entry can be identified, this would confine the vertical Guidelines to acquiring firms with rather larger market shares than at present. Similarly, the conglomerate Guidelines would be confined to acquisitions in which the acquired firm has substantial market power, as judged by a substantial market share and the existence of significant and specifically identified barriers to entry, and the acquiring firm was one of very few well-situated potential entrants.

As a general proposition, if the risks of foregone efficiency from a restrictive merger policy are judged significant, and if extensive, perhaps fruitless, efforts to assess potential efficiency gains in individual cases are to be avoided, the Guidelines should be less concerned with all mergers; they should adopt higher market share standards and should pay much more attention to direct evidence of significant barriers to entry.

Notes

I gratefully acknowledge the assistance of my colleagues Carln Boyer, Peter Bronsteen, A. J. Matsuura, and Valerie Sarris.

1. Undoubtedly they also embody certain legal and administrative principles.

2. The by now standard reference is F. M. Scherer, *Industrial Market Structure and Economic Performance* (Chicago: Rand McNally, 1980), pp. 3–6.

3. For an elegant treatment of the theory, see G. J. Stigler, "The Theory of Oligopoly," *Journal of Political Economy* 72 (February 1964), pp. 44–61.

4. Joe S. Bain, "The Relation of Profit Rates to Industry Concentration: American Manufacturing, 1936–1940," *Quarterly Journal of Economics* 65 (August 1951), pp. 293–324; H. Michael Mann, "Seller Concentration, Barriers to Entry and Rates of Return in Thirty Industries, 1950–1960," *Review of Economics and Statistics* 48 (August 1966), pp. 296–307; and Stigler, "Theory of Oligopoly."

5. For a comprehensive review of such studies up to 1974, see Leonard W. Weiss, "The Concentration Profits Relationship and Antitrust," in *Industrial Concentration: The New Learning*, ed. Goldschmid, Mann, and Weston (Boston: Little, Brown, 1974), pp.

184–233. More recent literature is thoroughly reviewed in Scherer, *Industrial Market Structure*, pp. 267–295.

6. Quoted in Yale Brozen, "The Antitrust Task Force Deconcentration Recommendation," *Journal of Law and Economics* 13 (October 1970), pp. 279–280.

7. Ibid.

8. Leading examples are: James W. Meehan and Thomas D. Duchesneau, "The Critical Level of Concentration: An Empirical Analysis," *Journal of Industrial Economics* 22 (September 1973), pp. 21–30; Stephen A. Rhodes and Joe M. Cleaver, "The Nature of the Concentration-Price/Cost Margin Relationship for 352 Manufacturing Industries: 1967," *Southern Economic Journal* 40 (July 1973), pp. 90–102; Lawrence J. White, "Searching for the Critical Industrial Concentration Ratio: An Application of the 'Switching of Regimes' Technique," in *Studies in Nonlinear Estimation*, ed. Goldfeld and Quandt (Cambridge: Ballinger, 1976), pp. 61–75; and James A. Dalton and David W. Penn, "The Concentration-Profitability Relationship: Is There a Critical Concentration Ratio?", *Journal of Industrial Economics* 25 (December 1972), pp. 133–142.

9. John Kwoka, "The Effect of Market Share Distribution on Industry Performance," *Review of Economics and Statistics* 61 (February 1979), pp. 101–109.

10. For Demsetz's analysis and empirical results, see his "Industry Structure, Market Rivalry, and Public Policy," *Journal of Law and Economics* 16 (April 1973), pp. 1–9 and "Two Systems of Belief about Monopoly," in *Industrial Concentration: The New Learning*, pp.164–184.

11. David Ravenscraft, *Price-Raising and Cost-Reducing Effects in Profits Concentration Studies* (Ann Arbor: University Microfilms, 1980).

12. Fisher and McGowan, "On the Misuse of Accounting Rates of Return to Infer Monopoly Profits," *American Economic Review* 73 (March 1983), pp. 82–97; Solomon, "Alternative Rates of Return Concepts and Their Implications for Utility Regulation," *Bell Journal of Economics and Management Science* 1 (Spring 1970), pp. 65–81; and Stauffer, "The Measurement of Corporate Rates of Return: A Generalized Formulation," *The Bell Journal of Economics and Management Science* 2 (Autumn 1971), pp. 434–469.

13. See, for example, Sam Peltzman, "Issues in Vertical Integration Policy," in *Public Policy toward Mergers*, ed. J. Fred Weston and Sam Peltzman (California: Goodyear Publishing Co., 1969), pp. 167–176.

14. See, for example, Willard F. Mueller, "Public Policy toward Vertical Mergers," in *Public Policy toward Mergers*, pp. 150–166.

15. Such a mechanism was hypothesized by the FTC to be at work in the cement and ready-mixed concrete industries in the early and mid-1960s. For further discussion see M. J. Peck and J. McGowan, "Vertical Integration in the Cement Industry," *Antitrust Bulletin* 12 (Summer 1967), pp. 505–531.

16. "Report of President Nixon's Task Force on Productivity and Competition," *United States Congressional Record* 115 (June 16, 1969) 91–1, pp. 15932–15937.

17. See, for example, Dennis W. Carleton, "Vertical Integration in Competitive Markets under Uncertainty," *Journal of Industrial Economics* 27 (March 1979), pp. 189–209; Oliver E. Williamson, "The Vertical Integration of Production: Market Failure Considerations," *American Economic Review* (Papers and Proceedings) 61 (May 1971), pp. 112–123; and Benjamin Klein, Robert Crawford, and Armen Alchian, "Vertical Integration, Appropriable Rents, and the Competitive Contracting Process," *Journal of Law and Economics* 21 (October 1978), pp. 297–326.

18. See Joe S. Bain, *Barriers to New Competition* (Cambridge: Harvard University Press, 1956); and Paolo Sylos-Labini, *Oligopoly and Technical Progress* (Cambridge: Harvard University Press, 1962).

19. For a useful review of these developments see Scherer, *Industrial Market Structure*, pp. 229–266.

20. See Joel B. Dirlam, "Observations on Public Policy toward Conglomerate Merger," in *Conglomerate Merger and Acquisition: Opinion and Analyses, St. John's Law Review* 44; and Willard F. Mueller, "The Rising Economic Concentration in America: Reciprocity, Conglomeration and the New American 'Zaibatsu' System (II)," *Antitrust Law and Economics Review* 4 (Summer 1971), pp. 91–104.

21. For views as to why reciprocity is unlikely to be anticompetitive and may be pro-competitive, see articles by Bork, Miller, and Posner in *St. John's Law Review* 44:9 (Spring 1970).

22. For a summary of relevant studies see Scherer, *Industrial Market Structure*, pp. 335–339.

23. Williamson, "Economics as an Antitrust Defense," *American Economic Review* 58 (March 1968), pp. 18–36.

24. The studies are cited and their findings summarized in Scherer, *Industrial Market Structure*, pp. 133–141. Arguments relying on such essentially adaptive responses to changing technology and market conditions as explanations for mergers and evidence consistent with that explanation were presented in J. McGowan, "International Comparisons of Merger Activity," *Journal of Law and Economics* 14 (April 1971), pp. 233–250.

25. Weiss, "Optimal Plant Size and the Extent of Sub-Optimal Capacity," in *Essays on Industrial Organization in Honor of Joe S. Bain*, ed. Robert T. Masson and David P. Qualls (Cambridge: Ballinger, 1976) pp. 123–141.

2

Competition and Antitrust in the Petroleum Industry: An Application of the Merger Guidelines

George A. Hay and Robert J. Reynolds

In issuing the 1982 Merger Guidelines, the Justice Department made it clear that the basic principle of merger policy would be to challenge only those mergers that contribute in a nontrivial way to the ability of one or more firms to profitably raise prices. In addition to communicating that basic principle, the Guidelines provide considerable detail on the methodology the department uses in applying the principles to specific cases. The hope was expressed that by stating its policy as simply and clearly as possible and by providing details on how the policy would be applied, the department would reduce the uncertainty associated with enforcement of the antitrust laws regarding mergers.[1]

The Guidelines have already been the subject of considerable commentary and criticism. The criticism includes attacks on the principle that economic theory ought to be the sole basis for merger policy, arguments that the Guidelines do not correspond completely with the relevant economic theory, and speculation that the Guidelines are unworkable as a blueprint for predicting the Justice Department's enforcement decisions because of, among other things, omitted assumptions or instructions and data-availability problems.[2]

This chapter deals with some of the same issues, but our approach differs from that of most previous work in that we base our discussion on a concrete application of the Guidelines to a real merger: the proposed acquisition in 1982 of Cities Service Company, the nineteenth largest oil company in the United States, by Gulf Oil Corporation, the sixth largest.[3] Our purpose is not to provide a how-to manual; rather, we think the approach adopted here—in exploring operational ambiguities, issues of data availability, and even some fundamental conceptual problems exposed in the process of attempted implementation—offers insights into the correspondence of the Guidelines with correct economic principles and into the likely success of the Guidelines in reducing uncertainty about the probable enforcement posture of government antitrust agencies toward individual mergers.

In this section we provide a brief summary of the proposed acquisition. After a short discussion of the refining process in the next section, we examine a key area of FTC concern: the supply of kerosene jet fuel. The other key area of concern, gasoline marketing, is considered in the section that follows, and our overall conclusions are reviewed in the last section of the chapter.

The Transaction

On June 17, 1982, Gulf Oil Corporation ("Gulf") and Cities Service Company ("Cities") entered into a merger agreement whereby Gulf agreed to initiate a cash tender offer of $63 per share for approximately 51 percent of Cities' stock. If the tender offer were successful, Gulf would consummate the merger by exchanging securities for Cities' remaining shares. The total value of the proposed transaction was $5.13 billion; if consummated, it would have been the third largest corporate acquisition in history as of that date.[4]

Gulf and Cities were both large, fully integrated companies involved in most aspects of the petroleum industry, including the exploration and production of crude oil, refining, transportation of crude oil and petroleum products, and marketing. In crude exploration and production, their individual and combined shares were far too small to raise an issue under the Guidelines. With respect to refining generally, Gulf and Cities' combined share of overall U.S. refining capacity in 1980 was less than 7 percent and the overall level of industry concentration quite low by most standards of comparison. The four-firm concentration ratio was less than 30 percent, and the Herfindahl-Hirschman Index (HHI) was less than 400.[5] Even if the geographic region is limited to PADD III (figure 2.1), where both Gulf and Cities had large refineries, their combined share of refinery capacity was still well below the level likely to raise concern under the Guidelines.[6] Gulf had 6.6 percent of PADD III refining capacity and Cities Service had 4.1 percent, yielding a change in the HHI of 54 and a post-merger HHI of about 600.[7]

Any serious competitive issue must, therefore, involve narrower markets.[8] In this chapter we focus on two specific petroleum products mentioned in the FTC complaint, kerosene jet fuel (kerojet) and motor gasoline. To understand properly the nature of these products and the competitive analysis that follows, a brief review of the refining process is appropriate.

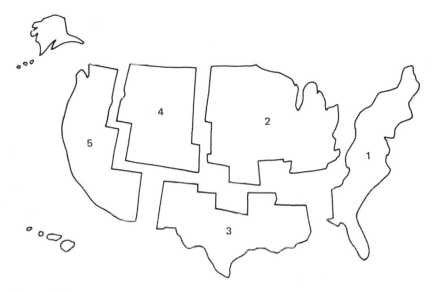

Figure 2.1
Petroleum Administration for Defense (PAD) Districts

An Overview of the Refining Process[9]

Refining is the process by which crude oil is converted into usable petroleum products (see figure 2.2 for a simplified view of the process).[10] The first step in the refining process is the fractional distillation of the crude input. The distillation process separates the crude into components of different boiling ranges. The initial composition of these refinery intermediate products from the distillation stage is relatively fixed and is determined primarily by the type and quantity of crude oil input. Each component is then directed to the appropriate equipment, where specified products are made. The final mix of products depends on where in the refinery the intermediate products are sent. There is some flexibility in the process, as a result of the options presented by the catalytic cracker, thermal cracker, or hydrocracker.[11] Not only do the various processing units produce different products but, by adjusting the operating characteristics of a processing unit, that unit can operate with a variety of feedstocks and a variety of product yields.

Hence, within limits, it is possible to alter proportions of various petroleum products obtainable from a barrel of crude oil. The time and expense needed to make the adjustment varies according to the magnitude of the desired change, the present configuration of the refinery,

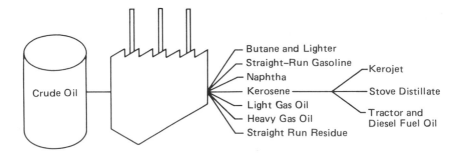

Figure 2.2
Crude Distillation and Product Disposition
Source: *Petroleum Refining for the Non-Technical Person*, 1979

and the characteristics of the available crude oil (or the ability to substitute a more suitable crude).

Notwithstanding some flexibility, the basic determinants of the amount of an individual product produced are the amount and quality of the crude throughput. Moreover, a decision to increase the amount of any one product by increasing the crude throughput has implications for the production of other refined products and, hence, cannot be based solely on the price of the product in question.

Kerojet

Preliminary Market-Share Calculations

Kerosene jet fuel (kerojet) is for all practical purposes the only jet fuel used by commercial airlines. Both Gulf and Cities were significant producers of kerojet. On a nationwide basis, however, it did not appear that the combined sales of kerojet by Gulf and Cities would result in a change in the HHI exceeding the threshold level specified in the Guidelines; hence, any potential problem in the kerojet market would have to involve a narrower geographic market. The FTC's complaint identified PADD III as a possible geographic market and the combination of PADD I (the U.S. East Coast) and PADD III as another. The press release accompanying the complaint indicated that the combined market share of the two companies in the latter market (PADDs I and III) was 17.6 percent.[12]

For our purposes here, we will examine both PADD III alone and the combination of PADD I and PADD III. In both cases, we will assume, for illustration, that the combined share is 18 percent and that this share is divided evenly between the two companies. Thus the maximum change in the HHI by combining the shares of the two firms is 162 points ($9 \times 9 \times 2$).[13] The FTC indicated that the post-merger HHI would be 1224 in PADD III and 1229 in the combined PADDs I and III. Under these assumptions, the merger is subject to possible challenge, unless there is some flaw in defining the relevant market or in measuring market shares.

Supply Flexibility

Although there seems little doubt that there are no good substitutes for kerojet on the demand side (i.e., kerojet is a relevant product market), the supply side of the equation warrants further inquiry. The central question is whether market shares based on production or sales in recent years provides an accurate barometer of the risk of collusion with respect to the price of kerojet. Notwithstanding apparently high market shares, successful collusion is unlikely if firms showing zero or small market shares can easily enter the market on a large scale or expand output significantly in response to an attempted price increase by firms currently producing the lion's share of the output.

Entry Because kerojet is produced jointly with other petroleum products, and because it amounts to only 5.8 percent of current refining product mix, it is unlikely that an increase in the price of kerojet (assuming other product prices are not increased) will induce any significant new entry into the refinery industry generally.[14] Hence, whereas the Guidelines provide for the possibility of substantial new entry, the issue is not relevant in the case of kerojet.[15]

Excess Capacity A second possible source of additional kerojet arises from the fact that, at the time of the proposed merger, there was substantial excess capacity among domestic refineries.[16] In response to an attempted price increase by the leading firms, firms with small current market shares might be able to expand output considerably and thwart the increase. The 1982 Guidelines contain no specific provision for this possibility.[17] The sections on market definition dealing with production substitution (Section II.B.1) and geographic substitution (Section II.C) indicate that any firm not currently in the market but able to sell the product to the customers in the geographic area affected by the monopoly will be taken into account by hypothesizing a 5 percent price increase and crediting the firm with the amount it would succeed in selling within one year were the price increase to remain in effect. Neither provision, however, seems directly applicable to a firm currently in the market yet which has substantial idle capacity—not being used to produce a related product or to sell in a different location.

Notwithstanding the fact that there is no specific provision for excess capacity, such a provision is critical in properly assessing the likelihood of effective collusion. If a firm currently selling nothing in the market can become a major seller if prices increase, surely firms currently selling a nominal amount, but with considerable excess capacity, are at least as much a threat to a leading firm's or group of leading firms' attempt to raise prices.[18] Clearly it would be inconsistent with the basic principle of the Guidelines not to take this into account.

Further, Section II.D, "Calculating Market Shares," while allowing for the fact that firms currently in the market may be able to sell more, fails to capture the essence of the excess capacity problem. Section II.D does indicate that, in some situations, market shares may be more appropriately measured by capacity rather than actual sales.[19] Measuring market shares by capacity instead of actual output, however, is not a satisfactory solution. For example, if all firms operate at approximately the same level of excess capacity, market shares will not change; yet the excess capacity in the hands of noncolluders is no less a threat just because the leading firms are also burdened with excess capacity. Finally, Section III.C, "Other Factors," while listing several factors that may influence the likelihood of the success of a conspiracy, makes no mention of excess capacity.

Although these ambiguities in the Guidelines' treatment of excess capacity are potentially troublesome, the joint-production nature of the refinery process, in conjunction with the relative unimportance of kerojet in the refinery mix (less than 6 percent), makes it unlikely that excess capacity would have much impact on the success of collusion for this particular product. A decision to increase capacity utilization by running more crude through the refinery would be based on the overall profitability of the entire product mix, not simply on whether kerojet were priced competitively. An increase in kerojet production, accomplished by raising refinery output, would be accompanied by a proportional increase in the output of all other petroleum products. Because the market demand for most of these products tends to be inelastic, the reduction in revenue caused by that additional production would tend to offset any additional profits earned on kerojet sales. One would need to know the demand elasticities of all petroleum products to calculate the profit impact precisely, but the incentive to produce more kerojet in this way is likely to be small.

Supply Substitution The Guidelines contemplate the possibility that additional kerojet will result from a decision by refiners to increase the *relative* amounts of kerojet produced from a given amount of crude input (i.e., a substitution from other petroleum products to kerojet).[20] Such a change in the product mix is technically feasible. Kerojet is derived from the refinery's production of kerosene. In some cases the kerosene obtained from the distillation of crude oil may be sold directly as jet fuel with no further processing; in other cases additional treatment may be required. Certain crudes have chemical properties that make kerosene from those crudes completely unsuitable for jet fuel. Kerosene can also be sold as No. 1 fuel oil or it can blended with heavier distillates to make No. 2 fuel oil, used for diesel fuel or home heating oil.[21]

Hence, some refineries that produce kerosene may not sell kerojet at all (since they are geared to a kind of crude that is not suitable for production of kerojet or are not capable of the additional processing that may be necessary), whereas others will sell only a portion of their kerosene output as jet fuel (either because a portion of the crude throughput is an unacceptable variety or because of a conscious choice to sell kerosene as fuel oil or to use it as a blending agent). Several types of substitution are thus suggested:

1. Some kerosene currently sold as fuel oil or used as a blending agent within the refinery is physically indistinguishable from kerojet. The added marketing expense of selling it as kerojet (assuming access to transportation) is minimal. The main cost is the profit foregone from the alternative use. A nontransitory price increase should provide sufficient incentive to expand kerojet sales.[22]

2. In theory, most refineries can adjust the cracking process to yield additional kerosene, which, in turn, is suitable as jet fuel. However, there are limits to this flexibility and, depending on historical price patterns, refineries might be at or near the maximum possible yield.

3. Notwithstanding suitable crude supplies, some refineries (primarily smaller ones) may currently produce no kerosene. Others may produce kerosene that requires additional treatment to be sold as kerojet. The expense of upgrading the refinery so it can produce kerojet will vary enormously depending on the initial conditions. However, from our inquiries it appears that the time limits imposed by the Guidelines for a nonproducing refinery to get an imputed market share (especially

given licensing requirements related to environmental concerns) are such that little additional output can be expected from this source.

4. Some refineries do not produce kerojet because some or all of the crude they have access to is not suitable. The ability of individual refiners to change the quality of crude input will vary across refiners, depending on contractual commitments or customary relationships (including vertical integration into crude production). Additionally, if a refinery is thoroughly oriented to a particular type of crude, physical changes may have to be made in the refinery to permit the processing of a different type. Therefore, the likelihood of substantial additional amounts of kerojet via changes in the crude quality mix may be limited.

Unfortunately, identifying the opportunities for supply substitution does not provide sufficient information to implement the 5 percent test suggested by the Guidelines. Some way is needed to quantify the possibilities for substitution more precisely. Our experience is that discussions with petroleum engineers are helpful in grasping the nature of the substitution possibilities; but because each refinery differs in its ability to perform the substitution, these discussions cannot be counted on to obtain any hard numbers. Moving to the other extreme, one might contemplate an econometric model from which the likely impact of a hypothetical price increase could be calculated. Although there is probably more data published for the oil industry than for any other, the opportunities for econometric modeling are limited. The availability of data at the level of detail needed is a problem, and the extensive regulatory structure (price and allocation) imposed on the industry over much of the past decade dictates a need for careful modeling and may even leave too few degrees of freedom to calculate the cross-elasticities of supply. Moreover, because the Guidelines' test contemplates a *nontransitory* increase, econometric procedures must be chosen carefully, or there is some risk that calculated cross-elasticities will underestimate the true substitution potential in the face of such a price change.[23]

To suggest the degree of supply substitution likely to be feasible, we indicate in table 2.1 the amount of reported kerojet production for 1981, plus the kerosene sold as heating fuel or motor transport fuel. This total overstates the amount of kerojet that could be readily marketed in the event of an increased price to the extent that some kerosene cannot be marketed as kerojet for technical reasons and to the extent that it would not be economically sensible for all refiners to

Table 2.1
PADD III Kerosene and Kerojet Production, 1981 (thousand barrels/day)

Month	Kerojet production	Kerojet plus kerosene production
January	375	496
February	355	466
March	378	470
April	399	489
May	426	511
June	395	479
July	418	484
August	377	450
September	363	426
October	342	406
November	364	448
December	400	504
Average	383	469

Source: *Petroleum Supply Annual*, 1981

withdraw kerosene from the fuel market. The total understates supply flexibility by ignoring the possibility of additional kerosene currently used for blending that can be sold as kerojet.[24]

It is not entirely clear how this total should be used in applying the Guidelines. The Guidelines suggest that firms which currently produce no kerojet will be ignored unless, in response to a small but significant and nontransitory price increase,[25] they can effect supply substitution so as to be producing and selling kerojet within six months.[26] Firms that pass the six month test receive "credit," in measuring market shares, for the amount of kerojet they would be likely to sell were the hypothetical price increase to remain in effect for one year.[27]

As in the case of excess capacity, the Guidelines are less clear on how to treat a firm with *some* kerojet sales but which, through supply substitution, could increase those sales in response to a nontransitory price increase. We infer that such a firm is somehow to be given credit for what it could produce over the course of a year in response to higher prices. Any other result would be anomalous, since a firm currently producing zero could receive an imputed share based on its potential sales, but a firm currently producing one unit but capable of the same expansion as the first firm would get credit for no additional sales.

The Guidelines, however, appear to contemplate that any upward adjustment to reflect the possibility of supply substitution would be made for all firms with kerosene production, even those most likely to implement the price increase. This is essentially equivalent to the traditional approach in which the market is redefined as "kerojet plus kerosene." As in the case of excess capacity, such an adjustment fails to capture the essence of the situation (i.e., the ability of fringe firms to thwart the leading firms' price increase by a dramatic expansion in production), where the leading firms also produce large amounts of kerosene. There is no reason to upwardly adjust the production capability of the hypothetical colluders, since they will be attempting to restrict output, not increase it. Indeed, even where the leading kerojet firms also account for the bulk of the kerosene production, the resulting ability to produce substantially more kerojet makes collusion more difficult to achieve, just as any excess capacity enhances the likelihood of cheating by participants in a cartel.

In attempting to amend the Guidelines methodology to account for these factors, several approaches are possible. One approach would add to the universe that portion of kerosene production likely to be converted to kerojet by noncolluders. Unfortunately, because the collusion is purely hypothetical and the potential colluders are not identified, the portion to be added is somewhat arbitrary. Moreover, such an adjustment fails to reflect the increased difficulty of collusion that results from excess capacity among the colluders.

One could follow the traditional market-redefinition approach (adjusting the universe and each firm's kerojet sales to include kerosene sales) but take into account the increased threat from noncolluders and the increased risk of cheating among the potential colluders as a nonmarket share factor, discounting the significance of whatever market shares emerge. This avoids arbitrary allocations between colluders and noncolluders but places a large premium on the nonmarket share adjustments, making the outcome difficult to anticipate.[28] Since the problem with the market-redefinition adjustment arises only when the leading producers of the product under investigation are also major producers of the supply-side substitute, following this approach at least has the advantage of permitting a consistent methodology to be applied in all cases.

Geographic Market Issues
The FTC's complaint indicated two possible geographic markets, PADD III alone and the combination of PADDs I and III.[29] Cities' only major

refinery was at Lake Charles, Louisiana (PADD III). Gulf had major refineries in both PADD III and PADD I. The press release accompanying the complaint indicated that in the larger market (I and III), the two companies accounted for 17.6 percent of production.[30]

Attempting to establish a narrow geographic market for kerojet raises a number of interesting issues In particular, the following are discussed:

1. Is price discrimination required to support the concept of separate geographic markets? Is such discrimination feasible?

2. Customers may be able to satisfy some but not all of their needs outside the suggested geographic markets. How can the extent of that substitution be determined, and how should it be factored into the Guidelines' computations?

3. Are imports of foreign kerojet feasible? Should they be given less weight than kerojet from domestic sources?

Geographic Markets and Price Discrimination Consider PADD III as a possible geographic market. An examination of PADD III discloses that shipments from other PADDs to PADD III are virtually nonexistent (see figure 2.3 and table 2.2). A major reason is that kerojet production in PADD III far exceeds consumption; PADD III is a net exporter to the rest of the country. Moreover, because nearby regions are deficit regions, and because pipelines are generally designed to flow from PADD III to these regions, it is unlikely there would be a significant amount of shipment from other parts of the United States into PADD III should prices there rise. The argument for PADD III as a relevant market, then, is that customers in PADD III have little choice but to buy from producers located there, and if those producers could avoid competition among themselves, a price increase would stick.[31]

The fact that PADD III is a net exporter to other regions, however, means that much of what it produces (more than 80 percent) competes with kerojet produced outside PADD III.[32] For this reason an across-the-board price increase by PADD III producers could jeopardize much of their sales.[33] More likely to be profitable, if feasible, is a discriminatory price increase limited to customers located in PADD III, with prices remaining competitive for customers in other regions. The Guidelines contemplate the possibility that price discrimination may justify narrow geographic markets; according to Section II.C of the Guidelines, "where price discrimination is possible, the Department

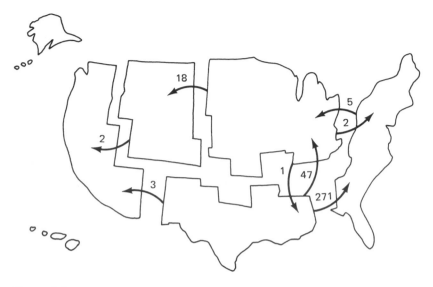

Figure 2.3
Domestic Movements of Kerojet, 1981
(Thousand barrels/day)
Source: *Petroleum Supply Annual*, 1981

Table 2.2
Sources of Kerojet Supply, by PADD, 1981[a] (thousand barrels/day)

PADD	Refinery output	Imports	Stock with-drawal	Supply from other districts	Supply to other districts	Supply for consumption
I	46	19	1	273	5	334
II	116	0	5	52	21	152
III	383	2	−1	1	321	64
IV	16	0	0	18	2	32
V	213	10	1	5	0	229
Total	775	31	5	349	349	811

a. Components may not sum to totals due to rounding.

Source: *Petroleum Supply Annual*, 1981

will consider defining additional narrower geographic markets oriented to those buyer groups subject to the exercise of market power." The question is whether such discrimination is feasible in the present context.

What makes discrimination against PADD III customers difficult is that many of those customers (airlines buying for airports located in PADD III) are also customers in PADD I and II. This suggests that a *minimum* condition for discrimination to work is that the refiners sell exclusively on a delivered price basis, with the price depending on the airport at which the fuel will be consumed and with the refiner providing transportation to the airport. Otherwise, airlines would easily be able to circumvent the discrimination by purchasing all requirements at the PADD I and II "competitive" price and, by taking possession at the (PADD III) refinery, diverting the kerojet to PADD III airports.[34]

It is unclear, however, whether refiners can lawfully insist on selling exclusively on a delivered price basis where the purpose and effect of such a scheme is to "facilitate" noncompetitive prices to PADD III customers. At least one recent FTC decision suggested that such a scheme would carry significant legal risks, even assuming it is practical from a business standpoint.[35] Is it legitimate to postulate a narrow geographic market if to do so would require assuming behavior by firms that may itself be an antitrust violation?[36]

Whatever the status of PADD III in this regard, the combination of PADDs I and III is an easier case. Only about 10 percent of production in the combined region is not consumed there; therefore, producers in this region arguably might not be deterred from raising prices across the board due to sales lost to producers elsewhere.

Airline Substitution Even if kerojet producers rigidly adhere to a price-discrimination scheme whereby customers for airports in one region are charged more than customers for airports in the remaining regions, some disadvantaged customers have an alternative means of circumventing the higher prices, at least in part. Commercial airlines do not necessarily fill their fuel tanks completely before taking off, since the typical intercity "hop" is only a fraction of the airplane's range. A calculation is made as to how much fuel is actually needed for the upcoming leg of the flight, plus a reserve to cover such contingencies as bad weather. Because this calculated amount normally falls well short of the actual fuel capacity, a decision may be made to carry additional fuel. The cost is added weight, which increases fuel consumption; the benefit is a savings in fuel cost if the price of jet fuel is higher at the destination airport, since the plane would reduce its purchases there. This process, which can be repeated throughout the entire journey of the aircraft, is referred to as "overflying" an airport, or "tankering" fuel.

This possibility is not just a theoretical one. Airlines routinely vary the proportion of their overall fuel needs across airports in response to changing conditions; on the margin, they would respond to a hypothetical price increase in the price at one airport by further reallocating business.[37] This results in a loss of sales by firms in a conspiracy limited to airports in PADDs I and III.[38]

Essentially, overflight is a geographic issue, but analytically it could be treated like a product-market issue, because customers are substituting one product (e.g., kerojet in PADD II) for another (kerojet in PADDs I and III). Either way, the Guidelines would postulate a 5 percent increase, then wait to see how much business would shift over the course of a year. There is some difference between the Guidelines' treatment of product and geographic markets. The former is regarded in the Guidelines as an all-or-nothing question (the market is either apples or apples plus oranges). For the latter, the outcome is a continuous variable, since the process involves deciding how much output from the neighboring region will be included in the universe for the purpose of calculating market share. If the market shares of the merging firms are on the low side to begin with, treating "overflight" as a geographic market issue may add enough to the universe to pull the combined share below the critical level, even if not enough to make a price increase unprofitable for a hypothetical monopolist.

Verifying the possibility of demand substitution unfortunately is much easier than quantifying it. In our limited survey, we found that airline personnel were emphatic about their ability to circumvent a price increase at any one airport. An across-the board price increase at all airports in a region as large as PADDs I and III, however, is difficult for them to conceptualize. In what is admittedly a crude effort (but not atypical of the empirical undertaking likely to occur in attempting to do a Guidelines analysis), we can try to get a feel for the outer limits of the overflight possibilities by exploring the extent to which planes cross geographic market boundaries. Figure 2.4 illustrates the calculation for a major airport in the PADD I and III regions. Of 744 domestic nonstop flights into Atlanta on a given day, 322 (43 percent) come from outside PADD I and 194 (26 percent) from outside the combined PADDs I and

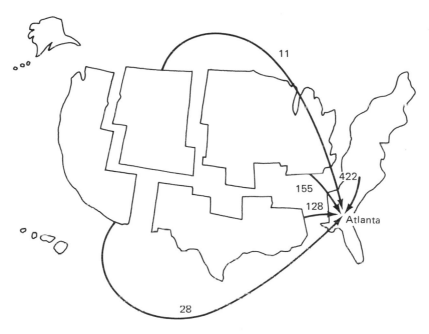

Figure 2.4
Nonstop Flights to Atlanta, 1982
Source: *Official Airline Guide*

III region. (Implicit in the use of this data is that the destination pattern of outgoing flights is similar to the origin pattern of incoming flights.) Given that overflying to circumvent the hypothetical price increase is feasible only for flights from outside the region, that for these flights only a portion of the fuel needs can be shifted, and that Atlanta probably has a relatively large percentage of cross-region flights because of its status as a major hub, these figures suggest that were the price increase as broad as the PADDs I and III region, the demand loss from overflight by itself may be insufficient to make the price increase unprofitable. In performing the 5 percent test, there is an implicit assumption that sales lost due to overflight are not "recaptured" by the colluders as a result of increased sales at airports in the adjacent regions. To the extent that there is some recapture, the risk to the colluders is diminished. "Recapture" is a potentially significant issue (which the Guidelines' methodology overlooks) any time the merging firms are also producers of the closest product or geographic substitute, yet overall concentration in the broader market is too low to trigger a challenge under the Guidelines.

Table 2.3
US Kerojet Imports, 1972–1981 (thousand barrels/day)

Year	Total kerojet imports	Kerojet imports from Caribbean	Caribbean imports as percent of total imports
1981	31	a	a
1980	49	39	80
1979	55	33	60
1978	67	39	58
1977	53	29	55
1976	62	41	66
1975	105	70	67
1974	135	94	70
1973	176	127	72
1972	162	124	77

a. Cannot be determined from available data.

Source: *Petroleum Supply Annual*, 1981; *Supply, Disposition, and Stocks of All Oils by PAD District, 1977–1980*; *Metals, Minerals and Fuel Yearbook*, 1971–1976.

Caribbean Imports An additional cause of demand loss from a price increase in PADDs I and III is imports of kerojet, primarily from the Caribbean region, a major center of refining activity. As indicated in table 2.3, the volume of kerojet imports into the U.S. has been modest in recent years. This can be traced to the substantial excess refining capacity in the United States and to the subsidy provided to domestic refiners derived from their ability to purchase U.S. crude oil at controlled prices. In earlier years, imports were more substantial, though the influence of allocation regulations under the Mandatory Oil Import Program makes it difficult to be completely confident about the inferences to be drawn from the data.

Perhaps the best indication of the potential for imports lies in the data on relative prices. Figure 2.5 plots the price of kerojet out of Rotterdam and the price out of the Caribbean as a percentage of U.S. Gulf Coast prices. Under the 5 percent test,[39] it appears that European imports would not be a factor but imports from the Caribbean would, since Caribbean prices are never more than 5 percent higher than U.S. prices. Transport costs from the Caribbean to terminal facilities in Florida and elsewhere up the East Coast would not be appreciably greater than transportation from U.S. Gulf Coast refineries.[40] For some interior points close to the Colonial Pipeline, kerojet shipped from the Gulf by Colonial would have a nontrivial cost advantage.

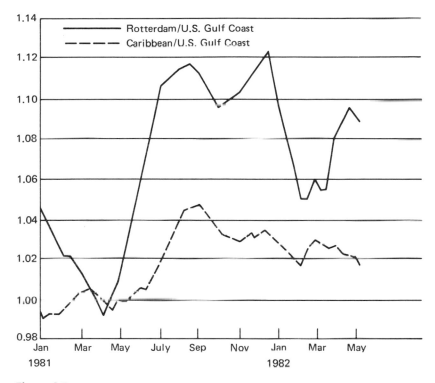

Figure 2.5
Ratios of Spot Kerojet Prices, Rotterdam/U.S. Gulf Coast and Caribbean/U.S. Gulf
Coast
January 1981–May 1982
Source: *Platt's Oilgram Price Report*

Although it seems clear that some imports are likely under the 5
percent test, the actual amount of imports is difficult to estimate. The
range of possibilities includes, but is not limited to, the following:

1. Actual Caribbean kerojet exports into all of the United States. This
assumes that kerojet exported to PADDs II, IV, and V could easily be
diverted into the region affected by the hypothetical increase.

2. Total Caribbean kerojet exports. This assumes that exports elsewhere would be diverted to the United States. A full diversion of
Caribbean exports would be unlikely if such diversion increased the
price of kerojet in the markets to which Caribbean refineries currently
export.[41] A large market is Western Europe (about 40 percent of non-
U.S.-destined Caribbean exports). Because these exports amount to less

Table 2.4
Domestic Kerojet Production and Import Potential, 1980

	PADD III	PADD I and III
U.S. kerojet production	388	438
plus Caribbean kerojet exports to U.S.	427	477
plus other Caribbean kerojet exports	472	522
plus other Caribbean kerojet production	524	574

Source: "Supply, Disposition, and Stocks of All Oils by PAD District, 1980," United Nations, *Yearbook of World Energy Statistics*.

than 5 percent of European production, the price effect may be slight. Evaluating the exact extent of diversion remains difficult in the absence of past changes in relative prices leading to diversion.

3. Total Caribbean kerojet production. This assumes that kerojet now consumed in the Caribbean would be exported, given the increased profitability of U.S. sales.

Table 2.4 indicates current domestic production in the proposed markets and the amount of kerojet that would be added under each assumption. The table includes no allowance for increased Caribbean kerojet production based on the supply-substitution possibilities already discussed. Once again, there is the question of how to adjust the domestic market share figures to account for the possibility of imports. The obvious candidate is to redefine the market to include Caribbean kerojet. Where the leading firms do not also control a portion of Caribbean production, this approach is satisfactory.[42] Such a redefinition, however, would not change market shares very much if the potential domestic colluders are the principal owners of Caribbean refining capacity, even though the amount not controlled by potential colluders is obviously a real threat to the viability of a conspiracy. Without a specific assumption as to the identity of the potential colluders, no precise estimate of noncolluder imports is possible.

Another question is whether foreign imports should be given full credit in making the Guidelines calculations. The 1982 Guidelines mention the question, but are inconclusive on the answer.[43] We note, however, that the most serious possibility for disruption of Caribbean supply would come from such an event as the Arab crude-oil boycott in 1973–74. Such a boycott would affect domestic refiners, for whom Arab crude is a major input, as much as it would Caribbean refiners.

Table 2.5
Illustrative Guidelines Calculation

Total kerojet sales (PADD I & III)	100[a]
Additions from supply substitution	20[b]
Additions from Flyover	5[b]
Additions from imports	19[b]
adjusted universe	144
adjusted HHI increase	78[c]

a. Normalized for ease of calculation.
b. Estimates made for illustrative purposes; see text.
c. $162 + 1.44^2$ (original HHI increase $= 162$)

Summary

We have identified several reasons why producers participating in a hypothetical kerojet conspiracy in PADD III or in the combined PADDs I and III region might experience a substantial loss of sales were they to attempt a nontransitory 5 percent price increase. It is possible that no reason, taken alone, is sufficient to frustrate the hypothetical price increase; yet all the factors working together would do so. In setting up a sequence of tests, the Guidelines should not be read as precluding the possibility of examining the *cumulative* impact of all factors.

To assess the cumulative impact we can construct a universe that includes all supplies that would be economically feasible in the event of a 5 percent price increase. Depending on the proportion of extra supplies under the control of the major producers of kerojet in the relevant geographic market, the impact on the HHI calculations could be dramatic. Adding 20 percent from supply substitution (see table 2.1; assume that the same percentages apply to the combined PADDs I and III region), 5 percent from losses due to overflight (treating overflight as a geographic issue), and 19 percent from imports (see table 2.5; assume that all current Caribbean exports are diverted) increases the total universe by 44 percent. If we assume Gulf and Cities have no kerosene sales,[44] and if we disregard Gulf's trivial Caribbean kerojet production, the change in the HHI in PADDs I and III attributable to the merger drops from our previously assumed value of 162 to 78, placing it outside the zone in which the Guidelines indicate a challenge is likely.[45]

Gasoline Marketing

In contrast to their analysis of the kerojet market, the FTC did not cite Gulf and Cities for their combined share of the *production* of gasoline (either in the entire United States or in a smaller region such as PADD III) but for their role in the *distribution and marketing* of gasoline at *wholesale* in various Gulf Coast and East Coast regions of the United States.[46] The FTC explained that the wholesale distribution of gasoline begins at terminals that store and dispense products received from pipelines or waterborne carriers. Terminals tend to be located near population centers where the demand for gasoline is greatest.[47] Gasoline is then trucked from these terminals to various retail and wholesale customers (FTC, Complaint, p. 4). Presumably, the FTC's concern is that in certain population centers Gulf and Cities each have high market shares measured not in terms of *retail* sales (i.e., sales at the gas station) but at an earlier stage in the distribution scheme, and that increased concentration at that stage raises the likelihood of noncompetitive pricing. The main issue is whether these market shares accurately reflect the potential for collusive behavior. The question is primarily one of geographic market definition, that is, whether wholesale gasoline prices in a particular region can be sustained at a noncompetitive level while prices elsewhere remain competitive.

Measurement is a second important issue. There are serious problems in attempting to measure gasoline market shares at the wholesale level in metropolitan areas. Total wholesale gasoline sales for an area can in principle be estimated from retail sales. There are no direct estimates, however, of total retail gasoline sales for such areas. An apparent source for these data is the 1977 Census of Retail Trade; but the census covers only gasoline sold through defined "gasoline stations"—retail outlets for which gasoline sales exceeded 50 percent of total dollar sales. Thus it omitted, for example, gasoline sales through convenience stores and direct sales to fleets. That the Census's coverage is deficient in measuring gasoline sales can be seen by comparing its figures for state sales with other sources of state data. For example, Federal Highway Administration gasoline sales estimates, based primarily on state tax data, exceeded the State Retail Census data by 119 percent in Alabama, 40 percent in New Jersey, 50 percent in Virginia, and 79 percent in Tennessee. One can attempt to overcome the deficiencies in the Census estimates by correcting for the coverage problem, by assuming the Census coverage ratio for the candidate area is the same as the ratio of the Census total for the state to FHA state gasoline sales. Alternatively, one can go directly to the FHA state data and estimate total sales in any SMSA by assuming the same per capita gasoline sales for the SMSA as for the state as a whole. (A more sophisticated version of the latter approach allows for the influence of other variables such as per capita income.) The FTC used the 1977 Census for one of its universes but apparently did not adjust for the coverage problems discussed above. That is, it adopted the 1977 SMSA Census data, simply adjusting it for changes in gasoline consumption between 1977 and 1980, based on changes in state consumption. Market share estimates based on such a universe are biased upward. In addition, with respect to individual firms' market sales, whereas various sources indicate that most trips by tank truck are within 50 miles of a terminal (see, e.g., the Congressional Reference Service Report, *National Energy Transportation*, May 1977, p. 249), many trips exceed this limit. Thus, trucks from a terminal typically serve areas larger than an SMSA, since the radius equivalent of the area (in square miles) of the average SMSA is 24 miles. Hence, comparisons of the merging firms' sales from terminals to estimated SMSA total retail sales typically cause overestimation of market shares. In principle, the merging firms could be asked to estimate the proportion of their terminal sales that are transported by tank truck for resale outside the SMSA, but the fact that many of the sales are made FOB terminal, with the customer providing the transportation, calls into question the reliability of such estimates.

Geographic Market Analysis

Two issues must be assessed in evaluating whether individual metropolitan areas constitute a geographic market. First is whether wholesale customers can shift their terminal source if local terminals attempt a small but significant price increase. Data on transportation costs suggest a trucking cost of 2 to 5 cents per gallon per 100 miles.[48] If the 5 percent test is employed, customers in the test SMSA might be served from terminals 100 to 200 miles distant.

The implications of the 5 percent test are indicated for some of the metropolitan areas identified in the FTC complaint in figure 2.6 (Atlanta) and figure 2.7 (Charlotte and Greensboro, North Carolina). In each figure we show the identified SMSA and a 50-mile radius around the central city of that SMSA, representing the location of the core customers of that terminal cluster at prevailing prices. To test the access of those customers to other terminal clusters at 5 percent higher prices, we have drawn 100-mile radius circles around significant alternative terminal clusters with pipeline or water access to refining centers and examined the degree of overlap between these circles and the SMSAs identified. As can be seen, the areas indicated result in substantial overlap with the

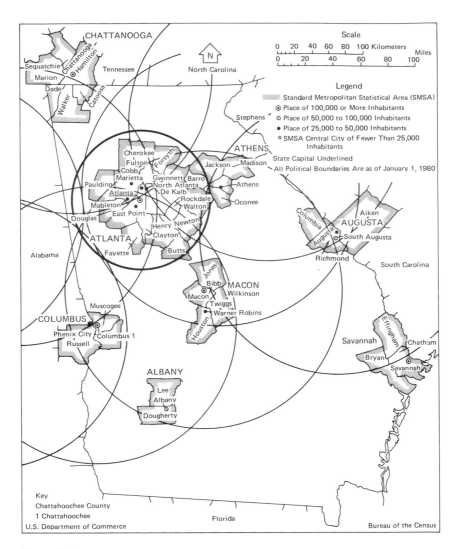

Figure 2.6
Georgia
Overlap of Wholesale Gasoline Markets

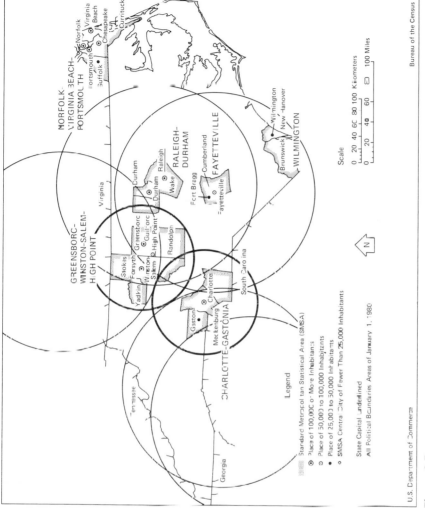

Figure 2.7
North Carolina
Overlap of Wholesale Gasoline Markets

SMSAs identified. Thus, under the 5 percent test, the metropolitan areas identified are doubtful candidates for geographic markets.

Further, the theory of spatial pricing suggests that, at current prices, the delivered price to fringe area customers is similar from each of two or more terminal clusters. Thus, in the absence of price discrimination, fairly small changes in the price at any one terminal will result in the loss of such fringe area customers.[49] The implications of fringe-customer switching for the profitability of a price increase can be estimated for various assumed price increases based on the population in the fringe areas versus the total population served by the terminal cluster.

The preceding analysis is based on responses to an assumed 5 percent price increase. Although simulations based on a hypothetical 5 percent price increase are suggested throughout the Guidelines, there are indications that this was intended for illustrative purposes, that for some industries a greater or smaller percentage increase would be a more appropriate test. Whereas the 1982 Guidelines provide no explicit advice on when to use a simulated increase other than 5 percent, it is worth noting that a 5 percent increase in the wholesale price of gasoline represents a substantial increase in the profit margin of the refiner (because the overwhelming portion of the wholesale price represents the cost of crude oil).[50]

The second issue related to the validity of metropolitan areas as relevant geographic markets stems from the fact that for most metropolitan areas, most of the gasoline originates at refineries located elsewhere. For most of the Southeast and East Coast cities served by Gulf and Cities Service, the bulk of the product is likely to come from refineries located in the Texas–Louisiana area, reaching these cities via the Colonial Pipeline.[51] Arguably, any refiner with access to Colonial, upon observing a higher wholesale price in a particular city, could reallocate shipments of gasoline, directing more to the high-price city until the refiner's activities (combined with arbitrage activities by nonrefiners) returned that price to a level of competitive equilibrium. If such reallocation is feasible, local metropolitan areas are not geographic markets for wholesale gasoline sales, and the smallest legitimate market might, at a minimum, include all of PADD III.

There may be limits to the ability to redirect gasoline to higher-priced areas arising from the ownership of key facilities by the Guidelines' hypothetical local monopolist. If the hypothetical monopolist owns or otherwise controls all the terminal facilities serving a particular metropolitan area,[52] newcomers would be hampered in their efforts to penetrate the market.[53] In most plausible scenarios, however, the leading firm or firms will not have complete control of the terminal facilities serving a particular city. This is significant because, although the size of the terminal facility tightly constrains the amount of gasoline that can be stored on its premises, the size of the facility imposes a less binding constraint on the flow of gasoline. A firm with relatively small terminal capacity (and historically small market shares) could increase sales dramatically if customers were available and would therefore disproportionately hinder the ability of the leading sellers to raise prices. As with the kerojet-excess-capacity issues already discussed, there are difficulties in using current shares in such a " market" to infer market power.

On could attempt to resolve all these issues by examining price patterns across cities to identify cities in which prices are unusually high at any given moment or to determine the extent to which prices have moved together or have diverged over time.[54] A number of empirical studies have attempted to identify cities in which retail gasoline prices appeared noncompetitive.[55] Marathon's expert in the Mobil–Marathon case, F. M. Scherer, in addition to citing these studies, noted certain patterns of prices that appear to be inconsistent with competitive behavior:

And I note in these, just taking a look at the prices of regular gasoline, that we find a large number of differentials that simply cannot plausibly be explained by differences in transportation costs from one region to another. For example, the price of regular gasoline in Hammond, Indiana, is half a cent higher than the price of regular gasoline at the Chicago terminal of Marathon. Now, that is quite peculiar, because the price leader in that area is Amoco, the Standard Oil Company of Indiana, and right next door to Hammond, Indiana, is Amoco's refinery, the biggest refinery in the whole Midwest, and gasoline has to be shipped up from the Amoco refinery into Chicago, about a distance of 30 miles, and yet the price in Chicago is half a cent lower than the price at Hammond, Indiana, right next door to the refinery.

Similarly, one finds that the price in Chicago, which was a dollar and three-tenths of a cent, is identical to the price at Birmingham, Alabama, even though Birmingham, Alabama, is located far south and very near crude oil deposits, and sitting right next door to the Colonial pipeline, a big product pipeline that allows Birmingham to obtain petroleum product at low cost. So you would expect about a 1 cent or so differential between the price of gasoline at Birmingham and the price of gasoline at Chicago, and that differential does not exist.

And one finds again that the price in Lima, Ohio, is 1.013 dollars for regular gasoline, and now Lima is the site of the Standard Oil Company of Ohio's largest refinery in its territory, and Marathon's gasoline has to go up from Robinson, Illinois, to Lima, and then continue to Cleveland. The price—and Sohio's gasoline—also has to move from Lima to Cleveland. This all is incurring additional transportation costs, and yet the price in Cleveland is identical to the price in Lima; so there are either equalities of prices where substantial transportation costs exist, or there are differences in prices that work in the direction opposite to those that would be expected on the basis of transportation costs.[56]

George Stigler, Mobil's expert, drew the opposite conclusions from essentially the same data, focusing less on differences that may be observed at a particular moment than on the tendency of prices in various cities to move together over time, with departures from the pattern being short-lived.[57]

The observation that flows into an area have eliminated price differentials in the past does not rule out the possibility that control of the facilities required for access to the area would allow significant price elevation. (This problem, of course, applies to any study based on historical price patterns.) Furthermore, such results (or those of other methods of correlating price changes across cities), generally still do not determine whether the degree of relatedness is sufficient to conclude that the city is or is not an *antitrust* market in terms of the Guidelines.

Summary
The role of terminal facilities in the wholesale distribution and marketing of gasoline gives rise to the possibility of geographic markets no larger than a metropolitan area, even though most or all of the gasoline sold in such an area is refined elsewhere. The argument would be that refiners who control the terminal facilities serving a metropolitan area could raise the wholesale price at those terminals, and it would not be economically feasible to truck in substantial quantities of gasoline from remote terminal facilities. Thus one might attempt to use the Guidelines' methodology to support the concept of such a small market.

The case for local wholesale markets displays certain weakness, however. The distance between many adjacent metropolitan areas seems not large enough to preclude the possibility of trucking in gasoline, at least if the 5 percent criterion is used. Moreover, no matter how insulated sales at the center of the metropolitan area might be, sales of gasoline to be consumed near the outer limits of the purported market are susceptible to competitive prices at the next-best terminal. Depending on the geographical distribution of sales, this could mean a substantial loss in sales for the hypothesized monopolist or cartel. In addition, if control of terminal facilities at a location is not complete, historically small sellers may be able to step up sales considerably in response to a price increase, since the flow of product is not totally constrained by the size of the terminal facilities. Unfortunately, although economists have examined actual prices across markets, they have been unsuccessful in resolving the likely impact of these factors.

Conclusion

The petroleum industry is an excellent vehicle for investigating the application of the Merger Guidelines to horizontal mergers. Most of the issues treated in the Guidelines (for example, product and geographic market definition, supply substitution, measurement of market share, foreign competition) come into play in a merger between two large, integrated petroleum companies. In addition, since more data has probably been collected on the petroleum industry than any other domestic industry, it should be easier to apply the Guidelines to large mergers in that industry than in other industries. Therefore, it is possible to attempt a number of the simulated calculations suggested by the Guidelines and to explore the problems that arise in the process. To the extent that the precise data called for are unavailable, it is possible to consider what substitute data or alternative tests might be suitable.

What is learned in attempting to implement the Guidelines is that several imaginative compromises are required to fit the Guidelines' procedures to the data likely to be available. Moreover, questions about the tests themselves arise which cannot be answered from a close reading of the Guidelines; rather, answers must be inferred from the principles that underlie the Guidelines. Thus, however appropriate to providing a broad conceptual framework for merger analysis, any notion that the Guidelines can be used like cookbook recipes—in which tests are applied in routine fashion to readily available data—is incorrect.

Notwithstanding certain problems and ambiguities in applying the Guidelines, it is clear just from the single example discussed in this chapter that doing merger analysis according to the 1982 Guidelines is a far cry from measuring actual past sales for some specified product in a specified section of the United States. At least in the petroleum industry the likelihood seems remote of establishing narrow product and geographic markets that stand up under a Guidelines analysis, as well as proving market shares that satisfy the Herfindahl criteria. As experience is gained in applying the Guidelines to other industries, it will be possible to determine whether that conclusion can be generalized.

Notes

The authors are grateful for comments and assistance from Barry Harris, Frank Lerman, and Lucinda Lewis and for suggestions from Franklin Fisher and an anonymous referee. The views expressed in this paper, however, are entirely our own.

1. Although the Guidelines do no more than suggest the Justice Department's likely enforcement stance, there seems little doubt that they are also intended to (and probably will) influence how the courts will decide cases brought before them. See Areeda, "Justice's Merger Guidelines: The General Theory," *Cal. L. Rev.* 71 (March 1983), pp. 306–307.

2. See generally, "Symposium: 1982 Merger Guidelines," *Cal. L. Rev.* 71 (March 1983); Schwartz, "The New Merger Guidelines? Guide to Governmental Discretion and Private Counseling or Propaganda for Revision of the Antitrust Laws?", *Cal. L. Rev.* 71 (March 1983); Ordover and Willig, "The 1982 Department of Justice Merger Guidelines: An Economic Assessment," *Cal. L. Rev.* 71 (March 1983); Harris and Jorde, "Market Discretion in the Merger Guidelines: Implications for Antitrust Enforcement," *Cal. L. Rev.* 71 (March 1983). For a discussion of the analytical underpinning of the 1982 Guidelines from the perspective of one of the drafters, see Werden, "Market Delineation and the Justice Department's Merger Guidelines," *Duke L. Journ.* (June 1983).

In response to some of the criticisms, the Guidelines were revised again in 1984. An earlier draft of this chapter was made available to the Justice Department while the revisions were being prepared, and some of the revisions are consistent with suggestions made in this chapter. Except where noted, citations correspond to the 1982 Guidelines.

3. The merger was investigated by the Federal Trade Commission rather than the Justice Department, and the FTC filed for a preliminary injunction to block the transaction, pending a full administrative hearing. At that point, Gulf elected to withdraw its tender offer, and Cities was subsequently acquired by Occidental Petroleum. Since the FTC has indicated its general agreement with the approach taken in the Guidelines, the decision as to which agency ultimately takes control of the investigation of a merger should not affect the relevance of the analysis contained herein. It should be noted that both authors were consultants to Gulf Oil for the proposed Gulf–Cities Service merger. The analysis, however, does not rely on any confidential data.

4. FTC Complaint, July 29, 1982.

5. M. Brannand and C. Beith, "Market Shares and Individual Company Data for U. S. Energy Markets: 1950–1980," *American Petroleum Institute Discussion Paper #014R.* Measuring shares by any other means (e.g., total refinery runs in the most recent year[s]) does not alter this picture.

6. PADD (Petroleum Administration for Defense District) III consists of the states of New Mexico, Texas, Louisiana, Alabama, Mississippi, and Arkansas.

7. Capacity percentage computed from DOE, *Petroleum Supply Annual* 1 (1981), pp. 103–125. In the portion of the Guidelines dealing with horizontal mergers, the Justice Department divides the spectrum of market concentration as measured by the HHI into three regions that can be broadly characterized as unconcentrated (HHI below 1,000), moderately concentrated (HHI between 1,000 and 1,800), and highly concentrated. Where a merger results in an HHI below 1,000, it will normally not be challenged. Where the resulting HHI is between 1,000 and 1,800, it is unlikely to be challenged if the increase attributable to the merger is less than 100. Where the resulting HHI is above 1,800, it is unlikely to be challenged if the increase is less than 50.

The HHI is calculated by summing the squares of the individual market shares of all firms included in the market. (Where one firm has 100 percent of the market, the HHI is 10,000.) The increase in the HHI attributable to any merger can be calculated independently of the overall market concentration by doubling the product of the market shares of the merging firms. For example, the merger of firms with market shares of 5 and 10 percent would increase the HHI by 100 ($5 \times 10 \times 2 = 100$).

8. An issue in the Complaint was that Gulf and Cities are two of the joint venture owners of the Colonial Pipeline, which has the largest capacity of any petroleum products pipeline in the United States. As a result of the merger, Gulf would control more than 30 percent of the voting shares of Colonial, sufficient under the shareholders' agreement to block any significant expansion of the pipeline's capacity. Since this issue is almost *sui generis* and is not amenable to a Guidelines type of analysis, it will not be discussed further. For overviews of the competitive issues relating to pipelines, see Edward Mitchell, ed., *Oil Pipelines and Public Policy* (1979); and John Hansen, *U.S. Oil Pipeline Markets* (1983).

9. See generally, Douglas Considine, ed., *Energy Technology Handbook* (1977).

10. Inputs other than crude oil, such as natural gas liquids, can serve as part of the basic raw material input to the refining process.

11. These units are expensive. A short-term change in relative product prices will not result in a change in the mix of these units. Short-term changes in the product mix occur within the limits of the existing units.

12. Neither individual shares of Gulf and Cities nor the overall level of concentration were provided in the public statements of the FTC, nor were the combined shares in PADD III alone made public.

13. Dividing the total into two equal parts produces the largest possible change in the HHI consistent with the total share equaling 18 percent.

14. *Petroleum Supply Annual* 1 (1981), p. 47.

15. "If entry into a market is so easy that existing competitors could not succeed in raising [the] price for any significant period of time, the Department is unlikely to challenge mergers in that market," Guidelines, Section III.B. It could be argued that some firms "on the margin" about whether or not to enter the refining industry would find the balance tipped by an increase in the price of kerojet. We assume this possibility

will not generate enough entry to affect the analysis. Our comfort in this assumption stems partly from our recognition that, given the current level of excess capacity, few firms are likely to be on the margin.

16. In 1981 United States refinery utilization averaged 69 percent of operable refinery capacity, with PADD III utilization of 67 percent; see *Petroleum Supply Annual* II (1981), pp. 135–146.

17. We assume that, during the time frame of the hypothetical conspiracy, excess capacity will not be eliminated by exit or demand increases. The 1984 revisions attempt to correct for this deficiency simply by defining entry to include significant expansion by fringe firms. (1984 Guidelines, footnote 20; also Section 3.43.)

18. This point is discussed generally in Landes and Posner, "Market Power in Antitrust Cases," *Harv. L. Rev.* 94 (1981).

19. Excess production capacity does not necessarily imply the ability to respond to a price increase if there are cost, product quality, marketing, or managerial problems that limit ability to increase sales.

20. The relevant passage reads: "The Department will include in the market the total sales or capacity of all firms (or plants) that are identified as being in the market" (Guidelines II.D.). The possibilities for supply substitution are discussed in the initial decision in another recent FTC merger case; see *In Re Weyerhaeuser Co.*, Docket No. 9150, FTC (October 10, 1983).

21. The quantity of kerosene yielded in distillation depends on the characteristics of the crude oil and the characteristics of the refinery. Because some of the quantity of kerosene yielded in distillation is used in blending, that quantity may differ from the sum of kerosene plus kerojet sold by refiners and reported in DOE figures of product leaving the refinery. The magnitude of this difference cannot be ascertained from public data. That it may be substantial is suggested by comparing DOE's reported kerosene plus kerojet shipments of 6.7 percent of total refinery products in 1982 with the industry rule of thumb of 10 to 15 percent kerosene distillation yield. See, for example, Nelson, *Petroleum Refinery Engineering*, pp. 216, 910–927, for kerosene yields from skimming and topping operations for U.S. crudes.

22. Presumably, as kerosene is withdrawn from the market, its price would increase, tending to eliminate the incentive to sell additional kerosene in the kerojet market. Once again, in addition to the relevant technological information, one would need all the relevant demand elasticities to calculate the precise amount of additional kerojet forthcoming. See Brennan, "Mistaken Elasticities and Mistaken Rules," *Harv. L. Rev.* 95 (1982), p. 1849.

23. Attempts to model the refinery process have employed econometric techniques and programming approaches. For examples of the former, see Dahl, "Refinery Mix in the U.S., Canada, and the EEC," *European Economic Review* (1981); and Dahl and Laumas, "Stability of U.S. Petroleum Refinery Response to Relative Product Prices," *Energy Economics* (1981). For examples of the latter, see Manne, "A Linear Programming Model of the U.S. Petroleum Refining Industry," *Econometrics* (1958); and Griffin, *Capacity Measurement in Petroleum Refining* (1971). Dahl focuses on the elasticity of the mix share of gasoline, finding it to be 0.2 for 1936–41 and 1947–75; Dahl and Laumas

examine the mix-share elasticity of kerosene but suggest that its insignificance arises from colinearity between the price of kerosene and distillate. (Combining kerosene plus distillate yields a share elasticity of 0.06 to 0.11 depending on whether observations during the controls period are or are not included.) This colinearity might arise if there is a significant substitutability between kerosene sold as a separate product and kerosene used in distillate blending. Griffin ("The Econometrics of Joint Production: Another Approach," *Review of Economics and Statistics* [1977]), using a pseudo-data approach, estimates a long-run supply elasticity of kerosene of 2.9, with significant cross-elasticities with gasoline and distillate.

24. Alternatively, one could identify, for each refinery, the observed maximum yield of kerojet (i.e., the ratio of kerojet production to total crude throughput) in the past several years and compute a kerojet universe based on the assumption that all refineries operate at maximum yield. Each refinery submits monthly production figures for individual products to the Department of Energy. Although these data are not publicly available, they can be obtained by the Justice Department or the FTC for litigation-related purposes (presumably to calculate the overall HHI, which requires the share of each firm). If relied on by the Justice Department or the FTC, they can probably be obtained, with appropriate confidentiality provisions, by counsel for the defendants if a lawsuit is filed. This, of course, is of no value to potential merger partners trying to decide whether a merger is likely to be challenged (a major purpose of the Guidelines).

25. The experiment suggested by the Guidelines involves a 5 percent price increase.

26. Guidelines, Section II.B.1. The 1984 revisions extend this period to one year.

27. Guidelines, Section II.D.

28. Under the 1982 Guidelines, other factors (with the exception of product heterogeneity) are invoked only for "close calls." (Hence, for example, mergers for which the HHI exceeds 1800 and the change in HHI exceeds 100 would not be affected.) Thus the traditional approach might undervalue the significance of excess capacity. The 1984 revisions do not limit consideration of other factors to close calls. That is, some factors (for example, ease of entry, changing market conditions) affect the analysis of any merger, whereas other factors enter only into close call situations under the 1984 revisions (Sections 3.2, 3.3, 3.4).

29. An additional issue, not discussed here, involved ownership of terminal facilities in southern Florida.

30. Market share figures based on *sales* within the market were not provided.

31. Hence PADD III would satisfy the LIFO (little in from the outside) test proposed by Elzinga and Hogarty for geographic market definition. "The Problem of Geographic Market Definition in Anti-merger Suits," *Antitrust Bulletin* 18 (Spring 1973).

32. Therefore, PADD III fails Elzinga and Hogarty's LOFI (little out from inside) test.

33. This is not to say that a price increase by PADD III producers would necessarily be unprofitable. The likelihood of its being profitable is more closely measured by PADD III's share of total United States production (or of total production in PADDs I, II, and III, since there is little flow across the Rockies), and the shares of two merging firms are more properly measured with respect to that larger universe.

34. A large portion of kerojet transport is by product pipeline (with a spur off the pipeline often leading right into the airport). Although most of the major pipelines are owned by the oil companies, they are required to operate as common carriers, which would tend to limit their ability to maintain the price discrimination by refusing pipeline access to airlines purchasing at the refinery.

35. In re *Ethyl Corp. No. 9128*, FTC (March 22, 1983). The Commission decision was reversed by the Court of Appeals. 729 F.2d 128 (1984). See also, Hay, "Oligopoly, Shared Monopoly, and Antitrust Law," *Cornell L. Rev.* 67 (March 1982).

36. Casual investigation suggests that, at present, kerojet is frequently sold on a delivered price basis, but if a customer insists on an FOB price, one is offered.

37. For a discussion of tankering, see, for example, Craig and Smith, "Aviation Fuel Usage—Economy and Conservation," *Canadian Aeronautics and Space Journal* (1978), esp. pp. 38–39.

38. To frustrate a hypothetical conspiracy it is not required that airlines take on no fuel at a particular airport, merely that they collectively shift enough business to make the hypothesized price increase unprofitable. The hypothetical colluders need not treat all of PADDs I and III in the same way; but arguably they could target the price increases at airports for which the possibilities for overflight are most limited.

39. Situations in which the 5 percent test can be quantitatively checked, rather than used as a mere thought experiment, are more likely to arise, as here, in a geographic market context.

40. In summer 1982 tanker rates from the Caribbean to Atlantic Coast ports amounted to about 2 percent of the value of kerojet transported (*Platts Oilgram Price Report*). The fact that Caribbean kerojet prices in early 1982 were about 2 percent above the Gulf Coast price indicates that Caribbean kerojet could be transported to either Gulf or Atlantic ports in the event of a 5 percent price increase.

41. See Brennan, "Mistaken Elasticities."

42. In this situation, Cities Service had no refinery in the Caribbean; Gulf had one small refinery in Puerto Rico amounting to only one-seventh of Puerto Rican refinery capacity (*Oil and Gas Journal*, Worldwide Refining issue, December 28, 1981). Further, Puerto Rican refineries as a group accounted for only 1.2 percent of Caribbean jet fuel production (United Nations, *Yearbook of World Energy Statistics*).

43. The 1984 revisions expand significantly the discussion of the proper treatment of foreign supplies with specific reference to situations where imports are subject to a quota (Sections 3.2.3 and 2.3.4).

44. Because Gulf and Cities' ratio of kerojet production to refinery capacity exceeded the industry average, it would not be surprising if the ratio of kerosene production to refinery capacity were well below the industry average (i.e., their shares in kerojet are high precisely because—at least during the year in which the measurements were made—they were emphasizing kerojet at the expense of kerosene).

45. Although we have emphasized the change in the HHI, it is important to note that the overall level of the HHI is also affected by expanding the universe, and the adjustment

might bring the overall index below 1,000, which is the so-called safe harbor. Because we lack data on other firms' market shares, we have not made these calculations.

46. The FTC identified nineteen metropolitan areas (SMSAs) (FTC Memorandum of Points and Authorities) in which it believed there was a lessening of wholesale gasoline competition. (It also identified three states which will not be examined here.) However, it did not publicly release the firms' market shares, the change in HHI, or the post-merger level of the HHI. In identifying these SMSAs in its complaint, the FTC indicated that it was relying on three different wholesale gasoline sales universes, one universe based on estimates contained in a Gulf document, a second universe based on the 1977 Census of Retail Trade, and the last universe based on data compiled by a private firm as a service to oil companies. The nineteen SMSAs cited by the FTC included any SMSA that appeared on any one of the three lists; only four SMSAs appeared on every list.

47. In the merger in question, most of the major pipeline terminals are adjacent to the Colonial Pipeline or the smaller, fairly parallel Plantation Pipeline; the water terminals are generally those serving cities on the East Coast.

48. For example, the FTC's Complaint regarding Mobil's attempted acquisition of Marathon Oil indicated trucking costs of 5 cents per gallon per 100 miles. "Memorandum of Points and Authorities in Support of the Federal Trade Commission's Complaint for Temporary Restraining Order and for Preliminary Injunction," p. 22. The secretaries of Energy and Transportation's *National Energy Transportation Study: A Preliminary Report to the President* (1980, p. 214) suggests 2 to 3 cents per gallon per 100 miles.

49. Many of the sales are made FOB terminal with customer pickup, which, if continued, would frustrate efforts at price discrimination.

50. The 1984 revisions are more explicit in indicating circumstances in which an increase other than 5 percent will be used. The revisions note, by way of example, that a larger increase might be appropriate if the "price" to be increased is a tariff (footnote 6) or commission that constitutes a small fraction of the price of the product being sold (footnote 7). The specific reference to tariff or commission is somewhat curious because the logic would seem to apply to any of the vertical stages involved in turning out a finished product. The implicit assumptions underlying such a modification are that one purpose of the Guidelines is to prevent mergers when the probability of collusion is significant *and* a judgment that the probability of collusion, for a given percent change in price, increases with the relative increase in profitability. The theoretical rationale for assuming that the probability of a price increase depends on the relative increase in economic profits is not clear, however. For example, if the difficulties of collusion do not increase proportionately with the size of the market, the probability of collusion would increase as the absolute size of the market increases (and, therefore, the absolute profits gain from a given percent increase in price). For a discussion of the 5 percent test, see Werden, "Market Delineation and the Justice Department's Merger Guidelines."

51. Some of the East Coast cities would be served by water transport from the Gulf Coast or from the New York or Philadelphia area refinery complexes.

52. If the validity of the metropolitan market turns on the ownership of terminal facilities, an additional measurement issue relevant to computing market shares is

raised. There appear to be two ways of measuring a firm's size in local areas: (1) sales (including internal transfers) by a refiner (or other wholesale entity) within the region; or (2) all movements through a company's own terminals in a region. The magnitudes may differ because a refiner may move gasoline through a terminal owned by an independent terminal operator or by another refiner without relinquishing ownership of the gasoline. In general, attributing movements through a terminal to the owner of the terminal results in a more concentrated market, since scale economies dictate a relatively small number of different terminals at any location.

53. For the sake of the present discussion, we assume that new terminal facilities would take a year or more to construct and, hence, would be ignored under the Guidelines' procedures for geographic market analysis. In addition, while pipeline ownership may possibly have an impact on the ability to utilize certain terminals, issues of pipeline ownership and access are not discussed here.

54. See, for example, the approach suggested by Horowitz to resolving market definition issues. I. Horowitz, "Market Definition in Antitrust Analysis: A Regression-Based Approach," *Southern Economic Journal* (1981).

55. See, for example, Edmund P. Learned and Catherine C. Ellsworth, *Gasoline Pricing in Ohio* (Boston: Harvard Business School Division of Research, 1959), p. 25, quoting a company policy statement. See also, pp. 42 and 83 of the same volume; Robert T. Masson and Fred C. Allvine, "Strategy and Structure: Majors, Independents, and Prices of Gasoline in Local Markets," in *Essays on Industrial Organization in Honor of Joe S. Bain*, ed. Masson and Qualls, pp. 155–180; and Howard P. Marvel, "Competition and Price Levels in the Retail Gasoline Market," *Review of Economics and Statistics* (May 1978), pp. 252–258.

56. Scherer testimony, pp. 241–243.

57. A recent paper attempts to examine wholesale gasoline price data for six cities in order to evaluate the cities that belong in the same market. Slade, "Causality Tests for Market Extent Applied to Petroleum Products," Bureau of Economics, Federal Trade Commission Working Paper, June 1983. Slade examines, for each city, whether the explanation of the city's price is improved by employing knowledge of contemporaneous prices in other cities. If the explanation is improved (and if the relationship is reciprocal), the cities are assumed to be in the same market. For the two cities in the Southeast considered, she finds evidence that they are in the same geographic market.

3 Anticompetitive Mergers: Prevention and Cure

William J. Kolasky, Jr.,
Phillip A. Proger, and
Roy T. Englert, Jr.

Mergers that are likely to lessen competition substantially are illegal.[1] Two federal agencies, the Federal Trade Commission (FTC) and the Department of Justice, have the statutory power to go to court to stop them.[2] In the past, however, these agencies were often unable to learn enough about a potentially anticompetitive merger before it took place to persuade a court to enjoin it. As a result, mergers have taken place, and afterward the government struggled, with indifferent success, to cure their anticompetitive effects.

Congress passed the premerger notification provisions of the Hart-Scott-Rodino Antitrust Improvements Act in 1976 to enhance the government's ability to block anticompetitive mergers before they occur.[3] As we will show in this chapter, that legislation has accomplished the desired end, though not by the means Congress probably expected. The government's record in obtaining preliminary injunctions in merger cases is no better today than it was before the act was passed.

What happened, instead, is that the act has caused both private parties and the government to take a more flexible, practical approach to mergers. Private parties now know that they must report any proposed merger to the government and that the government will have an opportunity, before consummation, to develop the information it would need to get a preliminary injunction. Therefore, the parties are less likely to be tempted into a clearly anticompetitive merger by the hope that, even if it is challenged, it will be several years before they will have to divest.

Conversely, the government, being in a position to conduct an extensive premerger investigation, is now better able to determine in which markets a merger is likely to have anticompetitive effects. Thus the government no longer faces the dilemma of having to seek a preliminary injunction against the entire transaction or, if it does not do that, engage in lengthy post-merger litigation to force divestiture of the assets that raise the antitrust problem. Instead, the government, through premerger negotiations, often can cause merging parties to restructure the merger to cure its anticompetitive aspects prospectively.

For the first two years that the Antitrust Improvements Act was in effect, neither the Department of Justice nor the FTC made fully effective use of the leverage the act gave them to extract such pre-merger concessions. Beginning with the administration of William F. Baxter, however, the Department of Justice—through what has come to be known as its "fix-it-first" policy—has begun to use this power more actively.

In this chapter we examine why restructuring transactions in advance of consummation is generally preferable to the alternatives of a preliminary injunction or a post-merger divestiture. We also examine how the Justice Department is currently applying its fix-it-first policy and offer some suggestions for improving use of the legislation.

The Failure of Traditional Remedies

The Traditional Remedies
The importance of relief to successful enforcement of section 7 has long been recognized. As early as 1947, in *International Salt Co. v. United States*,[4] the U.S. Supreme Court noted that a victory on liability was no victory without proper relief:

In an equity suit, the end to be served is not punishment of past transgression, nor is it merely to end specific illegal practices. A public interest served by such civil suits is that they effectively pry open to competition a market that has been closed by defendants' illegal restraints. If this decree accomplishes less than that, the Government has won a lawsuit and lost a cause.[5]

From the beginning, the principal goal for relief in section 7 actions has been to restore to the marketplace the competition lessened or eliminated by the merger. Once the government establishes that a merger or acquisition is illegal, courts have broad discretion to fashion equitable relief necessary and appropriate to achieve that goal.[6] A secondary goal has been to deter companies from attempting future unlawful acquisitions by denying the acquiring companies the benefits of an unlawful acquisition.[7]

Divestiture Divestiture traditionally has been the customary remedy.[8] As the Court observed in *du Pont II*, "the very words of §7 suggest that an undoing of the acquisition is a natural remedy."[9] Moreover, divestiture is "simple, relatively easy to administer, and sure."[10]

Divestiture may take many forms. Complete divestiture has been applied to remedy numerous illegal mergers or acquisitions.[11] Underlying complete divestiture is the premise that anticompetitive effects can best be counteracted by restoring the market to its preacquisition structure.[12] For example, when the FTC, in *Procter & Gamble Co.*,[13] found that P&G's acquisition of Clorox would lessen competition in the household liquid bleach market, it ordered complete divestiture. The FTC, applying *du Pont II*, rejected P&G's contention that the public interest could be protected by injunctive relief against enhancement of Clorox's dominance of the household liquid bleach market. The anticompetitive effects could be corrected only by restoring the market, as nearly as possible, to its premerger structure.[14]

Complete divestiture is not always necessary; the courts have found that often partial divestiture adequately serves the purposes of section 7.[15] This is most frequently true when a merger has anticompetitive effects in some markets but not in others. In such cases, divestiture may be confined to assets serving the markets adversely affected. For example, in *Union Carbide Corp.*,[16] after finding that Union Carbide's acquisition of the Visking Corporation would lessen competition in the manufacture of polyethylene, the FTC required Union Carbide to divest Visking's polyethylene manufacturing business but not its synthetic sausage casing manufacturing business. The FTC noted that "total divestiture is not an automatic remedy" and that the choice of remedies is "to be exercised with the goal of restoring and [ensuring] the preservation of healthy competition in the relevant markets."[17] Partial divestiture was found to achieve that goal because Visking could be an effective, strong competitor in the polyethylene film market without its sausage casing business.[18]

Injunctive Relief Enjoining an illegal merger or acquisition is the second equitable remedy traditionally available to the government. Section 15 of the Clayton Act authorizes the Department of Justice to sue in order to "prevent and restrain" illegal mergers or acquisitions.[19] Similarly, the FTC is empowered under section 13(b) of the Federal Trade Commission Act[20] to bring suit to "enjoin" violations of section 7 and other laws it enforces when the Commission has "reason to believe" that an injunction would be in the interest of the public.

Enjoining a merger, like complete divestiture, is a draconian remedy. Resulting delay often causes the parties to abandon the transaction altogether. There is little reason to be concerned about this impact in the case of a simple acquisition that affects only one market and that will unquestionably lessen competition in that market. But since the adoption of the original Merger Guidelines in 1968 and the related development by the Supreme Court of easy-to-apply presumptive rules for horizontal merger cases, few cases have been so straightforward. More common are cases in which the merger involves companies doing business in several different lines of commerce, not all of which will be adversely affected by the merger,[21] and cases where the effect on competition is relatively uncertain.[22] In such cases, courts have been reluctant to grant preliminary injunctive relief and have often resorted instead to hold-separate orders as a device for facilitating a later divestiture if the merger is ultimately found unlawful.[23]

An additional obstacle to injunctive relief in merger cases, at least before 1976, was that the government often did not learn about a proposed merger early enough to prepare a persuasive case on the merits. For both reasons, before 1976 preliminary injunctive relief, though theoretically available, was rarely sought and even more rarely granted.[24] Thus the success of merger enforcement depended heavily on the effectiveness of post-merger divestiture.

The Efficacy of Post-merger Divestiture

The efficacy of divestiture orders in achieving the goals of antimerger relief was reviewed in two empirical studies published in 1969 and 1972. Both studies concluded that divestiture orders frequently fail either to restore competition or to deprive the transgressor of the benefits of unlawful acquisition.

The Elzinga Study The 1969 study was adapted from a doctoral dissertation done at Michigan State by Kenneth Elzinga, a professor at the University of Virginia.[25] Elzinga studied thirty-nine merger cases filed between 1950 and 1960 and either settled by consent order or decided in the government's favor by the end of 1964.

Elzinga developed a set of criteria on the basis of which he rated these decrees as successful, sufficient, deficient, or unsuccessful. To be rated "successful," a decree had to require complete divestiture of the unlawfully acquired assets. The divestiture had to be to a person (other than one of the Fortune top 200 manufacturing or top 50 merchandising firms) able to provide adequate financing but with no previous ties, either horizontal or vertical, to the industry involved; and it had to be completed within three years after the acquisition. An order was rated "unsuccessful" if there was no divestiture at all, if the divestiture was de minimis, or if the divestiture was to a significant horizontal competitor, a vertically related company with foreclosure problems, or a nonviable firm.

Using these criteria, Elzinga found only three "successful" and thirty-one "unsuccessful" cases. Of the FTC cases in his sample, he found that the average time from acquisition to complaint was 19 months and the average duration from acquisition to divestiture 67.5 months. For the Department of Justice, the average time from acquisition to complaint was 10.6 months and the average from acquisition to divestiture 63.8 months.[26] To remedy these problems a low success rate and lengthy delays in divestiture—Elzinga recommended:

1. a presumption against partial divestitures. In his view, a "partial divestiture, since it consists of a 'line of commerce' as opposed to the operations of a once-going business, generally is not conducive to reestablishing a viable independent firm."[27]

2. that the government exercise greater supervision in the selection of a buyer for the divested assets because, "as a general rule, having resolved itself that divestiture is inevitable, it is in the divesting firm's interest to seek out or favor a buyer who will either be cooperative, phlegmatic in his rivalry, or destined to fail."[28]

3. not relying on injunctive provisions or bans on future acquisitions as a substitute for divestiture, on the ground that such provisions were a deviation from the ideal of antitrust enforcement because they involve the government in detailed regulation of markets, because the policing of such decrees is highly difficult, and because it is difficult for the government and the parties at the time they are writing the decree to anticipate the natural evolution of the markets involved.[29]

The Yale Study The second empirical study on the efficacy of divestiture orders was produced by Malcolm Pfunder, Daniel Plaine, and Anne Marie Whittemore, students at the Yale Law School.[30] In the study, Pfunder, Plaine, and Whittemore reviewed all section 7 cases begun after the 1950 amendments to the Clayton Act and terminated by

January 1, 1970. They found that of 227 cases, 137 (60 percent) resulted in an order of divestiture. From this group, they selected 114 cases for study.[31] Sufficient information concerning compliance was available to assess the completeness of relief in 103 of the cases. In eight cases, divestiture never occurred.[32] In an additional ten decrees, compliance occurred only after modification of the final order of divestiture, following the defendant's failure to comply fully with the original order.

By using a scale of preferences to classify the divestiture purchaser, the authors evaluated the success of decrees in which divestiture was accomplished. They regarded as most procompetitive a purchaser who was both small and a new entrant in the relevant market. Least desirable was a purchaser who was a competitor, supplier, or customer of the divested operation. Only sixteen cases resulted in sale of all or part of the assets ordered divested to a newly formed corporation backed by a group of independent investors or by the former independent owners. The authors also observed that "the most striking feature of compliance in Section 7 cases is the frequency with which *seemingly* anticompetitive corporate purchasers buy the assets ordered divested."[33] Moreover, in decrees requiring divestiture of only those assets used in the line of commerce in which the section 7 illegality was found, the assets were frequently sold to a buyer who turned out not to be economically viable.[34]

As Elzinga had done, the authors of the Yale study offered recommendations. They recommended that:

1. the entity ordered divested be required to be a complete economic package that is at least potentially profitable.[35]

2. a buyer not be considered acceptable unless its purchase would dissipate the effects of the illegal acquisition. In particular, they criticized the government's practice of approving any purchaser less anticompetitive than the divesting party. They proposed instead that a spinoff, public offering, or sale to a newly formed corporation be required whenever the divesting party is unable to locate an acceptable purchaser within the time provided by the decree.[36]

3. time limits in the decree be strictly enforced and that a divesting party be given no guarantee of a fair price for the divested assets. If the divesting party claimed inability to divest within the time allowed by the decree, modifications designed to ease the burden should not be granted unless compliance with the original decree was impossible at

any price. Instead, the party should be ordered to make the package of assets more attractive. If the party remained unable to obtain offers from any acceptable purchasers, and the possibilities of creating a marketable package had been exhausted, a trustee should be appointed to sell the assets for what they would bring.[37]

Some Thoughts on the Studies Viewed from the vantage point of a decade latter, some criticisms of the performance of the enforcement agencies in implementing divestiture decrees appear to have been misplaced. For example, from an antitrust perspective there is no need to prefer a newly formed company as a purchaser over a "conglomerate" entering the relevant market for the first time. Similarly, divestiture to a company with some vertical relationship to that market, or even to a much smaller competitor, may promote efficiency and might actually be preferable to divestiture to a new entrant.[38] And, as companies have come more and more regularly to buy and sell assets in particular lines of business,[39] the authors' objections to partial divestitures involving the sale of assets in particular lines of business now seem quaint.

Nevertheless, the core of the criticisms advanced in the two studies had merit. Many of the reforms advocated have since been incorporated in the practice of both enforcement agencies.[40] For example, both the FTC and the Justice Department now have general policies against including upset prices in decrees and against accepting detailed regulatory provisions as a substitute for divestiture.[41] In negotiating divestiture decrees, the agencies look more closely at the assets to be divested and have even employed financial analysts to evaluate their probable viability as a separate entity. Generally today, both agencies regularly insist on a veto power over the identity of the purchaser of the divested assets. Also, both agencies have developed a number of devices that promote timely compliance with divestiture orders, including (1) insistence on shorter deadlines for divestiture[42]; (2) periodic deadlines when, for example, the availability of the assets to be divested must be publicly announced, accompanied by periodic progress reports[43]; (3) built-in economic disincentives for delaying the divestiture[44]; and (4) provisions for appointing a trustee if the party fails to divest promptly.[45] Finally, both agencies have adopted tougher policies against modifying divestiture decrees to permit more time to complete the divestiture, and both have been quicker to seek sanctions for noncompliance.[46]

Whether these reforms have resulted in significant improvement in actual results is another question. No systematic empirical studies of compliance with divestiture orders have been published since 1972. Given the wide-ranging improvements made and the closer attention both agencies give to the entire remedy process, it is time to conduct a new empirical study. Until such a study is done, however, we can only say that the conventional wisdom—derived largely from the Elzinga and Yale studies—continues to be that divestiture may work but not without problems along the way which keep it from being a wholly satisfactory remedial tool.

A New Age: Premerger Notification

The empirical studies of the defects of divestiture did not go unnoticed. Members of the bar and the academic community soon began to echo Elzinga's and the Yale students' criticisms of divestiture orders.[47] As we have seen, both the Department of Justice and the FTC, in an effort to close the more obvious loopholes, began to include in their decrees some of Elzinga's and the Yale students' recommendations.

A more fundamental implication of these studies was also recognized, however. Even in the best of circumstances, divestiture is not, as the Supreme Court once claimed, "simple, relatively easy to administer, and sure."[48] In proverbial terms, divestiture is "a pound of cure": it is often painful to undergo, and the patient—competition in the relevant markets—may or may not recover his original health. Realizing this, and with a growing body of literature commending premerger relief,[49] Congress acted. In 1975 and 1976, the Senate considered the Hart-Scott Bill, which, with a few exceptions, provided for notification to the Department of Justice and FTC of mergers of a certain size, imposed a mandatory waiting period between notification and consummation, and made a stay of the merger automatic during any pending government suit to block the merger.[50] In testimony before the Senate Subcommittee on Antitrust and Monopolies, Assistant Attorney General Thomas E. Kauper said the premerger notification procedure would give the Justice Department "a meaningful opportunity to seek a preliminary injunction before a questionable merger is consummated. This is of great practical importance because divestiture of stock or assets after an illegal merger is consummated is frequently an inadequate remedy for a variety of reasons."[51] The subcommittee also heard testimony from Joseph F. Brodley, a professor who relied on the Elzinga and Yale studies to document the inadequacies of divestiture.[52]

In concluding that premerger notification should be enacted into law, the Senate Judiciary Committee noted:

Over the 20-year period from 1955 to 1975, the Department of Justice has sought only 62 full or partial preliminary injunctions against consummations of mergers. (FTC has had injunction authority only since 1973 and has used it in only three merger cases.) In the limited number of cases in which the Government sought a preliminary injunction, it was successful in obtaining it in less than one-third of the cases. After a court ruling on the merits, however, judgment for defendant was granted in only 10 instances—or in 16 percent of the cases. Of the 39 contested cases, the Department was ultimately successful on the merits in 31.

Despite the Department's impressive record after trial on the merits, the record reflects that the underlying purposes of section 7 have not been vindicated because of the lack of an effective mechanism to enjoin illegal mergers *before* they occur. The Committee believes that subsection (d) provides that mechanism.[33]

In 1976 the House considered a different premerger notification bill. This bill, introduced by Representative Peter W. Rodino, Jr.,[54] contained the same basic provisions as the Senate bill, except that the provision for an automatic stay of a merger during the pendency of any government suit was deleted. The House Monopolies Subcommittee heard testimony from Kauper and from FTC Chairman Paul Rand Dixon, as well as an independent statistical survey of merger relief presented by Willard F. Mueller, a former chief economist for the FTC.[55] The House Judiciary Committee, like its Senate counterpart, concluded that premerger notification was desirable to prevent anticompetitive mergers, and after some late-session maneuvering, Congress passed the Hart-Scott-Rodino Act.[56]

Commentators immediately noted that the Act "should significantly improve the Government's ability to obtain a timely preliminary injunction and thus make possible more meaningful relief in the case of mergers ultimately held violative of the antitrust laws."[57] But for nonbank mergers announced during the first five years that the Act was in effect (from August 30, 1978 to August 30, 1983),[58] the Department of Justice and FTC, between them, sought preliminary injunctions in only ten reported cases and obtained a preliminary injunction in only one case.[59] In one other case, the parties voluntarily postponed the merger pending adjudication of its legality.[60] In four cases a hold-separate order, not a full preliminary injunction, was entered.[61] In the remaining four cases, preliminary relief was denied.[62]

This record might lead one to conclude that premerger notification has not served its purpose, but such a conclusion would be hasty. The purpose of premerger notification is not to increase the frequency of preliminary injunctions but rather to prevent anticompetitive mergers. An anticompetitive merger abandoned because of a government threat to sue should be counted a victory for premerger notification.[63] The same is true of a merger restructured so as not to lessen competition after the government has studied it and has announced that it is prepared to bring suit.[64] As long as the government is neither too lenient nor too zealous in its demands, restructuring can preserve the public and private benefits of mergers[65] and, at the same time, prevent their bad effects. This is not to say that premerger notification is an unmixed blessing. An agency may in fact be too lenient or too zealous, and harm to competition or shareholders may result. Moreover, premerger notification is inevitably somewhat burdensome and therefore increases the costs of merging. Fortunately, the agencies need not, and do not, issue "second requests" for voluminous information when it is apparent that a merger poses no threat to competition.[66]

Available data suggest that the government has, in fact, been more successful since the Hart-Scott-Rodino Act became effective in persuading parties to restructure transactions. During the four-year period 1979–82, the Department of Justice entered premerger consent decrees in ten cases and the FTC entered premerger consent orders in twelve cases. By comparison, during the four-year period preceding the effective date of the act, 1974–77, there were only two such Justice Department decrees and no FTC orders. This increase in consent decrees, though perhaps not conclusive, tends to confirm that the act has had a greater impact than preliminary injunction figures alone suggest. The government is now better able to negotiate agreeable dispositions of most mergers without going to court, and private litigants are now less likely to force a matter to a preliminary injunction hearing unless the government's case is truly doubtful.[67]

Remedies in the New Age

Restructuring mergers prospectively has required changes in the policies and practices of both agencies. The FTC has long been willing to negotiate the terms of a consent settlement before filing a complaint, but in the past it rarely insisted that discussions be completed before the merger was consummated.[68] As a result, the FTC's consent orders usually involved post-merger divestiture. The FTC now more often attempts to reach a final decision before a merger is consummated, though its collegial structure makes difficult achievement of this result in every case.[69] Therefore, frequently the FTC still must be satisfied with post-merger relief.[70]

The Department of Justice, on the other hand, traditionally took the position that parties who propose an illegal merger could not obtain Department of Justice advice as to how to cure the illegality.[71] Even after the Hart-Scott-Rodino Act became effective, the Justice Department continued to refuse to enter into precomplaint negotiations: "The Division, as a matter of policy, does not make it a practice to discuss possible restructuring of proposed transactions to take place after consummation of the merger."[72]

That policy was wisely abandoned under Assistant Attorney General William F. Baxter. The Department of Justice now advises merging parties of its enforcement intentions and discusses with them alternative ways to cure any anticompetitive impact of the merger.[73] Through what has come to be known as the "fix-it-first" rule, the department has demanded in almost every case that parties submit to a consent decree, agreeing to restructure the transaction in a way satisfactory to the department, before they consummate a merger.

These premerger negotiations, backed by the threat of a government suit, have become a practical, efficient, and effective tool to remedy the anticompetitive aspects of a proposed merger prospectively. While Baxter was in office, the Department of Justice obtained premerger decrees in eight cases, and no preliminary injunction actions had to be litigated.[74] We hope, therefore, that the FTC will, to the extent possible, move toward the kind of fix-it-first policy the Department of Justice has adopted.

A General Approach: Accommodation of Interests

In structuring relief in a merger case, the primary focus of attention must be on maintaining (or, if necessary, restoring) competition. The surest way to achieve this goal is either to enjoin the entire transaction before it is consummated or to order a prompt and complete divestiture of all of the assets or securities that have been acquired.

If the only effect of mergers were to lessen competition, there might be no objection to such an approach; but as the late John McGowan showed in his article "Mergers for Power and Progress," mergers may enhance the efficiency of the firms involved in ways that clearly add to consumer welfare. This is especially likely to be the case with mergers involving two companies, each of which does business in several different markets and which compete with each other in only some of those markets. It is just as important that the government not interfere with the efficiency-producing aspects of such mergers as it is that their competition-lessening features be cured.

To preserve the efficiency-enhancing features of a merger while rooting out its anticompetitive effects, the government should always give the parties an opportunity to propose ways to restructure the transaction so as to eliminate its anticompetitive features. In determining whether the restructuring proposed is sufficient, the government should not be afraid to give consideration to what appear superficially to be "private interests" asserted by the merging parties, notwithstanding the U.S. Supreme Court dictum that "the pinch on private interests is not relevant to fashioning an antitrust decree, as the public interest is our sole concern.'[75]

This dictum was in cases involving *post-merger* remedies. In that context, the Court's concern is a valid one. Most private hardships that merged parties cite—tax consequences, the difficulty of unscrambling assets, the unfairness of being required to divest after-acquired assets—result from an unlawful transaction and would not have come about if the merger had been stopped or was restructured before closing. These are not interests that merit consideration by the government.

Interests asserted by not-yet-merged parties are likely to be very different and deserve a more sympathetic ear. Certainly, ineffective remedies should not be accepted to protect the private interests. Mergers that may lessen competition substantially are illegal, and no one should be able to buy a "little" substantial lessening of competition by claiming private hardship. Nothing in the law, however, requires that the government demand unnecessary sacrifice of private interests in the name of the public interest. Those private interests may be the very ones that, translated into consumer welfare terms, underlie the efficiency-enhancing features of the proposed transaction. Therefore, if the public interest in competition is served equally by any of several remedies, the one least injurious to those private interests should be selected.[76]

Guidelines for Merger Relief
Some of the enforcement agencies' policies concerning relief are well known to the bar, but they are not contained in either the Department

of Justice Merger Guidelines or any other official pronouncement.[77] For example, there are no official pronouncements on the amount of divestiture necessary to "fix" a competitive problem, or on when exceptions to the fix-it-first rule will be allowed. It would be useful for the agencies to develop a set of guidelines that would advise the public what standards they are likely to apply in framing relief. In this section, we suggest some guidelines.

1. *The restructuring should be sufficient to ensure that the affected markets are not substantially more concentrated after the merger than before.*

The overwhelming majority of mergers that give rise to legitimate antitrust concerns are those that involve companies that are direct competitors in one or more markets. In the case of such mergers the feared lessening of competition results from the reduction in the number of competitors, and the corresponding increase in concentration, in the markets affected.

Both for its own use in judging such mergers and for the guidance of the business community, the Justice Department recently revised its substantive merger guidelines, setting forth numerical criteria for the level of concentration it is prepared to tolerate before it will consider challenging a proposed merger.[78] These Guidelines provide, in effect, that a merger will not be challenged unless there is at least one market in which the parties compete that is sufficiently concentrated that the Herfindahl-Hirschman Index (HHI) is at least 1,000, and in which each party has a large enough market share that the merger will increase the HHI by at least 100 points.[79]

The simplest remedial guideline would be for the Justice Department to require that in any market in which a merger results in concentration levels above those permitted by the Guidelines, the acquiring party must agree to divest either the already owned or the acquired assets that are used in that market. This would have the appearance, at least, of preserving or restoring the status quo ante.

This guideline, while easy to administer, would be too simplistic, for there are some cases in which it would result in less divestiture than is necessary and others where it would result in too much. Such a rule might well result in too little divestiture—for example, if the assets used to compete in a particular market are operated by one or both parties to the merger as an integral part of a larger line of business. In such cases, those assets alone may be insufficient to allow the person acquiring them to compete efficiently in that market.

Thus, as the Elzinga and the Yale studies found, the enforcement agencies cannot simply identify the assets in the affected market and require, mechanistically, that those assets be divested. They must also determine whether those assets are part of a larger whole, some or all of which should also be required to be divested in order to ensure that the entity acquiring them becomes a meaningful competitive factor.

Conversely, there may be other cases in which divestiture of only a part of the assets used to compete in the affected market would be sufficient. This might be the case, for example, where a less-than-complete divestiture would be enough to return the post-merger concentration levels back below the Guidelines' thresholds.

A recent consent decree in the cigar industry shows that the government may, in some instances, be willing to accept more limited divestiture. Swisher, the second largest cigar producer in a national market, sought to buy Bayuk, the fourth largest producer.[80] Bayuk's shareholders had voted for complete dissolution of the company, which sold two brands of cigars. Before a scheduled preliminary injunction hearing, the parties settled by agreeing that Bayuk could sell the higher-volume cigar brand (Phillies) to any but the top four cigar companies and the lower-volume cigar brand (Garcia y Vega) to any but the top company (i.e., to Swisher or anyone else except Consolidated Cigar Company). As justification for this unusual decree, the government noted that the merger would raise the HHI above an objectionable level if and only if (1) both brands were sold to one of the top four companies; (2) the Phillies brand was sold to one of the top four companies; or (3) the Garcia y Vega brand was sold to Consolidated Cigar. In addition, the assets used to manufacture the two brands were easily separable and there were strong private equities—the desire of Bayuk's shareholders to liquidate their investment in a declining industry—at stake.

As the government recognized, this approach—modifying a proposed horizontal transaction in a single market to bring it within numerical bounds—should not lightly be carried over to other situations.[81] The basic numerical criteria used in the cigar case, and published four months later in the Merger Guidelines, are highly arbitrary simply because they are bright lines dividing a continuum. The government may challenge mergers causing a 101-point increase in the Herfindahl concentration index but not similar mergers causing a 99-point increase, not because they differ in competitive impact but because a line must be drawn somewhere.[82] A company buying certain assets, then selling just enough to bring the acquisition within numerical limits, may gain a significant but "slight" competitive advantage by its game of brinksmanship. In addition, the divested assets may not be as neatly severable as they were in the cigar case, and the divested assets may not be independently viable, or they may simply be much less of a competitive force than they were when attached to the company from which they were purchased.[83] In short, although there may be cases in which this sort of partial divestiture is appropriate, the government should scrutinize each case carefully and critically.

What this discussion shows most clearly is that no simple, mechanistic rule is available for defining what amount of restructuring should be required. Rather, enforcement agencies must judge, case by case, how much restructuring is necessary to ensure that the post-merger market structure is not substantially more concentrated than before. For the guidance of the business community, the agencies might indicate that, as a general rule, this means the post-merger concentration levels in the affected markets, after restructuring, must at least be restored to the levels deemed acceptable by the Justice Department's Merger Guidelines. Unless the parties are willing to agree to a restructuring that will satisfy this standard, the enforcement agencies should seek to enjoin the entire transaction.

2. There should be adequate assurances that the restructuring will be completed promptly.

a. *Where possible, the parties should either complete the restructuring before they merge or have a firm contract for the sale of the assets to be divested.* Once the parties to a merger have agreed to restructure the transaction in a way that satisfies the enforcement agencies, the inquiry shifts to how that restructuring should be administered. Ideally, one would like to see the restructuring completed before the merger goes forward. This, of course, may not always be feasible; so a rigid insistence on such a rule would defeat many otherwise desirable restructuring proposals.

The Justice Department's current fix-it-first rule is an alternative to requiring that the restructuring always be completed before the merger goes forward. This rule requires that merging parties, if they do not complete the restructuring before the merger is consummated, at least have a firm contract of sale for the offending assets before the merger is consummated. This policy is generally sound. It eliminates many problems identified in the Elzinga and Yale studies because the buyer will be known and evaluated in advance and the divestiture is certain to be completed within a brief, specified period of time. The current policy is not the only way to solve these problems, however, and in some cases it will not be the one that best accommodates public and private interests.

Where the parties will consent to a judicially enforcible divestiture order, other safeguards—such as hold-separate orders and trustee provisions—may, in appropriate cases, replace a firm contract of sale. These are discussed below; for now, the key point is that the government consider these alternatives whenever there is not enough time or it is not practical to find a qualified buyer, or delayed divestiture is likely to yield a more attractive buyer than immediate divestiture.

The first condition is most likely to be present in a tender-offer situation, whether it is a friendly or a hostile one. Recognizing that tender offers are part of the efficient working of capital markets,[84] the Department of Justice already excepts hostile takeover bids from the fix-it-first rule.[85] By not extending this exception to friendly offerors, the Department of Justice gives existing or incoming hostile offerors an arbitrary advantage in a takeover fight. Clearly, the department should adopt a more evenhanded policy and should except from the fix-it-first rule any offeror, hostile or friendly, in a tender offer where there is a hostile offeror.

The second condition—that delayed divestiture is likely to yield a more desirable buyer—will frequently be met because an acquiring company, forced to make a quick sale, will usually end up selling the assets to one of its own competitors. Unless the particular buyer is clearly unacceptable, the Department of Justice may back itself into a corner by insisting on the fix-it-first rule. A judge will be unimpressed by the government's complaints about a sale made, quickly, at the government's insistence. By agreeing to delay divestiture by a few months but retaining for itself the power to approve a purchaser, the government may be able to bring about a less potentially anticompetitive sale. The government, therefore, should require a firm contract for sale only when it is satisfied that there are a number of acceptable buyers, and a quick, forced sale can be made to one of them.

b. *If there is no firm contract, the merging parties should be required to agree to a set of standard safeguards to ensure that divestiture is accomplished promptly.* When merging companies present a convincing argument for an exception to the fix-it-first policy, the government must turn to some alternative set of safeguards to ensure that the necessary restructuring is accomplished in a manner that will preserve competition as fully as possible. In this section, we review the seven safeguards most commonly employed and offer some suggestions to enhance their effectiveness. These safeguards should, in every instance, be incorporated into a consent order that can be enforced either by the contempt powers of the federal courts or by substantial civil penalties.

(1) *The acquired assets should be required to be held separate pending divestiture.* A hold-separate order in a divestiture decree typically requires that assets to be divested be maintained separate from the other assets of the acquiring firm.[86] It appears that the Department of Justice, in consent decrees involving post-merger divestiture, now includes hold-separate orders as a matter of course.[87] The FTC usually acts after consummation of a merger; thus, hold separate orders are rarer in FTC consent decrees. Nonetheless, the FTC has issued hold-separate orders in some cases, particularly those in which the acquiring company has not acquired the entire stock of the acquired company.[88]

Hold-separate orders have four virtues. First, they make divestiture easier by preventing the scrambling of assets. Second, they help ensure that the divested assets will be an operable economic entity. Third, they limit the competitive harm that may occur during the post-merger, predivestiture period.[89] Fourth, in a tender-offer situation, they place the risk of failure of the offer on the acquiring company rather than the target.[90]

For these reasons, when agencies in premerger negotiations agree to post-merger divestiture, they should regularly insist on hold-separate agreements. Only in the unusual case will such an agreement be unnecessary.[91]

(2) *The decree should provide a firm but realistic deadline for divestiture.* Deadlines for divestiture vary widely.[92] This is as it should be. As has already been noted, one defect of the fix-it-first rule is that it usually attracts buyers who are already competitors and who can move more quickly than new entrants. The same problem inheres in a divestiture deadline that provides too little time. Thus the agencies should adjust deadlines for divestiture depending on the quantity and quality of likely buyers.[93] The more appropriate buyers there are available, the shorter the deadline should be.

In general, the government should be extremely reluctant to allow more than one year for divestiture to be completed. As the Elzinga and

Yale studies document, longer divestiture periods present too much risk of interim damage to the competitive vigor of the entity to be divested, without any countervailing benefit in terms of guaranteeing that the additional time will produce a more desirable buyer. Likewise, the government should make it clear that it will not grant extensions of the divestiture deadline except in unusual cases.

(3) *The decree should provide for the appointment of a trustee if divestiture is not completed by an agreed-upon deadline.* A consent decree may contain provisions requiring the appointment of a trustee, at the acquiring firm's expense, if divestiture is not completed by the acquiring firm itself within a specified time. The trustee may have absolute power to order the acquiring firm to divest assets (specified in the decree) to any purchaser the trustee selects. The trustee should, however, have a corresponding duty to find the purchaser who will provide the greatest compensation for those assets, so long as the purchaser is not itself anticompetitive.

The Department of Justice routinely includes trustee provisions in consent decrees.[94] The FTC rarely includes them.[95]

Trustee provisions are fair to the acquiring company and can be efficacious. That party has a reasonable time within which to divest the offending assets, and an incentive to do so within that time: if the acquiring company does not accomplish divestiture, it loses its choice among purchasers and also faces the expense of a trustee. Moreover, the trustee lacks the incentives to delay and to find a weak purchaser. The trustee may well accomplish the divestiture, whereas a company left to its own devices might not. Finally, if there is a trustee provision but divestiture is never accomplished, the court enforcing the consent decree can be confident that there are no willing buyers at a fair price, because it is the independent trustee, not the foot-dragging seller, who is making that claim. For these reasons, the FTC should abandon its present practice and adopt that of the Department of Justice.[96]

(4) *The decree should require agency approval of the purchaser.* Both the Department of Justice[97] and the FTC[98] usually require that divestiture be to a purchaser whom the agency has approved. And under the fix-it-first policy, the Department will not agree to a consent decree until it knows who the purchaser is going to be and has satisfied itself that that purchaser is an acceptable one.

Requiring agency approval is eminently sensible and should be a feature of every consent decree. The agency's power to approve the purchaser is a safeguard against a further anticompetitive transaction and also against a buyer who is too weak to be competitively adequate—two of the main problems identified in the Elzinga and Yale studies.

The more interesting question is what criteria the agencies should apply in approving a purchaser. First and foremost, because the purpose of relief is to restore competition, the agencies must be satisfied that the purchaser will use the assets it is acquiring to compete in the market in which the alleged lessening of competition was likely. Second, the agencies must be satisfied that the purchaser has the experience and resources to be a viable competitor in that market. Third, if the purchaser is already a participant in the relevant market, the agency should approve the sale only if the resulting increase in concentration falls within the limits permitted under the Merger Guidelines.

The Elzinga study suggested that the agencies should go beyond this and require that the assets be sold to the most procompetitive purchaser possible.[99] There is no legal authority supporting this degree of intervention, and a government agency is ill suited to make the kinds of comparative judgments this standard would require. Indeed, if the seller has solicited enough offers for its assets, and is selling the assets to the company that made the best offer (and meets the three criteria set out above), the market itself should operate to provide some assurance the company acquiring the assets can compete successfully and earn profits in that market.

The recent merger of Wheelabrator-Frye, Inc. and the Signal Companies provides an interesting example of how the government can use market mechanisms to test the qualifications of a proposed purchaser if, because of time constraints or other reasons, the merging parties have proposed to sell to a purchaser whose qualifications are questionable.[100] The Department of Justice required Wheelabrator to offer the divested assets to a group of companies identified by department investigation as potentially viable competitors in the market in question. The department agreed that if the original purchaser would meet the best offer received in this auction, the assets would be sold to it. The premise of this arrangement was twofold. If the prospective purchaser was willing to put as large a sum at risk as other purchasers who the department thought were more likely to succeed, that would be sufficient proof that the department's judgment was wrong.[101] If not, the high bidder would acquire the assets and should be a more effective competitor than the original prospective purchaser.

(5) *The decree should allow the divesting party to take back a security interest, with appropriate safeguards.* Especially in the case of a quick sale, a buyer may be unable or unwilling to arrange third-party financing for its purchase of the divested assets, and will agree to purchase the assets only if the seller supplies the financing. In these circumstances, the seller will naturally want to take back a security interest in the divested assets.

Such security interests pose two problems with respect to the effectiveness of the divestiture in preserving or restoring competition. First, if the buyer defaults on the loan, the seller may end up reacquiring the assets it was required to divest. Second, the seller and buyer may each have an incentive to compete less vigorously if there is a creditor-debtor relationship between them. Both problems are obviously most serious when the sale is highly leveraged and when the terms of the installment sale provide for a long payment period.

Consent decrees customarily contain a provision permitting a seller to take back a security interest but requiring that, if the seller reacquires those assets as a result of a default, it must redivest the assets promptly.[102] This type of provision may be sufficient as long as the agency, before it approves the sale, is satisfied that the payment period is not unduly long and that the sale is not so highly leveraged that the creditor-debtor relationship will itself discourage competition.

As an alternative, the government might require that the seller, in effect, divest the installment note within a relatively short period following the sale. This can be accomplished in almost every instance by selling the note to a bank or other investor. Private interests may be asserted against such a requirement because, if the buyer's likelihood of survival is uncertain, the note may have to be sold at a deep discount, reducing the consideration received by the seller for the divested assets. In most instances, this type of private interest should be given little weight; it is akin to the insistence on a "fair price" that led to the upset-price provisions that the Elzinga and Yale studies found often operated to defeat divestiture. More important, that very interest will give the seller an added incentive to find a buyer who has adequate resources to invest in the divested line of business, so that the financial markets will demand less of a discount.

(6) *The decree should give the enforcement agency inspection rights.* A standard part of every Department of Justice consent decree is a provision granting the agency the right to gain access to company records and personnel to review the extent of compliance with the

other provisions of the decree.[103] These provisions provide a useful shortcut for obtaining information in the event that an investigation into compliance becomes necessary, and should be a feature of every consent decree or FTC consent order.

(7) *Rescission as an alternative to simple divestiture.* At least one commentator,[104] one court,[105] and the FTC[106] have suggested rescission as an alternative way of assuring a prompt sale. There are reasons for resisting these suggestions.

It is the exceedingly rare seller who will, with open arms, greet the return of assets it has previously sold. However fair it may be to make the acquiring company divest the assets, the selling firm will generally not be a wrongdoer, and rescission will rarely be the best overall accommodation of public and private interests. In fact, the original seller—now an involuntary purchaser of unwanted assets—may be a much less effective competitor than a voluntary purchaser found through divestiture.[107] In addition, the apparent simplicity of rescission, like the apparent simplicity of divestiture in general, is deceptive. Indeed, in the one reported case in which a federal court ordered rescission, it never occurred.[108]

3. *There are several alternatives and supplements to premerger restructuring.*

a. *Hold-separate decrees.* Premerger divestiture agreements are not always the answer in section 7 cases. In a very limited class of cases, private equities are so strong and the legality or illegality of a merger is sufficiently uncertain, that a hold-separate order pending final adjudication may best accommodate the various interests involved. These unusual circumstances are exemplified by a recent decision of the United States Court of Appeals for the District of Columbia Circuit.

In *FTC v. Weyerhaeuser Co.*,[109] the court found and the private party did not dispute that the FTC would likely show that the merger was illegal.[110] The district court nonetheless denied a preliminary injunction and granted a hold-separate order, and the court of appeals affirmed. The appellate court carefully delineated numerous reasons why a hold-separate order was *not* appropriate in every case, but it rejected a rule that a hold-separate order is *never* appropriate in the face of a merger that is likely to be found illegal.[111] The D.C. Circuit then held:

Even when the Commission establishes a likelihood of success on the merits, a court may enter a hold separate order rather than a merger-blocking preliminary injunction if (1) strong equities favor the consummation of the transaction; (2) a hold separate order will check interim competitive harm; and (3) such an order will permit adequate ultimate relief.[112]

Applying its test, the court noted that the selling company had a small number of shareholders and that the acquisition was a rare opportunity to liquidate their investment. Finding there were also public interests favoring the transaction and that a hold-separate order should be effective in this case, the D.C. Circuit held that its test was satisfied.[113]

The enforcement agencies, too, should be willing to consent to a hold-separate order, in lieu of an injunction, when this test is met.[114] This is precisely what the FTC did in *FTC v. Exxon Corp.*[115] In *Exxon*, the same district judge imposed a hold-separate order with the blessing of the plaintiff, the FTC.[116]

Any evaluation of the FTC's reasons for accepting the hold-separate order is necessarily based on speculation, but two things are clear: (1) *Exxon* involved a tender offer, so time was of the essence, and a hold-separate order had the salutary effect of shifting risks from the acquired firm to Exxon.[117] (2) The FTC's section 7 theory was based on a view of Exxon as a potential entrant,[118] and the FTC has been notoriously unsuccessful in obtaining *any* relief in potential-competition cases. *Exxon*, therefore, is representative of a limited class of cases in which the equities favor consummation and the agency's theory is novel, so that it makes sense to permit the acquisition to proceed subject to appropriate checks and to a later adjudication of whether divestiture is necessary.[119]

b. *Conduct or marketing orders.* There may also be a limited class in which the merged firm should be required to deal on specified terms with particular parties in lieu of, or in addition to, divestiture.[120] For reasons stated in some detail by Professor Elzinga, such conduct or marketing orders are generally an unsatisfactory substitute for structural relief.[121] But in a few cases, an acquisition may be manifestly in the public interest, yet have a few troublesome competitive aspects that can be cured completely by an order directly regulating a company's manner of competing. For example, in a vertical merger the acquiring company might enhance the efficiency of, or provide greater operating capital to, the acquired company. There might, however, be potential foreclosure problems, particularly in industries that experience cyclical shortages.[122] An order requiring the acquired firm to deal on equal terms with the acquiring company and its competitors could conceivably cure the problems without preventing the merger.[123]

Not all vertical mergers will fit this description, and it is difficult to imagine a horizontal merger in which a marketing order will be an adequate substitute for structural relief. Conduct or marketing orders, therefore, should be used "parsimoniously,"[124] but there should be no per se rule against them.

c. *Acquisition bans.* The FTC generally imposes, as an additional condition to any consent order, a requirement that the defendant obtain prior FTC approval for any future acquisition in the line of commerce allegedly affected by the merger. The customary term of these acquisition bans is a period of ten years. In the past, similar acquisition bans were also a common feature of Department of Justice consent decrees.

During the administration of Assistant Attorney General Baxter, the department was more selective in imposing these bans. A review of the fifteen decrees filed while Baxter was in office finds acquisition bans in only nine of those decrees. Generally, the decrees in which Baxter sought acquisition bans were of two types:

First, those where the acquiring firm was the leading firm in the relevant market and had a market share greater than 35 percent.[125] In these cases, an acquisition ban served to reinforce the so-called "leading firm proviso" in the department's Merger Guidelines. That proviso states that "the Department is likely to challenge the merger of any firm with a market share of at least 1 percent with the leading firm in the market, provided that the leading firm has a market share that is at least 35 percent and is approximately twice as large as that of the second largest firm in the market."[126]

Second, those where the merger was in an industry characterized by local geographic markets, in which potentially anticompetitive mergers could occur without triggering the reporting requirement of the Hart-Scott-Rodino Act.[127] In these cases, an acquisition ban served to assure that the agency would be notified of potentially anticompetitive mergers that might otherwise go unreported.

Aside from these two situations, it is difficult to see any reason for the enforcement agencies to impose an acquisition ban. Before the enactment of the Hart-Scott-Rodino Act, such bans assured the agency of notice of at least some acquisitions.[128] Clearly, they are no longer needed to serve that purpose.

In addition, acquisition bans have, in the past, been viewed as a form of punishment, designed to deter companies from attempting unlawful acquisitions. If this is the reason for them, they clearly cannot be defended. There is no rational basis under the antitrust laws to apply harsher standards in reviewing future mergers by a company just because it has once proposed an acquisition that the agency considered unlawful.[129]

When an acquisition ban serves no useful purpose, it should not be imposed, because the imposition of such a ban may itself interfere with efficiency-enhancing, non-anticompetitive mergers. The delay inherent in the procedural requirement of prior agency approval may kill some efficiency-producing, procompetitive mergers.[130] In addition, fear of such a ban may well cause some companies to abandon mergers that may be efficiency producing and not anticompetitive because their lawyers cannot assure them that the agency will not challenge the acquisition and insist on a ban against future acquisitions. Accordingly, the FTC should follow the Department of Justice example and impose acquisition bans only when particular market conditions warrant their imposition.[131]

Conclusion

The U.S. Supreme Court was overly optimistic when it suggested that postmerger divestiture is "simple, relatively easy to administer, and sure." And the wisdom of lower federal court judges has prevented the enforcement agencies from routinely enjoining mergers that may have efficiency-enhancing effects in some markets that counterbalance their potential anticompetitive effects in others. Fortunately, the enactment of the Hart-Scott-Rodino Act has permitted the agencies to develop a means to restructure proposed mergers, before consummation, in a way that eliminates their anticompetitive features while preserving their efficiency-enhancing aspects.

In June 1982, the Department of Justice published a new set of Merger Guidelines which stated the substantive standards that would be applied in a premerger investigation to decide whether to challenge a proposed merger. The agencies should now consider adopting a similar set of guidelines to inform the antitrust bar and its clients about what standards will be applied by the agencies at the relief stage of a premerger investigation. The suggestions we have made in this paper may, we hope, serve as a starting point for the formulation of such a set of guidelines.

Notes

1. Clayton Act §7, 15 U.S.C. §18 (1982).

2. See Clayton Act §15, 15 U.S.C. §25 (1982) (Department of Justice); Federal Trade Commission Act §13(b), 15 U.S.C. §53(b) (1982); cf. Clayton Act §16, 15 U.S.C. §26 (1982) (injunctive relief for private parties). In this chapter we refer to the two agencies collectively as "the government."

3. For further discussion, see pp. 56–57.

4. 332 U.S. 392, 400–01 (1947).

5. Id., 401.

6. United States v. E.I. du Pont de Nemours & Co., 353 U.S. 586, 607–08 (1957).

7. See Pfunder, Plaine & Whittemore, "Compliance with Divestiture Orders Under Section 7 of the Clayton Act: An Analysis of the Relief Obtained," *Antitrust Bull.* 17 (1972), 19, 22, 27, 54 n. 38. One obvious result of *ineffective* section 7 relief is the encouragement of section 7 violations; if one person gets to keep some or all of the fruits of his illegal conduct, others are tempted to engage in similar conduct. Nonetheless, courts rarely discuss deterrence in section 7 cases, and they usually limit their remarks to the need to deter a particular party from repeating past conduct. See, e.g., United States v. Crescent Amusement Co., 323 U.S. 173, 186 (1944); see also National Commission for the Review of Antitrust Laws and Procedures, *Report to the President and the Attorney General*, 80 F.R.D. 509, 604 (1979).

8. United States v. E.I. du Pont de Nemours & Co., 366 U.S. 316, 326 (1961) (*du Pont II*).

9. Id., 327–29.

10. Id., 331; see also National Commission for the Review of Antitrust Laws and Procedures, *Report to the President and the Attorney General*, 80 F.R.D. 509, 602–04 (1979).

11. See, e.g., Ash Grove Cement Co. v. FTC, 557 F.2d 1368, 1379–80 (9th Cir. 1978); United States v. Carrols Dev. Corp., 454 F. Supp. 1215, 1223 (N.D.N.Y. 1978); United States v. Jos. Schlitz Brewing Co., 253 F. Supp. 129 (N.D. Cal.), *aff'd per curiam*, 385 U.S. 37 (1966); Brunswick Corp., 96 F.T.C. 151 (1980); Bayer AG, 95 F.T.C. 254 (1980).

12. The goal of relief is to restore effective competition; therefore, total divestiture may be appropriate even if the violation relates to less than the whole acquisition. OKC Corp. v. FTC, 455 F.2d 1159 (10th Cir. 1972). The Tenth Circuit stated that "[t]otal divestiture is not necessarily inappropriate even though the antitrust violation found relates to but one aspect of the company thus acquired, especially where, as here, total divestiture may be deemed necessary to restore effective competition." Id., 1163.

13. 63 F.T.C. 1465, 1584 (1963).

14. Id.; cf. United States v. Jos. Schlitz Brewing Co., 253 F. Supp. 129, 183–84 (N.D. Cal.) (Schlitz ordered to divest itself of all of the business and assets of Burgermeister Brewing Corp. acquired on or about December 31, 1961 and all shares of John Labatt Limited), *aff'd per curiam*, 385 U.S. 37 (1966).

15. See, e.g., RSR Corp. v. FTC, 602 F.2d 1317 (9th Cir. 1979), *cert. denied*, 445 U.S. 927 (1980); United States v. Reed Roller Bit Co., 274 F. Supp. 573, 584–92 (W.D. Okla. 1967); Brillo Mfg. Co., 64 F.T.C. 245, 261–64 (1964); Union Carbide Corp., 59 F.T.C. 614, 657–59 (1961). In addition, the government frequently has settled by accepting partial divestiture. See, e.g., United States v. Rockwell Int'l Corp., 1981–1 Trade Cas. ¶63,875 (W.D. Pa. 1980); United States v. Martin Marietta Corp., 1980–1 Trade Cas. ¶63,109 (N.D. Ill. 1980); United States v. Beneficial Corp., 1980–1 Trade Cas. ¶63,136 (N.D. Ill. 1979); United States v. Leggett & Platt, 1979–1 Trade Cas. ¶62,453 (S.D. Ohio 1978); United States v. Coca-Cola Bottling Co., 1978–2 Trade Cas. ¶62,277 (C.D. Cal. 1978); Owens-Corning Fiberglas Corp., 97 F.T.C. 249 (1981).

16. 59 F.T.C. 614, 657–59 (1961).

17. Id., 659.

18. Orders requiring divestiture, either full or partial, often contain ancillary provisions that either prohibit or mandate specified future conduct. Prohibitory injunctions usually involve acquisition bans. See, e.g., United States v. Merck & Co., 1980–81 Trade Cas. ¶63,682, at 77,667 (S.D. Cal. 1980). Mandatory injunctions may, in any of various ways, require a company to assist the purchaser of its divested assets. See, e.g., id., 77,665–67; United States v. Converse Rubber Corp., 1972 Trade Cas. ¶74,101 (D. Mass. 1972); see also United States v. Ford Motor Co., 315 F. Supp. 372, 378 (E.D. Mich. 1970). We discuss some forms of ancillary relief in the section below entitled "Remedies in the New Age."

19. 15 U.S.C. §25 (1982).

20. 15 U.S.C. §53(b) (1982). Even before the enactment in 1973 of section 13(b), the Supreme Court held that the FTC had standing to seek preliminary and permanent injunctive relief under the All Writs Act for section 7 violations. FTC v. Dean Foods Co., 384 U.S. 597, 606–12 (1966).

21. See, e.g., FTC v. PepsiCo, Inc., 477 F.2d 24 (2d Cir. 1973).

22. See, e.g., FTC v. Tenneco, Inc., 433 F. Supp. 105 (D.D.C. 1977); United States v. Black & Decker Mfg. Co., 430 F. Supp. 729 (D. Md. 1976).

23. See, e.g., United States v. Culbro Corp., 436 F. Supp. 746 (S.D.N.Y. 1977).

24. See S. Rep. No. 803, 94th Cong., 2d Sess. 72 (1976), quoted on p. 57 below. See generally United States v. Consolidated Foods Corp., 455 F. Supp. 142 (E.D. Pa. 1978).

25. Elzinga, "The Antimerger Law: Pyrrhic Victories?," *J.L. & Econ.* 12 (1969), 43.

26. Id., 46–53.

27. Id., 55.

28. Id., 65.

29. Id., 66–72.

30. Pfunder, Plaine, and Whittemore, "Compliance with Divestiture Orders Under Section 7 of the Clayton Act: An Analysis of the Relief Obtained," *Antitrust Bull.* 17 (1972), 19. We refer to this as "the Yale study" for convenience; we do not mean to imply that Yale University officially sponsored or endorsed the study.

31. Id., 32. In general, the cases they excluded were those that were (a) dismissed by the government, (b) terminated by an injunction banning a proposed acquisition, (c) litigated to a judgment for the defendant, (d) litigated to or settled by a decree that did not order divestiture, or (e) resolved by an order to divest trade names, commodities, or miscellaneous assets; to terminate leases; to dispose of notes; or to terminate joint operations. Id., 33, n. 19.

32. The majority of these cases involved divestiture orders that contained provisions purporting to assure the defendant a reasonable price by specifying an upset price or a formula for computing an upset price below which the defendant was not required to sell. Of the eight cases in which defendants never complied with their obligation to divest, six had such fair-price provisions. Id., 84–85.

33. Id., 38 (emphasis in original).

34. The authors also examined the length of time between consummation of the acquisition and completion of the required divestiture. They found, as Elzinga had, that "a comparison between the time limit specified in divestiture orders and the actual time required for compliance reveals a spotty record." Id., 92.

35. Id., 131.

36. Id.

37. Id., 131–33.

38. See R. Bork, *The Antitrust Paradox*, 219–22, 225–31 (1978); F.M. Scherer, *Industrial Market Structure and Economic Performance*, 133–38 (2d ed. 1980). See generally P. Steiner, *Mergers*, 58–69 (1975); Turner, "Conglomerate Mergers and Section 7 of the Clayton Act," *Harv. L. Rev.* 78 (1965), 1313, 1323–39.

39. See O'Toole, "Mergers and Divestitures: The New Growth Strategy," *Forbes* (June 6, 1983), 83.

40. Many of these reforms are discussed in *Hearings Before the National Commission for the Review of Antitrust Laws and Procedures* (July 12, 1978), 169–223 (testimony of Bernard M. Hollander, Chief, Judgment Enforcement Section, Antitrust Division) [hereinafter cited as *NCRALP Hearings*].

41. See Address by Donald F. Turner, Assistant Attorney General, Antitrust Division, to the Association of the Bar of the City of New York (Dec. 13, 1967).

42. See, e.g., United States v. ARA Servs., 1982–83 Trade Cas. ¶65,209 (S.D. Ohio 1982) (approximately three months); Godfrey Co., 97 F.T.C. 456 (1981) (six months). But see Godfrey Co., 100 F.T.C. 460 (1982) (after 17 months, deleting portion of divestiture requirement).

43. See, e.g., United States v. G. Heileman Brewing Co., 5 Trade Reg. Rep. (CCH) (1983–1 Trade Cas.) ¶65,399 (D. Del. 1983); Atlantic Richfield Co., 94 F.T.C. 1054 (1979).

44. See *NCRALP Hearings*, 172 (testimony of Bernard M. Hollander), citing *General Dynamics* decree, which required spinoff or public sale if timely divestiture not accomplished.

45. See, e.g., United States v. Stroh Brewery Co., 1982–83 Trade Cas. ¶65,037 (D.D.C. 1982); Atlantic Richfield Co., 94 F.T.C. 1054 (1979).

46. See, e.g., United States v. Work Wear Corp., 602 F.2d 110 (6th Cir. 1979); United States v. Louisiana-Pac. Corp., 1982–83 Trade Cas. ¶65,114 (D. Or. 1982) (FTC); United States v. American Technical Indus., 1982–2 Trade Cas. ¶64,890 (M.D. Pa. 1982); United States v. Papercraft Corp., 426 F. Supp. 916 (W.D. Pa. 1977) (FTC).

47. See, e.g., *The Antitrust Improvements Act of 1975: Hearings Before the Subcomm. on Antitrust and Monopoly of the Senate Comm. on the Judiciary*, 94th Cong., 1st Sess. pt. 1, 505–07 (1975) (prepared statement of Joseph F. Brodley, Professor of Law, Indiana University) [hereinafter cited as *Senate Hearings*]; National Commission for the Review of Antitrust Laws and Procedures, *Report to the President and the Attorney General*, 80 F.R.D. 509, 604–09 (1979); Note, "Section 7 Clayton Act Remedies—The Rescission Decision," *Cornell L. Rev.* 64 (1979), 736, 747–49. Not surprisingly, the Pfunder study, authored by two 1970 and one 1971 Yale law graduates, was contemporaneous with a sweeping, critical study of antitrust enforcement by two 1970 and one 1971 Harvard law graduates. See M. Green, B. Moore & B. Wasserstein, *The Closed Enterprise System* 184–93, 334–67 (1972).

48. United States v. E.I. du Pont de Nemours & Co., 366 U.S. 316, 331 (1961).

49. See, e.g., Lewis, "Preliminary Injunctions in Government Section 7 Litigation," *Antitrust Bull.* 17 (1972), 1; Schneiderman, "Preliminary Relief in Clayton Act Section 7 Cases," *Antitrust L.J.* 42 (1973), 587; Note, "Preliminary Relief for the Government Under Section 7 of the Clayton Act," *Harv. L. Rev.* 70 (1965), 391; cf. Elzinga, 47 (categorizing as "successful" cases in which anticompetitive effects are "stopped in their incipiency so that no restoration is necessary"); Elzinga, "Mergers: Their Causes and Cures, "*Antitrust L. & Econ. Rev.* (Fall 1968), 53, 84 ("an *optimum* antimerger enforcement program would presumably concentrate on stopping all anticompetitive mergers *before* their consummation").

50. S. 1284, 94th Cong., 1st Sess. §501, 121 Cong. Rec. 8134, 8146 (1975). The provision as originally drafted provided that if either agency during the waiting period filed an action alleging that the acquisition violated the Clayton or Sherman Act and "certifie[d]" to the appropriate district court that "it ... believes that the public interest requires relief pendente lite," then "the court *shall* enter an order that such acquisition shall not be consummated" until final judgment in the court action, which "shall be in every way expedited." Id. §501(d) (emphasis added).

51. S. Rep. No. 803, 94th Cong., 2d Sess. 65 (1976); see also id., 70. Kauper also supported the automatic stay provisions if the district court was given discretion "to lift the stay upon a showing of irreparable harm ... or that the suit is totally devoid of merit or is in some other way arbitrary or capricious." *The Antitrust Improvements Act of 1975: Hearings on S. 1248 Before the Subcomm. on Antitrust and Monopoly of the Senate Comm. on the Judiciary*, 94th Cong., 1st Sess. 82 (1975) (statement of Thomas E. Kauper). But the Ford administration withdrew its support for these provisions while the bill was still in committee. S. Rep. No. 803, 64 n. 27. See generally Kintner, Griffin & Goldston, "The Hart-Scott-Rodino Antitrust Improvements Act of 1976: An Analysis," *Geo. Wash. L. Rev.* 46 (1977), 1, 2 n. 2, 11–18.

52. S. Rep. No. 803, 71–74 and n. 31; *Senate Hearings*, 505–07.

53. S. Rep. No. 803, 72 (emphasis in original; footnote omitted).

54. H.R. 13,131, 94th Cong., 2d Sess. (1976), reprinted in *Merger Oversight and H.R. 13,131: Hearings Before the Subcomm. on Monopolies and Commercial Law of the House Comm. on the Judiciary*, 94th Cong., 2d Sess. 53–56 (1976) [hereinafter cited as *House Hearings*].

55. *House Hearings*, 1 52, 93–105. Professor Elzinga also testified. Id. at 105–17.

56. See generally H.R. Rep. No. 1373, 94th Cong., 2d Sess., reprinted in 1976 U.S. Code Cong. & Ad. News 2637; Kintner, Griffin, and Goldston, *Improvements Act of 1976*; and Pub. L. No. 94–435, 90 Stat. 1383 (1976). The premerger notification provisions are codified as Clayton Act §7A, 15 U.S.C. §18a (1982). For a comprehensive description of the entire act and its legislative history, see Kintner, Griffin, and Goldston.

57. See, e.g., Kintner, Griffin, and Goldston, 12.

58. The Act itself provided for effectiveness on February 27, 1977. Id. The FTC did not, however, publish final regulations until July 31, 1978, and the regulations carried an effective date of August 30. See 43 Fed. Reg. 33,450 (1978). The FTC had earlier published draft regulations, which received extensive public comment.

59. United States v. Hospital Affiliates Int'l, 1980–81 Trade Cas. ¶63,721 (E.D. La. 1980), *consent decree approved*, 1982–1 Trade Cas. ¶64,696 (E.D. La. 1982).

60. United States v. Household Fin. Corp., 602 F.2d 1255 (7th Cir. 1979), *cert. denied*, 444 U.S. 1044 (1980).

61. FTC v. Weyerhaeuser Co., 665 F.2d 1072 (D.C. Cir. 1981), *aff'g* 1981–1 Trade Cas. ¶63,974 (D.D.C.); FTC v. Exxon Corp., 636 F.2d 1336 (D.C. Cir. 1980), *modifying* 1979–2 Trade Cas. ¶62,972 (D.D.C.); FTC v. Southland Corp., 471 F. Supp. 1 (D.D.C. 1979); Carrier Corp. v. United Technologies Corp., 1978–2 Trade Cas. ¶62,393 (N.D.N.Y.), *aff'd per curiam on other grounds*, 1978–2 Trade Cas. ¶62,405 (2d Cir. 1978), *hold-separate order entered*, 466 F. Supp. 196 (N.D.N.Y. 1979). In United States v. Acorn Eng'g Co., 1981–2 Trade Cas. ¶64,197 (N.D. Cal. 1981), the government sued after the merger took place and got a hold-separate order. In one other case, the parties and the FTC staff entered a hold-separate agreement, and the FTC staff in return did not recommend a preliminary injunction. See Pfunder, "FTC, DOJ Modify Merger Enforcement Approaches," *Legal Times of Wash.* (Apr. 25, 1983), 12, col. 1, 16, col. 4 and n. 63.

62. United States v. Siemens Corp., 621 F.2d 499 (2d Cir. 1980), *aff'g* 490 F. Supp. 1130 (S.D.N.Y.); FTC v. National Tea Co., 603 F.2d 694 (8th Cir. 1979); FTC v. Great Lakes Chem. Corp., 528 F. Supp. 84 (N.D. Ill. 1981); United States v. Tracinda Inv. Corp., 464 F. Supp. 660 (C.D. Cal.), *final judgment for defendants*, 477 F. Supp. 1093 (C.D. Cal. 1979). In another case, the court denied a temporary restraining order without opinion, and the Department of Justice then did not seek a preliminary injunction. See Pfunder, at 12, col. 3, 15, col. 1 and nn. 16, 25; United States v. ARA Servs., 1982–83 Trade Cas. ¶65,209 (S.D. Ohio 1982) (consent decree). One other court never acted on a preliminary injunction request. See Pfunder, 12, col. 3 and nn. 4, 17; United States v. American Maize-Prods. Co., 5 Trade Reg. Rep. (CCH) ¶50,810 (M.D. Fla. filed Feb. 12, 1982) (proposed consent decree).

63. For citation of nine cases within a two-year period that apparently fit this description, see Pfunder, 12, col. 3, 16, cols. 3–4 and nn. 19, 58, 61–62. In another case, the original merger plans were abandoned, but a new buyer acceptable to the Department of Justice was found. See United States v. American Maize-Prods. Co., 5 Trade Reg. Rep. (CCH) ¶50,810 (M.D. Fla. filed Feb. 12, 1982) (proposed consent decree).

64. See generally Kolasky and Seidman, "DOJ Suggests Merger Parties Consider All Options," *Legal Times of Wash.* (July 12, 1982), 18, col. 1; Pfunder, at 12, col. 3, 15, cols. 2–3 and n. 20.

65. Professor McGowan, elsewhere in this volume, demonstrates from a theoretical standpoint some of the benefits of mergers. Recent empirical studies bolster the hypothesis that mergers tend to enhance the efficiency of capital markets. See, for example, "Successful Takeovers Boost Stock," *Washington Post* (April 16, 1983) D10, col. 8.

66. See 15 U.S.C. §18a(e) (1982).

67. For example, the Siemens case cited above was brought on a potential-competition theory, a frontier of antitrust law, and the Tracinda case involved a government theory so tenuous that judgment for defendants was granted within a year of the complaint. But see FTC v. Weyerhaeuser Co., 665 F.2d 1072 (D.C. Cir. 1981); entry of hold-separate order, rather than preliminary injunction, affirmed despite government's strong likelihood of eventual success.

68. See Kolasky and Seidman, 18, col. 2 and nn. 10–11.

69. Thirty-six percent (12 of 33) of all FTC consent orders entered in 1979–82 were announced before the merger took place.

70. See, e.g., ConAgra, Inc. [Federal Trade Commission Complaints and Orders 1979–1983 Transfer Binder] Trade Reg. Rep. (CCH) ¶21,951 (FTC Feb. 16, 1983); General Electric Co., 99 F.T.C. 422 (1982).

71. Kolasky and Seidman, 18, col. 1 and n. 1 (quoting statements by former Assistant Attorney General Thomas E. Kauper). The government once went so far as to argue (unsuccessfully) that a merger illegal when proposed could not be cured by a voluntary sale of offending assets before shareholder approval. See United States v. Atlantic Richfield Co., 297 F. Supp. 1061, 1069 (S.D.N.Y. 1969), *aff'd mem. sub nom.* Bartlett v. United States, 401 U.S. 986 (1971).

72. Remarks by Sanford M. Litvack, Assistant Attorney General, Antitrust Division, before the Fourteenth New England Antitrust Conference, Cambridge, Mass., Nov. 14, 1980.

73. A newspaper report summarizes this development:

Rather than rush to court when companies propose a merger with antitrust problems, antitrust chief William Baxter likes to work out a solution privately. He says he prefers "sitting down with them and saying: 'Look, let's turn this into an unobjectionable deal. Here's what you have to do.'"

Wall St. J., Feb. 9, 1983, 33, col. 4 (noting Baxter's policy and quoting both praise and criticism from former Justice Department officials); see Kolasky and Seidman.

74. But cf. United States v. Virginia National Bankshares, 1982–2 Trade Cas. ¶64,871 (W.D. Va. 1982) (Department sought permanent injunction against bank merger, which was automatically stayed pending decision).

75. Utah Pub. Serv. Comm'n v. El Paso Natural Gas Co., 395 U.S. 464, 472 (1969); see also United States v. E.I. du Pont de Nemours & Co., 366 U.S. 316, 326, 334 (1961). It seems clearly established that private interests are relevant at the *preliminary* relief stage of antimerger actions. See FTC v. Weyerhaeuser Co., 665 F.2d 1072, 1081–83 (D.C. Cir. 1981); FTC v. Weyerhaeuser Co., 648 F.2d 739, 741 (D.C. Cir. 1981) (per curiam).

76. See United States v. E.I. du Pont de Nemours & Co., 366 U.S. 316, 327 (1961) ("Economic hardship can influence choice only as among two or more effective remedies."); United States v. International Tel. & Tel. Co., 349 F. Supp. 22, 31 (D. Conn. 1972), aff'd mem. sub nom. Nader v. United States, 410 U.S. 919 (1973). Selection of this remedy, of course, is greatly facilitated by discussions between the merging parties, who will emphasize their interests, and officials of the agency involved, who should keep the public interest uppermost in their minds. Back-and-forth discussion may well yield creative solutions that will accommodate all relevant interests to the maximum extent possible.

77. U.S. Dept. of Justice, *Merger Guidelines* (1982), *reprinted in* 2 Trade Reg. Rep. (CCH) paras. 4501–4505. The FTC announced, simultaneously with the publication of these Guidelines, that it would give them "considerable weight." *Statement of Federal Trade Commission Concerning Horizontal Mergers* (1982). The Guidelines are silent on the subject of relief, despite the recommendation of commentators that revision of the 1968 Guidelines include addition of a section on relief. See Edwards, Joffe, Kolasky, McGowan, Mendez-Penate, Ordover, Proger, Solomon, and Toepke, "Proposed Revisions of the Justice Department's Merger Guidelines," *Colum. L. Rev.* 81 (1981), 1543, 1572. The omission is particularly ironic in light of the preeminent role the Department of Justice now plays in fashioning relief, and the acute need for consistency in exercise of the department's substantial powers.

78. The department's 1968 Merger Guidelines also contain numerical criteria for judging mergers. The new guidelines, however, are much more explicit than the old ones in treating those criteria as creating "safe harbors" so that businessmen can be reasonably assured that mergers falling within them will not be challenged.

79. This summary, of course, greatly oversimplifies the department's Guidelines. In more highly concentrated markets in which the HHI exceeds 1,800, for example, the department may challenge mergers that increase the index by as few as 50 points.

80. 47 Fed. Reg. 8423, 8424 (1982) (consent decree and competitive impact statement, published pursuant to 15 U.S.C. §16(b) (1982)). The rankings in text are, for expositional convenience, based on unit volume. As noted in the competitive impact statement, a more accurate picture of the industry would be obtained by examining both unit and dollar volume. Swisher is a subsidiary of American Maize-Products Company.

81. The Department of Justice explained:

This does not mean that increases in concentration of the magnitude possible under the decree are necessarily competitively benign. In another industry, or in other circumstances, the Department of Justice might oppose the acquisition of a company the size of Garcia y Vega by a competitor the size of Swisher or Culbro. Here, however, we believe that the risk of anticompetitive effect is acceptably low, in part because Garcia y Vega and Swisher compete primarily in different segments of the market.

47 Fed. Reg., 8425.

82. See generally U.S. Dept. of Justice, *Merger Guidelines*, 16–20 (1982), reprinted in 2 Trade Reg. Rep. (CCH) ¶4503.10-.101.

83. Suppose a firm with an 8 percent share in a moderately concentrated market bought a firm with a 7 percent share. Under the Guidelines, the Department of Justice would likely challenge this acquisition. The department would not likely challenge the same acquisition if the acquired firm had 6 percent; yet it hardly follows that purchase of the 7 percent firm, and sale of one-seventh of its assets, is not anticompetitive. If, as the Guidelines suggest, eradication of a 7 percent firm and creation of a 15 percent firm is anticompetitive, the competitive effect of creating 1 percent and 14 percent firms will not be much different, because the 1 percent firm will have nearly no competitive effect.

Of course, the 1 percent assets might not be spun off or sold to a new entrant; they might, instead, be sold to an existing company. In this case, there will be less of a problem of creating an insignificant firm but a greater overall competitive problem, for, as a result of the entire transaction, there will be one less firm in the market, and two firms will have increased their market shares, one by a very nearly anticompetitive amount.

84. See Statement of William F. Baxter, Assistant Attorney General, Antitrust Division, Before the Senate Subcomm. on Employment and Productivity 2 (Apr. 16, 1982).

85. In United States v. Stroh Brewery Co., 1982–83 Trade Cas. ¶65,037 (D.D.C. 1982) (consent decree), the government provided Stroh's one year from its acquisition of Schlitz to divest a plant, with a trustee designated to do so if Stroh's did not meet the one-year deadline. See 4 Trade Reg. Rep. (CCH) ¶45,082, at 53,538–39 (1983). More recently, the government allowed a hostile takeover of El Paso Co. by Burlington Northern, on the condition that the Department of Justice could later require a specified divestiture. See *Wall St. J.*, Feb. 9, 1983, 33, col. 4 and 6.

86. Occasionally, hold-separate orders *instead of* divestiture may suffice to solve antitrust problems. See United States v. GTE Corp., 5 Trade Reg. Rep. (CCH) ¶50,833 (D.D.C. filed May 4, 1983) (proposed consent decree); United States v. British Columbia Forest Prods. Ltd., 5 Trade Reg. Rep. (CCH) (1983–1 Trade Cas.) ¶65,280 (D. Minn. 1983) (consent decree). In addition, hold-separate orders are sometimes used when it is not certain that divestiture will be necessary.

87. *See* United States v. ARA Servs., 1982–83 Trade Cas. ¶65,209 (S.D. Ohio 1982); United States v. Baldwin-United Corp., 1982–2 Trade Cas. ¶64,788 (S.D. Ohio 1982); United States v. Beatrice Foods Co., 1982–1 Trade Cas. ¶64,698 (D. Minn. 1982); United States v. Harvey Hubbell, Inc., 1982–1 Trade Cas. ¶64,516 (D. Conn. 1981); United States v. E.I. du Pont de Nemours & Co., 1982–1 Trade Cas. ¶64,479 (D.D.C. 1981).

88. See Murata Mfg. Co., 96 F.T.C. 1116 (1980); Bendix Corp., 96 F.T.C. 352 (1980); Schlumberger Ltd., 95 F.T.C. 913 (1980); cf. Kennecott Corp., 98 F.T.C. 775 (1981) (division of acquiring company to be held separate pending divestiture); Cooper Indus., 93 F.T.C. 1051 (1979).

89. If the merger is vertical or conglomerate, the acquiring company's incentive during this period will be to make the held-separate assets as effective a competitive force as possible; this cannot diminish the acquiring company's competitive standing. If the merger is horizontal, the acquiring company will have conflicting incentives. On the one hand, it may want to promote its own competitive interests at the expense of those of its held-separate competitor. On the other hand, it will want to make the held-separate firm an effective competitor so that it will bring a good price when sold. Hold-separate agreements aid an agency to determine whether the acquiring company is yielding to the first of these incentives. The Department of Justice and FTC should include in consent decrees appropriate provisions allowing them to take corrective action in such situations.

90. See Kolasky and Seidman, 19, col. 2.

91. In United States v. Stroh Brewery Co., 1982–83 Trade Cas. ¶65,037 (D.D.C. 1982), the government evidently thought a hold-separate order unnecessary because the assets to be divested were an entire plant, which could not possibly be scrambled with other assets. Stroh was ordered to keep the two plants (of which it was to divest one) in good working order. In United States v. G. Heileman Brewing Co., 5 Trade Reg. Rep. (CCH) (1983–1 Trade Cas.) ¶65,399 (D. Del. 1983), the government apparently viewed various direct constraints on the operation of subsidiaries as sufficient protection during the brief period allowed for Heileman (rather than a trustee) to effect divestiture.

92. Compare United States v. ARA Servs., 1982–83 Trade Cas. ¶65,209 (S.D. Ohio 1982) (approximately three months), and General Elec. Co., 99 F.T.C. 422 (1982) (divestiture before entry of order), with United States v. CBS, 1982–1 Trade Cas. ¶64,478 (S.D.N.Y. 1981) (two years), and British Petroleum Co., 98 F.T.C. 128 (1981) (thirty months).

93. As discussed elsewhere in this section, the government should also insist on the right to approve the purchaser and should provide for the appointment of a trustee if timely divestiture is not effected. Only in these ways can it ensure that divestiture deadlines are taken seriously.

94. See United States v. American Brands, Inc., 5 Trade Reg. Rep. (CCH) (1983–1 Trade Cas.) ¶65,276 (S.D.N.Y. 1983); United States v. ARA Servs., 1982–83 Trade Cas. ¶65,209 (S.D. Ohio 1982); United States v. Stroh Brewery Co., 1982–83 Trade Cas. ¶65,037 (D.D.C. 1982); United States v. Acorn Eng'g Co., 1982–1 Trade Cas. ¶64,697 (N.D. Cal. 1982); United States v. Harvey Hubbell, Inc., 1982–1 Trade Cas. ¶64,516 (D. Conn. 1981); United States v. G. Heileman Brewing Co., 5 Trade Reg. Rep. (CCH) (1983–1 Trade Cas.) ¶65,399 (D. Del. 1983).

95. But see Atlantic Richfield Co., 94 F.T.C. 1054 (1979).

96. The Department of Justice occasionally does not insist on a trustee provision but does include similar requirements in the decree. See United States v. Baldwin-United

Corp., 1982–2 Trade Cas. ¶64,788 (S.D. Ohio 1982) (spinoff through "divestiture agent"); United States v. CBS, 1982–1 Trade Cas. ¶64,478 (S.D.N.Y. 1981) (CBS must enlist the aid of an investment banker).

97. See, e.g., United States v. Beatrice Foods Co., 1982–1 Trade Cas. ¶64,698 (D. Minn. 1982); United States v. Acorn Eng'g Co., 1982–1 Trade Cas. ¶64,697 (N.D. Cal. 1982); United States v. Wheelabrator-Frye, 1981–1 Trade Cas. ¶64,018 (D.D.C. 1981).

98. See, e.g., Coca-Cola Co., 3 Trade Reg. Rep. (CCH) ¶22,011 (FTC Aug. 3, 1983); Xidex Corp., 3 Trade Reg. Rep. (CCH) ¶22,067 (FTC July 1, 1983); Gulf & W. Indus. [Federal Trade Commission Complaints and Orders 1979–1983 Transfer Binder] Trade Reg. Rep. (CCH) ¶21,986 (FTC Apr. 14, 1983).

99. Professor Elzinga eliminated from the "successful relief category" all divestiture buyers with *any* ties, horizontal or vertical, to the industry of the divested firm, and even eliminated firms with *no* ties if they were "large." Elzinga, at 47–49. Moreover, at one point he appeared to suggest that there should be "ideal divestiture" to an "ideal buyer." Id., 61.

100. See "Wheelabrator-Frye to Sell Patent Rights to Solve Antitrust Division Objections," *BNA Antitrust & Trade Reg. Rep.* 44 (1983), 492.

101. Wheelabrator conducted the auction and received higher offers from other companies than the sale price it had originally agreed to, but the original purchaser agreed to meet the higher offer and ended up acquiring the assets in question.

102. See, e.g., United States v. ARA Servs., 1982–83 Trade Cas. ¶65,209 (S.D. Ohio 1982); United States v. Harvey Hubbell, Inc., 1982–1 Trade Cas. ¶64,516 (D. Conn. 1981).

103. See, e.g., United States v. Stroh Brewery Co., 1982–83 Trade Cas. ¶65,037 (D.D.C. 1982); United States v. Baldwin-United Corp., 1982–2 Trade Cas. ¶64,788 (S.D. Ohio 1982). The FTC usually requires periodic reports of compliance but does not reserve inspection rights. See, e.g., General Elec. Co., 99 F.T.C. 422 (1982); Gifford-Hill-Am., 99 F.T.C. 372 (1982).

104. See note 47 above.

105. FTC v. Weyerhaeuser Co., 648 F.2d 739, 740 (D.C. Cir. 1981) (per curiam).

106. Brunswick Corp., 96 F.T.C. 151 (1980).

107. See United States v. Reed Roller Bit Co., 274 F. Supp. 573, 590–91 (W.D. Okla. 1967).

108. See FTC v. Weyerhaeuser Co., 665 F.2d 1072, 1076 (D.C. Cir. 1981). In United States v. Coca-Cola Bottling Co., 575 F.2d 222 (9th Cir.), *cert. denied*, 439 U.S. 959 (1978), the court upheld an order of pendente lite relief designed to facilitate eventual rescission. There is no later published opinion indicating the final result on the merits. In Dunbar v. AT&T, 238 Ill. 456, 87 N.E. 521 (1909), a case involving sale of stock rather than assets, the state court ordered rescission, and it apparently was carried out.

109. 665 F.2d 1072 (D.C. Cir. 1981).

110. Id., 1087.

111. Id., 1085–87.

112. Id., 1087.

113. A strong dissent rejected the majority's statutory interpretation and its application of its test, and also warned that "the elevation of the hold-separate order to a worthy remedy under section 13(b) will thrust the courts into an activist supervisory role that ill suits them." Id., 1096 (Mikva, J., dissenting).

114. Application of this test by administrative agencies would meet some, but not all, of the concerns expressed in the dissent. Courts arguably are, but the Department of Justice and FTC are not, statutorily limited in their ability to choose among remedies that serve the public interest in §7 cases. In addition, the FTC at least is a regulatory agency, suited to a supervisory role. But cf. *Wall St. J.*, Feb. 9, 1983, 33, col. 4 and 6 (noting Thomas Kauper's criticism of Justice Department for "becoming more and more of a regulatory agency"). Finally, the agencies need not be insecure about undermining their position on the merits by agreeing to hold-separate orders, for in the Weyerhaeuser class of cases, the imposition of the hold-separate order depends on the equities rather than the merits.

115. 636 F.2d 1336 (D.C. Cir. 1980).

116. Id., 1339 and n. 8.

117. Id., 1343 and n. 26.

118. Id., 1338.

119. For another case that may fit this class, see Genuine Parts Co., No. 821–0025 (FTC Jan. 18, 1982), discussed in Pfunder, 18, col. 4, n. 63.

120. See, e.g., United States v. American Brands, Inc., 5 Trade Reg. Rep. (CCH) (1983–1 Trade Cas.) ¶65,276 (S.D.N.Y. 1983); United States v. GTE Corp., 5 Trade Reg. Rep. (CCH) ¶50,833 (D.D.C. filed May 4, 1983) (proposed consent decree); Allied Corp., [Federal Trade Commission Complaints and Orders 1979–1983 Transfer Binder] Trade Reg. Rep. (CCH) ¶21,978 (FTC May 17, 1983); Canada Cement Lafarge Ltd., 100 F.T.C. 563 (1982).

121. Elzinga, 66–71, 74.

122. See, e.g., Fruehauf Corporation, 91 F.T.C. 132 (1978).

123. See, e.g., Competitive Impact Statement pts. III(C), IV, United States v. GTE Corp., No. 83–1298 (D.D.C. filed May 4, 1983), reprinted in 48 Fed. Reg. 22,020, 22,030–31, 22,033–34 (May 16, 1983).

124. Elzinga, 74.

125. See, e.g., United States v. American Brands, Inc., 5 Trade Reg. Rep. (CCH) (1983–1 Trade Cas.) ¶65,276 (S.D.N.Y. 1983); United States v. Beatrice Foods Co., 1982–1 Trade Cas. ¶64,698 (D. Minn. 1982); United States v. Acorn Eng'g Co., 1982–1 Trade Cas. ¶64,697 (N.D. Cal. 1982).

126. U.S. Dept. of Justice, *Merger Guidelines* 21 (1982), reprinted in 2 Trade Reg. Rep. (CCH) ¶4503.102.

127. See United States v. Stroh Brewery Co., 1982–83 Trade Cas. ¶65,037 (D.D.C. 1982); United States v. Hospital Affiliates Int'l, 1982–1 Trade Cas. ¶64,696 (E.D. La. 1982).

128. See Elzinga, 72.

129. The courts' and agencies' fondness for acquisition bans seems to be a product of their peculiar view that deterrence operates only on those who proposed illegal acquisitions in the past, not those who might propose such acquisitions in the future. See note 7 above.

130. United States v. ARA Servs., 1979–2 Trade Cas. ¶62,861 (E.D. Mo. 1979), is an example of an enforcement action where the company, subject to a 10-year acquisition ban, made what was arguably an acquisition in a situation where pressing commercial necessity did not allow time to seek and obtain FTC approval.

131. Even since Baxter has been in office, there has been one consent decree imposing an acquisition ban although no justification for such a ban is evident. United States v. CBS, 1982–1 Trade Cas. ¶64,478 (S.D.N.Y. 1981). In this case, it appears that the ban may have been imposed as a tradeoff for otherwise very lenient divestiture terms. Such tradeoffs serve no public interest, but only salve an unsuccessful negotiator's ego. In the future, acquisition bans should not be imposed for such insubstantial reasons.

4   Market Definition and the SIC Approach

James W. McKie

Economists seek definitions and measurements of markets for a variety of purposes, among them the analysis of monopoly. They frequently make use of the data on economic activity organized under the Standard Industrial Classification (SIC) and its appended Census product classes in critiques of particular antitrust cases and in advising lawyers and judges on economically rational diagnoses of monopoly and competition.[1] But the SIC is an all-purpose classification not designed solely or even primarily to support definitions of markets. The shortcomings of the SIC for the analysis of markets have often been pointed out.[2] In this chapter we look again at the problem of reconciling the industry classification with certain requirements of market definition exemplified by recent antitrust proceedings.

The principal difficulty with the SIC as a surrogate for market classification is that it is a supply-oriented classification, whereas in economics, markets are usually defined in terms of demand substitution among products or services.[3] The empirical concept of an "industry" is a grouping of productive units on the basis of some observed characteristics of their activities, products, inputs, or relationships. Demand substitution among the products may be present, but it is a secondary consideration in industry definition. Only in abstract economic theory do the two concepts correspond exactly.

The supply-oriented SIC, however, has certain advantages of its own even for market analysis and often provides useful information on another aspect of market definition: supply substitutability.[4] Analysis of monopoly power in antitrust cases centers on the firm rather than the group or the market as such. Those firms that offer, or can offer, effective substitutes for a given firm's product are de facto in the same market with that firm, to a degree depending on the effective constraint of the substitute on its power or its decisions.[5] Those constraints can come from either demand substitutes or supply substitutes.

Supply Substitution and Potential Entry

Though the primary criterion used by U.S. antitrust policy for defining markets is demand substitution, it does make use of supply substitution. Contending parties sometimes invoke cross-elasticity of supply (though they hardly ever attempt to measure it),[6] and they frequently refer to the relative ease or difficulty with which firms other than the ones that now supply the products can begin to do so.

The nomenclature is a bit confusing. Viewed from the buying side, supply substitutability relates to the capability of firms that do not now produce a good to begin supplying it; and thus, from the point of view of producers, it is very likely to be associated with supply *complementarity*. That capability will be greater in firms that are already producing something similar or something that can share facilities, inputs, technology, or channels of distribution with the newly supplied product. Unused complementarities or potential subadditivities of cost are not strictly necessary conditions for supply substitutability, though when present they are likely to facilitate it.[7]

The Department of Justice Merger Guidelines of June 1982,[8] call for consideration of (1) supply substitution, when other firms can "easily and economically" produce the product in question with the same facilities within six months and (2) "de novo entry," when other firms may construct new facilities to produce the product. A better term for the latter might be "constrained de novo entry," since in a sufficiently long period capital and technology become fluid enough to move from practically any activity to any other; under those conditions, the Gross Domestic Product would be the ultimate boundary of the industry. Firms in the first category are included in the market. Firms that are possible de novo entrants are not included, but the possibility is taken into account in interpreting the significance of the shares of firms already in the market. It is practically impossible to predict or measure the quantitative results of de novo entry, of course, but the Guidelines do recognize the importance of constraints on market power arising from that possibility.[9]

Tabulations of statistical data on industrial production reveal little about short-run excess capacity in "existing facilities" that can easily and quickly be switched to production of other particular products. More detailed knowledge is needed about the productive processes and the internal organization of firms than is available in Census reports. If products are typically produced in the same establishment, however, or are grouped together because of complementarities in production or similar technologies, the data would reveal something about the likeliest sources of supply substitutability or de novo entry. Accordingly, a look at the Standard Industrial Classification and Census product classes, and their criteria for collection, is in order. (Because these are familiar research tools for many economists, some elementary details have been relegated to an appendix.)

The Standard Classification of Industries and Products

A system of classification should reflect real organization, but it also stamps its own character on the perception of reality itself. Ideally, the objective characteristics of products and activities should control classification at any given level of aggregation for any given use; in actuality, they do so only in part. Other aspects of classification are determined by a selected set of principles that are not generically compelling.

The critical question, of course, is: How are the products or activities grouped so as to define the industry or the product group? Scrutiny of the SIC reveals that, whereas products are grouped primarily on the basis of supply relationships, not all industries are defined in terms of product similarity even from the supply side.

The statisticians responsible for the SIC and its Census components sometimes claim, with some justification, that the classification reflects the observed characteristics of production: products are grouped together in the SIC because they are grouped together in the real process of production. It is true that the data categories in the Census of Manufactures are constantly checked by reference to the changing structure of activities. But the association of products in an industry or product group of the SIC does not mean that they are necessarily associated in production within the firm and still less that they are necessarily associated within the same establishment or factory. SIC industries are not uniformly coherent in this respect.

In classifying the flow of production in manufacturing, the SIC uses three main criteria. Foremost is similarity of products, but that in turn breaks down into several secondary criteria: technological or physical similarity; homogeneity of function; complementarity in production; complementarity in use; substitutability in use (which, in fact, is often present in the primary-product group but which is usually subordinate to the others). Frequent association *within the establishment* is regarded by the Census as a compelling reason for including those products within the same industry, and indeed it is usually good evidence of complementarity.[10]

The second basis for grouping products into an industry is similarity of inputs, especially material inputs. The products may be grouped for no other reason than they are made of the same material. The third criterion is similarity of process, especially when the process is the product, as in the Plating and Polishing industry (3471). A few miscellaneous industries show no persuasive common elements among products.

These three criteria for classifying products and activities are frequently observed together in an SIC industry. This is hardly surprising, considering the essential logic of any system of classification: to collect and divide *per genus et differentias*.[11] The classifiers use both primary (inclusive) and secondary (exclusive) criteria; the boundary lines drawn according to the various criteria or bases intersect each other. Therefore, one cannot generally say that industries or product groups defined primarily on the basis of similar materials are necessarily devoid of product complementarities or process similarities; those criteria may have been generated along another vector of distinctions.

For example: the entire major group 24 (Lumber and Wood Products) is an input-defined group, but the four-digit industries in it have to be distinguished from each other on the basis of product characteristics (Wood Kitchen Cabinets, 2434) or process (Wood Preserving, 2491). All three criteria are visible in 2421 (Sawmills and Planing Mills). On the other hand, product complementarity defines major group 25 (Furniture and Fixtures), whereas the adjacent industries within it, Wood Office Furniture (2521) and Metal Office Furniture (2522), are distinguished from each other primarily on the basis of material inputs. The Machinery major groups 35 and 36 are almost entirely product-complement groups in production, with both substitute and complementary relations in use, whereas secondary demarcations are very weak—again, usually differences in products. For contrast, nearly every process-defined industry in the SIC has a strong secondary criterion of exclusion, and frequently two, because the processes or stages have defined inputs and outputs—for example, Rice Milling (2044), Finishing Plants, Cotton (2261), Paper Coating and Glazing (2641), Blended and Prepared Flour (made from purchased flour inputs) (2045).

The demand and supply relationships of each SIC industry must be examined in determining whether it corresponds even roughly to a market grouping; no across-the-board characterization is possible. It is well known that some of the four-digit industries are too broad to be used as markets defined in terms of demand substitution; nonsubstitutable products are included, or the coverage is too low, or a nationwide total is not meaningful. The five-digit product class sometimes corresponds better to the economic market and might even qualify as a homogeneous "industry" from the supply side. Other four-digit industries or product groups are too narrow in scope and exclude significant demand-substitutable products: Refined Cane Sugar (2062-) and Beet Sugar (2063-) are well-known examples. Probably more four-digit groups are too inclusive than not inclusive enough of all close substitutes, but others are reasonably congruent with markets. Still others would have to be dissected and recombined to produce meaningful markets when judged by the criterion of demand substitution. Yet others include an array of demand-complementary products in the list that defines the industry, because some firms produce them together or merely because they share a common technology. It may turn out, however, that products that are complementary in use can also be substitutes when offered in different combinations.

What about supply substitution as a reinforcing criterion in market definition? The array of industries and product classes has never been comprehensively analyzed for the purpose of determining the opportunities for constrained de novo entry. Groups of products indicating complementarities in production are promising candidates for generation of supply substitution, but there are no good prima facie indicators of supply complementarities: those are revealed only by analysis. The Census approach, which uses establishments rather than firms as the basic unit, tends to overlook supply complementarities at levels of organization higher than the factory; nor does it reveal whether the product mix defining the class or industry is necessarily typical of establishments or firms included in the industry. Nevertheless, because the Census of Manufactures is a supply-side classification and the relations of production strongly influence that approach, one would expect to find useful indicators of supply substitution in the Census/SIC industry cells and product classes. Lacking a comprehensive analysis, we look at anecdotal illustrations.

Supply-Oriented Definition in Antitrust Proceedings

Share of a defined market is at best only one of several relevant clues to the constraints on the market power of a firm. Without dwelling on the limitations of market share as an indicator of monopoly, however, we must recognize that parties to antitrust suits do attempt to define markets and measure a firm's share of them. Let us see how the industry and product approach of the SIC might have helped in a few recent examples. The outcomes of those cases are of less interest than the arguments advanced.[12]

Constrained De Novo Entry—Military Equipment

Military equipment presents an obvious difficulty for market definition based on product substitution in use. It is usually produced to a special, unique design created between, or at least agreed upon by, seller and buyer. Characteristically, such equipment does not exist until the government calls it into being by assigning the tasks of designing (or developing it from a government design) and producing it to a contractor or contractors. Several, sometimes many, suppliers may develop alternatives at various stages in the process, or the government may go "sole source" from start to finish. It almost always chooses a single firm for the final development and initial production stages, though it may call on additional sources later. Meanwhile, any apparent monopoly of the product has been conferred by the buyer. Usually there are no substitute products of similar design and function unless the government has intentionally called them forth.

To assess the significance of the apparent monopoly we must tally the capabilities of other firms to produce the product; they will have no actual production at first. This capability is best determined by examining the adjacent technologies. If the SIC has set up a category of products complementary in supply and with interactive technology as the basic unifying element, then scrutiny of the five-digit class and the seven-digit products in the industry suggests the scope of supply substitutability or potential entry for the product in question, even though it may not support calculation of a potential market-share fraction for the military contractor.

A recent example involved in an antitrust case was the APX-72 transponder, a signaling and identification device for aircraft. Civilian transponders were available, but their design was different and they were not capable of sending and receiving cryptographed recognition signals. The design was developed by the Naval Research Laboratory and the final R&D and first production contracts were assigned in 1964 to the Bendix Corporation. An unsuccessful bidder for a subsequent contract (Wilcox) sued Bendix, charging monopoly of the APX-72.

The plaintiff, of course, opted for a narrow definition of the market: the APX-72 transponder itself, which at the time had no close substitutes and which Bendix alone produced for several years during which it was alleged to have monopoly power. In reply, Bendix pointed out that there were ten bidders on the development contract in 1964, and also that on a later reprocurement (1969) there were twenty-one bidders besides Bendix, one of which (Honeywell, which had never before manufactured transponders) actually got the contract. If, however, strict demand substitutability alone were used to define the market during 1964–69, there would have been only one supplier.[13]

At the critical points in the procurement process, the government in fact could choose among an even greater number of alternative suppliers with the ability to supply the transponder than the number who actually responded to its invitations to bid. How should we measure this range of potential alternatives and the share of the initially successful bidder (Bendix) in it? The Census industry that included transponders—3662 (Radio and TV Communication Equipment)—was probably too broad for effective supply substitution across the board or, of course, for demand substitution. A better case can be made for inclusion of product classes 36624 (Electronic Navigational Aids, including transponders) and 36625 (Electronic Search and Detection Apparatus).[14] Firms producing products in 36621 (Commercial, Industrial and Military Communications Equipment, Except Telephone) were also in a good position to enter production of transponders de novo. There were more than 1,000 firms in the four-digit industry, and at least 100 in the two most significant five-digit product classess; it would be surprising if there were not many more than 20 fully capable potential competitors throughout the relevant period. The government's tactics during the "monopoly" period showed that it was well aware of their availability. Bendix's efforts to renegotiate the contract to its advantage were frustrated.

Other episodes of military procurement may not be as clear-cut. The government may find itself locked in to a sole supplier for extended periods in procurement of a major weapons system. Nevertheless, its range of choice of alternate designs and alternate suppliers at critical points in the procurement process depends on potential capability or supply substitutability in a way that can be indicated, albeit imperfectly, by data on firms and products collected in industry categories on the basis of technological similarity and product complementarity.

Substitutes and Complements: Shared Technology in a
Dynamic Market

In its recent marathon antitrust case against IBM,[15] the government sought to demarcate a market that consisted of general-purpose digital computer systems. It excluded terminals, peripheral devices such as tape and disk drives that were sold separately, applications software sold separately, services such as those of service bureaus, and all special-purpose computers and computer systems including those which it claimed were designed for scientific purposes. The range of systems that qualified for inclusion in its market was strictly circumscribed. Excluded were large "number-crunchers," which were said to be largely scientific, and small and "mini" computers, said to be nonsubstitutable in the principal uses of the mainframes on a one-for-one basis. Also excluded were individual components not shipped as parts of systems. After the trial was under way, the government added more restrictive requirements: the systems in the market had to be members of a "family" of computers and had to be capable of operating in three modes—batch processing, interactive, and timesharing—and had to work with a single, integrated data base and management system. In short, the market was defined so as to include only the leading systems of the IBM line that were used primarily in business applications, and the systems that were very similar to them on a machine-for-machine comparison.[16]

IBM advocated a broad definition of the market. It claimed that its decisions and power were constrained by a broad range of alternatives, including computer systems of all types; leasing companies that owned IBM-manufactured and other equipment which they offered in competition with IBM's own leased and sold equipment; components of systems, including peripherals and terminals; software; and services of service bureaus, contract-service management companies, and systems engineering houses. These totals were not readily available from standard sources. In a joint program with the government and other plaintiffs, IBM developed this information from all the firms in these various categories that could be identified, added the total values in all categories annually from 1954 on, and determined its own share of this "EDP [electronic data processing] market." Some of these EDP data were presented in alternative forms to eliminate, for example, double counting of various kinds.

Let us now examine the SIC categories in the U.S. Census of Manufactures as an alternative measure.[17] Under the 1972 SIC, the industry was defined as Electronic Computing Equipment (3573). The product classes and products were:

35731   Electronic computers:
               11 Digital, general purpose
               13 Digital, special purpose [mostly military]
               22 Analog
               25 Hybrid

35732   Peripheral equipment for electronic computers
                    32 Direct access storage units [e.g., disk drives]
                    34 Serial access storage units [e.g., tape drives]
                    36–65 Input-output equipment [e.g., magnetic, optical, printers, graphic display]
                    71–75 Computer terminals [various types]
                    81–83 Digital interface equipment [modems, multiplexors]

35733   Parts and attachments for electronic computing equipment

35730   Electronic computing equipment n.s.k.

The SIC industry is considerably closer to the IBM definition of the market (though it includes only hardware) than to the government's market, which included only products from parts of several five-digit classes.[18]

Strong complementarities in production are one clue to the unifying principles of the SIC industry; another is complementarity in use. The government, of course, vehemently attacked the representation of the market by the SIC industry and even more strongly the IBM version that added service bureaus and leasing companies. The product (and service) mix obviously included both substitutes and complements. A single pair of products (tape drives and disk drives, for example) might illustrate both relationships simultaneously, but the true significance of complementarity in use could be seen against the background of the rich and varied product mix. Complements competed with each other *as parts of systems.* Computer systems were made up of components— "boxes"—and software, each element of which had substitutes, including incremental substitution from other elements. (Additional memory, for example was partially traded off against additional disk storage or better software.) This opportunity to substitute among components and systems, and the opportunities for reconfiguration, brought the entire range of electronic computer hardware within a market relationship.

Firms in the industry had something else in common: development of the technology along diverse and multiplicative lines. These firms, and firms newly entering from adjacent technologies, continually developed and marketed new devices, applications, and systems in a variety and volume that has elicited such descriptions as "torrential" and "bewildering."

Innovation is not usually considered to fit the definition of supply substitution, which is an essentially static concept; but in substance it is very similar if mastery of parts of a technology enables firms to enter other parts and to develop functional substitutes and extensions that change the competitive conditions for other firms producing other products. That, more than any other characteristic, has been the distinguishing mark of the electronic data processing industry. The market is scarcely the same, for any one firm or group of firms, from one day to the next. Yet the loose technological aggregation used by the SIC is not a bad approximation to identification of this industry, which generates those substitutions and extensions, though it leaves out such important complementary sources as electronic communications.

The market originally defined by the Department of Justice—mainframe systems of a certain capacity range for commercial applications—in fact became obsolete with dizzying speed. By the time the U.S. antitrust trial was well under way (1975), it must have been obvious to the department that all of the functions of a "mainframe" in 1969 could now be performed by "minicomputers"—and microcomputers were edging into that range of applications. New functions, devices, and combinations unknown in 1969 had taken over much of the EDP activity. These developments may have been what led the government to redefine the market in 1977; but even this attempt to resuscitate a narrow market was overtaken by events. (In early 1982, the government abandoned its entire case, presumably including its market definition, as being "without merit".) By 1982, for example, systems that once were on a board were now on a chip, and microprocessors were invading the mainframe range; Intel's model 432, a 32-bit processor, was becoming known as a "micromainframe." [19] The distinction between "commercial" and "scientific" systems had long been reduced to software and modular configurations, and even the line between data processing and communications was thoroughly blurred.

Meanwhile, the electronic computer "industry," defined largely in terms of technology and supply relationships, has been as good a representation of the market, especially a market centered on IBM, as any aggregation compiled in terms of demand substitution. Its boundaries have continually shifted outward with changes in technology.

Supply Substitutability Further Illustrated

Another illustration reveals supply substitution in a simpler form of parallel capabilities. Allis Chalmers' acquisition of Simplicity Manufacturing Company was attacked by the government under section 7 of the Clayton Act.[20] The government advocated a definition of the market restricted to "riding garden tractors and attachments and parts therefor." The defendants advocated a market definition including all mobile outdoor power equipment including powered walking lawn mowers, snowblowers, and powered tillers. The product group in such a market would be complements in part, substitutes in part, and in part unrelated in use.

The details are unimportant; the case turned on the choice of market definition. The court chose the broad one, partly on the basis of substitution in use but also on the basis of supply substitution, which brought in the suppliers of the products that were not demand substitutes. In the words of the court:

> The record does not establish that production facilities and engineering talent necessary for the development and manufacture of riding garden tractors, as defined by the plaintiff, differ from those necessary for other mobile outdoor power equipment. Rather, it appears that manufacturing techniques employed are similar, the same plant and assembly line or assembly line technique can be used, employees and development and research staffs can be interchanged.[21]

This element of the decision made the market practically conterminous with SIC Industry 3524 (Garden Tractors and Lawn and Garden Equipment), which itself had probably been grouped that way in large part for the very reasons mentioned by the court.

Market definition, as part of the assessment of monopoly power in any antitrust proceeding, quickly goes beyond the summary statistics of the Census of Manufactures as governed by the SIC, into detailed facts pertaining to the particular firms involved and their market circumstances. General-purpose classifications cannot be conclusive. We will never see a plenary industrial tabulation that reveals all we might want to know about particular industries and markets.

Nevertheless, because the elements of product complementarity and technological association are clearly significant in so many SIC/Census categories, they are a useful starting point for market definition, especially where there are no strong demand-side factors delineating market boundaries. Even where demand substitutability indicates a working definition for the market as a starting point, the evidence of SIC/Census categories is frequently useful as a supply-side modification of such definitions and is particularly helpful in avoiding the error of drawing the boundaries too narrowly.

Appendix

The Standard Industrial Classification covers the entire field of economic activity; this discussion is confined to manufacturing.

Under the SIC and Census product classification, individual products (seven-digits) are combined into five-digit product classes and these in turn into four-digit product groups. Establishments—plants, factories, shops, workplaces—producing these products are then allocated to the four-digit industries whose products account for a major share of the establishments' output or shipments. These are the "primary" products that define the industry, though most plants produce other, "secondary" products that belong (are primary) to other four-digit industries.

Data for four-digit industries are collected into broader aggregations, three-digit industry groups and two-digit major groups. Such data as employment, investment, value added, materials and fuels consumed, and geographical distribution of activity are available only for four-digit industries and larger aggregations of them. Product data—value of shipments, and sometimes physical totals—are available for four-digit product groups, five-digit product classes, and seven-digit products. "Shipments" means shipments *from* an establishment, whether to another establishment of the same firm or somewhere else. Products made and consumed within the same establishment are not counted.

Some data are published for *firms*, but in such form that the firms cannot be identified. For example, all the products of industry 0000 shipped by large multiplant firm A can easily be collected and combined with the total shipped by firms B, C, and D and published in the form of a largest-four-firm concentration ratio. This would not include the products of firm A that were primary to other industries, nor would its other establishments be included, for example, in value-added tabulations if they were classified in other industries.

The Bureau of the Census measures the cleanness of the four-digit industries with coverage and specialization tests. *Coverage* is the percentage of an industry's primary products shipped by establishments counted within the industry. *Specialization* is the ratio of primary product shipments to total shipments (primary plus secondary products) of those establishments. These tests are necessary but not sufficient criteria for the location of industry boundaries. The Census tries to achieve scores above 80 percent for both ratios. The average for all manufacturing industries is more than 90 percent.

It has long been the experience of the Census of Manufactures that efforts to improve the coverage and specialization of the four-digit industry units by extending the industry boundaries are usually self-defeating. Manufacturing is multiproduct, and the product mixes differ among establishments in an intractable way: no "clean" classification is possible short of tossing everything into one Gross Domestic Product category. Adding new establishments adds a new set of secondary products, even though it may bring more of the primary products within the industry boundary; converting secondary to primary products (redefining) pulls in yet other establishments, with new forms of product heterogeneity.

Although it is theoretically possible to form heterogeneous groups of products that meet the specialization and coverage tests but that are associated at random, the criteria for grouping discussed in this chapter are designed to produce acceptably homogeneous groups in terms of the criterion used. Unfortunately, what is homogeneous in terms of input may be heterogeneous in terms of product, and both may be irrelevant to the criterion of market demand substitution. Clearly, there must be prior judgments as to the *basis* of collection (of the smallest entities) or of subdivision (of the largest entities); mere observation does not dictate the result.

Notes

I am indebted to Professor Franklin M. Fisher and to an anonymous referee for helpful suggestions for improvement of this paper. Remaining defects are, of course, entirely my responsibility.

1. Here we consider the 1972 SIC, the latest comprehensive revision. Office of Management and Budget, Executive Office of the President, *Standard Industrial Classification Manual* (Washington, D.C.: U.S. Government Printing Office, 1972).

2. See, for example, *Studies of Industrial Concentration by The Conference Board, 1958–1972* (New York: The Conference Board, 1973), esp. sections II, III, and IX.

3. Peter O. Steiner, "Markets and Industries," *International Encyclopedia of the Social Sciences* (New York: Macmillan, 1968), vol. 9, pp. 575–581. In the article, Steiner says: "The focus of the SIC is on the supply side rather than the demand side, and SIC industries are more nearly appropriate to the identification of interrelated sellers than of alternatives to buyers" (p. 578).

4. Among other uses, the recently developed theory of "contestable markets" relies heavily on supply complementarities in multiproduct industries; it is a theory of industry structure, not just market structure. William J. Baumol, "Contestable Markets: An Uprising in the Theory of Industry Structure," *American Economic Review* 72, no. 1 (March 1982), pp. 1–15; Elizabeth E. Bailey and Ann F. Friedlander, "Market Structure and Multiproduct Industries," *Journal of Economic Literature* 20, no. 3 (September 1982), pp. 1024–1048.

5. Franklin M. Fisher, "Diagnosing Monopoly," *Quarterly Review of Economics and Business* 19, no. 2 (Summer 1979): "The fundamental question is that of constraints on power. Focusing on the question of relevant market can often lead to losing sight of that fact" (p. 16).

6. Cross-elasticity of supply of a given product is defined in terms of specific firms, usually as the percentage change in the quantity of good X that would be produced by firms not now producing it, divided by a percentage change in the price of good X by firms that are producing it; but to be reversible, it would have to include exit by firms now producing X if the price of X falls. The term is sometimes defined according to the reactions of a single potential supplier or in terms of supply of factor inputs. These definitions, however, seem to be more trouble than they are worth.

7. We are not concerned here with purely geographical supply substitution or potential entry into a restricted geographical market by producers of the same product from an area adjacent to it. These can be significant in practice—as in *U.S. v. Bethlehem Steel Corp. et al.*, 214 F. Supp. 501 (1963), 377 U.S. 271 (1964), although there were also issues of product groupings in that case. But they do not reveal the problems of product groupings and industry classification that characterize the accumulation of data on the nationwide basis typically used by those who gather industrial statistics.

8. Reprinted in Commerce Clearing House, 1 *Trade Regulation Reporter* 4501 at 4502.201.

9. This paragraph is based on Gregory J. Werden, "Market Delineation and the Justice Department's Merger Guidelines," EPO Discussion Paper 82–7 (December 1982), pp. 9–11.

10. In an earlier survey of the 1957 SIC, I counted 237 manufacturing industries (out of a total of 426) whose classification was primarily product association—functional similarity, substitutability, complementarity, technological resemblance—without

evident, strong secondary constraints. There were 119 more that showed product similarity with strong secondary constraints—similarity of inputs or processes. Most of the remaining 70 industries were grouped primarily on the basis of either processes or inputs, often with secondary product constraints; but they included a few wholly residual miscellaneous groups. See J. W. McKie, "Industrial Classification and Sector Measures of Industrial Production," U.S. Bureau of the Census Working Paper No. 20 (1965), p. 3. A similar breakdown is indicated in the 1972 SIC, though the number of manufacturing industries had increased to 450.

11. The essential logic is Aristotle's; his famous principle, "It is easier to define the particular than the universal, and therefore we must pass from the former to the latter" (*Posterior Analytics*, II, 13.28), is not consistently followed in the SIC, which evidently makes some Platonic prior designations of major categories, particularly those based on inputs, and then proceeds to define industries within them by division.

12. I participated in two cases, the Bendix Case (relating to the APX-72 transponder) and the IBM case, and gave advice as a witness for defendants on market definition.

13. *American Standard, Inc., v. The Bendix Corporation*, Civil Action No. 73-CV-670-W-B. (The case was settled before the actual trial began.) In 1967 the government directed Bendix to develop a second source (Wilcox) under a "leader-follower contract," which still left Bendix in charge of the essential elements of supply of the APX-72.

14. In 1967, Bendix's total shipments of products in the product classes most directly associated with transponders were less than 4 percent of the value of shipments by all firms. Plaintiff's Exhibit 2A-2Q, *American Standard, Inc. v. The Bendix Corporation*. This percentage is not a reliable indicator of Bendix's "share" of a total "market" consisting of potential competitors for the APX-72, but it helps refute any inference of dominance by Bendix of the technology and hence of the supply of electronic navigational and search apparatus.

15. *U.S. vs. International Business Machines Corporation*, Civ. No. 69-200, filed January 17, 1969. There were also some twenty private antitrust suits against IBM, whose plaintiffs adopted various narrow definitions of the "market" to suit their strategies.

16. Franklin M. Fisher, John J. McGowan, and Joen E. Greenwood, *Folded, Spindled and Mutilated: Economic Analysis and U.S. v. I.B.M.* (Cambridge, Mass.: The MIT Press, 1983), chapter 3. The government then proceeded to estimate IBM's share of this market, not of current production in each year but the "installed base," the inventory of systems in the hands of users. If a system had ever been produced by IBM, the undepreciated value of the entire system was counted in IBM's share of the market today, regardless of who owned it now and regardless of what peripheral attachments or software might have been provided by other suppliers. (For a critique, see ibid., chapter 4.) Needless to say, no system of production classification could provide such data.

17. U.S. Bureau of the Census, *1972 Census of Manufactures*, vol. II, part 3, p. 35-F-15. For convenience, some seven-digit products have been combined under a summary heading.

18. The Census of Manufactures tabulates current year totals, not installed base. It discovered early in the industry's history, however, that "total value of shipments" is

misleading; there is too much interplant shipment within the industry. To avoid counting the value of a disk drive, say, twice—once when shipped from the disk plant and again when shipped as part of a complete system from the computer plant—it is necessary to use a value-added basis for accumulation. Shipment value totals are reported for products but not for the industry. The high component of interplant shipments in industry totals indicates that the establishments are associated on the supply side by something stronger than product or process resemblance.

19. *Wall Street Journal*, December 24, 1982.

20. *U.S. v. Allis-Chalmers Mfg. Co., Simanco, Inc., and Simplicity Mfg. Co., Inc.*, 1970 CCH *Trade Cases* ¶73,341, pp. 89,348–355.

21. Ibid., p. 89,354.

5 Profitability and Market Share

M. A. Adelman and Bruce E. Stangle

Over the past two decades there has been extensive research in industry profitability as determined by industry concentration, advertising, and growth rates, among other things. An excellent summary (now, of course, incomplete) was provided by Weiss (1974). More recently, however, much research has focused not on industry but on individual firm profitability as it relates to firm market share.[1] An inquiry typically is formulated as follows. Let Pr_{ij} be the profitability for industry i and firm j; let C_i be concentration in the industry, MS_{ij} be the market share of firm j; and let a, b, and c be coefficients to be estimated with an equation of the type:

$$Pr_{ij} = a + bC_i + cMS_{ij} \tag{1}$$

Equation (1) can be interpreted as a statement that market structure can and should be analyzed into the component parts of concentration (and other industry variables) and market share. This involves an appeal to economic theory. Thus concentration is a proxy for fewness of sellers, which is said to make it easier to control production and prices in a market and to increase profits. Similar statements can be made about industry advertising, growth, and other variables.

The authors take *market share* as a proxy for economies of scale, or for the firm's own market power, or for some other factors that enable the firm to influence its costs or its prices or both, and hence, influence its profits. It seems to us that any statement in the form of equation (1) is inadequate to support a proposition about market structure, even the most tentative and limited; thus any conclusion drawn from it, to the effect that once we make allowance for market shares concentration does or does not have much effect on profitability, must be dismissed as altogether unfounded.

The reason is that profitability, as we hope to demonstrate, has a

strong effect on market share. Therefore, a profitability-share correlation will probably be found, and will be statistically robust, even in
the absence of economies of scale or market power. A single equation
cannot capture both the profitability-share effect and the share-
profitability effect. An econometric approach must be done by way of
simultaneous equations, or it had better not be attempted.

A quick look at three studies indicates the problem. Shepherd
analyzed a sample of 231 "Fortune 500" firms in various industries and
found market share variation to explain so much of profitability variation that there was little left for interindustry concentration to
explain. His sample and methods, however, were criticized by both
Weiss and Scherer. After making corrections, Bothwell and Keeler
confirmed the relation between share and profitability, then asked:
Why the association? Scherer and Ravenscraft suggest that superior
profitability in any industry must be partitioned into two elements: the
price effect, determined by concentration, and the *efficiency effect*,
determined by economies of scale. They use market share as a proxy for
scale economies; Scherer summarizes the results:

> Ravenscraft's simulation studies show that . . . the two structural
> variables do rather well disentangling price-raising and scale economy
> effects. . . .

The main point for the moment is that profit differences associated
with market share appear to embody a complex mixture of scale
economy, materials cost, selling price, and product differentiation
advantages.[2]

In business and popular discourse, market share is often assumed to
be an indicator of scale economy.[3] Nevertheless, market share is rarely a
valid proxy. It has no direct relation to the basic economic concept of
increasing returns to scale: over some range, an additional bundle or
module of inputs brings a greater than proportional increase in output.
In some markets operation may require large economies of scale, but if
the market itself is very large, a very large firm need be only a small
portion. There may be great economies of scale, but the firms achieving
them may have small market shares. Hence, in such a case, using market
share as a proxy for scale economies would not only be inadequate but
directly contrary to fact.

Thus far we have tried to show only what these studies aim to do. We
do not deny their validity for any purpose. For example, a stock market

analyst looking for companies likely to show unusually high profits would search among those with high market shares in a concentrated industry. The analyst would care not about the direction of cause and effect but only about correlation, and we see no error in such an inquiry.

Equation (1), however, is inadequate to show the effect of market share on profitability because, at any time, market share is largely a function of previous investment, determined by expected profitability, a proxy for which is observed profitability. We suggest a simple hypothesis to explain the observed connection between profitability and market share: *profits attract investment, losses repel*. Weak assumptions permit strong conclusions, and we have only two. First, we assume rational conduct, profit seeking even short of strict profit maximizing. In any given market, the firm that expects a higher return on a given investment will invest more. The second assumption is that the traditional supply curve and quasi-rents apply.

If these profit discrepancies persist—that is, if variations in profitability are anything more than an endless stochastic jiggle—then the more profitable firm will grow faster or shrink less than its less profitable rivals. If firms anticipating higher profit invest more than rivals while others disinvest to avoid loss, market shares will reflect these past expenditures. If profits stay below the cost of capital, the firm will quit and the market share will be zero. Therefore, even with no price-raising power nor economies of scale, more profitable firms will have higher market shares because the expectation of those profits induced the investment in capacity.

There is another reason why some regression studies tend to show a positive association between market share and profitability. The class of firms with very small market shares is like the lobby of a building, crowded with people coming and going but with nobody staying long. Many firms with low market shares are just entering the market. They are (or appear to be) less profitable because they have not yet paid their dues and absorbed all their start-up costs. Many others are persistent losers, not long for this world. Poor performance has cut off investment, and the owners are squeezing the last bit of value from plant and equipment, inventory, and organization, simply covering variable costs before giving up altogether.

The simplest way to test our proposition is to find a data set where there are neither economies of scale nor market power and test for the existence of the market share-profitability correlation. This would serve as a crucial experiment, compatible with one hypothesis while contradicting another.

We do have a small body of data on profits and market share for a single retail firm (A&P), one that operated in more than forty local markets during the years 1932–41. We can almost certainly eliminate differentials in market power, economies of scale, risk, or entry as explanations of differentials in profitability across local markets.

First, scale economies in (and other entry barriers to) food retailing are generally acknowledged to be low.[4] Perhaps economies cease with a single store, perhaps with a group of stores and a warehouse. We need not even reach the issue, however, because each of the forty-four units in our sample consists of many food stores grouped around a warehouse; there is no evidence in a voluminous company history of any hint of variations among units in scale economies. Average sales per store might indeed differ widely, but that would be attributable to better or poorer management and to luck.

Second, A&P's market shares were low. The mean share is approximately 10.2 percent in a typical year, with a standard deviation of 3.9 percent. At such low levels, the price-raising power of the individual firm is negligible.

The market share estimates were made by the firm for its own purposes, not for any public record. A&P knew its own sales, and sales in the area were from published estimates by the Department of Commerce. We have no data for concentration in these markets during this period. Presumably, A&P was one of the larger competitors in each of its markets, but there were many food retailers both locally and nationwide. By 1954 mean concentration in SMSAs for grocery stores was 45 percent at the four-firm level.[5] Our guess is that a comparable figure for 1935 might have been 10 percentage points lower. (Consider that if the largest four firms were of approximately equal size, on average, the concentration ratio would have been four times the A&P market share, or 41 percent; this at least sets a plausible upper bound, suggesting a real ratio that is somewhat lower.) It is possible—but, in our opinion, unlikely—that there is some systematic relation between market share and concentration in the forty-four sample markets. Unfortunately, this hypothesis cannot be tested.

The profit measure used is the net profit rate on sales, that is, sales less cost of goods (gross profit) less expenses (the sum of wages, rents, fuel and power, and miscellaneous operating costs), divided by sales, or

Table 5.1
Summary Statistics

Year	Net profit rate $(G - E)$		Market share (MS)	
	Mean	S.D.	Mean	S.D.
1932	0.025	0.018	0.101	0.040
1933	0.025	0.019	0.095	0.037
1934	0.021	0.016	0.105	0.040
1935	0.019	0.015	0.102	0.042
1936	0.020	0.012	0.098	0.039
1937	0.011	0.013	0.094	0.037
1938	0.019	0.013	0.100	0.040
1939	0.020	0.011	0.101	0.040
1940	0.019	0.011	0.107	0.042
1941	0.018	0.007	0.111	0.045
1932–41	0.020	0.014	0.102	0.039

Notes: $(G - E)$ = gross profit rate minus expense rate (rate of return on sales expressed as a decimal).

MS = A&P market share (expressed as a decimal).

Source: M. A. Adelman, *A&P: A Study in Price-Cost Behavior and Public Policy*, pp. 454–463.

simply $G - E$.[6] The gross profit rate, G, was, in effect, the price of retail services. Too high a gross profit rate—that is, misjudging demand response—led to lost sales and a higher expense rate, E, thereby yielding a lower net profit.

Table 5.1 shows that the average net profit rate fell over the period 1932–37, then recovered dramatically. Over the entire period 1932–41, mean net profits are approximately 2.0 percent of sales, with a standard deviation of 1.4 percent. The market share variable is fairly steady over the ten-year period, averaging 10.2 percent with a standard deviation of 3.9 percent; again, 1937 is the low point.

Table 5.2 gives detailed results for ten ordinary least squares cross-section regressions for each year between 1932 and 1941. Variations in market share in year t are explained by variations in net profit in the current year. The variation in market share explained by the net profit rate ranges from 21.1 to 46.9 percent, with the low point occurring in 1937. In each year the coefficients on both the constant term and the net profit rate are positive and are significantly different from zero as determinants of market share.

Table 5.2
Regression results for individual years, 1932–41 (*t* statistics in parentheses)

Equation	Dependent variable	Year	Independent variables		R**2	N	S.E.
			Constant	$(G - E)$			
1	MS	1932	0.065	1.487	0.439	43	0.031
			(8.06)	(5.66)			
2	MS	1933	0.066	1.160	0.343	43	0.030
			(8.53)	(4.63)			
3	MS	1934	0.077	1.316	0.286	43	0.034
			(8.83)	(4.05)			
4	MS	1935	0.070	1.675	0.365	44	0.034
			(8.45)	(4.91)			
5	MS	1936	0.062	1.778	0.323	44	0.032
			(6.55)	(4.48)			
6	MS	1937	0.081	1.288	0.211	42	0.034
			(12.15)	(3.27)			
7	MS	1938	0.072	1.492	0.251	42	0.035
			(7.61)	(3.66)			
8	MS	1939	0.055	2.267	0.387	40	0.032
			(5.11)	(4.89)			
9	MS	1940	0.058	2.561	0.469	40	0.031
			(5.89)	(5.80)			
10	MS	1941	0.040	3.895	0.345	39	0.037
			(2.29)	(4.42)			

Although we tested a pooled version of the year-by-year approach, we believe Table 5.2 provides much more information. Pooling seems wrong in this case, when the universe changes so much from year to year.[7] The years 1933 and 1934 were the nadir of the Great Depression; the period 1934–39 saw a painfully slow, incomplete recovery while there was a brisk approach to full employment in 1940–41. Furthermore, A&P was shaken by management mistakes in the early 1930s, and their rectification starting in 1936; this too must have distorted relationships. Note, for example, the extreme behavior of the slope coefficient that ranges from a low of 1.2 in 1933 to a high of 3.9 in 1941. The strength of Table 5.2 is that it permits these various factors to be examined separately.

We also tested a lagged specification in which profit is lagged by one year. Lagged profits may serve as a proxy for the profits expected at the time of the investment decision. Market share, in turn, is a proxy for investments made in earlier periods. The one-year lag is a crude guess;

Table 5.3
Regression results for individual years, lagged profits, 1933–41 (*t* statistics in parentheses)

Equation	Dependent variable	Year	Constant	$(G - E)$	R**2	N	S.E.
11	MS	1933	0.063 (8.30)	1.308 (5.25)	0.402	43	0.029
12	MS	1934	0.075 (8.76)	1.234 (4.50)	0.331	43	0.033
13	MS	1935	0.073 (9.18)	1.421 (4.80)	0.355	44	0.034
14	MS	1936	0.069 (9.02)	1.553 (4.94)	0.368	44	0.031
15	MS	1937	0.058 (5.96)	1.714 (4.30)	0.316	42	0.031
16	MS	1938	0.084 (12.2)	1.510 (3.70)	0.255	42	0.035
17	MS	1939	0.068 (7.16)	1.734 (4.23)	0.320	40	0.034
18	MS	1940	0.056 (5.14)	2.475 (5.24)	0.419	40	0.033
19	MS	1941	0.058 (5.00)	2.721 (5.30)	0.431	39	0.035

in this industry, buildings could be erected and equipped in a matter of months. The results for the lagged sample shown in Table 5.3 are virtually the same.

For both a test and an interpretation of the results, market share was set to zero. At that point, profit is equal to *minus* (a/b), where a is the constant and b the coefficient. It takes a certain level of loss, $-(a/b)$, to shake the firm out of that market. Thus, $-(a/b)$ is an estimate of the firm's shutdown point, which is also equal to fixed costs as a percentage of sales. A profit rate of less than $-(a/b)$ means the firm was not covering its out-of-pocket costs.

Table 5.4 shows that this number diminishes considerably, from 4 percent to 6 percent in 1930–38 to 1 percent in 1941. (In every year except 1941 the estimate of the shutdown point is significantly different from zero.) A loss rate that is not unusual, and therefore tolerable, in bad years is abnormal, and thus intolerable, in better times. Table 5.4 also shows that fixed costs as a percentage of sales declined dramatically in conjunction with A&P's recovery and management shakeup, suggesting that early in the decade of the 1930s there was considerable

Table 5.4
Fixed Cost as a Percentage of Sales

Year	Estimate of fixed cost as a percentage of sales[1]	A&P Real sales[2] (millions)
(in parentheses are ratios of estimates to asymptotic standard errors)[3]		
1932	4.37	1,363
	(3.49)	
1933	5.69	1,263
	(3.15)	
1934	5.85	1,176
	(2.91)	
1935	4.18	1,148
	(3.27)	
1936	3.49	1,191
	(2.76)	
1937	6.29	1,119
	(2.76)	
1938	4.82	1,198
	(2.58)	
1939	2.43	1,377
	(2.58)	
1940	2.26	1,526
	(3.03)	
1941	1.05	1,681
	(1.53)	

1. Estimate derived from table 5.2 regressions by dividing constant term by coefficient on profit variable.
2. From Adelman, *A&P: A Study*, pp. 436, 440.
3. We thank both Raymond Hartman and Neil Buchanan for the following approximation for the variance of the estimate (a/b):

$$V(a/b) = V(a)/b + (a^2/b^4)V(b) - 2(a/b^3)\text{Cov}(a,b)$$

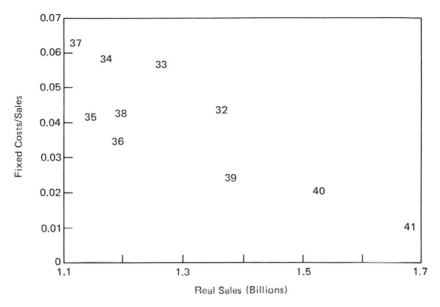

Figure 5.1
Fixed Costs vs. Real Sales 1932–1941
Source: Table 5.4

excess capacity. Figure 5.1 further illustrates the relationship: as output expands, fixed costs are spread over a growing sales base; consequently average costs flatten out.

These changing sales-profit relationships are to be expected, and hence strengthen the credibility of the results of tables 5.2 and 5.3.

Another test of data and their implications is less direct. Schmalensee points out that the familiar Lerner index,

$$(P - MC)/P = 1/E^f, \tag{2}$$

where E^f equals the absolute value of the price elasticity of demand facing the firm, under some simplifying assumptions,

can be restated for the jth firm as:

$$(P - MC)/P = MS_j/E^m \tag{3}$$

where MS_j equals the jth firm's market share and E^m equals the elasticity of market demand.[8] One interpretation of equation (3) is that a given market share may confer market power in one industry, but not in another. (Such interindustry comparisons, of course, are difficult to make.) If demand is relatively elastic, price will approach marginal cost even if a firm's share is large (recall that MS rarely exceeds 10 to 15 percent in our sample).

Let us assume that the net profit rate is approximately equal to the Lerner index, that is, average cost equals marginal cost such that all operating units are at or beyond minimum efficient scale and at or near minimum long-run average costs.[9] Under such conditions the coefficient on $G - E$ is an estimate of the elasticity of demand for food purchased at grocery stores. The years 1932–38 yield plausible estimates of this elasticity, that is, estimates ranging from approximately 1.2 to 1.8, but values in 1939–41 are implausibly high. If the early years are anywhere near accurate, the demand elasticity faced by A&P was considerably higher, ranging approximately from 12 to 18. Surprisingly, these estimates are in close agreement with calculations based on an altogether independent method, that is management's expectation in 1937 of response to price reductions.[10]

In our sample—where, by prior knowledge, both market power and scale economies are ruled out—a single equation confirms that profitability variations determine market share variations, as, in theory, they should for this simplest case. Hence, in the more complex case, if trying to test the *additional* hypothesis that market share has some effect on profitability—whether through economies of scale, market power, or anything else—one must somehow allow for, or remove, the effects of profitability on market share. Without prior knowledge, two-way, or mutual, causation must be the initial hypothesis. A single-equation system is simply wrong. It assumes away a pervasive relationship: even competitive industries with constant returns to scale should, in equilibrium, exhibit a positive association between share and profit if, as we contend, profits attract capital and losses repel. Where the profit-market share relation does not exist, it is prima facie evidence of new forces entering the market, for example, innovations or some other disturbance of the old regularities.

This puzzle in causation awaits methods for isolating the effects of profitability on market share. It seems to us that lagging profitability is not likely to be a useful expedient. Until an adequate methodology is developed, all statements about the effect of market share on profitability must be set aside as logically insufficient whether they are slogans in the business press that profits will surely follow achieving market share, or more cautious statements in the economic literature.

Notes

The authors thank F. M. Fisher, Raymond S. Hartman, Michael F. Koehn, H. Michael Mann, Stephen Martin, James L. Paddock, and participants in the Applied Microeconomics Workshop at MIT for helpful criticisms and suggestions, while remaining responsible for any and all errors.

1. See, for example, Bradley T. Gale, "Market Share and Rate of Return," *Review of Economics and Statistics* 54:4 (November 1972), pp. 412–423; James L. Bothwell and Theodore E. Keeler, "Profits, Market Structure, and Portfolio Risk," in *Essays on Industrial Organization in Honor of Joe S. Bain*, ed. Robert T. Masson and P. David Qualls (Cambridge, Mass.: Ballinger, 1976), pp. 71–88; John E. Kwoka, Jr., "The Effect of Market Share Distribution on Industry Performance," *Review of Economics and Statistics* (February 1979), pp. 101–109; David J. Ravenscraft, "Price-Raising and Cost-Reducing Effects in Profit-Concentration Studies: A Monte Carlo Simulation Analysis," Ph.D. diss., Northwestern Univ., 1980, William G. Shepherd, "The Elements of Market Structure," *Review of Economics and Statistics* 54:1 (February 1972), pp. 25–37; and Stavros B. Thomadakis, "A Value-Based Test of Profitability and Market Structure," *Review of Economics and Statistics* 59:2 (May 1977), pp. 179–185. Recently, Stephen Martin ("Market, Firm, and Economic Performance: An Empirical Analysis," Economic Report, Bureau of Economics, Federal Trade Commission), investigated the problem; Stephen A. Rhoades ("Structure-Performance Studies in Banking: An Updated Summary and Evaluation," Federal Reserve Staff Study No. 119 [August 1982]) provides a summary of studies in banking.

2. F. M. Scherer, *Industrial Market Structure and Economic Performance*, 2d ed. (Chicago: Rand McNally, 1980). pp. 283, 285.

3. For discussions of the "experience curve," see, for example, Buzzell, Gale, and Sultan, "Market Share A Key to Profitability," *Harvard Business Review* (January–February 1975), pp. 97–106; and Michael E. Porter, "How Competitive Forces Shape Strategy," *Harvard Business Review* (March–April 1979), pp. 137–145.

4. For analyses of the industry in the 1930s, see Clair Wilcox, *Competition in American Industry*, TNEC Monograph No. 21, cited in Federal Trade Commission, *Economic Report on the Structure and Competitive Behavior of Food Retailing* (Washington, D.C., 1966); and M. A. Adelman, *A&P: A Study in Price-Cost Behavior and Public Policy* (Cambridge, Mass.: Harvard Univ. Press, 1959), pp. 60–61, 70. A more recent study is National Commission on Food Marketing, *Organization and Competition in Food Retailing*, Technical Study No. 7 (Washington, D.C.: U.S. Government Printing Office, June 1966).

5. National Commission on Food Marketing, *Organization and Competition*, p. 51.

6. This measure would be wholly inadequate for an interindustry analysis except with a term registering capital intensity, but it is appropriate for the single firm in a single industry. A major controversy has developed over the use of accounting measures of profitability. See Franklin M. Fisher and John J. McGowan, "On the Misuse of Accounting Rates of Return to Infer Monopoly Profits," *American Economic Review* 73:1 (March 1983), pp. 82–97; and the "Comment" by Stephen Martin.

We need only maintain that the accounting fact—return on sales—and the true economic rate of return on prospective investment were so highly correlated among the units that one may properly be used as a proxy for the other. Certainly the former was the number used by management to judge performance. We also tested a second profit variable, net dollar profit per store, treating a store as a proxy for investment. The results did not differ greatly from those reported here, and are available from the authors.

7. The results for the pooled sample are:

$$MS_t = \quad 0.075 + 1.400\,(G - E)_t$$
$$\quad\quad\ (22.55)\quad (10.17)$$

Range: 1933–41 $R^2 = 0.233$
$N = 342$ S.E. $= 0.034$

A Chow test of the pooled versus unpooled results yields an F statistic of 2.20, which is different from zero at higher than the 1 percent significance level, thereby denoting that pooling is inappropriate.

8. William M. Landes and Richard A. Posner ("Market Power in Antitrust Cases," *Harvard Law Review* 94:5 [March 1981], pp. 937–996) subsequently developed a similar but more restrictive model for the case of the dominant firm with a competitive fringe.

9. In this sample it is likely that average cost and marginal cost are not equal. In the case where *MC* is underestimated, the resulting elasticity is also understated. Conversely, when *MC* is overstated, so too is elasticity.

10. See Adelman, *A&P*, p. 472, where a subjective long-run elasticity is reported for A&P of 10 to 14. These estimates should not be confused with the elasticity of demand for food from all sources, including, for example, restaurants, institutions, and other retail distributors. One would expect the elasticity for food from all sources, including grocery stores, to be considerably lower.

References

Adelman, M. A. *A&P: A Study in Price-Cost Behavior and Public Policy.* Cambridge, Mass.: Harvard Univ. Press, 1959.

Bothwell, James L., and Theodore E. Keeler. "Profits, Market Structure, and Portfolio Risk." In *Essays on Industrial Organization in Honor of Joe S. Bain*, ed. Robert T. Masson and P. David Qualls. Cambridge, Mass.: Ballinger, 1976, pp. 71–88.

Buzzell, Robert D., Bradley T. Gale, and Ralph G. M. Sultan. "Market Share—A Key to Profitability." *Harvard Business Review* (January–February 1975), pp. 97–106.

Demsetz, Harold. "Two Systems of Belief about Monopoly." In *Industrial Concentration: The New Learning*, ed. Harvey J. Goldschmid, H. Michael Mann, and J. Fred Weston. Boston: Little, Brown, 1974, pp. 164–184.

Fisher, Franklin M., and John J. McGowan. "On the Misuse of Accounting Rates of Return to Infer Monopoly Profits." *American Economic Review* 73:1 (March 1983), pp. 82–97.

Gale, Bradley T. "Market Share and Rate of Return." *Review of Economics and Statistics* 54:4 (November 1972), pp. 421–423.

Kwoka, John E., Jr. "The Effect of Market Share Distribution on Industry Performance." *Review of Economics and Statistics* (February 1979), pp. 101–109.

Landes, William M., and Richard A. Posner. "Market Power in Antitrust Cases." *Harvard Law Review* 94:5 (March 1981), pp. 937–996.

Mancke, Richard B. "Causes of Interfirm Profitability Differences: A New Interpretation of the Evidence." *Quarterly Journal of Economics* 88:2 (May 1974), pp. 181–193.

Martin, Stephen. "Market, Firm, and Economic Performance: An Empirical Analysis." Economic Report, Bureau of Economics, Federal Trade Commission.

Martin, Stephen. "The Misuse of Accounting Rates of Return: Comment." *American Economic Review* (June 1984), pp. 501–506.

National Commission on Food Marketing. *Organization and Competition in Food Retailing*. Technical Study No. 7. Washington, D.C.: U.S. Government Printing Office (June 1966).

Porter, Michael E. "How Competitive Forces Shape Strategy." *Harvard Business Review* (March–April 1979), pp. 137–145.

Ravenscraft, David J. "Price-Raising and Cost-Reducing Effects in Profit-Concentration Studies: A Monte Carlo Simulation Analysis." Diss., Northwestern Univ., 1980.

Ravenscraft, David J. "Structure-Profit Relationships at the Line of Business and Industry Level." *Review of Economics and Statistics* 65:1 (February 1983), pp. 22–31.

Rhoades, Stephen A. "Structure-Performance Studies in Banking: An Updated Summary and Evaluation." Federal Reserve Staff Study No. 110 (August 1982).

Scherer F. M. *Industrial Market Structure and Economic Performance*, 2nd ed. Chicago: Rand McNally, 1980.

Schmalensee, Richard. "On the Use of Economic Models in Antitrust: The ReaLemon Case." *University of Pennsylvania Law Review* 27 (April 1979), pp. 994–1050.

Shepherd, William G. "The Elements of Market Structure." *Review of Economics and Statistics* 54:1 (February 1972), pp. 25–37.

Thomadakis, Stavros B. "A Value-Based Test of Profitability and Market Structure." *Review of Economics and Statistics* 59:2 (May 1977), pp. 179–185.

Weiss, Leonard A. "The Concentration-Profits Relationship and Antitrust." In *Industrial Concentration: The New Learning*, ed. Harvey J. Goldschmid, H. Michael Mann, and J. Fred Weston. Boston: Little, Brown, 1974, pp. 184–233.

Wilcox, Clair. *Competition and Monopoly in American Industry*. TNEC Monograph No. 21; cited in Federal Trade Commission, *Economic Report on the Structure and Competitive Behavior of Food Retailing* (Washington, D.C., 1966).

6

Nonprice Anticompetitive Behavior by Dominant Firms toward the Producers of Complementary Products

J. A. Ordover,
A. O. Sykes, and
R. D. Willig

In a variety of market settings dominant firms have an incentive to engage in anticompetitive practices that disadvantage the producers of complementary products. (Here, we define "anticompetitive practices" as practices that exclude other producers from markets, to the detriment of economic welfare.) These incentives arise as a result of complementarities in consumption and in production. For example, cameras and film are complements in consumption, whereas basic and pay programming for cable television are complements in production, at least at the distribution level. Thus, contrary to conventional thinking, a firm with market power at one stage of production or over one component of a product may nonetheless have an incentive to extend its market power to other stages of production or to other product components.

As we will show, at least four sets of circumstances generate incentives for this kind of anticompetitive behavior. The resulting anticompetitive practices may consist of exclusionary vertical mergers, tie-ins, predatory product innovations, or the creation of other barriers to the ability of rivals to obtain needed complementary products. In recent litigation, for example, AT&T's practice of prohibiting the use of its local telecommunications equipment by rival sellers of long-distance services was alleged to have anticompetitive effects.[1] Whatever the underlying motives or anticompetitive tactics, the result is the same: inefficient supply of complementary products or services to the final customer.

In the first section we review conventional analysis that purports to demonstrate why a firm with market power over one product has no incentive to engage in anticompetitive behavior toward a rival producer of complementary products. This analysis suggests that a dominant firm can execute a perfect price squeeze and thereby earn all the monopoly profits available in the market for the package of complementary products.

In the second and third sections we delineate four sets of circumstances in which the dominant firm cannot execute a perfect price squeeze. Specifically, such a practice is infeasible if (1) there is an alternative albeit inferior source of supply for the monopolized product; (2) profit-maximizing implicit price discrimination requires a low price for the monopolized product and a high price for complementary products; (3) inflexible rules govern prices or the division of revenues between the dominant firm and the producers of complementary components; or (4) the dominant firm is subject to comprehensive rate-of-return regulation. In the last instance, anticompetitive behavior cannot increase market power, but the Averch-Johnson effect can nonetheless supply a motive for anticompetitive practices.

In the fourth section we briefly discuss how the cable television market exhibited several key elements of market settings (1) to (3) above during 1972–81, and thus how the cable industry may have been prone to anticompetitive behavior.

1. The Simple Economics of Price Squeezes

Modern commentary on both the economics of vertical integration and the economics of tying arrangements suggests that dominant firms have no incentive to extend their market power to complementary products.[2] Such commentary concludes that relations between the producers of complementary products should not be subject to intensive antitrust scrutiny because the resulting allocation of resources is governed by the pursuit of efficiency rather than the pursuit of monopoly profits.

In examining this proposition, we posit a market in which two products—components 1 and 2—are used jointly as a system by consumers.[3] Each system contains one unit of each component. Firm A is the sole producer of the first component, denoted A1. The constant unit cost of A1 is equal to c. An unspecified number of firms produce the second component, denoted A2, B2, and so on. These components have respective unit costs of a_A, a_B, and so on. We assume that all consumers are identical and have a willingness to pay equal to b per system, and that consumers have no preferences about the suppliers of components.

In this market the maximum conceivable profit from the sale of a single system is equal to $b - (c + a)$, where a is the minimum unit cost of the second component. Firm A can use its monopoly over the production of component 1 to realize that maximum profit, using any one of various tactics that result in a perfect price squeeze against the suppliers of the second component.

To see how such a squeeze might operate, assume for the moment that there are no barriers to entry into the production of the second component and that all producers of the second component are equally efficient. Component 2 will then be available in the market as long as its price at least equals its unit cost, a. To extract the available monopoly profit under these conditions, firm A can produce only A1 at a cost of c and set the price of A1 at $b - a$. Alternatively, firm A can manufacture A2 at unit cost a and sell systems for b, or it can sell unbundled components at prices a for A2 and $b - a$ for A1. In each case, firm A has no incentive to engage in anticompetitive behavior because it already earns the maximum possible profit per system. Thus, if we observe a tie-in of the components manufactured by firm A, for example, or some other form of exclusionary behavior, we must conclude that economic efficiency is the reason for such behavior.

This analysis is equally valid if the producers of component 2 are not equally efficient, assuming that no single firm or group of colluding firms has market power over the production of component 2. Firm A still has an incentive to select the most efficient supplier of the second component even if that supplier is a rival manufacturer. Suppose, for example, that firm B is one of several efficient firms that are more efficient than firm A; that is, $a_A > a_B$. If firm A refuses to sell A1 in the open market, and instead employs a tie-in between A1 and A2, its profit on each system is $b - (c + a_A)$, which is less than $b - (c + a_B)$. Firm A could realize a profit of $b - (c + a_B)$, however, by selling the monopolized component at $b - a_B$ and thereby forcing the most efficient suppliers—for example, firm B—to sell their components at a_B. Once again, an appropriate price for A1 suffices to extract all available monopoly profit through a perfect price squeeze.

In summary, if the dominant firm can execute a perfect price squeeze and thereby earn all the monopoly profit available in the systems market, it has no incentive to engage in anticompetitive behavior. Moreover, all systems sold in the market will incorporate components from the most efficient producers regardless of which firms produce the components complementary to those of the dominant firm.

2. Motives for Anticompetitive Practices in Systems Markets

The analysis above rests on several assumptions that may not be readily apparent. In this section we investigate three circumstances in which those assumptions do not hold, with the result that the dominant firm has an incentive to drive efficient rival producers of complementary products from the market.

Alternative, Inferior Source of Supply

In the hypothetical market described above, firm A has an unchallenged monopoly over component 1. Frequently, however, dominant firms confront rivals that can manufacture substitutes for their products, albeit at higher cost or lower quality. Such competition, actual or potential, from an "alternative, inferior source of supply" may constrain the price a dominant firm can charge for its products to the point where a perfect price squeeze becomes infeasible.

Suppose firm A confronts a rival producer of component 1—firm C—and that some producers of component 2 are more efficient than others (but that no producer of component 2 has market power). Let the unit cost of component 2 for a representative, efficient producer be a_B (thus, $a_A \geqq a_B$). Assume further that firm C can produce component 1 at unit cost c'. This prospect constrains the profits of firm A on each sale of A1 to $(c' - c)$, the cost advantage of firm A over firm C. Such a margin may be well below the maximum monopoly profit per system of $b - (c + a_B)$, which firm A could otherwise extract with a perfect price squeeze. Firm A then has an incentive for anticompetitive behavior toward rival producers of both components.

The simplest anticompetitive strategy is a horizontal merger with firm C, followed by an increase in the price of the first component, to $b - a_B$. This strategy may fail, however, perhaps because of legal restrictions on horizontal mergers or because potential entrants other than firm C can produce component 1 almost as efficiently.[4]

As an alternative, firm A can refuse to sell A1 in the open market, employing instead a tying arrangement in which the complete system is priced just below $a_B + c'$, the unit cost of a cost-efficient, competing system. This price may be above firm A's marginal cost, $a + c$,[5] but still it may suffice to drive rival producers of component 2 from the industry. In the presence of reentry barriers,[6] firm A can then raise its price and increase its profits. Of course, where, as in this simple model, all consumers have equal willingness to pay, no direct welfare loss arises from a refusal to sell A1 on the open market if firm A can produce component 2 as cheaply as anyone else; all value-increasing sales still occur. In markets where some consumers are priced out of the market after competing firms exit, however, the potential for direct welfare loss is obvious. Moreover, if $a_B < a_A$, a welfare loss arises because the tying arrangement leads to production of component 2 by an inefficient supplier.

Another anticompetitive tactic that can decrease welfare in the simple model above is "predatory systems rivalry." Firm A can introduce a new or redesigned system, say, A1' and A2', in which the new component, A1', is incompatible with existing versions of component 2. Simultaneously, firm A can discontinue A1 or greatly increase its price while pricing the new system low enough to divert all sales from rivals. Thereafter, if the costs of reverse engineering the new system pose sufficient "entry hurdles"[7] and reentry barriers to potential competitors, firm A can raise the price of the new system and reap monopoly profits. A study by Ordover and Willig shows that, because of the sunk costs of R&D for the new system, and the possible changes in unit costs and consumer willingness to pay, such behavior can decrease economic welfare. Their study also develops a method for distinguishing welfare-enhancing from welfare-decreasing design changes.

Finally, note that, in this model, a "vertical merger" between Firm A and an efficient rival producer of component 2—say, firm B—is not anticompetitive in and of itself. (Of course, if firm A produces A2, such a merger is, in fact, horizontal.) If firm B is subject to effective pre-merger competition, a horizontal combination with rivals of firm B or a post-merger tie-in is still necessary before firm A can raise the price of component 2.

Implicit Price Discrimination

Just as the presence of an alternative, inferior source of supply can prevent the use of a perfect price squeeze by a dominant firm, the structure of consumer preferences can render a price squeeze uneconomical. To facilitate profitable, implicit price discrimination, the dominant firm may wish to charge a low price for the products over which it has market power and a monopolistic price for complementary products.[8]

To make the analysis of this case more concrete, imagine that the dominant firm operates in the market for cable television viewing. (We do not suggest, however, that the simple model that follows is a correct

Table 6.1
Willingness to pay

Number of viewers	Basic	Pay
N_1	b_1	h_1
N_2	$b_2 > b_1$	$h_2 > h_1$

description of the complex cable industry.) Assume that only two types of programming are available in the cable television market, "basic" and "pay." The dominant firm controls delivery of basic programming; the number of pay programming networks is unspecified. Assume further that viewer preferences are such that type 1 viewers have a low willingness to pay for cable programming and that type 2 viewers have a high willingness to pay. Moreover, type 2 viewers have a greater willingness to pay for both basic and pay programming.

Table 6.1 summarizes the distribution of preferences in the population. The unit variable costs of basic programming and pay programming are c_b and c_h, respectively, where $b_1 > c_b$, but $h_1 < c_h < h_2$. Thus whereas both groups are willing to pay the costs of basic programming, only the second group is willing to pay the costs of pay programming.

The ideal pricing strategy for the dominant firm is a price of b_1 for basic service and a price of $b_2 + h_2 - b_1$ for pay service. With these prices the dominant firm can extract the entire willingness to pay from each group of viewers without explicitly discriminating between the two groups.[9] This strategy will not succeed, however, because, by hypothesis, pay programming is competitively supplied. Instead, unless the dominant firm can monopolize pay programming, it is limited to one of two pricing policies. First, it can set the price of basic programming at b_1 (to ensure that all potential viewers purchase the service) and earn profits of $R_1 = (b_1 - c_b)(N_1 + N_2)$. Or it can set the price of basic programming at $b_2 + h_2 - c_h$ (to squeeze all the surplus from type 2 viewers) and earn profits of $R_2 = [(b_2 + h_2 - c_h) - c_b]N_2$. The cost of the second policy is loss of profits from type 1 viewers; its benefit is added revenue from type 2 viewers. One cannot determine a priori which policy will yield a higher profit, but the first policy does yield greater economic welfare.

The dominant firm can improve on either policy if it can monopolize pay programming. For example, it can merge with one of the pay programmers and thereafter exclude other pay programmers from viewer homes; or, less blatantly, it can charge competing pay programmers a prohibitive price for access to viewer homes. In effect, the dominant firm uses the vertical merger to facilitate a tie-in of basic and pay programming, and its profits rise to

$$R_M = (b_1 - c_b)N_1 + [(b_2 + h_2) - (c_b + c_h)]N_2.$$

R_M clearly exceeds either R_1 or R_2.

Concededly, in this simple model no loss of economic welfare results from excluding other pay services except, perhaps, for the expenditures necessary to consummate the vertical merger. Indeed, there is potential welfare gain if, before the merger, type 1 viewers are priced out of the market, with the familiar, potential result that price discrimination is economically superior to a single-price monopoly.

In more complex markets welfare may decline. An obvious possibility of welfare loss arises where post-merger price discrimination is highly imperfect and, thus, its welfare consequences ambiguous. Alternatively, suppose that after the merger, a new pay service emerges that viewers prefer to the pay service of the dominant firm; or suppose that some viewers prefer a service excluded by the merger. If a horizontal merger between the dominant firm and such superior pay services is not feasible, then economic welfare may decline because the dominant firm profits from exclusion of the alternative service from its system. Interestingly, the pay programmer who, in the eyes of viewers, is inferior to his rivals gains the most from an exclusionary vertical merger. The inferior programmer fares poorly in head-on competition with his rivals but may retain a large share of viewers in markets where his rivals are excluded. As the next section suggests, this may have interesting implications for the choice of a target for a vertical merger.

Similarly, markets may exist in which predatory systems' rivalry is the best way for a dominant firm to exclude vertical competitors and thereby facilitate implicit price discrimination. Welfare may decline not only because the resultant price discrimination is imperfect but also because the added monopoly profits from price discrimination provide an incentive for economically excessive expenditures by the dominant firm on R&D and retooling. Indeed, if such a system facilitates price discrimination, the dominant firm may find it profitable to introduce a system with a smaller consumer surplus over variable costs.[10]

Pricing Rigidities and Merger Incentives
The analysis up to this point assumes that the pricing policies of the dominant firm and its rival producers are subject only to the con-

straints of competition and consumer demand and that each firm receives all revenue from its sales. In some markets, however, these conditions do not hold, thus creating yet another impediment to the execution of a perfect price squeeze. Such an impediment arises, for example, if the price the dominant firm can charge for its products is subject to a cap or if a rigid formula governs allocation of revenues among firms. An example is railroad interlining, where a single price is charged for freight shipped over independent, interconnected railroads. Before 1979, virtually all such "through rates" were capped and subject to inflexible revenue-division formulas. Another example is in the telecommunications industry, where local telephone rates are regulated and long distance revenues were until recently divided between local telephone companies and long-distance carriers by inflexible "separations and settlement" rules.

By way of illustration, let us consider again the market in section 2. Firm A is the sole producer of component 1, which carries unit cost c; firms B, C, and so on, not equally efficient, can produce component 2. We now assume that firm A does not produce component 2, that firm B is the most efficient producer, with unit cost a_B, and that firm C has a unit cost of $a_C > a_B$. Once again, consumers are identical with a willingness to pay per system equal to b. The maximum profit per system is $b - (c + a_B)$.

Suppose that the total revenue from the sale of a system is split between the sellers of each component according to a rigid formula that provides each seller with an amount in excess of its unit costs. As a result, the dominant firm, A, cannot capture the maximum profit $b - (c + a_B)$ per system even if firm B willingly sold components for a_B—the inflexible rule for division of revenue stymies the perfect price squeeze.

Under these conditions a merger between firm A and a producer of component 2 can increase the profits of firm A. Which producer will firm A choose as a merger partner? To answer this question, let us suppose that most of the systems sold before the merger combine a unit of A1 with a unit of B2, and that only a few system combine A1 with C2, D2, and so on. The reason for these consumer preferences is unimportant. Under these circumstances, we conjecture that firm A may prefer to merge with, say, firm C rather than firm B even though firm B is the lowest-cost producer of component 2. The new firm can then employ various anticompetitive tactics—tie-ins, predatory systems rivalry— to divert sales from firm B. The rationale for this conjecture is that a merger with firm C followed by an anticompetitive campaign against firm B can substantially increase the total profits earned by the merging firms, whereas merger with firm B will leave total profits virtually unchanged.

The reader might object that the level of profits is greater for the merged firm if firm A acquires firm B. Firm A would thus prefer to acquire firm B if it could do so on terms comparable to those for acquisition of firm C. Perhaps a *threat* to acquire firm C and subsequently to conduct an anticompetitive campaign against firm B would force the latter to capitulate to favorable terms. The problem with such a threat, however, is the prospect of an immediate injunction against merger with firm C, as well as the danger that issuance of a threat will generate evidence that can be used in civil and criminal actions if firm A carries out the threat. These difficulties may cause firm A to eschew efforts to secure favorable terms from firm B.

Diversion of sales from firm B after merger between firm A and firm C reduces the efficiency of resource allocation because firm B is the most efficient producer. The price paid by consumers remains at b per system, but society loses $(a_C - a_B)$ in real costs on each sale.

3. Rate-of-Return Regulation and Vertical Conduct

Rate-of-return regulation is another possible source of incentives for anticompetitive behavior. If the allowed rate of return, s, exceeds the true cost of capital to the firm, r, the potential flow of economic profits to the firm will reflect the margin between them, $s - r$, applied to the firm's total capital stock. Consequently, the firm may take actions to increase its capital stock (termed the Averch-Johnson effect) even if such actions are not otherwise profitable or efficient. In particular, the firm may use vertical mergers, tie-ins, predatory system rivalry, and other tactics to monopolize production of complementary products, notwithstanding that other firms may have a comparative advantage in production of those products.

This conclusion follows from a variant of the simple model already discussed. Let us assume that services 1 and 2 are complements or are vertically related and that each of Q identical consumers will pay an amount b for one unit of each service. Firm A has a protected monopoly position in the supply of service 1, as well as regulatory constraint on its overall rate of return equal to s, where $s > r$, the true cost of capital. To supply service 1, firm A has a capital stock valued at K_1, and it incurs unit variable costs of V_1. To supply Q units of service 2, firm A must invest in additional capital worth $k_{A2}Q$ and must incur variable costs of $V_{A2}Q$.

At the outset, firm A has rivals in the production of service 2. Let firm B be a representative, efficient rival and denote its unit cost, c_{B2}, which includes a flow of capital charges at the cost of capital, r.

To investigate the incentives for firm A to acquire control over the production of service 2, we examine the profits of firm A under various policies. First, suppose that firm A supplies only service 1 and that firm B supplies service 2. Because of its protected monopoly in service 1, firm A could, in the absence of regulatory constraint, charge price $b - c_{B2}$. At that price, firm B and its competitors would price service 2 at cost c_{B2}, and firm A would earn economic profits of $Q[b - c_{B2} - V_1] - rK_1$, with a corresponding rate of return equal to $Q[b - c_{B2} - V_1]/K_1$. If this rate exceeds the allowed rate of return, s, however, then the regulatory constraint would force firm A to charge no more than $V_1 + sK_1/Q$ for service 1. The corresponding profit figure is $(s - r)K_1$. Thus, by producing service 1 alone, firm A can earn a profit equal to min $[(s - r)K_1, Q[b - c_{B2} - V_1] - rK_1]$.

Now, suppose that firm B and its competitors are somehow excluded from the market for service 2. Absent the rate-of-return constraint, firm A could charge b for the package of services 1 and 2 and earn profits of $Q(b - V_{A2} - V_1 - rk_{A2}) - rK_1$, with a corresponding rate of return equal to $Q(b - V_{A2} - V_1)/[K_1 + Qk_{A2}]$. If this rate exceeds s, however, firm A must limit its prices for the package of services to $V_1 + V_{A2} + sk_{A2} + sK_1/Q$, with associated profits of $(s - r)(K_1 + Qk_{A2})$. Thus by producing both services, firm A can earn a profit equal to minimum $[(s - r)(K_1 + Qk_{A2}), Q(b - V_{A2} - V_1 - rk_{A2}) - rK_1]$. Comparing the profits of firm A when it produces only service 1 to its profits when it produces both services yields several possibilities, described below.

Case 1

In the simplest (and rather trivial) case, suppose that s is so large that the regulatory constraint never affects the pricing decisions of firm A. Then firm A will benefit from control over the production of service 2 if and only if $V_{A2} + rk_{A2} < c_{B2}$. This is precisely the condition, however, that must hold if the production of service 2 by firm A is to be efficient. Thus, if firm A is the most efficient producer, it can and will drive its rivals from the market even when it sells service 2 for an amount in excess of the service's true unit cost. Alternatively, if firm B and its rivals are more efficient, firm A will not wish to drive them from the market, but will instead execute a perfect price squeeze to extract the maximum profit that is available from the sale of service packages.

Case 2

A more interesting (and somewhat more complex) case arises where b is so large that the regulatory constraint binds firm A regardless of whether it supplies service 2. In that event, firm A can earn additional profits of $(s - r)Qk_{A2}$ from production of service 2 regardless of what firm (or firms) is the lowest-cost supplier of that service. Clearly, an incentive for monopolization of service 2 arises.

It is instructive to consider how, in this case, firm A might secure a monopoly over the supply of service 2 in the face of actual or potential competition. Suppose, first, that firm A offers service 2 at a price below c_{B2}, the unit production cost of its rivals. The apparent and true unit-production-cost figures for firm A are $V_{A2} + sk_{A2} = c'_{A2}$ and $V_{A2} + rk_{A2} = c_{A2}$, respectively, where the former reflects the allowed rate-of-return on capital and the latter reflects the true cost of capital. When $c'_{A2} < c_{B2}$, firm A can price service 2 at c'_{A2}, drive firm B from the market (in the long run), and earn maximum profits. Pursuit of profit by firm A accords with pursuit of economic welfare, however, because firm A is more efficient than firm B.

When $c_{A2} < c_{B2} < c'_{A2}$, firm A must price service 2 below its *apparent* unit costs if firm B is to be driven from the market.[11] Such behavior is still efficient, however, because the true unit cost for firm A is below c_{B2}.

Finally, when firm B is the more efficient producer of service 2 ($c_{B2} < c_{A2}$), firm A cannot win the market without engaging in anticompetitive practices. By permanently setting its price for service 2 below both the unit cost of firm B and its own unit cost, and by charging a high enough price for service 1, firm A can, however, drive firm B from the market and earn maximum profit.

Note that such a price structure fails the incremental-cost test, the stand-alone cost test, the burden test, and the Areeda-Turner test for cross-subsidy and predatory pricing. Thus, in this instance, these tests correctly indicate the presence of socially inefficient, anticompetitive behavior.[12] To avoid regulatory or antitrust sanctions as a consequence of such tests, firm A may employ one of several more subtle tactics to induce the exit of firm B and its rivals: tying the sale of service 1 to the sale of service 2; redesigning service 1 to make it incompatible with variants of service 2 produced by rivals; or combining services 1 and 2 in a physical package while refusing to sell service 1 to its rivals at a price that allows them to remain viable competitors. All such tactics facilitate extension of the market power of firm A to service 2, as well as lower economic welfare by excluding the most efficient suppliers of service 2.

Other Cases
The preceding analysis rests on the assumption that the rate-of-return constraint binds firm A whether or not it supplies service 2. We now relax this assumption in analyzing the remaining cases.

As a general proposition, if firm A is the lowest-cost supplier of service 2, it always has a profit incentive to supply it—either to capture a greater fraction of consumer willingness to pay or to earn $(s - r)$ on extra capital investment. Regardless of whether and how the regulatory constraint binds, firm A can gain control of the market for service 2 by pricing it at or above its true economic cost. Such behavior is always consistent with efficiency.

Thus, the only remaining cases arise when firm B and its rivals are more efficient producers. If firm B is more efficient than firm A, and if the rate-of-return constraint is binding on firm A when it produces both services, then the constraint is also binding when firm A offers only service 1. That is, $V_{A2} + rk_{A2} > c_{B2}$ and $(s - r)(K_1 + Qk_{A2})$ $< Q[b - V_{A2} - V_1 - rk_{A2}] - rK_1$ together imply $(s - r)K_1$ $< Q[b - c_{B2} - V_1] - rK_1$. Hence, if the rate-of-return constraint is binding when firm A produces both services, we are back to the analysis of case 2.

The sole remaining possibility is that firm B is more efficient than firm A in the production of service 2; the rate-of-return ceiling constrains firm A when it offers only service 1, but the ceiling does not constrain firm A when it offers both services. Here, one can show that the profits of firm A are maximized when it supplies a positive fraction of the market for service 2 given by $[b - c_{B2} - V_1 - sK_1/Q]/(c'_{A2} - c_{B2})$, where $c'_{A2} = V_{A2} + sk_{A2}$, as above.[13] Firm A can maximize its profits by selling that amount of service 2 at c_{B2}, which is below its own cost but equal to the unit cost of firm B, while selling service 1 at price $b - c_{B2}$.[14] Alternatively, firm A can sell packages of services 1 and 2 at price b to the above fraction of the market, and it can sell service 1 on the open market at price $b - c_{B2}$. Again, c_{B2} is the implicit price of service 2 in the package; such a price is detrimental to economic welfare because it is below the true unit cost of production for firm A. Firm B could supply the entire market at price c_{B2} and still cover its costs.

In sum, when a regulated firm is subject to a binding rate-of-return ceiling that exceeds its true marginal cost of capital, it has a profit incentive to expand into the production of vertically related services. A firm that has a comparative advantage in that market can compete successfully in the market with prices that cover its unit costs. If, however, the regulated firm is comparatively inefficient in producing vertically related services, it may still endeavor to extend its monopoly by means of such tactics as below-cost pricing, tie-ins, and predatory-systems rivalry—all to the detriment of economic welfare.

Ideally, regulators might fine-tune the allowed rate of return to eliminate incentives for anticompetitive behavior. Otherwise, policy-makers must try to devise regulatory judicial guidelines that will enable regulated firms to pursue efficient vertical market extension while cheaply and effectively discouraging anticompetitive conduct.

4. Possible Anticompetitive Practices in the Cable Television Industry

The cable television industry during the period 1972–81 affords an excellent example of a market with features that may have provided incentives for anticompetitive behavior of the sort discussed in section 2 above.[15] In broad outline, the structure of the industry during that period was as follows.

Dissemination of cable programming was controlled—subject to some regulatory constraints— by cable systems operators (CSOs) who, in virtually every instance, were locally franchised monopolists. Each franchise offered essentially two types of programming, basic and pay. The difference between the two types was somewhat blurred, except that the prices (subscriber rates) for basic programming were often subject to rate-of-return regulation, whereas the prices for pay programming were substantially unregulated. That is, the allowed rate of return applied only to the capital base and revenues associated with the production and dissemination of basic programming.[16] Although prices for pay programming were determined more or less freely by the CSO, the prices were influenced by the "rate cards" of pay television programmers. These cards specified a division of pay revenue between the CSO and the pay programmer.[17] Pay programmers, like the CSOs, benefited from a high degree of market concentration.[18]

As this brief summary indicates, the cable television industry exhibited characteristics that may have created incentives for anticompetitive behavior toward rival producers of complementary products. Specifically, notwithstanding CSOs' local monopoly, they were probably unable to capture all the monopoly profits available from cable system subscribers; rate-of-return regulation, as well as competitive bidding for franchises, placed a ceiling on basic subscription rates, which inevitably interfered with implementation of a perfect price squeeze.[19] As a consequence, CSOs and pay programmers had strong incentives for vertical integration followed by exclusionary tactics against competing pay programmers. Integrated CSOs could exclude competitors' programming from their systems or charge exorbitant prices to subscribers who wished to view the programming. Also the CSOs could devote little or no effort to the promotion and sale of competitors' programming. Indeed, the history of the industry suggests several examples of possible anticompetitive, exclusionary behavior. The most notable incident occurred when Showtime, following its acquisition by Teleprompter, replaced HBO in the affiliated systems, notwithstanding that Showtime may have been an inferior programmer (its share of the pay cable market never approached that of HBO, and it had only recently become profitable).

Concededly, no data are available for testing the hypothesis that vertical integration in the cable industry, on the whole, has been anticompetitive. In fact, exclusionary practices seem to be on the decline. CSOs increasingly include rival pay programming in their service offerings, perhaps because of competition for franchise renewal. It is difficult to predict whether this trend will persist; one must continue to scrutinize the prices charged for competing services. Thus, in view of the nature and history of the cable industry, we feel that the practices of cable programmers and operators may warrant ongoing scrutiny.

Our conclusion is both modest and challenging. We have shown that the behavior of dominant firms toward the producers of complementary products may not accord with the public interest. Such prevalent aspects of market structure as alternative, inferior sources of supply, opportunities for implicit price discrimination, price or revenue-division inflexibilities, and rate-of-return constraints can create incentives for anticompetitive behavior. The resulting conduct may include exclusionary vertical mergers, tie-ins, predatory systems rivalry, and a variety of other practices that are privately profitable yet detrimental to economic welfare.

We do not suggest that exclusionary practices are always undesirable or even that they are often undesirable; we suggest only that, contrary to an important body of legal and economic commentary, the behavior of dominant firms toward rival producers of complementary products may warrant serious antitrust and regulatory scrutiny.[20] The remaining challenge is to identify the instances of anticompetitive behavior without significant damage to incentives for efficient integration.

Notes

An early version of this chapter was presented at the Ninth Annual Telecommunications Policy Research Conference in Annapolis, Maryland, April 1981. J. A. Ordover and R. D. Willig would like to thank the National Science Foundation for its financial support.

1. See *MCI Communications Corp. v. American Telephone & Telegraph Co.*, 462 F. Supp. 1072 (N.D. Ill. 1978).

2. See, for example, R. Bork, *The Antitrust Paradox* (1978), 231–238; R. Posner, *Antitrust Law: An Economic Perspective* (1976), 173; Bowman, "Tying Arrangements and the Leverage Problem, *Yale L.J.* 67 (1957), 19. The commentators generally concede, however, that the desire to price discriminate may provide a motive for the extension of market power. See section 2 below.

3. For a detailed analysis of systems and system markets, see Ordover and Willig, "An Economic Definition of Predation: Pricing and Product Innovation, *Yale L. J.* 91 (1981), 8.

4. Firm A can attempt to drive firm C from the market with predatory pricing tactics, but such tactics may also be ineffectual for a variety of legal and economic reasons. See Ordover and Willig, 8, 40.

5. Thus a price of just below $a + c'$ will pass the Areeda-Turner test for predatory pricing. See Areeda and Turner, "Predatory Pricing and Related Practices Under Section 2 of the Sherman Act," *Harv. L. Rev.* 88 (1975), 697.

6. A reentry barrier is "the cost that a firm that has exited the market must incur to resume production" (Ordover and Willig, 8, 12). Such barriers may arise when the fixed cost investment that is required for reentry is substantial and at least partly irreversible. Id., 11.

7. See id., 11–12.

8. As noted, other commentators generally recognize this possibility. For an extended analysis of price discrimination as a motive for predatory systems rivalry, see Ordover, Sykes, and Willig, "Predatory Systems Rivalry: A Reply," *Col. L. Rev.* 83 (1983), 1150.

9. Type 1 viewers purchase only basic service for their willingness to pay of b_1, while type 2 viewers purchase both basic and pay service at a total cost of $b_2 + h_2$.

10. See generally Ordover, Sykes, and Willig, 1150.

11. Firm A can then price service 1 above $V_1 + sK_1/Q$, the apparent unit cost of service 1, without violating its rate-of-return constraint. Such a price structure does not entail true cross-subsidization, however, because firm A can win the market for service 2 without pricing below its true unit cost.

12. Faulhaber, "Cross-Subsidization: Pricing in Public Enterprise," *Am. Econ. Rev.* 65 (1975), 966; W. Baumol, J. Panzar, and R. Willig, *Contestable Markets and the Theory of Industry Structure*, 1982; B. Owen and R. Braeutigam, *The Regulation Game*, 1978; Areeda and Turner, 697.

13. The indicated fraction is smaller, the higher are firm A's costs relative to firm B's; but it is positive regardless of the cost differential.

14. Firm A will expand its capital stock to produce service 2 as long as it earns additional revenues from the sale of service 1 that suffice to cover the deficit on service 2 and provide a profit margin on the expanded capital stock.

15. We concede that the basic structure of the cable industry may have changed in recent years; thus we do not assert that the analysis in this section applies to the industry in its current state. Casual evidence suggests, however, that certain vertical practices in the cable industry may still have anticompetitive consequences. See Ordover, "Economics, Antitrust and the Motion Picture Industry," Economic Policy Paper No. 27, New York University (September 1983).

16. Partial regulation necessitated an allocation of capital between basic and pay programming. Given the common facilities for dissemination of all forms of programming, such an allocation inevitably lacked a firm economic basis, especially when standard accounting procedures were followed. See Coal Rate Guidelines—Nationwide, proceedings before the ICC, Ex Parte No. 347 (Sub-No. 1) (May 11, 1981) (statement of W. Baumol and R. Willig, economists); Braeutigam, "An Analysis of Fully Distributed Cost Pricing in Regulated Industries," *Bell J. Econ.* 11 (1980), 182.

17. In bidding for the franchise, however, some franchisees committed themselves to a structure of prices for pay programming for a period of time.

18. As of 1981, three pay programming services—HBO, Showtime, and The Movie Channel—served over 90 percent of pay TV subscribers. HBO was the dominant firm with approximately 60 percent of all pay subscriptions. In addition, pay programmers were vertically integrated into cable system ownership; in 1980, almost 30 percent of all pay subscribers were served by vertically integrated cable systems.

19. The creation of new programming services, such as The Movie Channel and Rainbow/bravo!, by large multiple system operators, further indicates the profitability of pay programming.

20. See also Salop and Scheffman, "Raising Rivals' Costs," *Am. Econ. Rev.* 73 (1983), 267; Williamson, "Wage Rates as a Barrier to Entry: The Pennington Case," *Q. J. Econ.* 85 (1968), 85; Advanced Notice of Proposed Rulemaking—Airline Computer Reservation Systems, Comments and Proposed Rules of the Dept. of Justice, CAB Docket 41686 (Nov. 17, 1983), 160.

Market Conduct under Section 2: When Is It Anticompetitive?

Robin C. Landis and Ronald S. Rolfe

With only a few exceptions, the courts have been reluctant to impose the penalties of Section 2 of the Sherman Act on firms that have gained substantial market positions without having engaged in conduct that otherwise violates the antitrust laws. The courts have reasoned, correctly, that to impose liability for market practices not clearly undesirable would discourage socially desirable initiatives and result in "soft" competition. Thus the law does not penalize firms that have succeeded by dint of "skill, foresight, and industry"; courts faced with a defendant possessing monopoly power must find that the defendant engaged in "anticompetitive" or "exclusionary" conduct before finding a violation of Section 2.

This approach assumes that firms can, in principle, engage in conduct that will either create or maintain substantial market power. It also assumes that the courts can, in practice, distinguish such conduct from procompetitive or competitively neutral conduct. All too often, the latter conduct has been challenged as violating the antitrust laws; it has been the subject of lengthy discovery and all too often has been submitted to the expense and uncertainties of a jury trial before having been declared blameless by an appellate court.

In this chapter we first propose a test to determine whether market conduct is anticompetitive or exclusionary and then apply the test to several kinds of market conduct, by which we exclude such nonmarket conduct as obtaining protective legislation or regulation. Of the kinds of conduct examined, we find that few are anticompetitive on the basis of the test proposed.

In first part of the chapter we lay out the general analytic approach, starting with the point that substantial market power—the ability to raise prices above marginal cost for a significant period of time without attracting entry or expansion by competitors—derives from market structure, chiefly barriers to entry. Consequently, unless conduct raises barriers to entry, it cannot increase market power. Market conduct that does raise barriers to entry enables the incumbent firm to raise prices above its own costs, thereby decreasing consumer welfare. In our view, such conduct is properly characterized as anticompetitive or exclusionary.[1]

Only conduct that satisfies this criterion can bolster a firm's market power. It is crucial to draw a sharp distinction between that kind of conduct and conduct that exploits or is made possible by market power. Unless this distinction is drawn, any analysis of market conduct for antitrust purposes runs a serious risk of mistaking effect for cause, and such confusion leads to unpredictable results or to the substitution of conclusory labels for careful analysis. Moreover, it leads to elimination of the "conduct" requirement of Section 2 of the Sherman Act.

Careful analysis suggests that most kinds of market conduct are either a way to exploit existing market power or an attempt to increase or retain market share. To exploit market power, a firm may charge prices in excess of the competitive level or restrict consumer choice in some other way that both decreases consumer welfare and increases the firm's profits. Although market power itself may be undesirable, exploitation of market power through, for example, high prices does not raise barriers to entry or even discourage or exclude competitors; rather, it makes entry more attractive. Nor do nonpredatory price reductions create a barrier to entry, though they may discourage or limit entry or expansion.

To increase or retain market share, however, a firm must offer a product whose combination of attributes and price is preferred by consumers to competitive offerings. Such offerings, if successful, lead to an increase in consumer welfare, furthering what most economists regard as the chief purpose of the antitrust laws.[2]

In the second part of the chapter we apply this method of analysis to several forms of conduct that have been attacked in lawsuits by the Department of Justice and by private plaintiffs, for example, tying, integration of function, long-term leasing of machinery (with cancellation penalties), "premature" announcement of new products, and the practices attacked in *United States v. Alcoa*.[3] Application of the test proposed here would both simplify and rationalize the analysis of conduct in antitrust cases and permit disposition of most claims in advance of lengthy discovery or trial. Moreover, by focusing the analysis of conduct on its effect on entry barriers, the test would help the antitrust laws to protect competition, not competitors.

Anticompetitive Conduct: A General Analysis

Our approach in this section is: (1) briefly discuss the requirement of anticompetitive conduct to establish liability under Section 2 of the Sherman Act; (2) establish two general criteria for anticompetitive conduct; and (3) elaborate on the criterion that the conduct must be a substantial cause of market power (that is, it must raise entry barriers).

Under current antitrust law, market power alone is not enough to establish liability under Section 2 of the Sherman Act. Additional requirements, in their most recent formulation by the U.S. Supreme Court, remain somewhat vague.[4] Market power obtained or maintained by anticompetitive conduct, however, is a clear violation of Section 2 of the Act.[5] Whether or not there should be a conduct requirement in Section 2, most courts are reluctant to subject firms to drastic antitrust remedies (such as divestiture or treble damages) without proof that the market power resulted from anticompetitive conduct.[6]

Two General Criteria for Anticompetitive Conduct

It appears that market conduct must satisfy two criteria to be anticompetitive or exclusionary. First, the conduct must not be of the sort that society seeks to encourage (such as nonpredatory price reductions or product improvements). Otherwise, the antitrust laws could be used to discourage socially beneficial conduct. For example, a patent confers a lawful monopoly as a reward for invention. If all conduct that led to monopoly power were treated as anticompetitive, then obtaining and enforcing a lawful patent would, if the invention were sufficiently novel to constitute its own market, necessarily offend Section 2.[7]

The second criterion is that the conduct attacked ought to be a substantial cause of the monopoly power under scrutiny. That is, the conduct must not merely exploit or manifest market power derived from other sources. Otherwise, any action by a firm with substantial market power could satisfy the conduct requirement,[8] with the practical effect that the requirement would be read out of Section 2 altogether.[9]

These two criteria for identifying anticompetitive conduct are essentially those proposed by F. M. Fisher, J. J. McGowan, and J. E. Greenwood:

First, the conduct must be other than that encouraged by and consistent with the competitive process.
Second, the conduct must also be substantially related to the main-

tenance or acquisition (or attempted acquisition) of monopoly power, in that it must have (or be expected to have) the effect of destroying or excluding competition.[10]

Areeda and Turner define exclusionary conduct similarly:

"Exclusionary conduct" is conduct, other than competition on the merits or restraints reasonably "necessary" to competition on the merits, that reasonably appear capable of making a significant contribution to creating or maintaining monopoly power.[11]

Conduct is neither anticompetitive nor exclusionary, as we use those terms, if it fails to satisfy either prong of the two-pronged test. The first prong—whether the conduct is inconsistent with competition on the merits—reaches most probingly into the area of pricing practices and the introduction of superior products, an area, however, not the primary focus here.

Market Conduct Must Raise Barriers to Entry

The second prong—whether the conduct helps a firm acquire or maintain market power—can be stated equivalently as whether the conduct raises barriers to entry (a term that must be carefully defined). The relationship between market power, barriers to entry, and anticompetitive conduct is implicit in the treatment of predatory conduct by Fisher, McGowan, and Greenwood, who state: "To be predatory, an action must not only be unprofitable in itself, it must also reasonably be expected to exclude competition so that monopoly profits can be earned later."[12] Because competition cannot be excluded in the long run unless there are barriers to entry, it would seem that the Fisher-McGowan-Greenwood formulation also requires that the action raise barriers to entry.

The equivalence arises because "market power," as we use the term, means the ability to raise prices substantially above the competitive level for some time without inducing new entry or expansion by competitors.[13] Because prices above the competitive level ordinarily induce competitive entry (driving prices down), a necessary condition for market power is the existence of entry barriers to block or deter other firms from entering the market if prices are raised above competitive levels.

The term "entry barrier" has been defined differently by different economists.[14] The most refined definition, and the one we adopt here, is that developed by C. C. von Weizsacker: "A barrier to entry is a cost of producing which must be borne by a firm which seeks to enter an industry but is not borne by firms already in the industry and which implies a distortion in the allocation of resources from the social point of view."[15] Thus, not every requirement of producing, distributing, or marketing a product that imposes costs should properly be considered an entry barrier, only those requirements that impose differentially higher costs on firms outside the market.[16]

The implications of this distinction have not been fully appreciated. For example, Bain listed capital requirements as a possible barrier to entry, considering that capital requirements might create an entry barrier if they imposed an absolute cost disadvantage on smaller firms seeking to enter.[17] High capital requirements, however, do not, by themselves, constitute entry barriers. By definition, an entry barrier exists when would-be entrants face higher costs than incumbent firms. Incumbent firms may have had to meet the same (or higher) capital requirements as would-be entrants. Would-be entrants may, in fact, be able to enter more cheaply if technological change has lowered the capital requirements. If, conversely, incumbent firms own patents or possess proprietary knowledge they are unwilling to license, that advantage may raise barriers to entry; but it does not depend on capital requirements. Unless the cost of capital of would-be entrants is higher than that of the incumbent firm, the capital requirements do not impose differential costs and hence do not raise entry barriers. A correct comparison of capital costs would also take into account differences in risk among the borrowers. Differences in capital costs that merely reflect differences in riskiness are wholly consistent with perfect capital markets and hence ought not to be viewed as barriers to entry.

Because the cost of capital to a firm depends, in large measure, on its overall credit-worthiness, and because many potential entrants are large, established enterprises, there is no reason to assume that incumbent firms always enjoy lower capital costs than would-be entrants.[18] This reasoning has led Stigler to conclude that capital requirements are not an entry barrier.[19]

For conduct to be anticompetitive in the sense of helping a firm acquire or maintain market power, it must raise entry barriers. Conduct that does not affect entry barriers may affect the incentives of rivals to enter or expand (since conduct that leads to high short-run profits tends to create incentives to enter, whereas conduct that leads to low short-run profits tends to reduce incentives to enter), but it does not affect the fundamental ability of the firm to charge monopolistic prices or earn monopolistic profits. Consequently, if conduct is to be subjected to antitrust scrutiny on the grounds that it contributes to market power, then the critical inquiry is whether it raises entry barriers.

The practical difficulties of measuring entry barriers need not, in most cases, lessen the usefulness of this prong of the test.[20] As we discuss below, many practices can be shown by theoretical analysis alone to have no effect on entry barriers. Empirical measurement of the effect of a practice on relative costs is wholly irrelevant if a theoretical analysis shows that the practice cannot, even in principle, raise entry barriers. Indeed, empirical measurement of the contribution of a practice to entry barriers is necessary only to determine its importance to the acquisition or maintenance of a firm's market power or, in private antitrust actions, to estimate the damage to competitors from the practice. From the perspective of injunctive relief based solely on antitrust considerations, empirical measurement would be unnecessary if the practice could be shown to have the unavoidable effect of raising entry barriers.

Analysis of Specific Practices

Tying

In general, "tying" is conditioning the sale of one good or service on the purchase of another good or service.[21] The practice may take a variety of forms.[22] For example, the goods may have separately stated prices but are not available separately at those prices (as in the practice of "block booking" of movies licensed to theaters,[23] or to television[24]); or one of the goods may not have a separately stated price and can be obtained only in conjunction with another good (as in the practice of "bundling," alleged by the Antitrust Division in its suit against United Shoe Machinery, whereby United Shoe provided maintenance at no additional charge on leased machinery).[25]

The practice has been condemned as anticompetitive.[26] Analysis, however, shows that although tying may be a method by which a firm exploits market power it already enjoys (for example, by charging less than the monopoly price for good A but conditioning its sale on the purchase of good B at a supercompetitive price),[27] it is not anticompetitive in the sense of raising entry barriers.[28]

It will be recalled that there are two parts to the test for anticompetitiveness. Assume that the first part is satisfied (i.e., that tying is not consistent with competition on the merits).[29] The second part is not satisfied, however, because tying is not a cause of monopoly power.[30]

Tying does not create barriers to entry because it does not impose differentially higher costs on potential entrants. That tying does not, of itself, raise barriers to entry is confirmed by analysis of the two main arguments made against the practice. First, it is sometimes alleged that a firm possessing market power in good A can acquire market power in good B by requiring consumers to purchase B if they want to obtain A.[31] It can, indeed, be shown that, under certain conditions, tying can deter entry into the market for good B, but that is not at all the same thing as raising barriers to entry.

For example, suppose that a monopolist in good A also supplies, at no additional charge, one unit of B for every unit of A purchased and that the quantity of B thus supplied equals the total amount of B demanded. Suppose, further, that the purchasers of A can resell (at no cost) any undesired units of B.[32] Then it follows that no other firm will find it profitable to supply B, and the monopolist in A will also be a monopolist in B. Nevertheless, that conduct does not confer any power on the firm in the market for B. That is, unless there exist other, independent barriers to entry into B, the firm cannot raise the price of B above the costs of producing B without inducing entry into the production of B.[33]

A somewhat more sophisticated variation of this incorrect argument hypothesizes that, to be competitively viable, rivals must produce both A and B and that, by making entry into B unprofitable, the firm can also deter entry into the profitable A market. That variation does not withstand analysis either. If firms can enter both markets simultaneously, entry will depend on the profits to be earned from production of both A and B together, and the fact that B is not separately profitable is irrelevant. As discussed above, the additional capital requirements are not a barrier to entry, because the need to produce B does not impose any costs on new entrants that are not already being borne by the monopolist of A. Even if firms must first produce B for some period before they can enter the market for A, the tie itself does not raise entry barriers because, given the hypothesized state of technology, the monopolist had to incur the same costs of producing the unprofitable B before it could enter the profitable (by hypothesis) market for A. That is, the new entrants face the same costs the monopolist incurred to enter.

Second, it is sometimes alleged that, by tying two products together, a firm can impose on would-be entrants the requirement of offering both products, with the result of increasing the capital required to enter and hence of raising entry barriers.[34] This argument suffers from at least two flaws. As a threshold matter, it is not, in general, true that one firm can force other firms to offer the two products together. Unless consumers actually desire to buy the products as a package, a firm that requires them to do so actually encourages other firms to enter and offer the products separately at separate prices.[35]

Even if that threshold could be crossed, because the incumbent firm somehow had conditioned consumers to purchase A and B as a package, higher capital requirements do not, in general, constitute higher entry barriers. As discussed above, these capital requirements must also be met by incumbent firms. It is only if the capital costs of outsiders are somehow higher than those of incumbents that capital requirements can form a barrier to entry.

Integration of Function

Various private plaintiffs in litigation against IBM[36] and against Kodak[37] have asserted that it is anticompetitive for an alleged monopolist to combine in a single product two or more products that were previously offered separately or that could have been offered separately. They argue that such combination restricts entry by competitors into an alleged market for one or both of the separate products. For example, when IBM brought out the 370/158 central processing unit in 1972, it contained main memory storage, whereas its predecessor, the 370/155, contained none, and the memory was offered in a separate box. Competitors alleged that failure to price the 370/158 memory separately precluded others from entering the "market" for main memory in the 370/158.

The defendants in those suits replied that the integration increases performance and is more efficient and economical; hence, it is socially desirable. Proof of such performance improvement or lower costs is, however, necessarily complex and difficult in high-technology industries, and courts have adopted different rules to avoid having to appraise product changes.[38] Nor is there any need for such proof or for courts to make such determinations.

Quite apart from the efficiency aspects, if one analyzes integration of function as a form of tying (as the competitor-plaintiffs did),[39] the foregoing analysis of tying leads to the conclusion that integration of function does not raise barriers to entry and hence is not anticompetitive.[40]

Long-Term Leases with Cancellation Penalties

One of the practices attacked in *United States v. United Shoe Machinery Corp.*[41] was that of making the machinery available only on long-term lease. Those leases also provided that the lessee paid a smaller cancellation penalty if the leased machine was replaced by another United Shoe machine than by a competitive machine. In his pioneering economic analysis of the *United Shoe* case, Carl Kaysen concluded that those leases discouraged entry by competitors into the shoe machinery business.[42]

The practice presents an interesting test of the analysis proposed here. On the one hand, it can be argued that the practice imposes higher costs on firms wishing to enter the market than on the firm already in the market. Particularly if the lease term is long and if the incumbent firm has a large market share, at a given time only a small fraction of the customers will be free to enter into new leases. That fraction may not be large enough to permit entry on an economic scale. The new firm could displace the incumbent by inducing customers to cancel their leases, but the new firm's prices would have to be substantially lower than those of the incumbent firm to make the switch economical, in view of the substantial cancellation penalties.

On the other hand, such long-term leases should not make entry any more difficult than the practice of selling the machines outright. Unlike leased machines, purchased machines never revert to the manufacturer but instead remain in use during their economic life. Consequently, to displace completely a purchased machine from the market, the new entrant's price must be low enough that it becomes economical to scrap the purchased machine. Such costs ought to be at least as great as any reasonable cancellation penalty.[43]

It is no answer to this argument to say that, if there is a market for second-hand machines, the customer who wishes to purchase from the new entrant can resell the machine he already owns. This "answer" merely assumes the problem away by positing a growing or unsatisfied demand for the machines, represented by the purchaser of the used machine. Otherwise, as long as the old machine stays in use, no effective displacement has occurred. If, however, there is growing or unsatisfied demand large enough to support new entry, it could also support new entry in a lease environment, because the new entrant could outcompete the incumbent firm for the new business.

If this analysis is correct, it suggests that the source of the difficulties to new entry is not the practice of long-term leasing (with or without cancellation penalties) but rather the durability of the machines.[44] Each machine provides a stream of future services, and production of enough machines to satisfy the market demand for machine-years of service is a competitive, not anticompetitive, outcome.

The existence of a stock of machines means that the demand for new machines at any given time is limited by the sum of new demand and replacement demand. If that demand is too small to support entry by a new firm, it is the result of market conditions, not of marketing practices.[45] The implication for antitrust policy is that the incumbent firm's marketing practices are not the deterrent to entry.[46] In other words, requiring the incumbent firm to offer its machines for sale or to require only short-term leases would not in fact affect the market structure, which is (in this case) determined by the durability of the product and by the static demand.

"Premature" Announcement of New Products

In some industries, firms announce new products that will become available only in the future. When done by a firm alleged to have a large market share, the practice has been attacked as anticompetitive under the rubric of "premature" announcement.[47]

It is alleged that dominant firms engage in this practice to discourage customers from switching to their competitors during the period before the new product becomes available. The firms under attack reply that such information enables consumers to plan their acquisition of major purchases and, in any case, leads to better-informed consumer decisions. The debate does not need to be resolved in court. Except under implausible assumptions, the practice cannot, even in principle, have any anticompetitive effect. The analysis is clearest if two separate cases are considered: first, that the new product does become available according to the announcement; second, that the firm repeatedly mis-forecasts (intentionally or not) the availability of new products. The first case can be summarily disposed of: the welfare of consumers can be increased only by having additional correct information that is relevant to their purchasing decisions. If competitors lose sales because consumers prefer to postpone their purchases until the new (and presumably more desirable) product becomes available, those lost sales are the result of competition and the appropriate response by the competitor is to offer better products or lower prices to induce consumers to buy from him. The practice creates no entry barriers because it imposes no differential costs on would-be entrants.

The analysis is somewhat more complicated in the case where the firm repeatedly fails to make good on the availability dates forecast. There it can be argued that both competitors and customers are injured by the mistaken forecasts. That injury does not, however, result in market power for the allegedly dominant firm, if consumers are intelligent. After the first mistaken forecast, intelligent consumers will view future product announcements by that firm with skepticism and those announcements will be given less weight in their purchasing decisions. Thus, at most, there may be a one-time impact of a mistaken forecast; it is most unlikely, however, that market power could be created by a series of such forecasts.[48] Indeed, one would expect such actions to result in loss of credibility and sales for the incumbent firm making the misrepresentation, and thus increase the opportunity for potential entrants.

Thus, even the practice of repeated incorrect forecasts cannot create entry barriers or enhance a firm's market position.

Practices Attacked in Alcoa

The opinion by Learned Hand in *United States v. Aluminum Co. of America*[49] is perhaps the best-known antitrust decision by a court of appeals.[50] Its holding that Alcoa had violated the Sherman Act has been repeatedly cited and frequently analyzed.[51] It is far from clear, however, whether the basis of the holding was simply Alcoa's market share or the means by which it maintained that share.[52]

We do not propose here to enter into that discussion but rather to apply our general analysis to the practices alleged by the government. Nor do we propose to discuss the factual basis of the allegations. Instead, we assume that Alcoa did engage in the practices in question, and ask, instead, whether the practices, in fact, enabled it to maintain its position of market dominance. Rather than analyze all the practices alleged, we focus on the two main ones.

First, Alcoa was alleged to have forestalled entry by building capacity ahead of demand. Judge Hand reasoned that

[Alcoa] insists that it never excluded competitors; but we can think of no more effective exclusion than progressively to embrace each new opportunity as it opened, and to face every newcomer with new capacity already geared into a great organization, having the advantage of experience, trade connections and the elite of personnel.[53]

Despite Judge Hand's eloquence, the practice does not create barriers to entry. If the capacity is planned and built so that its output can be sold as soon as the plant becomes operational, the expansion is both efficient and, from the standpoint of consumers, desirable. If, instead, the capacity is built so far ahead of the growth in demand as to sit idle, the practice imposes costs on Alcoa that are *not* imposed on would-be entrants. To be sure, in either case new entry is deterred by the prospect of being unable to make sales at a profitable price. That the practice *deters* entry no more makes it anticompetitive than the fact that low prices deter entry makes them anticompetitive. In both cases, the market position is the result of satisfying consumer demand, not of preventing entry that would benefit consumers economically. Consequently, it would appear to be a mistake to base antitrust liability on such a practice, whose effect is to benefit consumers and whose "harm" to potential entrants is that, because of low prices and sufficient quantities to satisfy consumer demand, there is inadequate incentive to enter.[54]

Second, Alcoa was alleged to have discouraged entry by buying bauxite deposits in excess of its needs and by obtaining the rights to all the low-cost hydroelectric sites that could be used to generate the large amounts of electricity needed for the production of aluminum.[55] Although that practice may not be effective, it could, in principle, be anticompetitive.[56]

That is, circumstances can be imagined in which that practice would raise entry barriers. To keep the analysis simple, suppose that the following (highly unrealistic) conditions existed: first, there were only enough hydroelectric sites available that if they were all used to generate electricity for use in aluminum production, the resulting output would be the competitive output; second, these sites could be, and were, acquired by Alcoa at a nominal cost; third, the additional cost of producing aluminum using electricity generated from some other source was X dollars per ton higher than the cost using electricity from the low-cost hydroelectric sites.

Under those conditions, acquisition of the hydroelectric sites would have the effect of raising entry barriers. Other firms seeking to enter the aluminum business would face costs X dollars per ton higher than those faced by the incumbent firm, and those additional costs would not have been necessary if all of the low-cost hydro sites had been available for the production of aluminum. Thus, the incumbent firm's actions in acquiring all of the low-cost hydro sites would be anticompetitive.[57]

In conclusion, our fundamental premise is that the single overarching purpose of the antitrust laws is—or, at least, ought to be—to protect the competitive process. From that premise it follows that conduct consistent with that process should be applauded, not condemned, even if, as a result of the conduct, existing competitors suffer losses or potential competitors decide not to enter. It also follows that, unless the conduct harms the competitive process (e.g., by raising entry barriers), it should not give rise to antitrust liability.

If market conduct is to be an element of liability under Section 2, only conduct that raises barriers to entry should give rise to such liability. Because such conduct enables an incumbent firm to acquire or maintain market power—i.e., to raise prices without attracting new entry—and thus to deprive consumers of the benefits of competition, such conduct deserves the label "anticompetitive."

As the analysis of specific practices suggests, most of the conduct examined here cannot properly be labeled anticompetitive. Because not every conceivable kind of conduct has been analyzed here, other conduct may well be anticompetitive according to the criteria we have proposed. It seems fair to conclude, however, that many practices in fact raise no entry barriers. Competitors, quite understandably, tend to view their rivals' practices as anticompetitive when those practices cost them sales and customers. If, in addition, the rival has a large market share, competitors have strong incentives to seek relief from those practices by means of antitrust lawsuits.

Nevertheless, if the purpose of the antitrust laws is to protect competition and not competitors, the appropriate test for anticompetitive practices is the one set forth here.[58] That test is clear; it is easily applied; and it is designed to increase consumer welfare. It cannot properly be rejected merely because many practices, when subjected to careful analysis, are found not to be anticompetitive. Rather, as we have suggested in this chapter, application of the test would clarify the role of market practices in antitrust analysis and simplify the resolution of antitrust disputes, leading to a reduction in litigation costs, as well as to greater consistency in judicial decisions. Moreover, application of the test proposed here would focus antitrust-enforcement resources where they can do the most good—on conduct that is truly anticompetitive.

Notes

1. It might be noted that a firm that develops a cost-reducing technological change not available to its competitors may appear thereby to have raised entry barriers. Because

society seeks to encourage cost reductions, however, that behavior does not fit the first prong of the test for anticompetitive conduct.

In general, in applying this definition of anticompetitive conduct, it is important properly to define "barriers to entry" rather than to assume, as over-zealous lawyers, economists, or courts sometimes do, that anything which makes it more difficult for a competitor to succeed is a barrier to entry.

2. See, for example, K. Elzinga, "The Goals of Antitrust: Other than Competition and Efficiency, What Else Counts?," *U. Pa. L. Rev.* 125 (1977), 1191; see also R. Pitofsky, "The Political Content of Antitrust," *U. Pa. L. Rev.* 127 (1979), 1051, 1058 (arguing that some non-economic values—but *not* protecting small businesses from the rigors of competition—should be fostered by the enforcement of the antitrust laws). But see L. B. Schwartz, "Justice and Other Non-Economic Goals of Antitrust," id., 1076 (arguing that antitrust policy does and should put more weight on non-economic goals that Pitofsky urges).

3. *United States v. Aluminum Co. of America*, 148 F.2d 416 (2d Cir. 1945).

4. In its most recent decision, the Court formulated the elements as follows:

The offense of monopoly under §2 of the Sherman Act has two elements: (1) the possession of monopoly power in the relevant market and (2) the willful acquisition or maintenance of that power as distinguished from growth or development as a consequence of a superior product, business acumen, or historic accident. (*United States v. Grinnell Corp.*, 384 U.S. 563, 570–71 (1966).

Perhaps because the district court had found flagrantly anticompetitive conduct, 236 F. Supp. 244, 258–59 (D.R.I. 1964), the Supreme Court did not elaborate on the second element of the offense.

5. Areeda and Turner, summarizing the law on monopolization, note: "It is clearly unlawful to achieve or maintain monopoly . . . by an exclusionary practice." P. Areeda and D. Turner, *Antitrust Law*, ¶613.

6. It is unnecessary to resurrect here the debate on the merits of the view that persistent market power, without anticompetitive conduct, should be held to violate the antitrust laws. Legislation has been proposed that "would replace the need for proof of conduct in government monopolization suits seeking divestiture with proof of persistent monopoly power alone." See National Commission for the Review of Antitrust Laws and Procedures, Report to the President and Attorney General (1979), viii–ix, 151–166; and Comment, "Draining the Alcoa 'Wishing Well': The Section 2 Conduct Requirement after Kodak and CalComp," *Fordham Law Review* 48 (1979), 291, 296 and notes 22–24; hereafter, cited as "Draining the Alcoa 'Wishing Well'." The article urges the adoption of such a standard in monopolization suits brought by the government; ibid., pp. 327–333. See also, F. M. Scherer, *Industrial Market Structure and Economic Performance*, 2d ed. (Chicago: Rand-McNally College Publishing, 1980), pp. 540–544.

7. C. C. von Weizsacker has analyzed this problem as a tension between competition in production (which would be increased if there were no patents) and competition in innovation (which would be decreased if there were no patents). He argues that the optimal policy must balance the different "levels" of competition. Von Weizsacker,

Barriers to Entry, A Theoretical Treatment (New York: Springer-Verlag, 1980), pp. viii–ix, 183–212.

8. As an oversimplified example, prices above cost hurt consumers and demonstrate market power, prices below cost are predatory, and prices at cost deter entry. Scherer notes that a dominant firm faces a hard choice between setting a high price that yields high short-run profits but induces entry and setting a low price that deters entry but sacrifices short-run profits. He does not, however, take a position on which choice is preferable from the standpoint of antitrust policy. Scherer, *Industrial Market Structure*, pp. 232–243.

9. Areeda and Turner agree that if the conduct requirement is to be eliminated, it should be done explicitly without the "charade [of] searching for bad practices":

Intellectual honesty should compel antitrust law to acknowledge that it is either (1) looking for a significant causal connection between power and challenged behavior or (2) condemning monopoly power as such (with possible exceptions). If the latter is the law's object, it should do so cleanly without burdening plaintiffs, defendants, courts and society with a meaningless but endless charade searching for bad practices. Areeda and Turner 3, ¶739.

Williamson notes that, when antitrust enforcement agencies file complaints against dominant firms,

the main effort is to scrutinize the behavior of dominant firms to discover evidence of offensive business conduct.... That, objectively, the conduct in question could not reasonably lead to the dominance result is simply disregarded.... That the process is regarded by outsiders, and even some insiders, as artificial and contrived is only to be expected (O. Williamson, *Markets and Hierarchies: Analysis and Antitrust Implications* [Glencoe, Ill.: Free Press, 1975, p. 212).

He argues that, if dominant positions arising from "market failure" could be reached directly by Section 2, "contrived proof of anticompetitive conduct would thereby be made unnecessary in order to obtain relief."

10. Fisher, McGowan and Greenwood, *Folded, Spindled and Mutilated: Economic Analysis and U.S. v. IBM* (Cambridge, Mass.: The MIT Press, 1983), p. 272.

11. Areeda and Turner 3, ¶626g.

12. Fisher, McGowan, and Greenwood, p. 276.

13. See, for example, F. M. Fisher, "Diagnosing Monopoly," *Quarterly Review of Economics and Business* 19 (Summer 1979), 7, 12.

14. For example, G. Stigler defines entry barrier as "a cost of producing (at some or every rate of output) which must be borne by a firm which seeks to enter an industry but is not borne by firms already in the industry." Stigler, *The Organization of Industry* (Homewood, Ill.: Richard D. Irwin, 1968), p. 67. To the extent that barriers to entry are always viewed as socially undesirable obstacles to the efficient functioning of markets, Stigler's definition runs afoul of the tension between competition in production and competition in innovation. His definition is similar to, but sharper than, that

given by J. S. Bain for conditions of entry: "the advantages of established sellers in an industry over potential entrant sellers, these advantages being reflected in the extent to which established sellers can persistently raise their prices above a competitive level without attracting new firms to enter the industry." Bain, *Barriers to New Competition* (Cambridge, Mass.: Harvard University Press, 1956), p. 3. Since potential entrants can make a profit by entering if their costs are the same as those of established firms and prices have been raised above those costs, the two definitions are similar in effect.

15. Von Weizsacker, "A Welfare Analysis of Barriers to Entry," *Bell Journal of Economics* 11 (1980), 388, 400. Von Weizsacker alternatively defines barriers to entry as "socially undesirable limitations of entry, which are attributable to the protection of resource owners already in the industry." See also his *Barriers to Entry*, p. 13.

16. See Fisher, McGowan, and Greenwood, pp. 165–67. For ease of exposition we assume that the firm whose market power is being assessed is the only firm in *the* market. Carefully stated, the correct proposition is that entry barriers confront only those firms that face differentially higher costs of producing the same good or service relative to some other firm or firms.

17. Bain, pp. 158–166.

18. Williamson has argued that "information impactedness" and "bounded rationality" hinder the capital market in disciplining inefficient management. See O. Williamson, *Markets and Hierarchies: Analysis and Antitrust Implications*, pp. 142–143. By extension, it might be argued that those same conditions enable incumbent firms to enjoy lower capital costs than do outsiders seeking to enter. To our knowledge, no empirical evidence suggests that such differences exist or are significant. In any case, firms that are now incumbent presumably faced the same differentials when they first entered the industry.

19. Stigler, p. 70. See also Fisher, McGowan, and Greenwood, pp. 183–191. Economists disagree whether capital costs can *ever* be a barrier to entry, but mere capital requirements are *not* a barrier. It is sometimes argued that capital market imperfections may cause the costs of capital to be higher for entrants than incumbents; Scherer, pp. 303–304. However, the authors of one of the few careful examinations of that hypothesis concluded that the market for venture capital, at least, operates without significant imperfections. Charles River Associates, *An Analysis of Capital Market Imperfections* (Cambridge, Mass.: Charles River Associates, 1976). Further, Scherer's reasoning that there must be capital market imperfections because "it is definitely more difficult or costly for small new entrants to raise capital than for established firms" (pp. 303–304) seems to be implicitly contradicted by his recognition that larger firms enjoy lower capital costs because they are less risky and because there are economies of scale in raising capital (pp. 104–105). Lower capital costs for large firms that reflect lower resource costs suggest that capital markets are functioning perfectly, not imperfectly. Large established firms are also potential entrants, so that the higher costs facing small entrants are not, in general, barriers to entry.

20. Some of the empirical work relating profit rates to entry barriers had classified entry barriers into broad categories (i.e., describing barriers as "low to moderate," "substantial," or "very high"), an approach that avoids the need for precise quantification. See, for example, Bain, pp. 192–200; H. Michael Mann, "Seller Concentration, Barriers

to Entry, and Rates of Return in Thirty Industries," *Rev. of Econ. and Stat.* 48 (1966), 296. That approach has been criticized on account of the "subjective character" of the classification. Scherer, p. 277. Other studies have developed indexes of entry barriers. See, for example, D. Orr, "An Index of Entry Barriers and Its Application to the Market Structure Performance Relationship," *J. of Indust. Econ.* 23 (1974), 39. That approach also avoids the need for precise measurements in terms of dollars per unit of output. In view of the difficulties inherent in defining and measuring actual costs, let alone potential costs, a test that depended on precise quantification of entry barriers would probably have a limited scope.

21. Areeda and Turner define it as "a tying arrangement [that] is the sale or lease of one item ('tying product') only on condition that the buyer or lessee take a second item ('tied product') from the same source"; Areeda and Turner, ¶733a. Scherer defines a "tying contract" similarly: "Under a tying contract, the purchaser of some article . . . agrees as a condition of purchase to buy the seller's supplies of some other commodity." Scherer, p. 582.

22. The discussion of these forms is intended only as illustration. We do not imply that any form is a tie that would be subject to the antitrust laws. Indeed, one of the inherent difficulties in the notion of tying is its presupposition that any particular good or service is a fixed, well-defined entity (i.e., in technical terms, is a fixed bundle of characteristics or attributes). In fact, product offerings are themselves variable and are frequently changed in response to or in anticipation of consumer demand. Changes that incorporate additional functions or products can be analyzed as a "tie," but it is not necessarily sensible to do so. For example, is it a "tie" for automobile manufacturers to include a heater as standard equipment? air conditioning? a radio? Each item could be priced separately or obtained from another source, as could, say, the spare tire or even the original tires. The examples could be multiplied or made more ridiculous; but the point is that attaching antitrust significance to the definition of a product (for example, the definition of an automobile) will inevitably lead to arbitrary distinctions that cannot form the basis of coherent antitrust enforcement.

23. *United States v. Paramount Pictures, Inc.*, 334 U.S. 131 (1948).

24. *United States v. Loew's*, 371 U.S. 38 (1962). See also G. J. Stigler, "A Note on Block Booking," in Stigler, pp. 165–70 (analyzing the hypothesis that offering packages of movies to an exhibitor or to television "is essentially a price discrimination technique").

25. *United States v. United Shoe Machinery Corp.*, 110 F. Supp. 295, 325, 344 (D. Mass. 1953), *aff'd per curiam*, 347 U.S. 521 (1954). See also J. McKie, *Tin Cans and Tin Plate* (Cambridge, Mass.: Harvard University Press, 1959). Both examples illustrate the problem of product definition. If the "product" in *United Shoe* is defined as a functioning machine, for example, then the service is simply part of the product. That the service *could* be priced separately does not mean it has to be priced separately. Similarly, if the product in the canning industry is defined as "closed cans," then the cans and can-closing machinery are parts of the same product.

26. See, for example, Areeda and Turner, ¶733c and 733e (tying arrangements may bring about a monopoly in the tied product and might, in some situations, reinforce a

monopoly in the tying product); Scherer, p. 582; C. Kaysen, *United States v. United Shoe Machinery Corporation* Cambridge, Mass.: Harvard University Press, 1956), pp. 250–55.

27. In summarizing the "key ideas" of the "Chicago school," Posner has noted that tying cannot be used to obtain a second source of monopoly profits, but that it may be a method of price discrimination. Posner, "The Chicago School of Antitrust Analysis," *U. Pa. L. Rev.* 127 (1979), 915, 926. The idea of tying or commodity bundling as a method of price discrimination was recently the subject of considerable theoretical attention. See W. J. Adams and J. L. Yellen, "Commodity Bundling and the Burden of Monopoly," *Q. J. Econ.* 90 (1976), 475; R. Schmalensee, "Monopolistic Two-Part Pricing Arrangements," *Bell J. Econ.* 12 (1981), 445; R. Schmalensee, "Commodity Bundling by Single-Product Monopolies, "*J.L. & Econ.* 25 (1982), 67. Empirically, in the context of block booking of motion pictures or of the sale of "sights" of uncut diamonds, Kenney and Klein argue that the hypothesis of price discrimination is not consistent with the facts and tying is practiced to economize on transaction costs. See R. W. Kenney and B. Klein, "The Economics of Block Booking," *J. L. & Econ.* 26 (1983), 497.

Neither price discrimination nor minimization of transaction costs is anticompetitive in the sense used here, because neither raises barriers to entry. Indeed, minimization of transaction costs is socially desirable; even price discrimination may lead to more efficient resource allocation than results from a single monopolistic price.

28. Here, we are not concerned with the legality of tying (e.g., the prohibition on tying arrangements under Section 3 of the Clayton Act or Section 1 of the Sherman Act; see Areeda and Turner, ¶733b), because we focus on the role of conduct in supporting market power. We might note in passing, however, that, because ties can, like high prices, be a form of exploiting market power, tying agreements among competitors are properly subject to Section 1.

29. This assumption will necessarily be true, as there are some instances in which tying is the competitive result (e.g., where no consumer wishes to purchase the tied goods separately or where the production or consumption technology makes it infeasible or inefficient to price the items separately). The competitive result—dictated by costs and consumer preferences—may be said to yield one definition of "product." There is no need, however, to investigate costs or consumer preferences on a case-by-case basis or to attempt to define *the* product, because, as we show below, tying does not create barriers to entry.

30. It might be argued that, where the tied product is not separately priced, the implicit price is zero, which is below marginal cost and therefore predatory. It would seem, rather, that where the two goods are so closely tied, they should be viewed as a single product. In that case, the correct inquiry is whether the combined price is below the combined costs. If the combined price is predatory, the effect may be anticompetitive, but the harm arises from the predatory price, not from the tie. Analytically, that is, the tie adds nothing to the anticompetitive effect of the predatory price.

31. See, for example, Scherer, p. 582.

32. This assumption, admittedly unrealistic, simplifies the analysis. If, on the contrary, unwanted acquisitions of B cannot be resold at no cost, the possibility arises that some consumers—i.e., those willing to pay a price for B higher than the costs of producing B, but who are not willing to pay the price of A to acquire both A and B—

would make it profitable for a firm to supply good B separately. That result would contravene the hypothesis that the monopolist in A will also be a monopolist in B.

33. It is also elementary that the firm cannot charge a price that is higher than the total price consumers would be willing to pay for one unit of A plus one unit of B. Thus, for example, if $P(B)$ is the competitive market price of B and $P^*(A)$ is the monopoly price of A, then the monopolist cannot charge a price for the package that is higher than $P(B) + P^*(A)$ without suffering unacceptable sales losses.

34. See Fisher, McGowan, and Greenwood, pp. 210–13, for an analysis of this argument in the context of *United States v. IBM*; see also Areeda and Turner, ¶733e.

35. See Fisher, McGowan, and Greenwood, pp. 212–13. To illustrate this proposition, suppose that the incumbent firm sells A and B at a combined price of $P = P^*(A) + P(B)$, where $P(B)$ is the competitive price of B (and therefore equal to its marginal cost). Suppose that, if the goods were separately priced, some customers would buy A at P^* but not B at $P(B)$. If a new entrant offered A separately at P^*, those customers would therefore prefer to buy from the new entrant rather than from the incumbent firm. The new firm would make as much profit on each additional unit of A sold as the incumbent firm makes. Under those circumstances, the tie encourages rather than discourages entry by competitors.

36. *ILC Peripherals Corp. v. IBM Corp.*, 458 F. Supp. 423 (N.D. Cal. 1978), *aff'd per curiam sub nom. Memorex Corp. v. IBM Corp.*, 636 F.2d 1188 (9th Cir. 1980); *California Computer Products Corp. v. IBM Corp.*, 613 F.2d 727 (9th Cir. 1979); *Transamerica Computer Products v. IBM Corps.*, 481 F. Supp. 965 (N.D. Cal. 1979), *aff'd*, 698 F.2d 1377 (9th Cir. 1983).

37. *Berkey Photo Co. v. Eastman Kodak Co.*, 457 F. Supp. 404 (S.D.N.Y. 1978), *aff'd in part and rev'd in part*, 603 F.2d 263 (2d Cir. 1979), *cert. denied*, 444 U.S. 1093 (1980); *GAF v. Eastman Kodak Co.*, 579 F. Supp. 1203 (S.D.N.Y. 1981). See comment, "Antitrust Scrutiny of Monopolists' Innovations: *Berkey Photo, Inc. v. Eastman Kodak Co.*," *Harv. L. Rev.* 92 (1979), 408.

38. Compare *ILC Peripherals Corp. v. IBM Corp.*, 458 F. Supp., 441 (product changes presumptively lawful unless clear lack of technical justification) with *Transamerica Computer Corp. v. IBM*, 481 F. Supp., 1002–1005 (product changes violate the law "if the design choice is unreasonably restrictive of competition"). See also Areeda and Turner, 1982 Supp., ¶738.4.

39. Areeda and Turner analyze integration of function as an "implicit tie." See Areeda and Turner, 1982 Supp., ¶738.4. See also note, "An Economic and Legal Analysis of Physical Tie-Ins," *Yale L. J.* 89 (1980), 769.

40. A related claim arises when changes are made in the design specifications of complementary products—e.g., the electronic interface between a peripheral device and its control unit or the photographic processing requirements of a new film. Courts have found it necessary to decide when such changes are anticompetitive. Even if it is assumed (contrary to the claims of defendants) that such changes do not benefit consumers, directly or indirectly, those changes are still not anticompetitive because they do not raise barriers to entry. In almost any realistic set of circumstances, it costs at

least as much to design and implement such changes as it does to imitate them. In that sense, the effect of such changes is to decrease barriers to entry, because the incumbent incurs *higher* costs than the new entrant or existing competitor.

One commentator has argued that such product changes can have long-run exclusionary effects if the average total costs of the innovating dominant firm are less than those of its competitor, because of the "spreading" effect on average fixed costs of a larger volume of output. See "An Economic and Legal Analysis of Physical Tie-Ins," *Yale L. J.* 89 (1980), 778–79. That analysis assumes that average total cost declines over the entire relevant output range; that is, that there are economies of scale over the entire range of output. Such economies of scale are rare indeed in unregulated industries. See Scherer, pp. 84–88, 93–98. To the extent that they occur, they are not a barrier to entry, as that term is used here, because efficiency in production requires that a single firm produce all the output. See von Weizsacker, "A Welfare Analysis of Barriers to Entry," pp. 401–405.

41. 110 F. Supp. 295 (D. Mass. 1953), *aff'd per curiam*, 347 U.S. 521 (1954).

42. Kaysen, *United States v. United Shoe Machinery Corp.*, 64–73. It has also been argued, for example, that United's lease-only policy prevented development of a market for second-hand machines and consequently contributed to its market power; *id.*, 113–14; Areeda and Turner, ¶735a, 735b. That argument mistakes exploitation of market power for maintenance of market power. If the "market" is viewed as one for machine services, then selling one machine is equivalent to leasing some large number of machines for a period shorter than their useful economic lives. That is, if a machine has a useful life of twenty years, then the sale of one machine provides twenty machine-years, while a ten-year lease provides ten machine-years of service. (These figures are meant only to be illustrative; the exact number of years of equivalent service depends on interest rates and depreciation rates.) Leasing a given number of machines can therefore be viewed as offering less output in the market than would be provided by the sale of the same number of machines. While the lower output may reflect a monopolistic decision to restrict output, it does not create barriers to entry by other firms but instead creates incentives for them to enter.

Recent theoretical work argues that monopolists of durable goods would prefer to rent rather than sell because purchasers of such goods take into account the possibility of a later decline in the value of the goods should the monopolist lower the price. See J. I. Bulow, "Durable-Goods Monopolists," *J. Pol. Econ.* 90 (1982), 314. Although Bulow suggests an interesting explanation for United Shoe's lease-only policy, he does not suggest that such a policy has anticompetitive effects. Indeed, even from the standpoint of social welfare, he notes that "it is unclear that the government should force durable-goods monopolists to sell"; ibid., p. 331.

43. It is theoretically possible that a true monopolist could exact unreasonable cancellation penalties as a term of the lease, though it is doubtful that a court would enforce such penalties if the customer cancelled the lease and refused to pay the penalty. See, e.g., Restatement, Second, Contracts §356(1): "Damages for breach by either party may be liquidated in the agreement but only at an amount that is reasonable in the light of the anticipated or actual loss caused by the breach and the difficulties of proof of loss." However, if the monopolist were able to do so, and if such clauses were believed to be enforceable, then under such conditions long-term leasing could deter entry.

44. See R. A. Posner and F. H. Easterbrook, *Antitrust: Cases, Economics Notes and Other Materials*, 2d ed. (St. Paul, Minn.: West Publishing Co., 1981), pp. 639–640.

45. It may be objected that demand is artificially small because the incumbent firm charges monopolistic prices. If it is true that, at competitive prices, there would be enough demand to support a new entrant, then (apart from inadequate information about the market demand schedule) a new entrant would perceive that it could survive by pricing at or slightly above the competitive level and would enter.

46. As discussed above, it is theoretically possible that marketing practices could be a deterrent to entry. In particular, if the cancellation penalties were unreasonably high and if they were enforced only when a machine was replaced by a competitor's machine, such long-term leases could deter new entry.

47. For example, *California Computer Products Corp. v. IBM Corp., Memorex Corp. v. IBM Corp., Transamerica Computer Products v. IBM Corp., Berkey Photo Co. v. Eastman Kodak Co., GAF v. Eastman Kodak Co.*

48. See Fisher, McGowan, and Greenwood, pp. 289–90.

49. 148 F.2d 416 (2d Cir. 1945).

50. Because there was not a quorum of six Supreme Court justices qualified to hear the case, the appeal from the district court decision was referred to the Second Circuit. See *Alcoa*, 148 F.2d at 421. Walter Adams called Judge Hand's decision "one of the most celebrated judicial opinions of our time." W. Adams, "The Aluminum Case: Legal Victory, Economic Defeat," *Amer. Econ. Rev.*41 (1951), 915, 917. The more expansive implications of *Alcoa* appear to have been rejected by the Second Circuit in *Berkey Photo, Inc. v. Eastman Kodak Co.*, 603 F.2d 263 (2d Cir. 1979), *cert. denied* 444 U.S. 1093 (1980). See, e.g., S. Robinson, "Recent Antitrust Developments—1979," *Col. L. Rev.* 80 (1980), 1, 1–13; M. Handler, "Reforming the Antitrust Laws," *Col. L. Rev.* 82 (1982), 1287, 1357–58. Our focus here is not on those implications but rather on the particular conduct at issue in *Alcoa*.

51. For example, it has been cited in more than 40 U.S. Supreme Court opinions, almost 200 opinions by federal courts of appeals, and over 250 federal district courts, as well as in numerous law review articles. It is also cited or discussed in a large number of articles appearing in economics journals and in texts and monographs. Notwithstanding that amount of attention, a former assistant attorney general for antitrust has remarked that the decision has been viewed as "something of an intellectual sport—the high watermark of overly zealous Section 2 enforcement—important to classroom and academic analysis, but . . . less important to the real world." Baker, "FTC's Use of Alcoa, DuPont Cases Puts More Businesses in Jeopardy," *Nat. L. J.* (April 23, 1979), p. 23, col. 2, quoted in comment, *Draining the Alcoa Wishing Well*, p. 301 n. 48.

52. There have been several interesting analyses of the extent to which "secondary" aluminum (e.g., aluminum recycled from scrap) competed with "primary" aluminum (refined from bauxite) and the extent to which the two should be included in the same market. See D. W. Gaskins, "Alcoa Revisited: The Welfare Implications of a Second-hand Market," *J. Econ. Theory* 7 (1974), 254; F. M. Fisher, "Alcoa Revisited: Comment," *J. Econ. Theory* 91 (1974), 357; P. L. Swan, "ALCOA: The Infuence of Recycling on Monopoly Power," *J. Pol. Econ.* 88 (1980), 76. That work does not relate directly to the practices alleged in *Alcoa*, however.

53. 148 F.2d, 431.

54. F. M. Fisher has pointed out to us that if Alcoa had sufficient excess capacity to credibly threaten a price war, the excess capacity might deter entry. In that case, the threatened predatory prices are the conduct that creates the entry barrier, in that the conduct would impose exit costs on the potential entrant not borne by the incumbent. It is questionable, however, whether such a speculative assumption of the threat of predatory pricing (labeled as "nuclear deterrence" by Scherer) should ever be considered an anticompetitive practice. To the extent that the idle capacity is necessary to the threat of such pricing, it could at least form part of an allegedly anticompetitive practice.

55. Because the alleged practices of buying up the best bauxite deposits and low-cost hydroelectric sites are analytically equivalent, we discuss only the latter practice. It should be noted that the trial court found that Alcoa had not engaged in these practices "for the purpose of preventing competition," and Judge Hand declared that the finding could not be set aside as "clearly erroneous." 148 F.2d, 432–434.

56. If, for example, the costs to Alcoa of stockpiling the hydroelectric sites were greater than the additional costs imposed on competitors, then Alcoa would be incurring higher costs than those of its competitors. In that case, the difference in costs would tend to encourage entry rather than block it.

57. The assumptions made here are unnecessarily restrictive, but they demonstrate that some practices can be anticompetitive. The analysis of a more realistic set of assumptions would be more complicated but would focus on the same question: Does the practice impose costs on would-be entrants that the incumbent firm does not have to bear?

58. See, for example, *Brown Shoe Co. v. United States*, 370 U.S. 294, 344 (1962).

8 Can Exclusive Franchises Be Bad?

Franklin M. Fisher

1. The Problem

Suppose the manufacturer of a certain product contracts with a dealer to distribute that product; the dealer is given an exclusive franchise making him the only distributor in a given area. Does this constitute a restraint of trade, and if so, a harmful one?

The answer depends in the first instance on the competitive position of the manufacturer himself. Where there is substantial competition for the manufacturer's product ("interbrand competition"), the manufacturer, even if fully integrated, has no market power and can confer none on the dealer. In this type of situation an exclusive franchise may be granted for efficiency or marketing-incentive reasons (for example, to avoid the free-rider problem), but it can have no anticompetitive implications.[1]

The situation in which interbrand competition is either weak or absent is more complex. In that case, an antitrust interest in limiting exclusive distribution arrangements may appear warranted on the basis of the following argument: An exclusive franchise eliminates rivalry among distributors in the sale of the manufacturer's product (intrabrand competition). As with all reductions in competition, this is contrary to the public interest. Although it may be true that the manufacturer could legally achieve the same reduction in competition by integrating forward and acting as his own exclusive distributor, there is no reason for making it easy to reduce competition in distribution by allowing market power to be passed on to an independent distributor. Indeed, such an arrangement risks permitting the franchisee to exercise some market power of his own. It may permit him to restrict sales of the manufacturer's goods and attempt to reap monopoly profits in reselling the goods; such a restriction is both inefficient and harmful to consumers.

This argument is inadequate, however, for the matter is deeper than it might appear. Where a monopoly franchisee restricts output, the ultimate customers will not be the only ones affected, for the profits of the manufacturer will also be reduced. Because the manufacturer will realize this before granting the franchise, an exclusive franchise will be given only if such an output restriction by the franchisee is in the manufacturer's interest or if the negative effect on profits is overcome by such efficiencies as may be involved in such a setup. If there is reason to believe that the manufacturer has the same interests as does society in avoiding output restriction by the franchisee, there will be no occasion for antitrust action as the fact that the manufacturer chooses to set up an exclusive franchisee shows that reasons of efficiency must outweigh any anticompetitive effects resulting from the arrangement.

Is there, then, a reason for believing that the interests of the monopoly manufacturer in avoiding output restriction by his franchisees coincides with those of society? The growing literature on the subject claims that there is and thus that it should be presumed that any such arrangement is in the interests of society if it is freely entered into by the manufacturer.[2] The reason given is that output restriction by the dealer shifts the manufacturer's derived demand curve inward; thus, at any given price charged the dealers, the manufacturer's output will be greater if the dealers compete to resell the product than if a monopoly dealer deliberately restricts output. Because this situation cannot be in the manufacturer's interest, efficiency rather than avoidance of competition must account for his granting such a franchise.

Although this reasoning is undoubtedly correct as far as it goes, it does not go far enough, for it fails to take into account the possibility that the manufacturer's profits may not consist only of the profits to be made by selling to dealers. If the manufacturer sets up a monopoly dealer who then earns monopoly profits, the manufacturer may be able to extract some or all of those monopoly profits from the dealer as a franchise fee. This raises the possibility that the manufacturer may be better off with a monopoly, output-restricting franchisee than with competitive dealers, even though society is worse off. The remainder of this chapter is devoted to an examination of this possibility.[3]

In that examination it is important to bear in mind that we are always operating under the assumption that the manufacturer is a monopolist. This means that the first-best case of full competition at all levels is not attainable, so that we are comparing second- and third-best situations.

2. Costs and Supply Curves

In order to study the issue in its purest form, I consider a situation in which the costs of distribution do not depend on the way the manufacturer organizes the distribution function; thus, efficiency considerations do not arise. I assume, therefore, that the costs of selling and distributing any given output are the same whether selling and distribution are done by a single monopoly dealer, by a group of competitive dealers, or by the manufacturer himself integrating forward. Particularly because it turns out that the question of the existence and nature of decreasing returns in distribution plays a crucial role, this assumption requires discussion.

In the long run, a competitive industry exhibits some attributes of constant returns to scale. This can occur if each enterprise, in fact, operates under conditions of constant returns; more generally, though, it occurs because, in long-run equilibrium, each firm operates at the minimum point on its average-cost curve. Provided the minimum cost output is small enough, the latter situation resembles constant returns if the cost curves are all the same, and this is ensured by definition: differences among firms are defined as rents rather than costs.

Despite the appearance of constant returns at the industry level, however, and despite the fact that competitive supply curves coincide with marginal-cost curves, the long-run supply curves of competitive industries generally are not flat. This is so for more than one reason.

First, the definition that treats interfirm differences as rents rather than costs is merely a definition. However such differences are treated, they may be real ones. In that case, at low prices, only the most efficient or most favorably situated firms will enter the industry. Unless there are constant returns at the firm level, only a limited output will be produced by such firms. As price rises, additional firms (the less efficient or less favorably situated ones) will be attracted; thus higher prices are required to call forth greater output.

Second, even though firms are all the same, the costs of different units of output may differ. In distribution, for example, it may be easy to find or attract some customers but progressively more difficult to find or attract others. This may be related to the first phenomenon—for example, if stores in population centers naturally have lower selling costs than stores in outlying areas—but it need not be.

Third, negative externalities may be involved. In the case of distribution, for example, sending out many salespeople may create a situation in which the salespeople interfere with each other. The necessity of providing enough taxis to keep rider waiting time to some minimum may mean that the waiting time of taxis between customers rises when there are more customers to be served. Such cases lead to rising industry costs.

The final case also involves an externality, although here the phenomenon involved is an externality only to the industry involved, not to the production system as a whole. As price rises and output expands—either through expansion of existing firms or through new entry—the demand for the inputs necessary to produce the expanded output will tend to bid up the prices of those inputs. The firms in the industry will experience this as an upward shift in costs; it is an important part of the process that leads average costs in competition to equal price. From the viewpoint of the economy as a whole, however, such factor-price increases simply produce a rising supply curve for the product in question.

In each of these four somewhat related cases, then, it is possible to have costs the same for a monopolist as for a competitive industry. If this occurs with rising marginal costs, increasing output creates inframarginal rents; that is, it costs less to produce earlier units of output. In the first three cases listed above, such rents under competition will accrue to the competitive firms; in the last case (that of rising factor prices), they will accrue to the factors of production.

By setting up an exclusive franchise rather than competitive dealers, the monopoly manufacturer creates a situation in which such rents can be captured by the exclusive franchisee in the first three cases and siphoned off by the manufacturer himself through a franchise fee. If this siphoning cannot occur with competitive dealers, the acquisition of such rents may provide a reason for divergence between the interests of the manufacturer and those of society.

In the first case listed above (real differences among firms), the manufacturer may be able to extract the rents in question from competitive dealers by discriminating in the price charged different dealers for the product or, more simply, by charging different dealers different franchise fees. To do this, of course, the manufacturer must know how much rent will be earned by each dealer, but that involves precisely the same knowledge he would need to arrive at the optimal franchise fee to charge a monopoly dealer: rents earned by each dealing enterprise whether or not they are separately owned and operated. Further, the manufacturer may be able to set the fees optimally by auctioning off the franchises. Thus, unless there is some reason why different franchise fees cannot be charged to differently situated dealers, this case is not one in which the manufacturer's interests differ from those of society and will not be discussed further.

I shall also not consider at length the fourth case listed above, rising input prices. In that case, rents accrue initially to the factors of production; they can be captured by the manufacturer only if the exclusive franchisee can exercise monopsony power over one or more *input* markets. An exclusive franchise that gives rise to the creation of such monopsony power might well be contrary to antitrust policy; but, whereas it is important to note the possibility, it is not directly related to the problem under discussion, which involves monopoly in the *output* market. This possibility does, however, provide an example in addition to that below of a case in which the manufacturer's interests in deciding on franchising arrangements do not coincide with those of society.

The two remaining cases (different costs for different units of output, and negative externalities in distribution) are the ones of substantial interest for the remainder of this paper. In those cases, the rents accrue initially to the dealers rather than the factors of production. Moreover, although the manufacturer may be able to siphon off rents earned by a monopoly dealer, generally he will not be able to accomplish the same end if there are competitive dealers. This is because, in these two cases when there are competitive dealers, while everyone may realize that rents are there to be earned, it will not be known in advance which dealers will earn them (and this may remain true even in later years). Thus, to siphon off the rents, the manufacturer must generally integrate forward or set up a single dealer to act as an identifiable conduit (in the externality case, he must internalize the externality involved).

I now analyze these two cases in detail, although there is no further need to distinguish them. I thus assume that the costs of distribution are the same under any form of market organization and that, whereas the manufacturer can acquire any inframarginal rents in distribution if there is a monopoly dealer, he cannot do so if there are competitive dealers. I shall also assume that there are no fixed costs to distribution; this is sensible, since we are dealing with a long-run decision and, in any case, the assumption makes relatively little difference in what follows. The marginal costs of distribution are assumed to be either constant (constant returns to scale) or rising (decreasing, returns to scale). Under competition, the marginal cost curve becomes the supply curve.

The following analysis is largely a mathematical one; the nontechnical reader, however, will find heuristic discussion interspersed with the mathematics.

3. Model and Notation

Let x denote the output sold by the manufacturer to the dealer or dealers and then to the ultimate customers; let p denote the price paid by the customer. Price and quantity are related by the inverse demand curve, $p = D(x)$, which I assume to be three times continuously differentiable. In accordance with the fact that the manufacturer is a monopolist and that there is no interbrand competition, $D'(x) < 0$. Total revenue at retail is denoted by $R(x) \equiv px$.

In the case where there is a monopoly dealer (or the manufacturer is fully integrated forward), the costs of dealing are given by the function $C_2(x)$. Because there are no fixed costs in dealing, $C_2(0) = 0$. It is assumed that $C_2(x)$ is three times continuously differentiable, with $C_2'(x) > 0$ and $C_2''(x) \geq 0$, so the technology of distribution exhibits either constant or decreasing returns to scale. (For convenience, I assume that whichever kind of returns to scale is involved holds everywhere in the relevant range; this makes no essential difference.) Because costs are assumed to be independent of market organization, the marginal cost curve for distribution, $C_2'(x)$ is the industry supply curve when there are competitive dealers.

The manufacturer's own costs of distribution are given by $C_1(x)$, assumed to be twice continuously differentiable. The behavior of his marginal costs is unrestricted, except by (3.2) to (3.4) below.

In addition to the assumptions already made, I assume the following:

$$R''(x) < 0, \tag{3.1}$$

so that marginal revenue is decreasing in output.

$$R''(x) - C_1''(x) - C_2''(x) < 0, \tag{3.2}$$

so that, although there can be increasing returns in manufacturing, they are limited so as to ensure strict concavity of overall profits. Further,

$$R''(x) - C_1''(x) - 2C_2''(x) - xC_2'''(x) < 0, \tag{3.3}$$

which, as we shall see, ensures strict concavity of manufacturing profits when there are competitive dealers. All three assumptions—(3.1) to (3.3)—can be weakened to hold only in the relevant regions, but there seems little point in doing this, as they are not very special.

I also assume that at the point at which the first-order conditions for profit maximization by a manufacturer facing a monopoly dealer are satisfied:

$$2R''(x) - C_1''(x) - 2C_2''(x) + xR'''(x) - xC_2'''(x) < 0 \tag{3.4}$$

This is the appropriate second-order condition; it need not be assumed to hold elsewhere.

4. Full Integration versus Competitive Dealers

It will be convenient to compare three situations. In addition to considering the case in which the manufacturer sets up an exclusive franchise and that in which he encourages competition among dealers, I consider the possibility that the manufacturer integrates forward and takes over the distribution function himself. In such a fully integrated case, the manufacturer obviously can capture all the profits that exist in the system; he will prefer that case if there are no other reasons not to integrate. It is helpful to begin by comparing this case to the case in which the manufacturer sells to competitive dealers at a fixed price.

In the fully integrated case, the manufacturer's profits are given by:

$$\pi^1(x) \equiv R(x) - C_1(x) - C_2(x). \tag{4.1}$$

Denoting the profit-maximizing output by x^*, that output must satisfy:

$$R'(x^*) = C_1'(x^*) + C_2'(x^*). \tag{4.2}$$

The second-order condition is given by (3.2).

Now suppose instead that there are competitive dealers. Let the price at which the manufacturer sells to the dealers be denoted by p_m. Because the dealers receive $(p - p_m)$ before their own costs, and because their competitive supply curve is given by $C_2'(x)$, the price the manufacturer must offer to get the dealers to sell any given output x must satisfy:

$$p_m = D(x) - C_2'(x), \tag{4.3}$$

which thus gives the manufacturer's own derived inverse-demand curve.

In this case, the manufacturer's profits are given by:

$$\pi_m^2(x) \equiv p_m x - C_1(x) = R(x) - C_1(x) - x C_2'(x). \tag{4.4}$$

Let x_c be the profit-maximizing output; the first-order condition for a maximum is:

$$R'(x_c) = C_1'(x_c) + C_2'(x_c) + x_c C_2''(x_c). \tag{4.5}$$

The second-order condition is given by (3.3).

We can now prove theorem 1.

Theorem 1 (A) If there are constant returns to scale in distribution $[C_2''(x) \equiv 0]$, then the competitive case and the fully integrated case yield the same outputs, the same retail prices, and the same profits to the manufacturer.

(B) If, on the other hand, there are decreasing returns to scale in distribution $[C_2''(x) > 0]$, then the competitive case yields *lower* profits to the manufacturer and results in a *lower* output and a *higher* retail price than does the fully integrated case.

Proof: (A) If $C_2''(x) \equiv 0$, then, from (4.5), x_c satisfies (4.2). Since, by (3.2), x^* is unique, $x_c = x^*$, and $D(x_c) = D(x^*)$. Finally, since $C_2(0) = 0$ and $C_2''(x) \equiv 0$, $C_2(x)$ is a ray through the origin, and $x C_2'(x) = C_2(x)$. Comparison of (4.1) and (4.4) now shows $\pi^1(x^*) = \pi_m^2(x_c)$.

(B) In this case, $C_2''(x) > 0$, so that (4.5) implies:

$$R'(x_c) > C_1'(x_c) + C_2'(x_c). \tag{4.6}$$

The concavity of overall profits, (3.2), then shows that $x_c < x^*$, so that $D(x_c) > D(x^*)$. Since $C_2(0) = 0$ and $C_2''(x) > 0$, marginal costs exceed average costs, so that $x_c C_2'(x_c) > C_2(x_c)$. It follows from the fact that x^* is the unique overall profit-maximizing output that:

$$\pi^1(x^*) > \pi^1(x_c) = R(x_c) - C_1(x_c) - C_2(x_c) \tag{4.7}$$

$$> R(x_c) - C_1(x_c) - x_c C_2'(x_c)$$

$$= \pi_m^2(x_c),$$

and the theorem is proved.

Thus, in choosing between the fully integrated and competitive cases, the interests of the monopoly manufacturer coincide with those of society.

It is easy enough to give a heuristic explanation of what is going on.[4] Consider the case in which there are decreasing returns. With competitive dealers, there are inframarginal rents that cannot be captured by the monopoly manufacturer. If the manufacturer fully integrates forward, he can make these rents his own. Thus it is not surprising that his profits are greater in the latter case.

To put it another way: with competitive dealers, the manufacturer must allow the dealers a retail margin sufficient to pay them the marginal cost of the last unit of output. He must do this in order to induce the dealers to put forth the necessary effort and resources to distribute that output. Further, he must pay that same marginal cost on each unit of output. Because marginal costs are increasing, a profit (rent) on the inframarginal units is created, since the manufacturer will be paying more than is needed to call forth the necessary effort and resources to get those inframarginal units distributed. By integrating forward, the manufacturer can internalize these profits; in effect, he can price discriminate in what he pays for the resources involved in distribution, paying only what is necessary for each unit.

This is closely related to the more surprising result that retail price will be less and output greater under full integration than with competitive dealers. Under full integration the monopolist considering expanding output by one unit must recognize that marginal revenue falls short of price because price on all previous units must be lowered in order to sell the next one. With competitive dealers, the manufacturer must not only take that same phenomenon into account but must also realize that selling the next unit of output will involve raising the amount dealers are paid per unit.[5] In effect, at any output, the marginal revenue corresponding to the manufacturer's derived demand curve falls short of the marginal revenue corresponding to the retail demand curve because of the increasing marginal costs that must be paid to dealers. This naturally leads to a lower output and a higher retail price than result when those increasing marginal costs are internalized.

To put it another way, the monopoly manufacturer with competitive dealers can be thought of as a monopsonist in the purchase of dealer services. This provides a reason for him to restrict output in addition to that provided by the downward sloping retail demand curve he takes into account in either case. In the fully integrated case, the monopoly manufacturer can be viewed as a perfectly discriminating monopsonist so that there is no output restriction.

When there are constant returns in distribution, however, all these phenomena disappear. There are no inframarginal rents to be extracted and no increasing marginal costs to be paid. The manufacturer, whether integrated or with competitive dealers, must pay the same constant marginal distribution cost per unit on all units. He receives all the profits in either case and has no incentive to prefer one to the other, setting the same output and thus the same retail price in both.

5. Competitive Dealers versus a Monopoly Dealer

These results, though interesting, do not bear directly on the main question: the manufacturer's choice between competitive dealers and an exclusive franchise monopoly dealer. Because profits are greatest in the fully integrated case, this choice assumes that full integration is not possible for efficiency or other reasons. (For example, the particular product may customarily be carried by supermarkets or mass marketers, and it may not make sense for the manufacturer to engage in such activities directly.)

To begin our examination of this choice, suppose there is a single, monopoly dealer. As in the competitive case, the monopolist sets a price, p_m, at which he sells to the dealer. The dealer takes this price as given and maximizes his own profits:

$$\pi_d^3(x) \equiv R(x) - C_2(x) - xp_m. \tag{5.1}$$

In doing so, the dealer will, of course, set the retail price, p, but this is equivalent to his choosing an output, x, so we may as well consider that he chooses x directly. This means the dealer chooses x to satisfy:

$$p_m = R'(x) - C_2'(x) \tag{5.2}$$

which is thus the manufacturer's derived inverse-demand curve for this case.

Given (5.2), the manufacturer's profits are given by:

$$\pi_m^3(x) = p_m x - C_1(x) = x\{R'(x) - C_2'(x)\} - C_1(x). \tag{5.3}$$

The manufacturer chooses p_m to maximize this; that choice is equivalent to a choice of x. Let $\hat{x}$ be the profit-maximizing output. The first-order conditions for a maximum are:

$$R'(\hat{x}) = C_1'(\hat{x}) + C_2'(\hat{x}) + \hat{x}C_2''(\hat{x}) - \hat{x}R''(\hat{x}). \tag{5.4}$$

The second-order conditions are given by (3.4).

The total profits available to the manufacturer in this case, however, are not merely $\pi_m^3(\hat{x})$. By charging the dealer a franchise fee for the privilege of having the monopoly at retail, the manufacturer can extract $\pi_d^3(\hat{x})$ from him and achieve *total* profits:

$$\pi_T^3(\hat{x}) \equiv \pi_m^3(\hat{x}) + \pi_d^3(\hat{x}). \tag{5.5}$$

We must investigate whether the manufacturer would prefer this to having competitive dealers and achieving $\pi_m^2(x_c)$.[6]

Postponing discussion until after the results, we prove theorem 2.

Theorem 2 The competitive case always results in a *greater* output and a *lower* retail price than does the case of a monopoly dealer. However, while profits *at the manufacturing level* are always greater in the competitive than in the monopoly case, *total* profits, including the franchise fee in the monopoly case, can be either greater or less, so that the manufacturer's interests need not coincide with those of society in choosing between the two cases.

Proof: By (3.1) and (5.4), we find:

$$R'(\hat{x}) > C_1'(\hat{x}) + C_2'(\hat{x}) + \hat{x}C_2''(\hat{x}). \tag{5.6}$$

The concavity of profits in the competitive dealer case, (3.3), now shows that $\hat{x} < x_c$, so that $D(\hat{x}) > D(x_c)$. Since $R'(x) < p = D(x)$, comparison of (4.3) with (5.2) shows that, for any given output, p_m is lower in the monopoly dealer case than in the competitive dealer case. Thus:

$$\pi_m^2(x_c) > \pi_m^2(\hat{x}) > \pi_m^3(\hat{x}), \tag{5.7}$$

where the first inequality follows from the fact that x_c is the unique output at which $\pi_m^2(x)$ is maximized.

It remains to show that $\pi_T^3(\hat{x})$ can be either greater or less than $\pi_m^2(x_c)$. Here, it suffices to provide examples.

(A) To see that $\pi_T^3(\hat{x}) < \pi_m^2(x_c)$ is possible, suppose that there are constant returns in distribution $(C_2''(x) \equiv 0)$. By theorem 1, $\pi_m^2(x_c) = \pi^1(x^*)$. But

$$\pi_T^3(\hat{x}) \equiv \pi_m^3(\hat{x}) + \pi_d^3(\hat{x}) \tag{5.8}$$

$$= \{R(\hat{x}) - C_2(\hat{x}) - \hat{x}p_m\} + \{\hat{x}p_m - C_1(\hat{x})\}$$

$$= R(\hat{x}) - C_1(\hat{x}) - C_2(\hat{x}) \equiv \pi^1(\hat{x}).$$

since $x_c = x^*$ is the unique output which maximizes $\pi^1(x)$, and $\hat{x} \neq x_c$, it follows that $\pi_m^2(x_c) > \pi_T^3(\hat{x})$. Evidently, this will also be true under decreasing returns, provided returns do not decrease too sharply.

(B) To see that $\pi_T^3(\hat{x}) > \pi_m^2(x_c)$ is also possible, suppose that the inverse (retail) demand curve, $D(x)$, is:

$$p = 1 - x, \tag{5.9}$$

and that the manufacturer has zero marginal costs and a fixed cost, $F \geq 0$, so that

$$C_1(x) = F. \tag{5.10}$$

(By continuity, the results will also hold if marginal costs are positive but low enough.) Finally, suppose that the cost of distribution, $C_2(x)$, is given by:

$$C_2(x) = x^2. \tag{5.11}$$

In the competitive case, the manufacturer chooses x_c to satisfy (4.5), which now becomes

$$1 - 2x_c = 2x_c + 2x_c, \tag{5.12}$$

so that $x_c = 1/6$ and $p = 5/6$. From (4.3), $p_m = 1/2$. Profits, $\pi_m^2(x_c)$, are given by (4.4) evaluated at $x = 1/6$, and they are readily seen to be $1/12 - F$. The competitive dealers receive inframarginal rents amounting to $R(1/6) - C_2(1/6) - (1/6)p_m = 1/36$.

In the monopoly case, on the other hand, the manufacturer chooses $\hat{x}$ to satisfy (5.4), which now becomes:

$$1 - 2\hat{x} = 2\hat{x} + 2\hat{x} - (-2)\hat{x}, \tag{5.13}$$

so that $\hat{x} = 1/8$ and $p = 7/8$. From (5.2), $p_m = 1/2$, as before (this is not a general property). Profits at the manufacturing level, $\pi_m^3(\hat{x})$, are given by (5.3) evaluated at $x = 1/8$ and are readily seen to be $1/16 - F$, so that $\pi_m^3(\hat{x}) < \pi_m^2(x_c)$, as must be the case. However, total profits, $\pi_T^3(\hat{x})$, are given by:

$$\begin{aligned} \pi_T^3(\hat{x}) &= R(1/8) - C_1(1/8) - C_2(1/8) \\ &= 3/32 - F > 1/12 - F = \pi_m^2(x_c). \end{aligned} \tag{5.14}$$

Thus the dealer monopoly profits extracted by the manufacturer through a franchise fee are $1/32$, enough to make the manufacturer's total profits (including the franchise fee) greater than the profits he would earn in manufacturing if he had competitive dealers. The theorem is proved.

For the sake of completeness, in the example used in part (B) of the proof, x^*, the profit-maximizing output in the fully integrated case, satisfies (4.2), which now becomes:

$$1 - 2x^* = 2x^*, \tag{5.15}$$

so that $x^* = 1/4$ and $p = 3/4$. Total profits are then given by (4.1)

Table 8.1

	Full integration	Competitive dealers	Monopoly dealers
Output (x)	1/4	1/6	1/8
Retail price (p)	3/4	5/6	7/8
Wholesale price (p_m)	—	1/2	1/2
Manufacturing profits	—	$1/12 - F$	$1/16 - F$
Dealer profits or rents	—	1/36 (rents)	1/32
Total profits or rents	$1/8 - F$	$1/9 - F$ (manuf. profits plus dealer rents)	$3/32 - F$

evaluated at $x = 1/4$, and they are readily seen to be $\pi^1(x^*) = 1/8 - F$. The example is summarized in table 8.1.

Once again it is possible to give a heuristic explanation of the results. The fact that in the competitive case output is greater and retail price lower than in the case of a monopoly dealer reflects the monopoly dealer's motivation to restrict output. Even though the manufacturer takes this motivation into account in setting the price at which he himself sells to the dealer, the effect cannot be overcome completely. As compared with the competitive case, the manufacturer who contemplates expanding output must not only take into account the rising (or constant) marginal cost of the dealer, but also the fact that the dealer will regard the payment he receives for selling the next unit of output as less than the retail margin on that unit by the reduction in revenue that will be incurred on the inframarginal units. This gives the manufacturer an added incentive to reduce output, for marginal revenue from his derived demand curve is lower than in the competitive case.

The reason that manufacturing profits must be lower in the case of a monopoly dealer than in that of competitive dealers is straightforward. Manufacturing profits will be lower because the manufacturer's derived demand curve will be lower at any price he sets when there is a monopoly dealer than when dealers compete to sell that output. That is the reason the literature gives for believing that the manufacturer will prefer competitive dealers if there are no counterbalancing considerations of efficiency.[7]

The catch, of course, is the behavior of the franchise fee; when this fee is taken into account, the manufacturer may prefer either arrangement. When, for example, there are constant returns to scale in distribution, there are no inframarginal rents to be captured, and no dealer will pay a franchise fee. In this circumstance, the fact that manufacturing profits are lower in the case of the monopoly dealer will be controlling (particularly since, by theorem 1, the manufacturer can achieve maximum profits by using competitive dealers). By continuity, the same will be true if returns to scale in distribution do not decrease too sharply, so marginal costs do not rise too quickly. When returns are decreasing and marginal costs are rising fast enough, however, the rents that can be captured through a franchise fee in the monopoly dealer case can be large enough to offset the lower manufacturing profits to be made, compared with the case of competitive dealers.

6. A Monopoly Dealer versus Full Integration: Implicit Contracts

Before proceeding to the implications of these results for antitrust policy, one other matter must be considered. In the analysis of the monopoly dealer case, I assumed that the manufacturer proceeds as follows: Knowing that the dealer will act so as to maximize his own monopoly profits, the manufacturer sets the price at the manufacturing level (p_m) to maximize his own profits at the manufacturing level, extracting the dealer's profits through the franchise fee. The question arises whether the manufacturer can do better than that—indeed, whether he can achieve the maximum profits of full integration—by setting his manufacturing price, p_m, taking into account its effects not only on manufacturing profits but also on the size of the franchise fee the dealer will be willing to pay, thus maximizing total rather than simply manufacturing profits. If so, then, under decreasing returns in distribution, a monopoly dealer will always be preferred to competitive dealers by the manufacturer. Further, such a preference will be in society's interest, since achievement of the same profits that accrue under vertical integration necessarily requires the same output and retail price; as we have seen, these are better for consumers than the output and retail price that occur in the case of competitive dealers.

Ignoring for a moment the question of whether such actions are feasible, the simplest way for the manufacturer to set his manufacturing price and franchise fee to obtain the maximum total profits would be to set the manufacturing price competitively, that is, at the marginal cost of manufacturing. This would enable the monopoly dealer to earn all possible monopoly profits, and the manufacturer could then extract the profits as a franchise fee.

Formally, suppose the manufacturer sets $p_m = C_1(x^*)$. The monopoly dealer then chooses x according to (5.2), so that x satisfies:

$$R'(x) - C_2'(x) = C_2'(x^*). \tag{6.1}$$

Obviously, by (4.2), this is satisfied at $x = x^*$; further, it is satisfied nowhere else, in view of (3.1) and the assumption that $C_2''(x) \geq 0$. Thus the resulting output and retail price are the same as in the fully integrated case; the dealer earns all the profits that can be earned, and the manufacturer can extract those profits as a franchise fee.

Whether this is possible depends on the formal and implicit relations connecting the manufacturer and the monopoly dealer. Suppose, for example, we are considering an arrangement that will last only one year and will never be repeated. In this case, no dealer would agree to pay such a franchise fee without an enforceable contract specifying the level of p_m. Any dealer would know that once the franchise fee is agreed on it will be in the manufacturer's interest to set p_m so as to maximize his profits at the manufacturing level—that is, to set p_m to satisfy (5.4), which would leave the dealer with profits lower than the agreed-on franchise fee. Thus, unless the manufacturer can bind himself to charge only marginal cost $[C_2'(x^*)]$, the policy under discussion will not be feasible. Because a similar statement holds for any franchise fee higher than $\pi_d^3(\hat{x})$, the best the manufacturer can do is to follow the policy described in the preceding section.

Obviously this problem does not arise merely in short-lived relationships. No matter how long an arrangement is to last, if the franchise fee is fixed at the outset, any dealer will require a binding commitment as to manufacturing-level price before agreeing to any fee higher than $\pi_d^3(\hat{x})$, the maximum profits that can be earned in distribution when the manufacturer sets p_m to maximize manufacturing profits. What matters is not the length of the arrangement but whether it is to be repeated.

If the arrangement is not a one-time affair, however, then it is at least possible that the policy under discussion could work without an explicit binding commitment on the part of the manufacturer as to the level of p_m. This is so because knowingly imposing losses on the dealer by extracting a very high franchise fee and then departing from an implicit commitment to charge marginal cost will lead the dealer to terminate the relationship and will warn other dealers not to take his place. Knowing this, the dealer may be willing to rely on the manufacturer's long-run self-interest to enforce marginal cost-pricing, thus enabling the manufacturer to earn the maximum possible profits in the way described. The more frequent the setting of the franchise fee, the more likely this is to occur.

Just how likely it is to occur at all may depend on circumstances, however. In complex situations where there is uncertainty as to demand and costs, where change is expected to occur, and where the dealer cannot monitor the manufacturer's costs, the dealer and his potential replacements may be unable to tell whether his losses come from the manufacturer's departure from an implicit agreement or from some other source. Knowing this, the manufacturer may be tempted occasionally to cheat on such an agreement. In such circumstances, potential monopoly dealers may not be willing to agree to franchise fees much above their estimate of what they can earn if the manufacturer does cheat. Even though the manufacturer may still be able to earn higher profits with a monopoly dealer than he could in the noncooperative case analyzed in the preceding section, he may not be able to come close to the profits, output, and retail price that would occur under full integration. Thus it will still be true that cases exist in which society, but not the manufacturer, would be better off with competitive dealers.

The case we have been discussing is one in which the manufacturer seeks to set a very high franchise fee and bind himself as to the price at the manufacturing level. It is also possible that the manufacturer will seek to bind the dealer to a minimum output and a maximum price at the retail level in exchange for a low franchise fee and the award of the franchise (or the threat of its termination). This would enable the manufacturer to move all profits to the manufacturing level (as opposed to the previous case, where they are moved to the retail level) and thus attain the equivalent of the fully integrated case.

Again what matters is the observability of behavior—in this case, the behavior of the dealer. If the selling and promotion of the product is not simple but requires a multidimensional effort on the part of the dealer, then the manufacturer may not be able to tell whether the dealer is living up to an implicit agreement, and an explicit agreement may be difficult or impossible to write or monitor. In such cases, the manufacturer may still prefer an unrestricted or imperfectly restricted monopoly dealer to having competitive dealers even though doing so runs counter to society's preferences.

Conclusions

I now summarize the results and consider their relevance for the antitrust treatment of exclusive franchising.

Where full integration is possible and easy, or where there are constant returns or near-constant returns to scale in distribution, the interests of the manufacturer coincide with those of society. In such cases it is to be presumed that setting up a monopoly dealer occurs for reasons of efficiency.

When, however, full integration is not possible and returns to scale in distribution appear to be decreasing, the conclusion reached may be different. In such cases, the question arises whether the manufacturer is achieving results equivalent to those of full integration in some way other than actually integrating. In the simplest case, for example, because the problem faced by a manufacturer with a monopoly dealer is one of output restriction, is the manufacturer imposing a minimum output or a maximum price restriction on the dealer? If so, the manufacturer may simply be achieving the fully integrated result in a different way; both he and society will prefer that result to one achieved with competitive dealers even if no efficiency considerations are involved.

Note the implication here. Although it is true that an important and sometimes controlling question is whether the manufacturer could have done the exclusive distributing himself, in cases in which that is not possible, certain kinds of *more* restrictive arrangements are to be preferred to less restrictive ones. This is particularly important when one leaves the simplest case of a single homogeneous good with all costs known and considers the possibility that selling a complex product line may involve the dealer exerting efforts in several dimensions, some of which may be observable to the manufacturer only imperfectly. In such a case, the advantages of full integration may not be achievable at all. If they are achievable, achievement may require placing quite detailed restrictions on the dealer. The analysis in this chapter suggests that, so long as manufacturer-imposed restrictions require the dealer to put forth greater rather than less effort, they are positively desirable.

Especially in complex cases, however, restrictions on the dealer may not allow the manufacturer to come close to achieving the equivalent of full integration. Where they do allow him to do so, and thus guarantee that society's interests are protected (in this second-best situation), franchise fees cannot be substantial, for the agreements will themselves siphon off dealer rents.

Where franchise fees are substantial, the principal result discussed in this chapter comes into play. A high franchise fee is a mechanism through which a manufacturer can extract rents from his monopoly dealer. Where rents that arise from decreasing returns in distribution due to externalities or different costs for different units of output, such an arrangement may be preferred by the manufacturer to a system of competitive dealers, even though no efficiency or marketing-incentive reasons are involved. Whereas it *may* be true that such preferences coincide with those of society, that result certainly is not inevitable. Such arrangements, therefore, should not be considered presumptively lawful; rather, the presence of a high franchise fee should signal the need for further investigation.

Notes

I am indebted to R. L. Bishop, P. A. Diamond, J. Farrell, G. Hay, E. Rasmusen, L. Solomon, and L. White for helpful comments but retain responsibility for error.

1. The possible relevance of the "free-rider" problem goes back to Telser's discussion of fair trade. See L. Telser, "Why Should Manufacturers Want Fair Trade?" *Journal of Law and Economics* 3 (October 1960), pp. 86–105. The discussion in the text ignores the possibility that the manufacturer enters into an exclusive dealing arrangement because the dealer himself has monopsony power either over the manufacturer's product or over other inputs needed to sell or service that product. In such a case, such monopsony power might itself raise antitrust questions, but those questions would not arise solely (or even primarily) because of the exclusive franchise itself.

2. See R. Bork, "The Rule of Reason and the *Per Se* Concept: Price-Fixing and Market Division (II)," *Yale Law Journal* 75, pp. 397–405, esp. 402–403; R. Posner, "Antitrust Policy and the Supreme Court: An Analysis of Restricted Distribution, Horizontal Merger and Potential Competition Decisions," *Columbia Law Review* 75 (1975), pp. 283–88; Case Comment, *Harvard Law Review* 88, (1975), p. 641; R. Bork, *The Antitrust Paradox* (New York: Basic Books, 1978), pp. 288–291; P. Areeda and D. Turner, *Antitrust Law* (Boston: Little, Brown, 1978), vol. 3, paras. 734a, 734d.

3. See G. F. Mathewson and R. A. Winter, "An Economic Theory of Vertical Restraints," *The Rand Journal of Economics* 15 (1984), pp. 27–28 (which appeared while this book was in press) for an analysis of the various instruments available to the manufacturer.

4. There is a strong family resemblance here to the variable proportions literature on vertical integration. See Richard Schmalensee, "A Note on the Theory of Vertical Integration," *Journal of Political Economy* 81 (1973), pp. 442–49; and Frederick R. Warren-Boulton, "Vertical Control with Variable Proportions," *Journal of Political Economy* 82 (1974), pp. 783–802. The constant-returns case can be thought of as one in which distributor input is required in fixed proportion to manufacturer output while the decreasing returns case corresponds to variable proportions.

5. All these "payments" of marginal costs, in fact, come from allowing the dealers a larger retail margin. The manufacturer sets that margin by setting the price to dealers and calculating what the resulting competitive-dealer retail price will be. In practice, the manufacturer may be able to offer dealers special incentives for special effort, thus, in effect, price discriminating in the margin offered for the distribution of different units of output. Such price discrimination is unlikely to be perfect, however. I ignore such phenomena.

6. Note that the strategy which leads to (5.5) appears to yield the maximum profits the manufacturer can obtain with a monopoly dealer. The question of whether this is so and of whether the manufacturer can do better and even attain the results of vertical integration with such an arrangement is discussed in the next section.

7. See note 2 above.

9

Mixing Regulatory and Antitrust Policies in the Electric Power Industry: The Price Squeeze and Retail Market Competition

Paul L. Joskow

John McGowan taught my first graduate course in antitrust policy and government regulation in the spring of 1969 when I was a student at Yale. He was also a reader of my Ph.D. thesis. As both a teacher and an advisor, John was a source of ideas and criticism, and he helped increase my interest in teaching and research in the areas of antitrust economics and public-utility regulation.

As recently as 1970, antitrust policy and public utility regulation were treated as vastly different subjects. Antitrust policies were (in theory, anyway) supposed to promote competition, whereas regulatory policies frequently restricted price competition and competitive entry. As a legal matter it was generally understood that regulated industries were immune to antitrust sanction.[1]

Beginning in the early 1970s the U.S. Supreme Court issued a number of decisions, which held that the antitrust laws could be applied to regulated industries lacking clear statutory exemptions, that regulation and antitrust policy (competition) are not necessarily repugnant, and that these policies may very well be complementary.[2] In recent years such regulated industries as telecommunications, electric power, and insurance have increasingly come under antitrust scrutiny, with the result that an extensive body of antitrust law has developed which deals with anticompetitive activities of regulated firms. During this same period there has been considerable discussion of regulatory and institutional changes that would allow market forces to replace economic regulation. Dramatic changes have taken place in telecommunications, and there is continuing interest in deregulation of certain components of the electric power industry.[3]

Efforts to mix antitrust policies designed to promote competition with regulatory policies that restrict it can cause numerous difficulties.

Although antitrust policy and regulatory policy are not necessarily "repugnant," conflicts between these public policies can and do arise. One of the strangest and most confusing sectors in which the antitrust laws were mixed with pervasive economic regulation is in the electric power sector. It is the application of the antitrust laws to the electric power industry that is discussed in this chapter.

The first section provides a brief discussion of the structure and regulation of the electric power industry. It is impossible to understand and evaluate the application of antitrust law to this industry without a complete understanding of the structure of the industry and its regulation. Here, the unusual mixture of private and public firms and the overlapping jurisdictions of state and federal regulatory authorities play a particularly important role in the evolution of antitrust policy. In this section I try to lay out all the relevant industry and regulatory characteristics necessary for understanding what *really* motivates antitrust litigation in this industry as well as for evaluating antitrust policies. In the next section I discuss what appears to be the basis for applying antitrust sanctions to the electric power industry, the general thrust of antitrust policy, and how antitrust responsibilities are shared by the courts and various regulatory agencies. The institutional setting for applying antitrust policies in the electric power industry is quite different from other industries, in part reflecting the fact that it is heavily regulated. Antitrust enforcement responsibility lies both with several federal regulatory agencies, which themselves have overlapping regulatory responsibilities, and the federal courts.

Next, I focus on a specific antitrust abuse—the price squeeze—which has been the source of substantial litigation since 1976. In the fourth section I evaluate the price-squeeze doctrine as it applies to regulated electric utilities and the underlying concern with promoting competition in retail electricity markets that has been the primary foundation for applying antitrust laws to the electric utility industry. I conclude that the conceptual framework within which antitrust policy has evolved is seriously flawed. The great quantity of litigation motivated by concerns about "price squeezes" in particular and retail market competition in general has had no positive efficiency consequences; it is at best a waste of time and litigation expense and at worst a source of inefficiency. In reality, application of the antitrust laws to the electric utility industry has had little to do with competition. Primarily it reflects conflicts between public and private firms and efforts to use the threat of antitrust litigation to exact rate concessions in regulatory proceedings and force low-cost suppliers to share their resources with less efficient firms. Antitrust policy can play a productive role in this industry, but it must proceed from a different conceptual framework, one that recognizes where competition can play a productive role in increasing economic efficiency and where it cannot, one that must be much more sensitive to the limited efficiency-enhancing role competition and associated antitrust policies can play in this industry, given its current structure and regulation.

Structure and Regulation of the Electric Power Industry

It is impossible to understand or evaluate the application of the antitrust laws to the electric utility industry without first understanding the peculiar structure of the industry and the various local, state, and federal regulations that define the arena in which competition does or can take place. In this section[4] I discuss what I believe are the critical industry and regulatory characteristics for understanding and evaluating the application of the antitrust laws. I will draw on many of these facts in the remainder of this chapter.

The firms that make up the electric power industry are diverse with regard to size, extent of vertical integration, and form of ownership. About 3,500 firms play some role in supplying electricity. They include privately owned utilities (IOUs), municipal utilities (munis), cooperative utilities (coops), federal agencies, and state and county power authorities and utility districts. Normally defined, the industry includes everything from firms that distribute electricity to several thousand residential and small commercial customers and that rely on others to provide generation and transmission services, to large integrated utilities that serve millions of residential, commercial, and industrial customers and that own and operate the generating and transmission facilities that make up large, coordinated electric power networks spanning several states.[5] (I refer to the former as distribution companies and to the latter as integrated firms.)

IOUs account for over 75 percent of power produced and number of customers served at retail. The term "retail sales" refers to all electricity sales except transactions between utilities. When I refer to "retail markets," I am talking about sales by utilities to final consumers. Sales by one utility to another are referred to as "wholesale transactions," or quite commonly, "sales for resale." When I refer to "wholesale markets," I am talking about sales between utilities. There are about 250

IOUs, although the 35 largest account for over 60 percent of IOU generating capacity. The top 100 account for about 95 percent of IOU generating capacity. The IOUs that account for the great majority of industry sales are vertically integrated firms that own and operate generating plants, transmission networks, and distribution systems. They produce electricity for sale to their own retail customers as well as to other utilities (wholesale customers), including extensive sales to unintegrated municipal and cooperative distribution companies.

Most of the antitrust litigation in the industry involves behavior at the wholesale level, which supposedly restricts competition at the retail level. It is difficult to estimate precisely how much of the electricity produced by IOUs is associated with wholesale transactions. For reporting purposes, wholesale transactions are grouped in two categories: sales for resale and interchange transactions. The former includes various transactions in which the buyer and the seller have a conventional "one-way" sales/purchase relationship; the latter includes ongoing short-term power exchanges between interconnected utilities in which one party to the transaction may be buying power one day from a neighboring utility and selling it another day to that utility. These exchanges are both a natural and a necessary consequence of the economic operation of interconnected systems and power pools made up of separate corporate entities that are generally much smaller than is necessary to achieve all supply-side economies. The Department of Energy (DOE) reports "sales for resale" equal to 18 percent of total sales by IOUs and about 20 percent of net generation. This figure includes all sales under "requirements' contracts as well as one-way transactions under a variety of coordination contracts. About 60 percent of sales for resale involve transactions between IOUs, primarily coordination transactions of various types. Thus about 8 percent of IOU generation is attributable to sales for resale to publicly owned utilities.[6] It is these sales that have been a major focus of antitrust litigation in the electric power industry.[7]

There are over 2,000 municipal utilities, state and county power districts, and municipal joint-action agencies. Municipal utilities account for less than 4 percent of total U.S. electricity generation. They are frequently (but not always) small, unintegrated distribution entities that rely on other public and private producing entities to provide them with all or substantially all of their power requirements.[8] State and county power authorities, power districts, and joint-action agencies account for over 5 percent of industry generation. The systems that fall in this category are diverse and include utilities that are primarily distributors as well as utilities that are primarily wholesale power suppliers. Municipal utilities are exempt from federal and, generally, state and local income and property taxes, and they can raise capital in the municipal bond market. In lieu of tax, payments are sometimes made.[9]

Some 1,000 cooperative utilities are organized under the Rural Electrification Act (REA) of 1936. This category includes cooperative distribution companies which generate none of their own power as well as cooperative generation and transmission (G&T) companies which produce power for resale to cooperative (coop) distribution companies. Coops account for less than 3 percent of total industry generation. Coop distribution companies rely heavily on power supplied by federal power systems and IOUs. Historically, these entities have been eligible for federally subsidized investment funds; as nonprofit organizations, they are exempt from federal and, generally, state and local income taxes.

Finally, there are six federal power systems, which account for over 10 percent of total industry generation. About 70 percent of their production consists of sales for resale, primarily to munis and coops; about 30 percent is accounted for by sales to large industrial customers. Five of these systems market power produced by federal dams for resale by public and private utilities engaged in retail distribution; they also make direct sales to large industrial customers. The facilities are financed by federal appropriations. Pricing policies are determined by statute, which provides that prices be the lowest possible consistent with sound business practice.[10] The sixth system is the Tennessee Valley Authority (TVA), which is engaged in the production and transmission of electricity over a seven-state region. Like the other systems, TVA originally relied exclusively on hydroelectric sites; but it is now primarily a coal and nuclear steam-generating utility. TVA supplies power to about 160 cooperative and municipal utilities for resale, to about 50 large industrial customers, and to federal agencies.[11]

In terms of retail sales, a substantially larger fraction of IOU retail load tends to be accounted for by large industrial and commercial customers taking power at high voltage than is the case for the typical small muni or coop involved in antitrust litigation. The munis and coops tend to serve primarily residential, agricultural, and small commercial customers. About 40 percent of IOU KWH sales go to large industrial customers. Excluding direct sales to industry by federal agencies and the Power Authority of the State of New York (PASNY), about 24 percent of the public sector's retail load is industrial. The munis and coops typically involved in antitrust cases frequently have few large industrial customers.

The Federal Power Act contains various preference provisions that affect allocation of "cheap" hydroelectric power and the relicensing of hydroelectric sites.[12] As a general matter, publicly owned utilities have first preference for power produced by federal hydroelectric projects. Usually this power is substantially less expensive than power produced by conventional power plants, since federal hydroelectric power, though scarce, is sold to recover operating costs (nil) and low historical book investment plus interest amortized over many years. Controversy over the allocation of "preference power" between publicly owned and privately owned utilities, as well as direct-service industrial customers, has increased over time as the demand by preference customers has increased and hydro sites licensed to and developed by private utilities in the 1920s and 30s have begun to come up for relicensing. Conflicts over access to preference power sometimes plays an important role in motivating antitrust litigation.

State and local laws (at least de facto) generally preclude direct competition by utilities for retail customers in a particular geographical area.[13] With a few exceptions, customers can purchase electricity at retail from only one utility. Monopoly supply at the retail level generally reflects the widely held belief that distribution is a natural monopoly in any geographical area and that allowing multiple distribution companies to serve an area is inefficient.[14]

The details of restrictions on entry and direct competition vary from state to state. IOUs generally operate under state charters and distribute electricity to municipalities and other government subdivisions pursuant to local franchises and various state authorizations (certificates of convenience and necessity, territorial restrictions, allocation of unincorporated territories, approvals of acquisitions of other utilities with operating franchises, and so on). The technical terms and conditions of distribution franchises vary substantially from state to state, however. In some states franchises are exclusive and of indefinite duration. In most states franchises technically are nonexclusive and, depending on the state and time the original franchise was awarded, have durations varying from ten years to an indefinite term. In many states the geographical boundaries of service territories are fixed by state law or regulations. Although distribution franchises are frequently nonexclusive, multiple franchises are rarely awarded and utilities typically operate with de facto exclusive distribution franchises. State laws frequently bar the granting of multiple franchises if a firm is already providing service to the area. Procedures for terminating franchises and refranchising practices are usually subject to both local and state regulations. In about forty states a certificate of convenience and necessity from the state public utility commission is required for an IOU to serve an area or extend service into another area [15] In short entry into the business supplying electric power to a particular geographical area (especially for IOUs) is sharply constrained by state law.[16] Transfers of distribution franchises by government entities with franchising authority, arising from competition between two or more alternative distribution companies (this excludes mergers of IOUs), occur rarely, and actual head-to-head competition for retail customers between two or more utilities permitted to serve the same geographical area is extremely unusual.

IOUs are subject to economic regulation by state public utility commissions and the Federal Energy Regulatory Commission (FERC, formerly the Federal Power Commission). Retail rates are subject to the exclusive jurisdiction of state regulatory commissions (except for some provisions of the Public Utility Regulatory Policy Act of 1978). All states with IOUs have set up independent regulatory agencies to regulate rate levels, rate structures, and service quality. Most state commissions operate under the general mandate to set rates that are just, reasonable, fair, and nondiscriminatory. Basically, both the average level and the structure of prices are supposed to be based on the "prudent" costs of providing service, including a fair return on equity investment. Different prices are normally set for customers with different demand characterisitcs (voltage level at which power is taken, peaking characteristics, average load factor, and so on), based on a wide variety of "fully allocated cost" techniques. Application of marginal cost-pricing techniques for determining rate structures has been on the increase, but they have not received wide acceptance. The per-kwh "delivered" price typically is highest for residential and small commercial customers who take power at low voltages, requiring investment in low-voltage distribution facilities with relatively large line losses, and who have relatively poor load factors. Rates are lowest for large industrial customers who take power at high voltages, make no use of the bulk of the distribution system, and have relatively high load factors.

The price differences (at least roughly) reflect differences in costs between customer classes.

An IOU's financial performance typically depends primarily on state regulation, since most of a typical IOU's operating costs, capital facilities, and revenue are associated with serving its retail customers. The volume of wholesale power transactions has been increasing over time, however, and it is likely to increase further in the future. This increase is most likely to take place in the area of sales between integrated utilities rather than sales under requirements contracts to publicly owned distribution systems. Despite the legal distinction between "retail sales" (regulated by the states) and "wholesale sales" (regulated by the FERC), essentially there is no functional distinction between generation and transmission facilities dedicated to retail and wholesale transactions. Distinctions made to satisfy dual regulation of integrated utilities, depending on whether a particular rate schedule is for sales to retail customers directly (state regulation) or for sales to another utility (federal regulation), are based on complicated accounting conventions designed somehow to allocate joint costs between federal and state jurisdications to reflect cost responsibility. Because wholesale transactions involve transfers of power at high voltages, costs associated with distribution and retail customer costs (metering, billing, etc.) are never allocated to wholesale rates. Unlike the traditional practice followed by the Federal Communications Commission in setting long-distance telephone rates, no costs associated with the "local loop" for distributing electricity to retail customers are allocated to wholesale transactions subject to federal jurisdiction.

Wholesale transactions by IOUs (purchases and sales of electricity between utilities) are subject to rate regulation by the FERC under the Federal Power Act. As with the state regulatory statutes, the Federal Power Act contains a broad requirement that rates be just, reasonable, and nondiscriminatory. For "conventional" wholesale contracts (full and partial requirements contracts), the FERC uses rate-making techniques similar to those used by most of the states. A customer purchasing power under these wholesale tariffs typically is a coop, muni, or small private distribution company that does not maintain sufficient generating capacity to satisfy its own load. Because generation or transmission facilities are rarely dedicated exclusively to the wholesale market, the FERC must allocate a utility's costs between the wholesale market (jurisdictional) and the retail market (nonjurisdictional), taking into account the load characteristics of wholesale customers as a group.[17]

The FERC then establishes wholesale rates for different types of wholesale customers, based on differences in their costs of service. Overall, wholesale rates are set to cover "prudent" costs, including a fair rate of return on investment.

Because any individual utility normally has a relatively small number of wholesale requirements customers, the FERC encourages negotiated settlements of changes in the terms of wholesale power contracts, which require commission approval but help reduce administrative delay. Historically, negotiated contracts were frequent and rate increases rare (indeed, long-term, fixed-price contracts were not infrequent during the 1950s and 60s), but litigation seems to have increased in recent years as cost increases and associated wholesale rate increase requests have become more frequent. It is these wholesale requirements contracts that have been the subject of substantial antitrust scrutiny under the price-squeeze doctrine.

The FERC also regulates a wide variety of other wholesale power transactions involving sales by IOUs (unit power sales, economy exchanges, emergency power contracts, short-term energy and capacity transactions, power pooling arrangements, etc). These contracts usually are referred to as "coordination transactions" to distinguish them from "requirements contracts." Typically, they involve transactions between utilities that ordinarily maintain sufficient generating capacity (via sole ownership or joint ownership) to meet their own loads and include transactions categorized as sales for resale as well as all interchange transactions. These contracts typically involve transactions between integrated IOUs rather than transactions between IOUs and the various publicly owned entities. These wholesale transactions often are consummated as a result of negotiation between the parties involved. Although the FERC requires that the terms and justifications (including cost justifications) of the contracts be filed with the commission, they are rarely challenged unless a third party (such as a state PUC) objects and are often approved upon staff review without lengthy administrative procedures.

The FERC had developed general guidelines for evaluating this wide array of (nonrequirements) IOU wholesale contractual arrangements and has, by design or accident, permitted evolution of contract terms which in a number of cases (especially for short-term transactions not involving capacity charges and in the case of unit sales contracts) lead to prices roughly based on the relevant incremental costs of a particular type of transaction. (Unfortunately, this is not true of full and partial requirements contracts.) Although there is still room for improvement, the terms of these wholesale transactions come closer to being based on the relevant marginal costs of the exchange than in any other aspect of electric power rate-making, whether wholesale or retail.[18] Wholesale transactions other than the typical requirements type of contract also occur in the closest thing to a market that exists anywhere in the electric power industry. Relatively loose regulation of nonrequirements transactions and encouragment of bilateral negotiation have allowed a wholesale market of sorts to develop for consummating this type of transaction. This "regulated market" is becoming increasingly important as a mechanism for allocating bulk electricity supplies efficiently among the many firms engaged in the production of electricity.

Rates charged on sales by the federal power-marketing agencies are subject to limited FERC scrutiny.[19] Prices charged by REA G&Ts are not regulated by any federal agency, and the U.S. Supreme Court recently held that a state may regulate such wholesale transactions.[20] Wholesale transactions by municipal utilities and other state and federal agencies are exempt from FERC rate regulation.

Economic regulation of municipal utilities varies substantially from state to state. In some nine states, municipal utilities are subject to rate regulation by the state public utilities commission. In about twenty-two states municipal service to customers outside the geographical boundaries of the municipality (sometimes with a three- to five-mile exclusion zone) is subject to state rate regulation.[21] Cooperative utilities are subject to the rules and regulations of the Rural Electrification Administration. In several states coop distribution company rates are regulated by the state public utilities commission. In about twenty-five states coops require a certificate of convenience and necessity to provide service to a particular area.

Application of Antitrust Laws to Electric Utilities

It is now established law that regulated firms are subject to antitrust laws unless there is a clear statutory exemption. The pre-1970s view that the behavior of regulated firms is subject to an implicit "state action" immunity has been narrowed considerably.[22] The courts *may* determine that certain behavior that might otherwise be deemed a violation of the antitrust laws in an unregulated industry is immune from antitrust prosecution if the behavior is approved by a regulatory agency with the intent of overriding the antitrust laws or is compelled by a state or federal regulatory agency and is actively supervised by that agency.[23] A mere showing that the subject behavior is, in principle, subject to regulation is not enough. The narrowing of regulated firms' immunity to the antitrust laws, absent specific statutory exemption, reflects the belief that regulation is imperfect, that any residual competition not restricted by regulation is likely to be beneficial and not inconsistent with regulatory objectives, and that the regulatory process can be manipulated to restrict competition, permitting regulated firms to obtain and exercise monopoly power.

IOU's are subject to antitrust scrutiny in several different forums. The government and private parties can bring Sherman Act (and almost certainly Robinson Patman Act) cases against IOUs.[24] Mergers are subject to approval by the FERC (Section 203 of the Federal Power Act) and in the case of public utility holding companies by the SEC under the Public Utility Holding Company Act of 1935 and state laws which give state PUCs the power to approve mergers and acquisitions.

The Atomic Energy Act requires the Nuclear Regulatory Commission to consider the effects of licensing new nuclear power plants on competition in areas where the plants are to be built; and the commission may attach terms and conditions to licenses to ameliorate existing or potential restrictions on competion.[25] The prelicensing review process requires the Department of Justice to review each application for a license to construct and operate a nuclear power plant regarding its antitrust consequences and to provide advice to the NRC. The Justice Department has interpreted this mandate broadly, and prelicense reviews frequently have become comprehensive reviews of a private utility's relationship with "competing" utilities (typically small munis and coops that purchase power from the applicant).[26]

In addition to specific statutory provisions for regulatory agency antitrust review contained in some regulatory statutes, the courts have interpreted the public interest and just, reasonable, and nondiscriminatory provisions of the Federal Power Act and provisions of the Public Utilities Holding Company Act (e.g., 15 USC 79) to require the FERC and the SEC to evaluate the antitrust consequences of their decisions regarding, for example, rates, securities issues, mergers, interconnections, and power pools.[27] Thus antitrust issues can be raised before these federal regulatory agencies in the context of virtually any utility action that requires regulatory agency approval. The agencies' decisions necessarily are subject to review by the federal courts. Regulatory commission review of particular antitrust issues in the context of a rate proceeding or approval of a securities issue *does not* preclude traditional antitrust remedies. In the case of price-squeeze charges, FERC cases and Sherman Act cases are sometimes brought concurrently.[28]

The complex, overlapping web of antitrust scrutiny of regulated electric utilities that has evolved in the past decade provides parties who feel they have been damaged by the alleged anticompetitive behavior of an electric utility many more legal opportunities to challenge that behavior than are afforded parties who purchase from, supply to, or compete with unregulated firms. Essentially, all antitrust litigation in the electric power industry pits small muni or coop distribution companies against integrated IOUs. The companies can: raise antitrust objections in FERC rate proceedings; appeal an FERC decision through the federal courts; raise the same issues with the Justice Department in a NRC prelicensing antitrust review; or bring an antitrust suit in the federal courts.[29]

If any general competitive rationale underlies application of the antitrust laws to the electric utility industry during the past ten or fifteen years, it appears to be something like the following. Competition has an important supplementary role to play in constraining pricing and the costs of regulated electric utilities, especially at the retail (distribution) level. The increasing concentration that has characterized the electric utility industry since early in the century, but especially in the twenty years after World War II, threatened the viability of these competitive market forces. Integrated IOUs often had monopoly power at both retail and wholesale levels and were engaged in a variety of activities to increase that power. Mergers between private firms and takovers by IOUs of muni and coop distribution franchises were leading to increased concentration and diminishing retail and wholesale competition. Large IOUs were engaged in a wide range of activities to drive smaller competing utilities from the market. As we will see, this rationale is based on faulty understanding of the role of retail competition in this industry and does not provide a sound basis for antitrust policy. This conceptualization of the issues, however, has led to two broad policies that have been pursued to maintain "competition":

1. Mergers between integrated private utilities were to be discouraged unless a persuasive case could be made that the merger would lead to lower costs and rates and not reduce competition.[30] To the extent that firms were too small to achieve all economies of scale and

coordination internally (as they almost always are), regulatory authorities assumed that joint ventures and power pooling generally are
superior alternatives to mergers that would help to achieve these
economies without increasing concentration and (supposedly) maintaining competition at both the wholesale and the retail level.[31]

2. Small distribution companies that purchased all or substantially
all of their power from neighboring, integrated IOUs had to be protected in order to maintain competition in the retail market. These
companies were too small to economically produce their own power
internally. If they were to survive, they had to have access to power
supplies from larger, integrated firms and power pools. The large,
integrated IOUs supposedly had much to gain by reducing competition
in the retail market and could use their monopoly power in the wholesale market (assuming they had such power) to drive small distribution
companies from the market (forcing them to sell out to their integrated
suppliers), increasing the integrated IOUs monopoly power at the retail
level.

Merger policies aside, historically, almost all antitrust disputes involving electric power firms have been disputes between relatively
small munis and coops and integrated IOUs. The result is that most of
the antitrust law that has evolved in the last ten years has focused on
preserving what I believe is largely nonexistent competition in the
retail market by maintaining the viability of small publicly owned
distribution companies. To accomplish this, antitrust authorities have
tried to constrain the use of various alleged "foreclosure" and "predatory" practices by IOUs that supposedly have monopoly power in
both wholesale and retail markets. The evolution of the price-squeeze
doctrine applied to electric utilities is the starkest conceptualization of
the public interest associated with preserving retail competition and
the need to use antitrust sanctions to constrain predatory behavior by
IOUs aimed at monopolizing retail markets.

Application of the Price-Squeeze Doctrine to Electric Utilities

I have chosen to focus on the price-squeeze doctrine here for several
reasons. It represents an antitrust issue the consideration of which was
imposed on the FERC by the U.S. Supreme Court (rather than by statute)
and which subsequently became a source of considerable conventional
antitrust litigation. The evolution of this doctrine also provides some
interesting insights into the problems of dual application of the anti-

trust laws to regulated electric utilities by federal regulatory agencies and the courts. These problems include the administrative delay and confusion engendered by imposing new antitrust responsibilities on an existing regulatory process, difficulties the courts and regulatory agencies have in harmonizing regulatory rules and procedures with conventional antitrust doctrines and real conflicts between the primary statutory requirements under which regulatory agencies operate and court interpretations of additional antitrust responsibilities. In this particular case dual regulation of electric utilities by state and federal agencies raises additional public policy conflicts. Finally, I believe that the concern about price squeezes as a source of anticompetitive harm in this industry and the enormous amount of litigation that has resulted in the past few years are the result of a misunderstanding of the nature of competition in the electric power industry and the role competition now plays or can play in promoting economic efficiency. The price-squeeze doctrine as applied to the electric power industry represents a body of antitrust law in search of a real anticompetitive problem. Similar problems pervade the current application of the antitrust laws generally to the electric utility industry.

The concept of the "price squeeze" as a monopolizing device was introduced into antitrust law by Learned Hand in the *Alcoa* case.[32] As it is generally conceptualized, for a price squeeze to take place we need a firm with substantial monopoly power in an upstream market (virgin ingot, in the case of Alcoa) that integrates forward into one or more downstream markets which use the upstream product as an input (the production of aluminum sheet, in the case of Alcoa). The firm with monopoly power in the upstream market then becomes both a supplier to firms in the downstream markets it has integrated into and a direct competitor with them. A price squeeze is said to take place when the monopoly input supplier charges a price for the input to its down-stream competitors that is so high they cannot profitably sell the downstream product in competition with the integrated firm. The integrated firm implicitly charges itself much less for the input than it charges its competitors. By engaging in a price squeeze, the integrated firm can drive its downstream competitors out of the market and "extend" its monopoly in the upstream market into the downstream market.

In *Alcoa*, Judge Hand proposed what has become known as the "transfer price test," designed to determine whether the integrated firm had engaged in a price squeeze. Simply put, this test required that the courts examine whether the integrated firm could have sold its downstream output profitably at prevailing prices, *assuming* it had to pay the same price for the input it produced internally as it charged to its downstream competitors. A price squeeze would be said to exist if the integrated supplier could not sell its downstream products (the production of aluminum sheet, in the case of Alcoa) profitably, assuming it had to pay a "transfer price" equal to what it was charging for the input (virgin ingot, in the case of Alcoa) in the market. Judge Hand's notion was that if the monopoly supplier of the input was able to market a downstream product profitably, based on its internal costs of production, but could not produce its downstream output profitably if it purchased the input at the prices it charged to its competitors, neither could its competitors, and they would be "squeezed" from the market as a result of the higher market prices for the input.[33]

Alcoa's vertical integration into the fabrication market and the price-squeeze has sometimes been cited in the antitrust literature as a way for monopolists to "foreclose" competition and "extend" their monopoly power from one market to another. Critics of this view have often argued that vertical integration and foreclosure are not necessary for a firm with a monopoly in an upstream market to fully exercise its monopoly power. They claim that the monopoly can extract all the monopoly rents simply by charging the monopoly price directly for the input (in this case, exploiting the derived demand for ingot) and that vertical integration is likely to be a consequence of increased efficiency which has nothing directly to do with monopoly power in the upstream market, rather than a vehicle for fuller exploitation of monopoly power. Both the traditional "foreclosure" doctrine and the initial critiques of it are now generally acknowledged to be incorrect. Although standard efficiencies often associated with vertical integration may be the primary motivation for integration by an upstream monopolist, a firm with monopoly power over an input will find it profitable to integrate forward, lacking conventional integration efficiencies, when the downstream production process uses inputs in variable proportions and, more relevant to the *Alcoa* case, as a vehicle for engaging in price discrimination.[34]

A comprehensive, theoretical analysis of the price-discrimination argument for vertical integration has recently been provided by Martin K. Perry.[35] In Perry's model a monopolist in an upstream market will find it profitable to integrate forward into certain downstream markets when the final goods have different demand elasticities. In particular, the monopolist will integrate into markets where demand elasticity is greatest and will sell on the open market where elasticity of demand is smallest. The price for the inputs sold on the open market is higher than the price the monopolist would have charged had it not been integrated and higher than the "implicit" transfer price that supports the prices charged for downstream products produced internally. This permits the monopolist to exploit differences in elasticity of demand in *different* downstream markets, rather than working with the derived demand for the input in the aggregate, to engage in third-degree price discrimination, thus increasing its profits. In principle, the unintegrated upstream monopolist could do this by charging different prices for ingot to downstream buyers producing different products but with no way to prevent resale, such a strategy would fail. By vertically integrating, the monopolist avoids the resale problem.

As a *consequence* of vertical integration and downstream price discrimination, the integrated firm also "squeezes" its competitors in the markets it has integrated into, because they can buy only the input in the open market at the higher prices set to exploit the low-demand elasticities of the remaining, unintegrated downstream markets. As a result, they are unable to compete in the downstream markets the monopoly supplier has integrated into. The welfare consequences of this integration, given the existence of an upstream monopolist and ignoring income distribution effects, is unclear. However, the resulting price squeeze is not itself a predatory tactic designed to reduce or "foreclose" competition in downstream markets; it is a result of monopoly power in the upstream market and the use of vertical integration as a vehicle for price discrimination to more fully exploit monopoly power in the upstream market.

Price squeezes such as those identified in *Alcoa* have not proven to be an important source of antitrust litigation in unregulated industries; nor, apparently, is it considered a serious anticompetitive problem there. A leading industrial organization text neither mentions price-squeezes in general nor with regard to *Alcoa*.[36] Until the Supreme Court's decision in *Conway* in 1976, the price-squeeze problem was, for all intents and purposes, a moribund antitrust issue.

Price-Squeeze Considerations within the Regulatory Process

In 1976 the U.S. Supreme Court, in a unanimous decision, resurrected the price-squeeze issue as an antitrust concern in evaluating the regulated prices charged by integrated electric utilities to their wholesale customers.[37] *Conway* involved a suit brought by nine small municipal and cooperative distribution companies which purchased all or most of their power at wholesale from Arkansas Power & Light Company (AP&L) at rates regulated by the Federal Power Commission (now the FERC).

In 1973 AP&L filed new wholesale rate proposals with the FPC that would have increased wholesale rates to Conway and others by 22 percent to 35 percent. AP&L's wholesale customers intervened to oppose the rate increases, and the FPC suspended the new rates for review pursuant to section 206(a) of the Federal Power Act. In addition to the normal objections to a proposed rate increase raised by wholesale customers in an FPC proceeding (e.g., allowable costs, allocation of costs between wholesale and retail jurisdictions, fair rate of return, rate base items), the intervenors asked that the rates be set aside because they represented "an attempt to squeeze petitioners or some of them out of competition, and to make them more susceptible to the persistent attempts of the company to take over the publicly owned systems in the state." In particular, they argued that they competed with AP&L for large industrial customers, that AP&L's wholesale rates were above the retail rates charged to its large industrial customers, and that, as a result, the petitioners were being squeezed out of the market to serve large industrial customers at retail. Although the focus was on comparative wholesale/retail rates for large industrial customers and the associated competition for such customers (as have most subsequent price-squeeze cases), both the complaint and the courts were apparently concerned with *retail* competition in general.

The FPC accepted the petitioners' motion to intervene based on the conventional objections to wholesale rate changes but rejected an evaluation of the new wholesale rates based on the relationship between the wholesale rates and the retail rates for large industrial customers and the associated anticompetitive effects of the alleged price squeeze. The FPC argued that since it had no jurisdiction over retail rates regulated by the states and therefore could not control the level of retail rates, such a comparison was beyond its statutory mandate.[38] All it could do was try to set "just and reasonable" wholesale rates that appropriately reflect the cost of providing wholesale service. Once the FPC determined that a particular wholesale rate schedule appropriately reflected the cost of providing service, the commission reasoned that it would violate its statutory responsibilities under the

Federal Power Act to reduce the rate below cost to alleviate any squeeze.

An appeals court agreed that the FPC had no jurisdiction over retail rates.[39] However, it rejected the FPC's claims that it could not consider the anticompetitive effects of the alleged price squeeze resulting from a disparity between jurisdictional (wholesale) and nonjurisdictional (retail) rates. The court held that AP&L was both a supplier of the municipal and cooperative utilities and a competitor for retail customers, and that by allowing AP&L to maintain wholesale rates above retail rates, it would be "impossible for petitioners to maintain parity with AP&L in competing for retail customers." The difference between wholesale and retail rates would "inevitably and immediately affect the context in which long-term contracts will be bargained for, and relatively irrevocable location decisions will be made by potential industrial customers. "The court argued further that without FPC consideration of the issue there would be a "regulatory gap," with no agency considering "undue preference between wholesale and retail rates, even where the preference was deliberately instituted for the purposes of clogging competition...." As a result the appeals court held that the FPC must consider the alleged price-squeeze resulting from a disparity between wholesale and retail rates and that if a price-squeeze were found must reduce wholesale rates to try to eliminate it. The court suggested that there is not a single "cost-recovering rate" but a "zone of reasonableness" and that the commission could reduce the wholesale rate to the lower end of the zone to mitigate the disparity between jurisdictional and nonjurisdictional rates. The court left open the question of what would happen if the rate disparity could not be eliminated by setting wholsale rates at the lower end of the zone of reasonableness. The U.S. Supreme Court affirmed the Court of Appeals and ordered the FPC to consider the existence and anticompetitive effects of disparities between wholesale and retail rates.[40]

Since 1976 the FERC and the federal courts have been moving down a circuitous, time-consuming and confusing path to develop procedures for implementing *Conway*. At the time *Conway* was decided by the U.S. Supreme Court, the FERC had a large backlog of wholesale-rate cases pending in various states of consideration, as well as new rate filings coming in regularly. Following *Conway*, municipal and coop wholesale customers raised price-squeeze objections in many pending cases as well as in new filings. The FERC was now required to make findings on the price-squeeze charges before any rate cases could be disposed of.

As a result, some rate filings have been in litigation for nearly a decade. Conflicting interpretations of ever-changing FERC price-squeeze criteria by administrative law judges have been common and have resulted in considerable confusion. At least one federal appeals court became so confused that it had to substantially alter its decision in one case upon rehearing.[41] Substantial litigation expenses have been incurred by utilities supplying power to muni and coop customers at wholesale, by the FERC, and by customer-intervenors. The price-squeeze claims before the FERC have frequently spawned simultaneous Sherman Act cases in the federal courts. Despite all this litigation, as this is written, the FERC has found a price-squeeze situation to exist only once and in that case identified mitigating circumstances which led it to conclude that no remedies were required.

The efforts of the FERC to integrate the courts' concern about the anticompetitive effects of price squeezes in the regulatory process provides an interesting case study of bureaucratic adaptation to court-imposed administrative procedures which the regulatory agency felt it did not and should not have responsibility for dealing with and which was perceived to conflict with its primary, statutory mandate. Because the FERC had to consider price-squeeze charges in pending rate cases and new rate cases during a period of time when it was inundated with wholesale rate increase requests, it moved quickly (perhaps too quickly) to develop general guidelines for resolving the price-squeeze charges.

In Order No. 563 the commission provided guidelines for establishing a prima facie price-squeeze case.[42] The commission proceeds in two stages. Under the guidelines it requires wholesale customers who object to a rate on price-squeeze grounds to show that a price-squeeze situation may exist by showing that the filing utility and the wholesale customer are in competition with one another, by specifying which retail rate schedules the wholesale customer competes with, showing that the retail rates identified are lower than the *proposed* wholesale rates, and indicating the reduction in the wholesale rate required to bring the retail and wholesale rates into parity.[43] If the wholesale customers can establish that the conditions identified by the guidelines exist, more complete price-squeeze procedures are triggered which allow the parties and the staff to completely litigate the issue.[44] The threshold necessary to trigger a more complete investigation appears to be quite low.

In a series of cases beginning in 1977, the FERC and the courts have wrestled with questions involving exactly what the FERC had to take into account, once a prima facie case had been made, to determine whether a price squeeze existed, whether a price-squeeze situation resulted in any competitive harm (undue discrimination), whether there were mitigating circumstances that might justify an apparent price squeeze, and what remedies to apply if an anticompetitive price squeeze was found.

Initially the FERC suggested the need for a broad inquiry into the extent of competition between the parties, the measurement of anti-competitive effects, the intent of the supplying utility, the appropriate way to measure a price squeeze, the role of state commission regulation in creating the price squeeze, remedies and so on.[45] This quickly became an administrative nightmare, as each case began to look like a full-blown Sherman Act investigation with records being developed on numerous issues of competition, measurement, dual regulation, and remedies.

Over time the FERC has substantially narrowed its inquiry. The commission has held that the issue of anticompetitive intent was not relevant under *Conway* and eliminated it from the inquiry.[46] The commission has minimized the inquiry into the extent of competition by effectively assuming that a wholesale supplier and its customers are in competition with one another for retail customers if they are in geographical proximity to one another and can potentially supply power to both new and existing customers.[47] The standard here is loose, and there is a de facto presumption of competition between suppliers and their distribution system customers. Likewise, the issue of competitive harm has been sidestepped; for all intents and purposes, competitive harm is presumed if the supplier and its wholesale customers are found to compete for retail loads and a price squeeze lasting more than a few months is found to exist.[48] As I shall argue, these developments, while administratively convenient, are unfortunate in terms of appropriate antitrust evaluation, because meaningful competition at the retail level is the exception rather than the rule.

Assuming that a prima facie price-squeeze case can be made by a distribution company customer, the presence of a price squeeze turns on the appropriate measurement criteria and circumstances under which the price-squeeze, if one is found, arose. The FERC has not yet had to deal with appropriate remedies. The primary issue the FERC and the courts have had to address is the proper empirical method to use for identifying a price squeeze. Two subissues are involved here: (1) What should be the *structure* of the price-squeeze computation? (How should the "transfer price test" in *Alcoa* be applied?); and (2) Which wholesale and retail rates should be used for comparison purposes, filed wholesale rates in effect subject to refund plus interest or the final "reasonable but for price squeeze" rates?

Wholesale customers initially argued for a simple variant of the "transfer price test" used in *Alcoa*. This normally involved a simple comparison between the wholesale rate and the retail rate for large industrial customers which the distribution company would "qualify" for by virtue of its minimum billing demand. In some cases this proposed test has involved a simple comparison between wholesale and "equivalent" retail rates, and in some cases adjustments have been made to subtract the distribution-cost component of the retail rate used for comparison. Superficially, such an approach makes sense. Distribution-system customers argue that they can't possibly compete for retail customers if they have to purchase power at a rate higher than the rate charged to large industrial customers at retail by the supplying utility.[49]

The commission has rejected this approach and similar variants, however, taking (correctly) the position that it is inappropriate to make simple, direct comparison between retail rates available to various classes of industrial customers and the wholesale rate available to different types of wholesale customers (a supplying utility often has different rates for full- and partial-requirements customers, different rates for munis and coops, and so on, each incorporating a "rate profile" that yields a different average price for purchasers with different demand characteristics). The commission and its staff have argued that rates for large industrial customers and wholesale customers are not necessarily comparable merely because a wholesale customer "qualifies" for the rate by virtue of its minimum billing demand. Implicitly, the commission has taken the position that, unlike the situation in *Alcoa*, the "product" being sold under a wholesale-requirements contract is not necessarily the same as the "product" being sold to large industrial customers. The two products may have different costs, and any such cost differences should be taken into account in determining whether price discrimination exists and whether it results in a price-squeeze situation. As a class, the munis and coops that normally bring price-squeeze charges tend to have very different demand characteristics than large industrial customers. The demand characteristics of a wholesale customer depend on the aggregate demand characteristics of its retail customers. Muni and coop intervenors tend to serve primarily residential and small commercial customers with different peaking and load-duration characteristics than large industrial customers.[50]

In setting wholesale rates and for evaluating price-squeeze charges, the commission attempts to account for differences in the demand characteristics of different classes of customers (wholesale and retail), the relationship between different demand characteristics and the cost of serving different groups of customers, and attempts to allocate costs among customer classes to take into account "cost responsibility." A price squeeze resulting from price discrimination between wholesale and retail customers now will be found only if the commission finds that the rate differential *is not cost-justified*.

To perform its price-squeeze test the commission does a fully allocated cost study in which it allocates capital, as well as operating and maintenance costs, to different classes of retail and wholesale customers and compares the rate of return on book investment associated with the wholesale and retail rates. For a price squeeze to be found, the rate of return on investment for retail service must be less than the rate of return on wholesale service. This general approach appears to be a sensible way to implement the transfer-price test in this case, and the courts have generally accepted as reasonable the approach for purposes of FERC review.[51]

In addition to discussion of the basic structure of the price-squeeze test to be used, there has been considerable debate over precisely which rates should be used to make comparisons. Essentially, this issue required the commission to determine how to factor in the effects of regulatory lag and differences in rate-making policies between state and federal regulatory jurisdictions.

When a utility files new wholesale rates the commission typically encourages the filing utility to negotiate a settlement with the wholesale customers affected by the rate change to avoid the time-consuming and expensive administrative process. If a rate-increase request is agreed to by the parties affected, the FERC normally will allow it to go into effect without a lengthy, formal administrative review. If there is no agreement—that is, if wholesale customers challenge the new rates—the commission can, by statute, suspend the new rates for not more than five months. After that, the filed rates must go into effect, subject to refund (including interest) pending a final decision on the proposed rates. Typically, the commission allows the filed rates to go into effect immediately, subject to refund (including interest) pending a full investigation *if* the filed rates are no more than 10 percent higher than the staff's initial recommendation.

A final determination of "just and reasonable rates" (exclusive of price-squeeze considerations) can take two years or more. In almost all cases the rates allowed are lower than the temporary rates in effect, in which case the utility is required to refund to the wholesale customers the difference between the revenues collected under the temporary rates and what would have been collected had the final accepted rates been in effect (plus interest). Because of the long lag between initial filing and final acceptance of new rates, and because the rate-making process does not, aside from fuel-adjustment clauses, build general escalator provisions into rates to reflect inflation, it is necessary to file for frequent rate increases if costs increase rapidly as they did in the 1970s. As a result, a utility may have two or more temporary rate increases in effect, subject to refund, at the same time (this is sometimes called "pancaking") pending final commission approval.

Individual state commissions follow a variety of different procedures for dealing with *retail* rate-increase requests. Statutory suspension periods vary from about six months to as long as the commission cares to suspend new rates. Some commissions have the authority to allow temporary rates under certain circumstances; others do not. Some commissions may allow rates to go into effect subject to refund; others may not. In general, the lag between filing and even a temporary rate increase tends to be longer for rate increases subject to state jurisdiction (retail) than to FERC juridiction (wholesale), although final rate determination probably takes place more quickly at the state level than at the federal level if a wholesale rate is litigated.

Wholesale distribution-system customers have argued that the FERC should move quickly to evaluate the price-squeeze issue based on the *filed rates* rather than waiting for a full review of all contested issues associated with the wholesale rate proposal. These customers claim that the high *filed* rates cause the price squeeze, that the refunds plus interest provide inadequate protection. They argue that by evaluating the price squeeze as part of a lengthy administrative proceeding based on the final rates accepted by the commission as just and reasonable except for price-squeeze issues, "the monopolist is able to cripple the municipality with the unjustified discriminatory wholesale rate."[52]

The FERC, in turn, has taken the position that the provisions for refunds plus interest protect the municipalities, and that if there were evidence of a severe price squeeze in specific cases, they could take action to reduce the delay. The FERC has sought to minimize the burden placed on municipalities by high, filed rates subject to refund by developing a procedure for keeping the price-squeeze investigation itself from delaying the primary-rate determination longer than is absolutely necessary. Rates are now evaluated in two phases when price-squeeze charges are made. First, the FERC goes through its standard rate evaluation and develops final rates that go into effect before the price-squeeze charges have been resolved. This triggers any refunds due based on differences between temporary and final rates. The FERC next evaluates the price-squeeze charges based on the final rates, "but for price-squeeze considerations" that have been put into effect as a result of the first phase of the investigation.[53] If a price squeeze is found, additional refunds can be made.

The courts have approved the FERC's procedure for evaluating the price-squeeze issue *within the regulatory process*, using the "but for" final rates determined during the proceeding. They have made it clear, however, that "traditional antitrust remedies are also available to price-squeeze victims" and that it is expected that the commission will guard against strategic use of the regulatory process (filing very high temporary rates) to squeeze wholesale competitors.[54]

The FERC has also dealt with the problem of changing retail rates during a proceeding. Wholesale customers have argued that the retail rates in effect when the temporary wholesale rates go into effect should be the basis for comparison and that subsequent retail rate increases should be ignored. The commission appears willing to take into account retail rate increases subsequent to the time temporary wholesale rates go into effect if the difference in timing is fairly short. The courts have affirmed its discretion to do so.[55] The commission, however, has stated as well that a price-squeeze situation lasting 11.5 months and subsequently eliminated by a retail rate increase is of "a sufficient magnitude and duration that, in the absence of mitigating circumstances, we would find it undue and require a remedy."[56]

After several years of confusion and much litigation, the FERC has moved from interpreting *Conway* as a broad requirement to consider anticompetitive effects of wholesale/retail rate disparities to a series of mechanical cost and revenue computations. Price-squeeze charges routinely have been brought and have occasioned considerable litigation. Establishing a prima facie price-squeeze case is fairly simple because most of the elements are assumed effectively to be satisfied, and temporary filed rates without cost adjustments can be used for comparison. Actually, however, making a price-squeeze charge stick at the FERC has been extremely difficult. Obtaining remedies is even more difficult. Indeed, in the recent *Penn Power* case (on appeal as this is written), the FERC has tightened its requirements for obtaining remedies by suggesting that if the price squeeze results from differences in state and federal regulatory policies rather than by conscious actions by the supplying utility, it has no obligation to provide even the limited remedies suggested in *Conway*:

Rate-setting authority depends on the statutes conferring it, and there may be explicit differences in the standards imposed on various agencies. Even where the standards are identical, however, the state and federal interests sought to be achieved may vary significantly. For example, it may be the state's interest to keep retail industrial rates relatively low in order to attract new business. But the federal agency, charged with maintaining the reliability of the interstate power grid, may have an interest in maintaining high rates of return on jurisdictional rates to [ensure] that adequate revenues are available for proper plant maintenance, replacement and the like. Under such circumstances would it be appropriate for the federal interest to yield to competing state interests [?] The question virtually answers itself. *To permit such a result would be an abdication of the federal agency's duties under its statutory charter* (my emphasis).[57]

After eight years of litigation the FERC has almost come back to where it was before *Conway*. It will go about its primary business of determining appropriate rates and will guard against strategic use of the dual regulatory system by a utility to create a price-squeeze situation. If, however, a state regulatory agency fails to set retail rates at a level to cover the cost of service, the FERC will not be dragged along and lower wholesale rates accordingly.

This position appears to conflict with *Conway*, where there was concern about the "gap" created by dual regulation. Further, *Conway* does not require that the FERC do anything more than reduce rates to the lower end of a "zone of reasonableness." The FERC appears to be saying that it will not do even this unless it can be shown that the utility's actions caused the price squeeze, especially if its responsibilities under the Federal Power Act would thereby be hindered. Perhaps this case will give the U.S. Supreme Court the opportunity to reconsider the wisdom of *Conway* in light of the experience of recent years.

Although the primary concern motivating the price-squeeze inquiry was the potential for adverse competitive impact, issues associated with the actual extent of competition in particular markets (wholesale and retail), the likelihood that a price squeeze would consciously be used to restrict competition given the structure of the industry and the regulatory process, and the actual anticompetitive effects of wholesale-retail rate differentials have all but disappeared from the FERC's procedure for evaluating price squeezes. This situation appears to reflect the impossible administrative burden that would be imposed by dealing with these basic issues in every rate case, and the perception by an agency intimately familiar with the structure and regulation of this industry that price squeezes actually are not a public policy problem, that there is nothing the FERC can do about a price squeeze anyway without implementing procedures that conflict with its responsibilities under the Federal Power Act, and that wholesale-retail rate disparities result from fundamental conflicts between state and federal regulation that the FERC cannot resolve.

Price Squeeze in the Traditional Antitrust Context

Wholesale customers have available two forums for making price-squeeze claims. They can argue their claims before the FERC in rate proceedings (as discussed above), with the opportunity to appeal FERC decisions to the federal courts; and/or they can bring an antitrust suit against the utility, arguing that it has violated Section 2 of the Sherman Act. As far as I can tell, no conventional antitrust case against an IOU involving price-squeeze charges was ever litigated before *Conway* required the FERC to devote its attention to the issue. Clearly, the requirement that the FERC evaluate price-squeeze charges does not give the FERC exclusive jurisdiction, and conventional antitrust cases can be and have been brought that raise the same price-squeeze issues.[58] By requiring the FERC to investigate price-squeeze charges while recognizing that the commission had only limited power to remedy a price squeeze, the U.S. Supreme Court appears to have provided a signal suggesting that it believes price squeezes are a serious, potential, antitrust abuse that merits general antitrust scrutiny.

To prevail in a Section 2 case a plaintiff must, in principle, do much more than show it was placed in a price-squeeze situation by virtue of a disparity between wholesale and retail rates. The plantiff must show that the utility has monopoly power or a dangerous probability of obtaining monopoly in the relevant product and geographical markets, and that it has engaged in practices which show an intent to monopolize these markets. In evaluating the intent to monopolize charge, "it is the mix of the various ingredients of utility behavior in a monopoly broth that produces the unsavory flavor."[59] In principle, a price-squeeze claim alone is not enough to prevail in a Section 2 case. The alleged price squeeze must be part of a larger series of activities aimed at obtaining or maintaining a monopoly position in the relevant markets, although price-squeeze charges appear to have been the major "bad" alleged in several recent Section 2 cases.[60] The litigation strategy of plaintiffs seems to be to package price-squeeze charges with charges involving refusals to wheel power,[61] refusals to make certain wholesale rates available, restrictive terms and conditions of power pooling arrangements, and so forth—all with the intent to restrict competition at the retail level. These happen to be the kinds of charges that led to a finding of a violation of Section 2 by an IOU in *Otter Tail*,[62] except for the price-squeeze issue, which was not raised.

In a recent antitrust case (*City of Mishawaka*) in which the plaintiffs prevailed, price squeeze was a primary element of the anticompetitive behavior underlying the monopolization charge and, at the district court level, the source of the damage calculation.[63] This case demonstrates how the price-squeeze doctrine has led to antitrust liability based almost entirely on a utility's efforts to comply with state and federal regulatory procedures, as well as how difficult it is to apply the antitrust laws to this industry without a proper understanding of the nature of competition, price formation, and regulation that characterize the electric power industry. Furthermore, dual application of the price-squeeze doctrine by the FERC and the federal courts has led to very different interpretations of what constitutes a price squeeze. A utility could easily pass the FERC's price-squeeze tests while failing the tests established in *City of Mishawaka*.

In *City of Mishikawa* ten municipal utilities in Indiana and Michigan which purchase substantially all their power requirements from Indiana and Michigan Electric Company (I&M, a subsidiary of American Electric Power Co., a holding company) initially charged that I&M had violated Section 2 of the Sherman Act by implementing a price squeeze. The charge was subsequently expanded to include other practices that supposedly restricted plaintiffs access to wholesale power supplied by I&M, with the objective of restricting competition in the retail market.

The district court found that I&M had monopoly power in both retail and wholesale markets (I will accept these findings for purposes of discussion, though I am troubled by the market definitions, the measurement and use of concentration ratios to measure market power, and the lack of a thorough discussion of alternative wholesale power-supply opportunities). The court also found that the municipalities were in competition with I&M for franchise areas and for new and existing retail customers. In addition to relying on the general presumption of competition, to show that there was active competition for retail customers the court pointed to I&M's purchase or lease of the distribution facilities of five municipalities between 1957 and 1979, the fact that I&M served nine large retail customers within the municipalities' boundaries,[64] that both I&M and the municipalities offered to serve customers at the boundaries of the municipalities, and the fact that, by using their powers of annexation to expand their boundaries, the municipalities could simultaneously take over retail customers from I&M.

There is considerable doubt that the district court's finding of fact regarding competition is consistent with the actual extent of competition between I&M and the plaintiffs. It is useful to note that the rates charged by I&M to these wholesale customers did not come under federal jurisdiction until 1963 and that the initial wholesale tariffs under which these customers were served did not go into effect until 1968.[65] I&M did not apply for a wholesale rate increase until 1973, with two subsequent requests for rate increases in 1976 and 1978. The price-squeeze claims related only to the last two federal rate filings. During this same period, five retail rate increases went into effect in Indiana, and three in Michigan. I&M acquired no municipal franchises after 1966 (it acquired franchises in 1957, 1960, 1962, and 1966, before the initial federal rates were approved). I&M did lease one franchise in Indiana in 1975 in a municipality in which there were overlapping, duplicative, distribution facilities. The lease was approved by the Indiana Commission, which found that duplication of distribution facilities was not in the public interest. Thus minimal evidence of franchise competition was presented.

With regard to competition for individual customers, the primary fact relied on was that I&M served a few large industrial customers in the service areas of some of the municipal utilities. I&M, however, had served these customers for many years and had not in recent years obtained any new industrial customers similarly situated. The municipalities presented no evidence that they had ever lost customers in competition with I&M or that they had tried to extend service to the large industrial customers served by I&M within their municipalities. They did not know when or how I&M came to serve these customers. It is doubtful that some of the municipal utilities even had the necessary distribution facilities to serve large industrial customers. Thus the evidence on actual competition for large industrial customers is almost nonexistent.[66]

The court focused on two types of behavior that I&M supposedly engaged in to monopolize the retail market and damage the municipal utilities. The primary charge was one of price-squeeze. The second charge (actually, a package of charges) involved statements and FERC filings made by I&M in the early 1970s, suggesting that it might withdraw from the wholesale market, that in the event of a power shortage it wanted to serve its retail customers first, a request to limit the quantity of power available to some wholesale customers, a request that it serve wholesale customers under renewable three-year contracts rather than longer-term contracts, and, apparently, that the municipalities seek alternative sources of supply. Most of the requests were subsequently rejected by the FERC.[67] The court found that this behavior, viewed in its entirety, violated Section 2 of the Sherman Act. Damages were assessed based entirely on the alleged overcharges associated with the price-squeeze. No specific damages were identified with the other "exclusionary acts."

These other charges do not themselves suggest any anticompetitive intent. Like many utilities in the early 1970s, I&M and its parent, American Electric Power, were concerned about the possibility of capacity shortages in the coming decade. I myself had raised similar concerns.[68] I&M's actions essentially involved efforts to encourage its municipal customers to seek alternative sources of supply and to put mechanisms in place that would allocate supplies between wholesale and retail customers if shortages occurred. Unlike the situation in *Otter Tail*, I&M never refused to wheel power to the municipalities from alternative suppliers; indeed, it offered to wheel such power, along with its request that the munis seek alternative supplementary supply sources. The combination of rising electricity prices and substantial reductions in economic growth ultimately led to much lower increases in electricity demand than had been anticipated in the early 1970s. Rather than a shortage, a surplus emerged; but this was not generally anticipated early in the decade.

With regard to the price-squeeze charge, the district court held that the

rates plaintiffs pay are the wholesale rates *unilaterally* set by defendants' . . . filings before the Federal Energy Regulatory Commission. Under the Federal Power Act . . . in filing new wholesale rates I&M must compare those rates against its retail rates, consider their possible anticompetitive impact, and not require any of the plaintiffs to pay more at wholesale than it would pay under I&M's retail rates then in effect without justifying the higher wholesale rate. Defendant have ignored this obligation.[69]

The court found that the defendant had overcharged the plaintiffs as a result and that the practices identified were designed to promote the defendant's policy to take over the municipal utilities and monopolize the retail market.

The district court found it especially offensive that the defendant was permitted to charge "unregulated" rates as a result of the FERC procedure allowing rates to take effect (subject to refund) long before setting final rates, that I&M filed an additional rate increase that went into effect before the previous one had been fully adjudicated, and that after a full FERC hearing the temporary rates filed were in effect reduced when final rates were set by the FERC. "Not once during the entire period at issue have defendants charged a wholesale rate that the Commission has determined to be just and reasonable. On each occasion when a Commission Administrative Law Judge has examined I&M's wholesale rates, he has concluded that they were excessive, unjust and unreasonable and has ordered them lowered."[70] The district court never mentioned that the filed rates were in effect subject to refund, including interest.

The district court assessed damages by comparing the *filed* (rather than final) wholesale rates in effect from 1976 to 1978 with I&M's "equivalent" retail rates, which amounted to a difference of $4 million and treble damages of $12 million. No adjustments for cost differences were made and the refunds plus interest the municipal utilities received were simply ignored. The district court also enjoined the defendant from engaging in various wholesale-rate policies that purportedly singled out or discriminated against wholesale customers; it also enjoined the defendant from putting wholesale rates into effect that were greater than retail rates then in effect until such wholesale rates are approved by the FERC.

The appeals court affirmed the district court's Section 2 liability finding, including the price-squeeze analysis, but had trouble with the damage calculation and injunctive relief.[71] First, the appeals court recognized that it was wrong to assume that in the absence of a price squeeze "just and reasonable" wholesale and (presumably large industrial) retail rates should be equal, since the costs of serving different types of customers may differ. The court included a vague statement that the "fixed and variable costs" that must be recovered may differ for different customer classes. Indeed, the court noted that *after FERC review*, the *final* wholesale rates allowed were substantially *less* than the defendant's retail rates after refunds were taken into account.[72] No analysis of cost differences, however, was conducted by the district court for the appeals court to rely on. Second, the court concluded that if an overcharge analysis is the proper method for calculating damages, the appropriate damage measure is the difference between filed rates and accepted rates—the amount the FERC orders refunded. But then the court noted that, since the "monopolistic overcharges" were refunded with interest, an overcharge analysis yielded *no damages:*

Thus, the federal regulatory statute provides the municipalities with a system by which the utility's overcharges are automatically and necessarily restored to them with interest.

Given this federal regulatory system which is designed to curb the utility's abuse of its monopoly power and which guarantees ultimate restoration to the wholesale customers of the "overcharge" unlawfully extracted from them, we are not convinced that the utility's temporary monopolistic overcharge is an accurate measure of antitrust damages.[73]

The court concluded that to obtain damages, proof of specific injuries resulting from the overcharges and other practices had to be obtained. It offered two suggestions (loss of customers, higher capital costs) as to where the municipalities might find damages. Finally, the court vacated the injunctive relief ordered by the district court partly because it encroached far too much on the rate-making powers given the FERC by the Federal Power Act. The case was remanded to the district court and, along with twelve other FERC and court proceedings involving I&M and its muni customers, was settled in September 1981.[74]

It should be noted that, although the courts in *Mishawaka* found that an illegal price squeeze had taken place, it is unlikely that the FERC's procedures for evaluating a price-squeeze claim would come to the same conclusion. The FERC would have compared the final rates (not the temporary filed rates) with the retail rates, adjusted for cost differences. Apparently, using the accepted rates, the wholesale rates were lower than the retail rates.[75] Even if there had been a difference, it appears that I&M had satisfied the obligation in *Penn Power* to mitigate any squeeze by filing promptly for retail rate increases. During the period 1968–78, I&M filed for seven rate increases in Indiana and four in Michigan but filed only three wholesale-rate-increase requests. If there was a squeeze, it probably would have been justified as a result of differences in state and federal regulatory procedures.

Thus there appears to be a profound inconsistency between FERC price-squeeze procedures (accepted by the courts) and the court's procedures for evaluating a price-squeeze in a conventional anti-trust case. Furthermore, the decision of the appeals court in *City of Mishawaka* seems to have lost sight of the regulatory gap *Conway* sought to fill. What it found objectionable was not that I&M's effective wholesale rates were higher than its adjusted retail rates (with a result-ing price squeeze) but that it was permitted by the FERC to put rate increases into effect (subject to refund plus interest) that were higher than the rates ultimately approved. In the end, it never really evaluated the price-squeeze charge itself. In the context of an antitrust case, the appeals court effectively found it illegal for a utility to follow the FERC's rate-making procedures mandated by the Federal Power Act, which allows new rates to go into effect subject to refund at most five months after filing, unless it filed for rates so low that it could be assured they would be accepted in toto. Yet these same procedures have been accepted by appeals courts reviewing them directly, and the maximum five-month suspension period is provided for by statute in the Federal Power Act. Even assuming that the courts' analysis of "market definition," "market power," and "retail market cmpetition" are correct, it is hard to avoid the conclusion that the ultimate result is strange.

Evaluation of the Price-Squeeze Doctrine

The Role of Retail Competition in Promoting Economic Efficiency

Although the debate continues over a precise definition of the goals of the antitrust laws, it seems to be generally accepted that one important goal of the antitrust laws is to promote an efficient allocation of society's scarce resources. Have the antitrust laws as applied to the electric power industry—*given the prevailing structure of the industry and the nature of state and federal regulation*—helped promote economic efficiency? Have the antitrust laws been a useful complement to the regulatory process, preserving and promoting a competitive process that leads to a more efficient allocation of resources under the regulatory umbrella? Where regulatory policy and antitrust policy conflict, have the antitrust laws helped steer the electric power industry toward greater efficiency?

I believe that antitrust policy, applied to the electric power industry, got off on the wrong foot because of a general misunderstanding of the role retail market competition can play in the electric power industry *as it is currently structured and regulated*. Development of the price-squeeze doctrine, as well as most other aspects of antitrust law applied to the regulated electric power industry, is based on the assumption that small distribution companies (generally munis and coops) are in active competition with integrated investor-owned utilities which both produce and distribute electricity and often sell power at wholesale to adjacent nonintegrated distribution companies. The legal and economic analyses have focused on preserving and promoting *retail* competition. Restrictions on particular types of supplier behavior in the wholesale market are perceived as means to that end.

This concept of the role retail competiton plays in allocating resources and promoting economic efficiency in the electric power industry is wrong. Opportunities for relying more on competitive market forces to allocate resources at the *wholesale* level are real but uncertain, whereas prevailing regulatory institutions restrict the role competition can play at the retail level, particularly with regard to small distribution companies that purchase wholesale power. It is the *wholesale* market (buyers, sellers, price formation), not the retail market, that should be the focus of antitrust law applied to the electric power industry, with appropriate sensitivity to the constraints placed on competition by the structure of the electric power industry, the economics of efficient electricity supply, and prevailing regulatory policies.

The courts tend to focus on three dimensions of actual and potential retail competition: (1) competition for distribution franchises; (2) competition for new industrial loads based on location decisions; and (3) fringe-area competition.

Franchise Competition It is generally recognized that distribution of electricity within a particular area is a natural monopoly. Multiple distribution companies serving the same geographical area would lead to wasteful duplication of capital facilities.[76] It should be clear from the discussion thus far of the structure and regulation of the industry that state and local laws have deliberately been structured to minimize competition for existing and, in many cases, new distribution franchises. With a few exceptions, IOUs operate with de facto exclusive franchises granted under long-term contracts, with regulatory protection from municipal condemnation absent appropriate compensation.

When the courts speak of franchise competition presumably they are referring to the ability of a municipality to take over the franchise currently licensed to a private utility and either substitute a municipal utility or award the franchise to a competing private utility. They are also apparently referring to the ability of an investor-owned utility to convice the voters in a municipality to transfer the franchise from a municipal utility to the IOU. The potential for this type of competition to emerge is necessarily constrained by state laws governing the terms, duration, and takeover opportunities of municipal franchises. In some states, franchise laws and procedures for obtaining certificates of convenience and necessity make it almost impossible for the IOU holder of an existing franchise to be forced by a municipality to give it up. In other states municipal takeovers are much easier, but real opportunities for a municipality to condemn a franchise and then offer it to a competing *private* utility are for all intents and purposes nonexistent. Even when franchises expire I have been able to find no evidence that they are picked up by a competing IOU. Where practical takeover options do exist, a municipality usually must compensate the current franchise holder for the value of the property lost.

What passes for franchise competiton nearly always involves municipalities that are trying to take over the distribution function from an IOU within the municipality or that are considering offers by one or more investor-owned utilities to take over the distribution facilities owned and operated by a muni. Typically, it is only a distribution system, not generating or transmission services, that is the focus of the franchise "contest." The municipalities involved require that generation and transmission services be provided by a proximate utility or that a proximate utility provide transmission capacity (wheeling) to secure power from a third party—most frequently preference power from a federal power project. The municipality's choice is between owning and operating a distribution system and purchasing power from a neighboring IOU or from some other wholesale supplier, or selling off the distribution franchise to a neighboring utility to provide integrated service. Cooperative utilities are not a serious franchise threat to existing integrated companies, because REA-subsidized loans are not available in areas already served with central station power.[77]

Given the thousands of municipalities and other government sub-divisions that have franchising authority, it is surprising to find that there are relatively few transfers of franchises involving municipalities or cooperative utilities. In the last twenty years there have been fewer than thirty municipal takeovers of the distribution properties of integrated investor-owned utilities.[78] These takeovers nearly always are motivated by an interest in obtaining low-cost federal preference power available only to municipal and cooperative utilities. Since 1973, as fossil fuel prices rose, the economic-transmission distance for preference power has increased, which has prompted some municipalities to take over local distribution facilities in order to obtain it.[79]

During the same period, about one hundred municipal systems were acquired by investor-owned utilities, though approximately 75 percent of these acquisitions took place before 1970. The systems involved generally have been small, too small to generate power efficiently, and in several cases the municipal properties were in a state of disrepair.[80] Interestingly, *cooperative* systems are rarely taken over by integrated investor-owned utilities.[81]

Whereas in theory the threat of municipal condemnation or rebidding of expired franchises may be an important spur to efficiency, which supplements state and federal regulation, in practice, this threat has not played such a role in this industry. Access to scarce federal preference power, rather than inefficient production or monopoly pricing by integrated private utilities, has been the primary motivation for municipal takeovers in recent years. To the extent that franchise competition has had efficiency consequences, it probably flows in the other direction. Constraints are placed by IOUs on unregulated municipalities to operate their systems efficiently and constrain their ability to supplement municipal tax revenues from municipal utility profits by charging monopoly prices. On balance, one must conclude that in the electric power industry franchise competition plays little if any supplemental role to regulation in promoting efficient production and constraining monopoly prices of the IOUs. Choices for or against municipal or cooperative distribution are dominated by interest rate subsidies, tax subsidies, and access to preference power, not the relative efficiencies of alternative franchisees.

Even if there were more vigorous franchise competition, and ignoring the various subsidies available to publicly owned firms, opportunities are minimal for increased efficiency associated with competition by the type of muni and coop system that typically has sought protection from price squeezes and other alleged anticompetitive behavior. The municipal distribution companies that bring these charges are almost always involved primarily in distributing electricity produced by others (in some cases they have minimal amounts of subtransmission capacity). In the typical price-squeeze case the assumed competition is between the muni distribution company and an IOU assumed to be its sole economical source of bulk power supplies and that happens to distribute power as well in neighboring areas. To the extent that there is actual or potential competition between them *for the right to distribute power* (retail sales), opportunities to reduce electricity costs and prices are minimal. Less than 6 percent of the costs of operating and maintaining an integrated utility are attributable to distribution; about 30 percent of the investment in plant and equipment is attributable to distribution. On average, 15 percent to 20 percent of the total cost of providing electricity to ultimate consumers is associated with distribution (including taxes, interest payments, profits, and depreciation). Most of these costs are the carrying charges on electrical poles, transformers, distribution lines, meters, maintenance equipment, and so forth.

Possible tax benefits aside, there is little room for a municipality that must rely on its assumed competitor for 80 to 85 percent of its costs to reduce the cost of electricity by operating a distribution system more efficiently than the IOU competitor might. On the contrary, there are at least some economies of sale in maintaining distribution plant and equipment that small distribution systems may be too small to exploit fully. Furthermore, the distribution function is not technologically sophisticated and is a relatively mundane activity that makes use of well-understood technology that changes only slowly. Distribution-system economies appear not to have been an important source of productivity growth in the electric power industry. All commentaries concerned with the efficiency of the electric power system have focused on generation, transmission, and coordination, not distribution, If there are efficiency problems on the supply side in the electric power industry, the distribution system is just not where the action is. Also, there is no evidence that muni or coop distributors are more likely to *price* electricity more efficiently (peak-load pricing, marginal cost-pricing, etc.) then do IOUs.[82]

If franchise competition is to play a significant role in promoting the efficient supply of electricity, it must involve competition between alternative, bulk-power supply sources, not competition for distribution franchises alone. Franchise competition involving *integrated* firms could, in principle, yield these efficiencies; but that type of franchise competition is almost nonexistent; most of the antitrust cases involving electric utilities do not involve claims that this form of competition is being restricted.

Retail Competition for Large Industrial Loads In price-squeeze cases, franchise competition is often mentioned, but it is competition for customers—particularly, large industrial customers—that gets the most attention as a source of retail competiton. "Load competition" is also mentioned as part of broader antitrust charges brought by municipalities against integrated IOUs. As long as franchises provide de facto territorial exclusivity to serve existing retail customers once a utility has the franchise, it has these customers. Therefore, the courts and the FERC have focused on retail competition aimed at attracting new customers to a particular service territory and on keeping customers from moving to another service territory. Based on the assumption that location decisions of residential and small commercial customers are not influenced significantly by relative electricity prices of adjacent distribution system, the courts and the FERC have focused on competition aimed at attracting new *industrial* customers and retaining existing industrial customers—industrial-location competition as an important source of retail competition.[83]

Obviously, the cost of electricity is one of many factors that goes into *any* consumer's decision about where to locate. To the extent, however, that electricity costs are a sufficiently important source of expense to play an identifiable role in locational decisions, it must be expectations about the price of electricity *in the long run*, not temporary variations in relative prices, that influence decisions. Other things being equal, any consumer would rather locate where the price of electricity is lowest. But other things are rarely equal, and many factors other than relative electricity prices can affect location decisions.

It is generally agreed that except in electricity-intensive industries such as aluminum, location decisions are not very sensitive to relative electricity prices. (That's why the entire population has not chosen to locate in the Pacific Northwest, though many aluminum plants have). At least one court seems to have recognized this, but not in a price-squeeze case.[84] The fact that electricity accounts for less than 1 percent of cost on average in manufacturing, combined with the small fraction of electricity costs that the typical muni or coop plaintiff actually has control of by virtue of its distribution operations, makes it extremely unlikely that competition between munis/coops and integrated IOUs to attract industrial customers to locate in their service territories will serve as a potent force promoting more efficient production and lower costs. If the muni distributor can reduce its distribution costs (tax advantages aside) 10 percent compared to an integrated IOU distributor, it can reduce the average electricity price by 2 percent (actually, much less for a large industrial customer) and reduce the typical manufacturing firm's total costs by 0.02 percent. In light of all the other factors that influence location decisions, these considerations are trivial.

The potential for this type of competition to spur a reduction in the cost of service is especially unlikely in typical price-squeeze cases. In those cases, the municipal distribution company typically purchases all of its power from the supplier it is supposedly in competition with, for "resale" to large industrial customers. Large industrial customers, however, generally take power at relatively high voltages, frequently directly from the subtransmission system, and can make little use of the bulk of the facilities composing the municipality's distribution system. Indeed, large *public* agencies such as TVA, Bonneville, and PASNY supply power to both muni and coop distribution systems and serve large industrial loads directly. This is so because these customers can economically take power off the transmission system, and there is no need for a distribution system "middleman." Lacking a subtransmission system, a municipality is not in a position to serve the largest industrial customers in the first place. If it invests in subtransmission capacity and can serve industrial customers off the primary (higher-voltage) distribution lines, it can serve these customers; but the value added to the power purchased from the IOU is likely to be insignificant.

There simply are no significant economic costs (tax and interest rate subsidies aside) that the municipality could hope to conserve on in competing for large industrial customers with its sole power supplier. In such cases the IOU is accounting for nearly all the costs of serving large industrial loads, whether it serves them directly or through the municipality. Indeed, I suspect that many industrial customers would prefer not to be served by an unregulated muni distribution system because they are concerned that they will be forced to pay a fraction of the distribution costs despite the fact that they don't use the distribution system.[85] In the typical price-squeeze case this type of retail competition can have no significant supplementary effects on the efficiency with which power is supplied to industrial customers.

If this kind of industrial location competition actually is of some significance under current institutional arrangements (a dubious proposition), it is most likely to be an important spur to lower costs and a constraint on monopoly power when each of the competing distributors has its own sources of generating and transmission capacity either because both are integrated or because one or both have access to alternative wholesale suppliers *who, in turn, are in competition with each other and wholesale prices are determined as a consequence of that competition.* This is not the situation in the typical price squeeze context.

Meaningful competition for industrial customers (or any other type of retail customers) can take place only in the absence of de facto territorial exclusivity. As long as customers must obtain power from a single franchisee authorized to provide service to the area where the customers are located, the opportunities for significant load competition are small. Usually, territorial exclusivity and meaningful competition for industrial customers are inconsistent with one another except perhaps in electricity-intensive industries. If large industrial customers could shop around for power from alternative suppliers, meaningful price competition might emerge, since it would not be restricted to effects on industrial location. Whether it would be a good idea to abandon territorial exclusivity and encourage large industrial customers to shop around for power supplies is another question. Problems of facility duplication, effectiveness of competition, wheeling possibilities and compensation arrangements, and the effects of such rivalry on the efficiency with which the transmission and distribution systems operate must be dealt with. Although I do not intend to answer these questions here, it seems to me that if encouraging this kind of competition makes any sense at all, it would only be for very large industrial customers who take power from the high-voltage transmission system. The proper way to analyze the pros and cons of opening up the market to such customers is to think of them (with appropriate adjustments for differences in load characteristics) as though they were small distribution systems shopping for power in the wholesale market. Thus, although such large industrial customers technically are retail customers, they may be functionally equivalent to what we now categorize as wholesale distribution system customers. The pros and cons of introducing competition into the wholesale market could then be applied to large industrial customers taking power directly from the transmission system. It should be noted that if such a market were allowed to emerge, the muni and coop distribution companies that obtain generation and transmission services from others would have no role in such a market, since they provide a service these customers don't need.

Except in those areas where multiple generating companies can compete head to head for existing industrial customers, the assumption should be that this type of competition is not a significant spur to lower prices or costs or to economic efficiency generally.[86]

Fringe-Area Competition Fringe-area competition is also mentioned in some antitrust cases and in the antitrust literature, so I will discuss this concept briefly. Fringe-area competition appears to refer to the expansion of competing distribution companies (in principle, either integrated or unintegrated) into adjacent areas that fall between the geographical boundaries of existing franchisees. It is effectively a form of franchise competition. For example, new subdivisions in unincorporated areas may be able to choose among two or more adjacent utilities (including an adjacent muni) interested in expanding their service territories. Presumably, these customers will try to choose among alternative suppliers the one they except to provide service at the lowest cost. If an adjacent utility is a muni, it may be able to serve areas outside the municipal boundaries if requested to do so. In many states the rates charged by a muni to customers outside municipal boundaries are regulated by the state public utility commission. If a private utility is given the franchise, rates too are regulated by the state commission.

Most states have discouraged this variant of franchise compeition either by fixing utility boundaries or developing rules to assign new customers to particular franchises. In a few states this type of franchise competition is permitted, but in general it is not an important phenomenon in the electric power industry.[87] Furthermore, competing utilities usually may not truly "compete" with each other in the sense of negotiating a special deal (a special long-term contract) with the new area. In many states, rates are regulated in the case of private utilities and in the case of munis outside their municipal boundaries, and usually these rates are based on the average historical cost of the utility as a whole and are not permitted to differ from one municipal franchise area to another served by a single utility.[88]

Adjacent utilities may have different average historical costs for reasons having nothing to do with relative efficiency or differences in marginal costs.[89] As a result, where such fringe-area opportunities exist, there is no guarantee that the more efficient supplier will be chosen in the long run, because regulated rates based on average historical cost do not provide the right price signals to consumers. In addition, to the extent that the competition is between an unintegrated muni or coop and an integrated IOU, the ultimate choice depends more on the availability of various subsidies and preferences than on relative efficiencies in providing electricity. Fringe area competition is fairly rare; where it does occur, efficiency considerations play a minor role.

Overall, it seems to me that retail competition plays essentially no role in promoting economic efficiency—on the cost side or on the price side—in today's electric power industry. This is especially true when the assumed competition is between an integrated utility and one of its full-requirements customers, as it is in the typical price-squeeze case. Thus one of the primary assumptions on which price-squeeze charges and other antitrust concerns that arise in the electric power industry are based is largely wrong: that retail competition can and does play an important role in allocating resources. Rather than assume that retail competition is important, as is done now, the assumption should be just the opposite; under current institutional arrangements, the burden of proof should be on those who contend that there is significant competition at the retail level which affects the behavior of consumers and alternative suppliers.

Are Intentional Price Squeezes Rational Predatory Actions?

The underlying theory motivating the price-squeeze inquiry also assumes that a rational, profit-maximizing, integrated utility will find it advantageous to institute a price squeeze to drive competing retail distribution systems from the market through acquisition by the "competing" IOU or by making it uneconomical for them to serve certain types of customers, in order to obtain or maintain a monopoly position in the retail market. A price squeeze is viewed by enforcement authorities either as a predatory tactic aimed at forcing competing distribution systems to sell out to their integrated supplier or as a foreclosure device to make it uneconomical for the distributing systems to serve certain classes of customers. For predation to be a rational strategy one also must assume that an IOU distribution company can charge higher prices and earn higher profits if "competing" retail distribution companies are eliminated either completely through acquisition of distribution systems by integrated IOUs or as competitors for certain types of retail customers (new industrial customers, for example).

In this section I shall argue that in the typical situation in which price-squeeze cases arise, it would almost certainly be irrational for an IOU regulated by both state and federal authorities to *consciously* implement a price squeeze to drive muni or coop distribution systems from the market with the goal of reducing retail competition. This result emerges because to successfully drive out "competing" firms, an IOU supplier must sacrifice short-run profits. For such a sacrifice to be rational, the supplier must assume that as a result of its actions it can earn enough more in profits after the competitors have been driven from the market and/or new industrial customers secured to more than make up for the short-run profit loss associated with implementing the strategy. In the typical situation where price-squeeze charges arises, however, an IOU would almost certainly find no way to make up the revenue loss from implementing the squeeze in the short run. I focus first on alternative methods for implementing a squeeze and the associated short-run profit losses; then I discuss the opportunities an IOU faces in making up these losses if its muni customers are driven from the market or shorn of their large industrial customers.

What must an integrated supplier do to *consciously* squeeze its customer/competitor out of the market? Let's focus on the situation in which we compare final (rather than temporary) wholesale and retail rates. Very simply, the IOU must somehow manipulate its rate requests so that wholesale rates are higher than retail rates properly adjusted for cost differences. This means the relevant rates must be set so the profit per unit of electricity sold in the wholesale market is higher than the profit per unit sold in the retail market. We must assume that the FERC, but for price-squeeze considerations, will use its conventional criteria to set wholesale rates and that the IOU will, in any event, try to get rates approved that yield the highest profits the FERC will allow. Therefore, to consciously implement a price squeeze, a utility must ask the state PUC to set retail rates so they yield a *lower* return than the maximum it otherwise could obtain, which, in turn, must be lower than the return it expects to be allowed by the FERC on wholesale sales.

There are several ways a utility could try to do this. First, it could delay making a request for a general increase in retail rates at the time it files for a general increase in wholesale rates, so that it ends up earning a lower return on its retail sales than on its wholesale sales. It is in the context of intermittent and overlapping wholesale and retail rate increases, reflecting rapid increases in electricity costs during the 1970s, that all price-squeeze cases have arisen to date. To implement this strategy, the utility must sacrifice some retail revenues today in order to create a disparity between the unit prices of wholesale and retail service.

This would be a costly strategy for a typical IOU to adopt; the average IOU's sacrifice in retail revenues necessary to create a significant disparity between wholesale and retail rates in this way must be large compared to the losses its unintegrated distribution system customers must sustain to "meet the competition." Consider the following example.

On the order of 90 percent of a typical IOU's net kwh sales are retail sales subject to state regulatory jurisdiction or wholesale transactions under coordination contracts with other integrated IOUs.[90] Assume that an IOU has $1 billion in total revenues per year (equal to its total costs) if it does not try to implement a price squeeze. These revenues are distributed as $900 million in retail revenues at 5 cents per kwh and $100 million in wholesale (requirements contracts) revenues at 4 cents per kwh. The IOU is the sole supplier to its publicly owned requirements customers; both the IOU and its customers have distribution costs of 1 cent per kwh. Thus both the IOUs and their wholesale customers can charge 5 cents per kwh at retail and cover their costs (the wholesale customers then have *total* revenues of $125 million).

Let's assume that the IOU tries to impose a price squeeze by reducing retail prices to its own retail customers so that they are 10 percent lower than the total costs incurred by its wholesale customers. This requires a price reduction of 0.5 cent per kwh and a reduction of $90 million per year in total revenues. To match these lower prices (assuming they had to do so to meet the "competiton"; in practice, tax and interest rate subsidies that give the munis a cost advantage probably would make a competitive rate cut unnecessary), the munis would also have to cut prices by 0.5 cent per kwh and lose $12.5 million in revenue per year (I have assumed that demand is perfectly inelastic for simplicity). Thus, for every dollar its wholesale customers lose in the aggregate as a result of the assumed price squeeze, the IOU loses about $7.20. Furthermore, for the squeeze to be effective the IOU must keep the rate disparity in effect for a fairly long time, because the kind of franchise-transfer and industrial-location decisions that are supposedly the source of retail competition are based on long-run-cost comparisons, not temporary rate disparities, and the IOU must convince potential customers that the low rates are in fact permanent.[91] Thus the IOU must sacrifice substantial revenue over a period of years to attract new retail customers on account of rate disparities or to drive "competing" distribution system customers from the market.

Presumably, one way an IOU can reduce the short-run revenue loss is to "target" the retail price reductions on particular classes of "competitive" loads. Then it might apply for an increase in its residential and small commercial rates to yield the highest return it can get from the state commission, except for a smaller increase for its large industrial rates, concentrating the revenue sacrifice on large industrial customers. (To my knowledge, there is no suggestion in the actual price-squeeze cases that such a strategy has been used.) It is extremely unlikely that a state PUC would permit new rates to go into effect that provided for a significant difference in the returns allowed for different classes of customers. Indeed, it would be illegal under most state laws lacking a sound public-interest justification (perhaps helping promote employment or industrial development, as suggested in *Penn Power*).[92] The revenue sacrifice would still be significant, since, on average, 40 percent of IOU kwh sales are to large industrial customers. Furthermore, a state PUC is likely to allow such a disparity only as a temporary measure for pursuing some public-interest goal that could be defended on appeal to a state court. Finally, the losses that would have to be sustained to "meet the competition" by the typical muni that is the target of the squeeze would be minimal since it would only have to respond by reducing its own rates below cost for large industrial customers as well. No "competitive" price reduction need be incurred for residential or commercial sales which make up a much higher proportion of small muni/coop loads (as well as the voters who must oust the muni) than for IOUs.

To rationally make this kind of short-run revenue sacrifice, the integrated supplier must anticipate that it will gain additional profits, by driving from the market wholesale customers, with a present discounted value greater than the short-run profit losses. This is the essence of a rational predation story. Let's say the IOU ultimately obtains all the municipal franchises it now serves at wholesale as a result of this strategy, after paying the municipality for the distribution system at something close to book value, and thereby eliminates this assumed source of retail competition. The only way the short-run revenue sacrifice can be profitable is for the IOU to now be in a position to obtain higher retail rates than it could previously have obtained in the presence of this retail competition. Also, the increased profits must be large enough to more than make up for the short-run profit loss required to implement the strategy.

Unlike the traditional predatory pricing situation, the IOU cannot unilaterally raise its rates to exploit an increase in retail market power obtained in this way. To "exploit" its assumed increased market power arising from acquisition of its retail distribution company customers/competitors, it must now go to the state regulatory commission for a rate increase. But why should we expect the state regulatory commission to allow it a higher rate of return now than it would have received in the first place? Retail competition isn't determining prices or profits here, the state regulatory commission is. Even if the state regulatory commission is very lax, it would also have been lax before the demise of the "competing" unintegrated distribution systems. Acquisition of all distributors being served as wholesale requirements customers merely increases the IOU supplier's rate base by 3 percent to 5 percent and shifts jurisdiction from federal to state regulation over about 10 percent of its rate base, since it is adding distribution investment (30 percent of total investment) only for the equivalent of about 10 percent of its retail sales. Even if state regulators are much more lax in controlling profits than federal regulators (the opposite is more likely to be the case), the difference must be enormous, so large that court reviews of either state or federal decisions would find returns to be unreasonable, for it to be profitable to sacrifice so much in retail revenues in order to shift the regulatory jurisdiction over a relatively small fraction of its business from the FERC to the state commission.

There is just no way the alleged predator utility can make up the short-run-revenue sacrifice necessary to rationally implement a price squeeze in this way from the additional revenues associated with adding the new distribution systems. Lacking significant retail competition—elimination of which would allow the integrated supplier to maintain its retail rates persistently above what they would have been in the presence of such competition, that is, retail rate regulation is ineffective in constraining prices—engaging in a conscious price squeeze is irrational. I have already argued that such competition is minimal to nonexistent as a factor in the determination of retail rates. Furthermore, the typical price-squeeze case arises as a result of state regulation that is *more* constraining than federal regulation, not *less*.

There is only one possible situation I can think of in which a conscious price-squeeze strategy involving short-run retail revenue sacrifices could be a rational strategy. It requires that the expected return earned under state regulatory jurisdiction be significantly higher than the expected return under FERC jurisdiction, that a large fraction of a utility's sales are wholesale requirements transactions subject to FERC jurisdiction, *and* that municipal takeover of distribution franchises cannot easily be accomplished once the franchises have been transferred to the IOU (otherwise, any subsequent price increases would merely generate muni takeovers again). Here, the intent of the price squeeze is to get muni distribution franchises to sell out in order to shift regulatory jurisdiction from the federal government to the states and thereby increase profits in the long run. It is not the elimination of retail market *competition* that motivates this behavior but disparities in expected profits between state and federal regulatory jurisdictions.

Neither of the first two assumptions necessary for this scenario to be realistic is generally satisfied. Wholesale sales to muni and coop distributors generally are a small fraction of total sales, and state regulation is not noticeably less lax than federal regulation. Indeed, in the past few years any apparent price squeeze was more likely to be the result of excessively stringent state regulation and regulatory delays at the state level than the conscious efforts of an IOU interested in monopolizing the retail market for loss or gain.

The problem here lies with the conceptualization of the price squeeze as a predatory tactic. In *Alcoa*, for example, the price squeeze is now understood to be a result of a desire to exploit upstream monopoly power by engaging in price discrimination in downstream markets. This is accomplished by vertical integration into some fabricated product markets (the most elastic) and the sale of ingot in the open market to fabricators selling products with less elastic demands. To accomplish the profit-maximizing third-degree price discrimination in downstream markets, the internal transfer price in the integrated markets is low than the external sales prices. The difference is so great that Alcoa's competitors in the integrated markets get squeezed out but not those in unintegrated markets. There is no short-run revenue sacrifice involved here, however; the low internal transfer price and the higher external market price are permanent parts of the strategy to engage in price discrimination. The price squeeze is a consequence of vertical integration and price discrimination by an upstream monopolist, not an overt predatory act.

The antitrust concern as it is viewed in electric power price-squeeze cases is much more akin to a conventional predatory pricing situation.[93] (If it were merely concern about price discrimination and not the effect on competition, regulatory statutes would deal with this issue directly and there would be no need to resort to the antitrust laws.) In the classical predatory pricing situation, below cost pricing involves short-run profit sacrifices that are made up in the long run by raising prices and profits once the competition is driven from the market. But here there is no significant retail price competition to begin with and short-run revenue sacrifices that must be made to eliminate some retail "competitors" cannot be made up in the long run lacking unrealistic assumptions involving competition for regulatory jurisdiction rather than conventional price competition. A strategy of consciously squeezing a wholesale distribution company customer by deferring retail rate increases will not be profitable in the kind of situation where a price-squeeze charge has arisen.

Any rational strategy for implementing a price squeeze requires behavior that does not entail the substantial short-run sacrifices in retail revenues that previous strategies do. In *Mishawaka*, the courts suggested that the strategy involved filing repeated wholesale-rate-increase requests which the company knew would never be completely approved but would go into effect temporarily subject to refund plus interest. The result of putting temporary wholesale rates into effect immediately, plus pancaking multiple increases, it was argued, can put the wholesale customer distribution company in a position where it is always paying rates higher than those that will ultimately be approved and always passing these higher rates on to its customers, with periodic refunds, of course. The result, it is argued, is that the large industrial customers and voters notice the high temporary rates and will tend to locate in the integrated competitor's area and/or vote to turn the franchise over to it. It costs the integrated IOU nothing (except, perhaps, interest charges) to implement this strategy.

I find this view of a price squeeze a dubious source of competitive disadvantage. Contests for franchise awards and decisions on industrial location are long-run decisions entailing commitments lasting many years. One would expect that, if a franchise contest arose for an existing muni system, the municipality would try to demonstrate that its rates are actually low by incorporating the refunds obtained plus interest and passing refunds along to customers and comparing rates over a long period of time. Given the minimal retail competition that actually exists in these situations, it is difficult to imagine that there would ever be any competitive harm resulting from the FERCs procedures, which allow temporary rates subject to refund to go into effect before a final set of rates is approved. Let me note that this also suggests that the cases in which the FERC or the courts have found that a price-squeeze situation lasting less than a year is of "long enough duration" to find undue discrimination and create a presumption of anticompetitive impacts are inconsistent with the unrealistic view of retail competition on which the price-squeeze theory is based.[94] Decisions on franchise and industrial location simply are not going to be effected by temporary disparities in wholesale and retail rates of the type that might arise due to differences in state and federal regulatory procedures.

If the FERC and the federal courts must be concerned about the price-squeeze issue, the analysis should be based on rate comparisons averaged over several years, not just an isolated rate filing. Rate comparisons should reflect cost differences, and final rates, not temporary rates subject to refund, should be the basis for comparison. In calculating damages, the courts should follow the remand of the Court of Appeals in *Mishawaka* and require proof of specific competitive damages resulting from the price squeeze. That court, however, should have remanded the entire price-squeeze issue, since the district court did not provide the necessary information to infer a price squeeze.

There is a final, conscious, predatory price-squeeze strategy that has not yet come up in any of these cases but which theoretically might be profitable. Rather than sacrifice retail revenues in the short run, the IOU might try to distort its retail-rate structure so it earns nearly the same aggregate profit but sets below-cost rates for some "competitive" customer classes and above-cost rates for others. Once competitors are driven (permanently) from the market, the utility readjusts its rates to maximize profits, subject to the regulatory constraints it faces. This is a cross-subsidy argument similar to the more conventional concern that firms operating in both regulated monopoly and competitive markets will use revenues from sales in the regulated markets to subsidize sales in competitive markets, thus driving competitors out of the competitive market at little or no net cost to the monopolist.[95]

Thus an IOU might file a new retail-rate structure that reduces prices for residential customers below cost while raising prices to commercial and large industrial customers to cover the revenue loss. The IOUs retail residential rates must be low enough, compared to its wholesale rates, that its "competing" unintegrated distribution customers cannot profitably match the retail rates. This requires that the muni and coop distributors have a substantially different mix of customers than the IOU. In this case they must make a larger fraction of their sales to residential customers than to large commercial or industrial customers. The IOUs low residential rates then induce voters to sell the municipal franchise to the IOU, because the muni cannot profitably match the retail residential rates of the IOU.

This situation conceivably could be profitable if the expected rate of return on the G&T assets (rate base) currently allocated to these whole-sale transactions were increased by making assets subject to state jurisdiction rather than to federal (FERC) jurisdiction. Alternatively, if expected returns in the two jurisdictions are approximately equal and above the cost of capital, the IOU could increase its profits by adding distribution assets to its rate base.[96] (We could try this the other way around: depress industrial rates and raise residential rates; given the customer mix of the typical muni or coop, however, that would impose no burden on them.)

In implementing this strategy the utility faces the difficult problem of convincing the state PUC that the rate structure change is justified on either cost grounds or public interest grounds. Industrial customers would almost certainly challenge the proposed rate structure changes in court. Furthermore, to make the acquisition of the additional retail (heavily residential) customers profitable—given the associated trans-fer of assets currently subject to federal jurisdiction, plus acquisition of new distribution assets and customers with a larger proportion of residential customers—the IOU would have to readjust the rate struc-ture and increase rates to residential customers after the acquisition takes place. Thus the initial distortion in the rate structure would have to be at least partially reversed once the goal of acquiring the new distribution franchise is achieved—even more difficult to accomplish than the initial distortion.

None of the cases litigated suggest that such a strategy (designed to exploit imperfections in the regulatory process and differences be-tween state and federal jurisdictions) has ever been attempted. The difficulties in implementing it—plus the small or negative profit incre-ment that can be expected unless state regulation is much more lax than

federal regulation, which was quite unlikely during the past decade—
make such a strategy highly improbable.

It is interesting to note that this "price-squeeze" strategy would not
be picked up by conventional price-squeeze procedures in any event,
since they focus on comparing wholesale rates with retail *industrial*
rates. In a typical case this strategy requires industrial rates *higher* than
wholesale rates, properly adjusted for cost difference. No price-
squeeze case has suggested that such a strategy was implemented.
Probably the best way to guard against this unlikely strategy is court
review of the reasonableness of regulated retail rates.

Unintentional Price Squeezes

Now let us turn to situations where a price squeeze, as defined by the
FERC and the courts, might arise due to differences between state and
federal regulatory policies rather than to a conscious effort of an IOU to
reduce competition by driving its distribution company customers
from the market with the aim of exploiting some assumed reduction in
retail competition to raise prices and increase profits. I call this the case
of regulatory "capture," though there may be numerous reasons why
differences in regulatory policies lead to an apparent price squeeze.
Here, we might think of the IOU "capturing" the FERC so that prices
are set at a level which allows wholesale suppliers to earn more than
their cost of capital on wholesale transactions, and, as a result, wholesale sales are always more profitable than retail sales. Another variant
might involve "capture" of the state regulatory commission by consumer groups so that the PUC routinely rejects rate increases and
causes the integrated utility to earn less than a fair rate of return on
investments supporting retail sales while federal regulators strive to set
rates so that returns track the cost of capital reasonably closely. In
either case wholesale transactions are more profitable than retail transactions, and a price-squeeze situation, as it is normally defined, could
easily result.

If such a situation were to persist, it would be irrational for the
integrated supplier to use the rate disparity to take over its wholesale
customers or make an effort to attract new customers from them. On the
contrary, it would be in the IOU's interest to divest itself of its distribution franchises at book value (with conventional regulatory accounting procedures that use a depreciated original cost-rate base, if investors expect a state regulatory agency to persistently set prices at a level
that does not yield profits greater than or equal to the cost of capital, the

price of the utility's stock will be below book value) and sell power to the independent distribution companies so created under more profit able wholesale rates. The integrated IOU will, in any event, effectively serve the same customers, so it makes sense to serve them under a more profitable regulatory regime. (Of course, state commissions probably will not permit the divestitures and loss of regulatory jurisdiction of 80 percent of the costs of electricity sold at retail, but they can't force the utility to actively solicit muni franchises or industrial customers).

If there is a problem here it is not one of antitrust; it is one of regulation. The apparent price squeeze has nothing to do with the IOU trying to drive competing firms from the market for some resulting monopoly reward. The most productive thing the courts could do is enforce state and federal regulatory statutes to ensure that neither state nor federal regulatory agencies persistently allow returns (or otherwise discriminate in rates) substantially above or below the cost of capital without good public policy justification (for example, bonuses or penalties for efficiency or inefficiency). The federal courts frequently are asked to review FERC determinations, though generally they defer to commission findings on such issues as allowed rate of return unless they are clearly arbitrary or obviously at variance with the facts presented to the commission. If the disparities are not large enough to cause the courts to overturn the offending regulatory disparities, then, I suggest, this is a regulatory gap we will have to live with, one which the antitrust laws do not represent a suitable mechanism for filling.

Consequences of Price-Squeeze Litigation
It appears that all the recent price-squeeze litigation, at both the FERC and the courts, has been at the very least a waste of time as far as its impact on competition and economic efficiency is concerned. The foundation for price-squeeze consideration, based on concern for the maintenance of retail competition and an assumption that integrated utilities can and will use the price squeeze as a mechanism for mono-polizing retail markets to restrain price competition, is based on an incorrect understanding of the structure, regulation, and competitive opportunities in the electric power sector as it exists. As a practical matter all the price-squeeze doctrine has done is create another forum for wholesale customers to try to get their regulated rates reduced. The doctrine, as it is applied in this industry, has nothing to do with promoting competitive processes that spur efficient production and pricing.

This would be enough to raise serious questions about the desirability of applying antitrust sanctions that turn on price-squeeze evidence to the regulated electric utility industry. I think, however, that *Conway* as implemented by the FERC, as interpreted by the courts in reviewing FERC decisions, and as a stimulus to numerous conventional antitrust cases has been a waste of time, and worse. It has had an undesirable effect on the regulatory process and the ability and willingness of utilities and regulators to make electricity rates more efficient.

Price-Squeeze Litigation Price-squeeze litigation has added unnecessary delay and expense to FERC proceedings at a time when the FERC has had to cope with many difficult rate-making issues involving rate structure, efficiency incentives, the use of marginal cost-pricing techniques, approriate accounting treatment of new plant and equipment when nominal interest rates and inflation are high, and so on. It has discouraged voluntary, timely settlement of rate disputes which the FERC has been trying to encourage to reduce regulatory costs and delays. Substantial regulatory resources have been devoted to an issue of no consequence during a period when they could have been deployed much more effectively.

Price-Squeeze Rules The price-squeeze rules have had the unfortunate result of sanctifying the use of fully allocated cost studies and the determination of rates based on average historical costs, because such a method is now required for implementing price-squeeze criteria used by the FERC and approved by the courts reviewing these procedures. Critics of the regulatory process have argued for years that both state and federal regulators should try to move toward the use of marginal cost-pricing techniques and adopt time-of-day rates and interactive rates in an effort to privide consumers with more efficient price signals. Sales to wholesale customers and large industrial customers are the most likely places for implementing innovative rate-design proposals. Concern that innovative rate proposals at either the federal or the state level will trigger antitrust suits based on price-squeeze charges or other charges that turn on the impact of wholesale rates or large industrial rates on retail competition has helped delay such innovations. In a recent case, a utility proposed an interesting wholesale rate which apparently would have given wholesale customers much better signals about the cost of providing electricity at different times of the day and year than do conventional wholesale rates. The FERC eventually rejected the new rate, and it became a key issue in an antitrust suit.[97]

IOUs Discouraged Perhaps the greatest irony is that this litigation discourages IOUs from becoming involved in taking on new requirements customers, especially if they lie outside their service territories; currently they have no formal obligation to extend service. Once an IOU offers power to new muni and coop customers, it must anticipate the likelihood of expensive, time-consuming antitrust litigation down the road if it tries to increases rates or otherwise change the terms of wholesale contracts.

The end result of these rules is likely to be restriction of *wholesale* market competition, the one area where opportunities for efficiency-enhancing competition seem possible, by discouraging IOUs from voluntarily extending wholesale service to new customers under requirements contracts. (Current FERC rate-making practice for requirements contracts, which relies on average historical costs rather than long-run marginal cost which is often higher, provides another constraint and is the source of considerable friction between IOUs and their requirements customers.)

Threat of Costly Antitrust Litigation The threat of costly antitrust litigation arising to some extent from price-squeeze claims but more generally from a body of antitrust law built on preserving nonexistent retail market competition and focusing on protecting small munis and coops has probably had more extensive undesirable effects on the structure and operation of the electric power industry. Antitrust suits by munis and coops are threatened whenever there is a dispute of any kind between an IOU and its publicly owned wholesale customers. These cases have become a nuisance; they reflect the use of antitrust sanctions as a bargaining tool in contract negotiations rather than a constraint on anticompetitive activity. Utilities have responded by trying to avoid *any* relationship or behavior that would set the stage for antitrust litigation even if such a relationship could reduce costs.

Cautious participation in the wholesale market, especially regarding efforts to expand the traditional geographic boundaries of wholesale transactions, is only one such undesirable response to current antitrust policies. Because of prevailing antitrust theories, merger activity, especially acquisitions of small munis, has virtually come to a halt despite the fact that mergers and acquisitions of small utilities could help reduce costs. Mergers of integrated IOUs have been discouraged as well, based on similar theories despite the likelihood that the industry is characterized by too many small firms to fully achieve all economies of scale and coordination.[98] Finally, the threat of antitrust suits by small munis and coops appears to be a major reason why the creation of formal power pools almost stopped during the 1970s. More pooling and better coordination of generation and transmission facilities is where the action is on the production-efficiency front. By discouraging both mergers and formal pooling by integrated utilities, current antitrust policies have served merely to restrict the attainment of all available supply-side economies in order to preserve the illusion of competition at the retail level.

The extensive price-squeeze litigation spawned by *Conway* has been much ado about nothing in terms of legitimate concerns about competition, and it has had several undesirable consequences as well. The U.S. Supreme Court would be doing electricity consumers a favor if it narrowed considerably the FERC's responsibilities in this area and removed the impression *Conway* gave that this is an issue the courts should be especially concerned with in applying the antitrust laws to this industry. The likelihood that a price squeeze would or could be used to restrict competition at the retail level is so slight and the expected costs of reduced competition so small that it makes good sense to simply eliminate it as a source of antitrust litigation in the electric power industry. At the very least, the FERC should be permitted to stop considering price-squeeze issues on a case-by-case basis in the context of rate proceedings. After eight years of litigation without finding persistent disparity between wholesale and retail rates, the FERC should be able to make a generic determination that price squeezes are not a problem and are not worth so much administrative delay and litigation expense. The burden of proof should be shifted to the wholesale customers and price-squeeze investigations should not be initiated unless customers can show that the alleged rate disparities arise in a situation in which they really are likely to restrict competition in the long run. Rather than assuming that retail competition is important in each case, the assumption should be just the opposite. The burden of proof should be shifted to those who contend that retail market competition is significant to show that state laws and prevailing economic conditions in fact allow for real competition for customers or franchises. More generally, sensible antitrust enforcement in this industry cannot be based on promoting competition at the retail level which local and state laws have almost completely eliminated and federal and state rate-making procedures, interest rate subsidies, and unequal allocation of scarce hydroelectric power would severely distort in cases where residual competitive rivalry exists. If the antitrust laws are to promote competition and economic efficiency in this industry, they must focus on those areas where meaningful competitive opportunities exist. Under current institutional arrangements, that area certainly is not at the retail level.

If antitrust policies based on preserving retail competition in the electric power industry are so seriously flawed, does this mean that the antitrust laws should not be applied to electric utilities, given the current and likely future regulatory environment? I believe the answer is no. Bad antitrust policy need not be replaced with no antitrust enforcement. At least some opportunities exist for increasing the role of competitive market forces in allocating electricity supplies and determining prices of electricity. These opportunities, however, lie at the *wholesale* level, not the retail level. While these opportunities too are sharply constrained by current regulatory practice, antitrust policies that focus on wholesale market competition can help promote the competitive opportunities that now exist; they may play a more important role in the future if a larger fraction of wholesale transactions is deregulated or large industrial customers are permitted to shop around for bulk power supplies; and they can help structure regulatory reforms aimed at increasing wholesale market competition.

At the present time the allocation of wholesale power supplies is not governed by the forces of supply and demand in a competitive market but is subject to pervasive price regulation by the FERC. This is especially true of full and partial requirements contracts whose prices are based on average historical costs. As I have noted, however, a market of sorts *has* evolved for a variety of coordination transactions negotiated on a case-by-case basis, primarily between integrated IOUs. There appear to be opportunities to deregulate wholesale transactions further and several commentators have, with varying degrees of enthusiasm, supported efforts to at least experiment with additional deregulation of wholesale transactions in situations where competitive markets appear likely to emerge.[99]

Antitrust laws alone can only promote as much efficiency-enhancing competition as state and federal laws permit. By focusing on competitive opportunities in the wholesale market, however, antitrust analysis may help federal regulators develop rules and regulations regarding wheeling, tariff availability, pricing, and power pooling, which could at least simulate the outcomes that would emerge in a unregulated, competitive market and suggest areas where deregulation might be desirable.

Notes

I would like to thank Frank Fisher, Richard Schmalensee, Reiner Lock, Joe Pace, and John Burton for helpful comments on an earlier draft of this chapter. Sam Huntington and John Landon provided me with useful information at an earlier stage. I am grateful for support from the MIT Center for Energy Policy Research and the Department of Economics Energy Research Fund. The responsibility for the views expressed here is, of course, entirely my own.

1. *Parker v. Brown* 317 U.S. 341 (1941).

2. *Otter Tail Power Co. v. U.S.*, 1973 Trade Cases (74,373) and 1971 Trade Cases (73,692); cited hereafter as *Otter Tail*. *Cantor v. Detroit Edison Co.* 428 U.S. 579 (1976); cited hereafter as *Cantor*.

3. See generally Joskow and Schmalensee, *Markets for Power: An Analysis of Electric Utility Deregulation* (Cambridge: MIT Press, 1983); cited hereafter as Joskow and Schmalensee (1983).

4. Much of the material found in this section is drawn from Joskow and Schmalensee (1983), chap. 2. Detailed references can be found there. I have provided additional references for material not contained there.

5. There are about ten "nonexempt" (under the Public Utility Holding Company Act) electric utility holding companies that own more than one individual operating company located in two or more states. Under the Public Utility Holding Company Act of 1935, a holding company's operating subsidiaries must be in geographical proximity and must be operated as an integrated system. The largest holding company accounts for about 4 percent of total U.S. generating capacity; the largest four account for about 12 percent.

6. U.S. Department of Energy, "Statistics of Privately Owned Electric Utilities—1981 Annual," pp. 28–29; and Edison Electric Institute, "Statistical Yearbook of the Electric Utility Industry, 1980," p. 43. Most discussions of FERC regulation focus on requirements contracts, perhaps because these transactions tend to be contested and are heavily regulated. Yet requirements contracts account for only about a third of the kwh sales subject to FERC regulation (but probably a larger fraction of revenues generated by wholesale power transactions). Wholesale transactions are often expressed as a fraction of total sales either by the IOU sector or the industry as a whole. There is an apparent double-counting problem here since all wholesale transactions eventually appear as sales to ultimate customers. The EEI yearbook separates wholesale transactions between IOUs and publicly owned systems. Sales by IOUs to publicly owned systems account for about 40 percent of IOU sales for resale. It is these transactions that are the focus of price-squeeze cases. For an informative discussion of the wide array of "coordination transactions" regulated by the FERC, Wilbur C. Early, "FERC Regulation of Bulk Power Coordination Transactions," unpublished draft staff working paper, Federal Energy Regulatory Commission, Office of Regulatory Analysis (December 1982).

7. IOUs also engage in numerous joint ventures with each other and with publicly

owned utilities to build and finance new generating and transmission capacity. Wholesale transactions have, in the aggregate, been increasing over time.

8. Relatively large integrated municipal utilities such as the Los Angeles Department of Water and Power are atypical, but there are a few municipal utilities that provide a large fraction of their own power requirements. These companies are not typically involved in price-squeeze cases.

9. The tax and financing subsidies available to publicly owned utilities are discussed in Joskow and Schmalensee (1983), pp. 17–20.

10. 16 USC 825s. This means that revenues are supposed to cover operating costs plus amortization and interest payments on the government's investments. Some power-marketing agencies have fallen behind in their payments to the federal government in recent years. See, for example, *Electric Utility Week* (September 12, 1983), p. 8.

11. TVA projects were originally financed by congressional appropriations. More recently, TVA relies primarily on long-term bonds to finance its facilities. Section 15d of the TVA Act authorizes TVA to issue bonds up to a total of $30 billion. As of 1982, TVA had debt obligations of about $14 billion, most of which was financed through the Federal Financing Bank. See 1982 TVA Annual Report, part II, p. 11.

12. 16 USC 825s and 16 USC 800. The result of increasing electricity demand, plus dramatic increases in fossil fuel prices since 1973, led to an increasing fraction of preference power going to munis and coops during the 1970s. Beginning in 1973 the Bonneville Power Authority (the largest federal power-marketing agency) curtailed firm power sales to IOUs and interrupted sales to direct service customers in order to meet its commitments to its preference customers. See 96th Congress, House Report No. 96-976. The Pacific Northwest Electric Supply & Conservation Act of 1980 made provisions for the IOUs in that region to share in the cheap hydro resources marketed by Bonneville by allocating a share of that power to IOUs to be "dedicated" to residential customers and small farm customers. P.L. 96-504 (1980) and House Report No. 96-976. This is accomplished by allowing the private utilities to "sell" power to Bonneville at their average system cost and to "buy" it back at preference customer rates. Purchases and sales are limited by an IOUs residential load. (There are no new physical transactions, it is merely an accounting transaction.) The difference is made up by increasing prices to direct service customers (large industrial customers served directly by Bonneville; primarily aluminum companies). The Niagara Redevelopment Act of 1957 allocated 50 percent of Niagara Project power (operated by the Power Authority of the State of New York—PASNY) to public bodies and nonprofit cooperatives. PASNY's allocation policies are currently the subject of litigation regarding the meaning of "public body" and the legality of PASNY's original contracts with private utilities for a share of that power. See *Municipal Electric Utilities of the State of New York v. Power Authority of the State of New York, et al.*, FERC Opinion No. 151 and 151-A (October 13, 1982 and April 6, 1983), Utilities Law Reports (12,629 and 12,693).

13. There are some exceptions, however. See the discussion of direct competition in Joskow and Schmalensee (1983), pp. 60–62.

14. See Joskow and Schmalensee (1983), pp. 59–62.

15. Detailed information on regulatory practices in various states can be found in *1981 Annual Report on Utility and Carrier Regulation*, National Association of Regulatory Commissioners (NARUC), Washington, D.C. Cited hereafter as NARUC Annual Report.

16. See James E. Meeks, "Concentration in the Electric Power Industry: The Impact of Antitrust Policy," *Columbia Law Rev.* 72, no. 64 (1972), pp. 95–96. This article appears to have been influential in fashioning the views of the federal courts regarding competition in the electric power industry, though Meeks actually places less emphasis on retail market competition than have the courts.

17. Several nuclear plants are owned jointly by two or more utilities and are organized as separate, wholesale power companies. These nuclear plants "sell" power to their owners under tariffs subject to FERC regulation. There are also at least two holding companies organized with separate, wholesale generating and transmission companies which sell power under FERC regulated tariffs to wholly owned distribution company subsidiaries which are in turn subject to state regulation of retail rates. In these cases the state regulatory commissions must treat purchased-power costs subject to FERC regulation as prudent expenditures and pass the costs through in retail rates. See Joskow and Schmalensee (1983), chap. 11, note 24.

18. This depends to a large extent on the type of coordination transaction. For example, long-term contracts for capacity reflect rate-making principles similar to those in requirements contracts. Unit power sales, short-term energy transactions, economy interchange transactions, and so forth come much closer to reflecting the relevant marginal costs. Although the FERC requires that fairly detailed filings accompany negotiated rates which include cost justifications, the requirements do not appear to be rigid, and extensive reliance on negotiation between utilities for this type of transaction suggests that market forces are playing an important role in allocating resources in the wholesale market. FERC cost-justification requirements probably tend to restrain the full evolution of these market opportunities, though such regulation may be necessary to restrain monopoly power in the wholesale market. For a discussion of rate-making practices for coordination transactions, see Early, "FERC Regulation." For a discussion of competitive opportunities in the wholesale market see Joskow and Schmalensee (1983), chap. 12.

19. 16 USC 825s and Section 7(a) of the Pacific Northwest Electric Power Planning and Conservation Act of 1980 (see note 12 above).

20. *Arkansas Electric Cooperative Corporation v. Arkansas Public Service Commission,* ____U.S.____ (May 16, 1983).

21. See 1981 NARUC Annual Report, table 4, inc. notes.

22. *See Parker v. Brown, Otter Tail* and *Cantor.* Unlike most of the other antitrust cases involving electric utilities, *Cantor* does not involve a dispute between an IOU and muni or coop distribution companies. The issue in *Cantor* was the competitive effects of Detroit Edison's policy of giving away "free" light bulbs to residential customers. It is interesting to note that Thomas Edison started the policy of bundling light bulbs with electricity in the 1880s.

23. Phillip Areeda, *Antitrust Analysis* (Little Brown, 1982), Supplement, section 212.6.

24. See *City of Kirkwood v. Union Electric Co.*, 1982-1 Trade Cases (64,574); cited hereafter as *City of Kirkwood*.

25. A detailed analysis of these antitrust review procedures is contained in "The Nuclear Regulatory Commission's Antitrust Review Process: An Analysis of the Impacts," Transcomm, Inc. June 1981. Prepared for the Department of Energy Under Contract No. DE-AC01-79PE-70025. Cited hereafter as Transcomm (1981).

26. The review focuses on the utility's general bulk power (wholesale) supply behavior (interconnection policies, availability of wholesale tariffs, wheeling policies, power pooling policies, etc.) and its effects on hypothesized competition at the retail level, not simply the implications of construction of the nuclear power plant at issue. In most NRC licensing cases, where the Justice Department identified competitive problems (normally assumed to be adverse consequences for retail competition resulting from restrictions on wholesale transactions), utilities have agreed "voluntarily" to change some of their policies and, with the associated commitments attached to the license application, Justice then recommends against a formal NRC antitrust hearing. In a few cases an agreement with the Justice Department was not reached by the utilities involved, and full-scale antitrust hearings were held by the NRC. Almost all the largest utilities in the country have been subject to this broad antitrust scrutiny. The required commitments to munis and coops include ownership participation in particular facilities, wheeling services, tariff availability, power pool membership, interconnection and coordination, and so forth.

27. See *Gulf States Utilities v. Federal Power Commission et al.* 411 U.S. 774 (1973), cited hereafter as *Gulf State Utilities, Vermont Yankee Nuclear Power Corp. et al.*, 43 SEC 693 (1968), *Federal Power Commission v. Conway Corp* 1976-1 Trade Cases (60,912) and 1975 Trade Cases (60,272); cited hereafter as *Conway*.

28. Although the courts require regulatory agencies to consider the antitrust consequences of their decisions, these agencies are not given exclusive jurisdiction in such situations. Some courts have given the FERC primary jurisdiction over issues raised concurrently in FERC proceedings and Sherman Act cases, however, in deference to the regulatory commission's expertise. *Borough of Ellwood City v. Pennsylvania Power Co.* 1979-2 Trade Cases (62,852); cited hereafter as *Borough of Ellwood City*. Neither does a finding by the FERC that a price squeeze has not taken place also immunize a utility from further litigation on the same issue in an antitrust case. See "New Antitrust Developments Give Munis Greater Clout in Power Purchasing," *Electric Utility Week* (October 10, 1983), p. 9.

29. Indiana & Michigan Electric Co. had 13 FERC, FERC appeals, and antitrust cases pending in 1981, involving essentially the same set of plaintiffs and the same issues. See *Electrical Week* (April 24, 1981), p. 2.

30. See *Power Pooling in the United States*, Federal Energy Regulatory Commission (FERC-0049) (December 1981) (Washington, D.C.); and *Commonwealth Edison Company* 36 FPC 927,931 (1966).

31. *Eastern Electric Energy Systems*, 45 SEC 684 (1975).

32. *U.S. v. Aluminum Company of America et al.* 1945 Trade Regulation Reports (57,342), 57,689-691, 148 F.2d 416 436-38; cited hereafter as *Alcoa*.

33. The Court found that during the period 1925–32, if Alcoa had paid what it charged its competitors for ingot, its profits on rolled sheet would have been negligible for most types of rolled sheet and negative for several types. The Court concluded that the profits were too low to sustain a rolled-sheet manufacturer in business. It should be noted that the Court did not attempt to determine directly what a "fair profit" would be; rather, it used the transfer price test to simulate profits for the 1925–32 period when the squeeze was alleged to be in effect, then compared the simulated profits with actual profits during the 1933–37 period when Alcoa lowered its ingot prices allegedly in response to the announcement of an antitrust investigation by the Department of Justice. *Alcoa* 1945 Trade Regulation Reports, cited at 57,690–691.

34. See Richard Schmalensee, "A Note on the Theory of Vertical Integration," *Journal of Political Economy* 81 (March–April 1973), pp. 442–449; and Frederick R. Warren-Boulton, "Vertical Control with Variable Proportions," *Journal of Political Economy* 82 (July–August 1974), pp. 783–802.

35. Perry, "Price Discrimination and Forward Integration," *Bell Journal of Economics* 9, no. 1 (Spring 1978), pp. 209–217; and "Forward Integration by Alcoa, 1880–1930," *Journal of Industrial Economics* 29, no. 1 (September 1980), pp. 37–53.

36. F. M. Scherer, *Industrial Market Structure and Economic Performance*, 2d ed. (Chicago: Rand McNally, 1980).

37. *FPC v. Conway* 1976-1 Trade Cases (60,912); and *Conway v. FPC* 1975 Trade Cases (60,272).

38. Section 206(a) of the Federal Power Act requires the commission to set just and reasonable rates when, after a hearing, it finds that the rate filed "by any public utility for any transmission or sale *subject to the jurisdiction of the Commission* . . . is unjust, unreasonable, unduly discriminatory or preferential." Similarly, Section 205(b) of the Federal Power Act prohibits any public utility from maintaining rates *subject to the jurisdiction of the commission* where there are "any unreasonable difference in rates, charges, service, facilities, or any other respect, either between localities or as between classes of service" (my emphasis).

39. *Conway v. FPC* 1975 Trade Cases (60,272). Meeks (1972) appears to have been especially influential in convincing this court that retail competition is important. Meeks contains no empirical evidence supporting the importance of retail competition as a supplement to regulation constraining monopoly pricing and promoting economic efficiency at the retail level. See *Conway v. FPC*, at 66,053.

40. FPC v. *Conway*, 426 U.S. 271 (1976).

41. *Illinois Cities of Bethany et al. v. Federal Energy Regulatory Commission* 670 F. 2d 187 (1981); cited hereafter as *Bethany*. The original appeals court opinion (August 17, 1981, slip opinion) is cited as *Bethany I*.

42. 18 CFR 2.17 (March 25, 1977 as amended May 3, 1982 47 FR 190511).

43. *Southern California Edison Co.*, FERC Opinion No. 62 (August 22, 1979), *Utilities Law Reports* (12,233), at 14,206–207.

44. *Cities of Batavia et al. v. FERC et al.* (D.C. Court of Appeals, February 9, 1982),

Utilities Law Reports (12,540), at 16,209–210; cited hereafter as *Cities of Batavia*, *Bethany* 670 F. 2d 195.

45. *Boston Edison Company* FPC Opinion No. 809 (July 6, 1977).

46. *Missouri Power & Light Company*, FERC Opinion No. 31 (October 27, 1978), *Utilities Law Reports* (12,517), at 13,517. In a recent decision the FERC seems to be moving away from this position. See *Pennsylvania Power Company Phase II* FERC Opinion No. 157 (December 21, 1982), *Utilities Law Reports* (12,674); cited hereafter as *Penn Power*.

47. *Connecticut Light & Power Company*, FERC Docket No. ER78-517 (August 20, 1979).

48. *Penn Power*, at 16,984.

49. *Cities of Batavia*, at 16,212; and *Bethany*, at 190–91.

50. *Penn Power*, at 16,984; *Cities of Batavia*, at 16,210–213, *Bethany*, at 198–199.

51. *Cities of Batavia*; and *Bethany*.

52. *Cities of Batavia*, at 16,211.

53. *Southern California Edison Company*, FERC Opinion No. 62 (August 22, 1979), *Utilities Law Reports* (12,233), at 14,208; and mimeo of full opinion, at 29–30; *Commonwealth Edison Company* FERC Opinion No. 63 (September 14, 1979) *Utilities Law Reports* (12,234), at 14,216.

54. *Cities of Batavia*, at 16,211.

55. *Bethany*, at 196.

56. *Penn Power*, at 16,984.

57. *Penn Power*, at 16,985.

58. *Borough of Ellwood City et al. v. Pennsylvania Power Company*, 1979-2 Trade Cases (62,852), at 78,935; cited hereafter as *Borough of Ellwood City*. This case is the antitrust case spawned by *Penn Power*. Now that *Penn Power* has been resolved by the FERC, the antitrust case will once again become active. See also *City of Kirkwood*, at 73, 145–147; and *City of Mishawaka et al v. American Electric Power Co.* (63,193) 1980-1 Trade Cases, at 77,928. See 1979-1 Trade Cases (62,447) for the district court opinion. Cited hereafter as *City of Mishawaka*.

59. *City of Mishawaka*, at 77,930.

60. *City of Groton, Borough of Ellwood City, City of Kirkwood, City of Mishawaka*. The district court in *City of Groton* seems to have understood better than anyone else what is going on in these cases. "Throughout this action the [plaintiffs] have persisted in [what] might charitably be considered the 'shotgun' approach to antitrust litigation: they have challenged everything and now hope to hit something"; 1980–81 Trade Cases, at 78,399. The district court rejected all the municipal plaintiff's claims. The appeals court affirmed everything except the rejection of the price-squeeze claim, which was remanded for further findings; 1981–2 Trade Cases (64,329), at 74,502, 74,509.

61. Wheeling refers to the provision of transmission services by a third party when a buyer purchases power from a seller to whom the buyer is not interconnected.

62. In *Otter Tail* an integrated private utility refused to sell power at wholesale or to wheel power from a federal hydro source or from several cooperative G&Ts to municipal distribution systems previously served at retail by Otter Tail but which subsequently had taken over Otter Tail's municipal distribution assets when its franchises expired. By refusing to deal in this way, Otter Tail was accused of using its control over "bottleneck" subtransmission facilities to monopolize the retail market. Although the domain of competition and concern about Otter Tail's monopoly power focused on the retail market, its control over certain "bottleneck" (subtransmission) facilities was critical to a finding that its refusal to deal constituted a violation of the antitrust laws. It is clear, however that the courts conceived of its intent as being to monopolize the retail market. Plaintiffs have not been particularly successful in sustaining the kinds of charges made in *Otter Tail*. See *City of Groton, Borough of Landsdale v. Philadelphia Electric Co.* (3rd Circuit) 1982–83 Trade Cases 65,025. The latter is cited hereafter as *Borough of Landsdale. Town of Massena v. Niagara Power Corp.*, 1980-2 Trade Cases (63,526).

63. See also *Borough of Ellwood City, City of Kirkwood*, and *City of Groton*, where price-squeeze charges have figured prominently.

64. I&M turns out to be one of the few utilities that serves some large industrial customers inside the service territory of a municipal utility to which it sells power. This reflects long-standing historical relationships. No evidence was presented of active competition for existing or new industrial loads in the recent past. To the extent that large industrial customers take power at subtransmission voltage, the muni distribution companies may not be in a position to compete for such customers. Indeed, industrial customers who cannot be served by an IOU which, because the municipality has de facto exclusivity, may be forced to pay for distribution facilities they actually don't require. Although the district court pointed to an ongoing program by I&M to purchase municipal distribution systems, it appears that I&M had not acquired any since 1966. See brief for Defendants—Appellants filed April 4, 1979, pp. 44–50.

65. Until the early 1960s the states often regulated intrastate wholesale transaction. The FPC asserted jurisdiction over these transactions at that time.

66. In this case, the district court appears to have adopted the plaintiffs' proposed findings of fact almost word for word (including typographical errors) despite conflicting evidence in the record.

67. *Indiania and Michigan Electric Company*, FERC Opinion No. 95 (September 2, 1980), *Utilities Law Reports* (12,360).

68. See Paul L. Joskow and Paul W. MacAvoy, "Regulation and the Financial Condition of the Electric Utilities in the 1970's," *American Economic Review* 65 (May 1975), pp. 295–301; and M. L. Baughman et al., *Electric Power in The United States* (MIT Press, 1979), chap. 9.

69. *City of Mishawaka* (1979), at 76,631 (emphasis added).

70. *City of Mishawaka* (1979). The maximum five-month suspension period is a statutory requirement, not an administrative procedure adopted by the FERC under broader statutory authority. In addition, the statute requires that a utility file proposed rate

changes at least sixty days before they are scheduled to go into effect. Thus there is actually a period of seven months within which the FERC can keep a new rate from going into effect. If rate reviews have not been completed within five months after the rates are scheduled to go into effect, by statute, the rates must be allowed to go into effect subject to refund. See 16 USC 824d(e). Interest is now credited at the prime rate (18 CFR 35.19 (a) (2) (iii)). The statute does give the FERC authority to develop procedures to shorten the suspension periods and develop specific procedures for calculating refunds plus interest. *As regulatory procedures* per se, the FERC's policies here have been approved by the courts. See *Municipal Light Boards of Reading and Wakefield Mass. v. FPC* 450 F. 2d 1341 (1971); and *Wisconsin Electric Power Co. v. Federal Energy Regulatory Commission* 602 F. 2d 452. A charitable interpretation of the court's concern here is that I&M abused these procedures in an effort to drive competitors from the market. But the only evidence discussed by the court is that I&M used the procedures and, as is almost always the case, got less than it asked for in the final rates.

71. *City of Mishawaka* (1980).

72. *City of Mishawaka* (1980), at 77,931 note 15.

73. *City of Mishawaka* (1980), at 77,932.

74. Settlement agreements with the "Mishawaka cities," as well as settlement agreements for "clone" cases with the cities of Anderson and Auburn, Indiana, are on file with the FERC (settlement agreements dated September 30, 1981). The settlements covered thirteen cases involving these cities relating to both price-squeeze charges and various vertical restraints. See *Electrical Week*, (August 24, 1981), p. 2.

75. See note 72 above. This comparison, however, does not appear to reflect cost differences. When cost differences are included in most of the cases, the wholesale rates are even lower relative to retail rates.

76. See Joskow and Schmalensee (1983), chap. 6. The general literature on competition in the electric power industry focuses on six dimensions of competition, five retail and one wholesale. In addition to the three dimensions of retail competition discussed here, the literature discusses direct competition where there are duplicative or overlapping franchises and "yardstick" competition. Neither type of competition has played a significant role in the evolution of the price-squeeze doctrine. As I have mentioned, direct competition is rare. Yardstick competition seems to be an especially silly concept here, since the "yardstick" comparison is between vertically integrated systems that produce, transport, and distribute electricity and small unintegrated distribution systems. Any yardstick comparison would be like comparing apples and oranges. For further discussion see Joskow and Schmalensee (1983); and Pace and Landon (1982).

77. 7 USC 904.

78. Joe D. Pace and John H. Landon, "Introducing Competition into the Electric Utility Industry: An Economic Appraisal," *Energy Law Journal* 3, no. (1982), p. 57. Cited hereafter as Pace and Landon (1982).

79. See *MEUA v. PASNY* FERC Opinions 151, 151-A (October 13, 1982, April 6, 1983), *Utilities Law Reports* (12,629 and 12,696).

80. Pace and Landon, pp. 48–50.

81. There may be several reasons. Municipal utilities are in some cases used as a vehicle for generating additional revenues for a municipality. Cooperative utilities are independent, nonprofit organizations which cannot be used by a municipality as a supplementary source of tax revenues by charging monopoly prices and using net revenues for other municipal services. Cooperatives are also more frequently subject to regulation of prices, profits, and service quality by state regulatory commissions than are municipalities. This gives municipal governments more freedom to charge above-cost prices for electricity and siphon off revenue for municipal services rather than invest in maintaining the distribution system and thereby use the municipal utility as a source of supplementary tax revenue. The primary constraint on such behavior is the threat that a proximate regulated IOU will convince the voters to transfer the municipal franchise to it. Also, cooperative distribution companies historically have been much more aggressive than municipals in providing for their own generating capacity through creation of cooperative generation and transmission entities that serve many coop distribution companies. Municipal utilities have begun to cooperate to build or own generating capacity through joint-action agencies but not always with great success. Cooperatives have also had access to much more favorable interest subsidies under the REA than have municipals (see Joskow and Schmalensee [1983]) and tend naturally to have been formed in areas near sources of preference power.

82. See Joskow and Schmalensee (1983), pp. 163–166.

83. When we are talking about location decisions involving a choice of living or engaging in business in some municipality served by a municipal utility, rather than an *adjacent* area served by an IOU supplier (as opposed to interregional location decisions, for example), I see no obvious reason why most industrial location decisions should be more sensitive to electricity prices than are residential or commercial-location decisions. The evidence on the effect of electricity prices (and energy prices more generally) on industrial location reflect larger interregional differences in prices, not small differences within a narrow geographic area.

84. *City of Frankfort, Indiana v. Federal Energy Regulatory Commission* (7th Circuit, May 17, 1982), *Utilities Law Reports* (12,586), at 16,487 note 16. This case is one of a series of related cases involving charges of anticompetitive discrimination between different classes of wholesale customers rather than wholesale/retail discrimination as in the price-squeeze cases. See also *Boroughs of Chambersburg and Mont Alto, Pennsylvania v.FERC*, 580 F.2d 573 (1978), *Public Service Company of Indiana v. FERC* 575 F.2d 1204 (1978), *Town of Norwood v. FERC* 587 F.2d 1306 (1978), *Towns of Alexandria et al. v. FPC* 555 F.2d 1020 (1977), *Central Illinois Public Service Company*, FERC Opinion No. 142 (July 12, 1982), *Utilities Law Reports* (12,619). Unlike the price-squeeze case, the FERC has jurisdiction over all rates at issue. However, although the issue of "competitive harm" arises in these cases as it does in price-squeeze cases, the FERC and the courts have rejected the use of "price-squeeze standards" for determining undue discrimination. Here, the assumed competitive problem is that different sets of wholesale customers compete with each other for retail customers, and some may be disadvantaged in the competition if they are charged higher wholesale rates than others by the IOU supplier. See *Central Illinois Public Service Co.*, at 16,658. In these cases the FERC and the courts appear to tolerate differences in wholesale rates that are not cost-justified if there are other factual differences that justify the rates or the rate differences do not result in any

competitive harm. *City of Frankfort*, at 16,487. Differences over long-term contracting policies over time and the use of fixed price versus adjustable contracts are often at issue in these cases. The standards for rejecting jurisdictional wholesale rates based on concerns about the anticompetitive effects of discrimination are much tougher than are the standards for evaluating wholesale/retail rate disparities. Also, there is considerably more skepticism about the existence of competition at the retail level.

In the price-squeeze cases, a showing that there is a difference between wholesale and retail rates leads to the assumption that there are anticompetitive effects; the burden of proof is on the utility to show that there are none. In the wholesale rate discrimination cases, even if there is a noncost-justified difference in rates, the burden of proof is on the wholesale customers to show evidence of competitive harm; a showing of *possible* competitive harm is not enough. See *Central Illinois Public Service Co.*, at 16,658.

85. In *Connecticut Light & Power Co.*, FPC Opinion No. 761-A (July 20, 1977), a large industrial customer served by a municipal utility customer of CL&P complained about being squeezed and requested a special industrial wholesale rate to be flowed through to muni industrial customers. The munis themselves did not bring a price-squeeze claim before the FERC in this case, though they subsequently did bring a Section 2 case (*City of Groton*).

86. For example, rivalry between two utilities with generation and transmission facilities for providing electric service to an isolated shale oil production facility in Utah appears to reflect a dispute over territorial exclusivity. See "Shale Oil Project Sparks Territorial Dispute between Utah P&L and a Co Op," *Electric Utility Week* (December 5, 1983), p. 4.

87. See Pace and Landon (1982), pp. 48–50. It is interesting that since *Mishawaka*, the State of Indiana has further restricted the opportunities for fringe-area competition. See Indiana Public Law No. 69-1900 effective March 1, 1900.

88. The FERC and most states evaluate rates based on the "cost of service." However, they use accounting formulas for determining costs which yield costs for pricing purposes that may have little relationship to the *economic* costs of providing more or less electricity in the long run. In particular, rates reflect the depreciated original cost of plant and equipment, straight-line depreciation based on original cost and the average coupon rate of existing long-term debt obligations. Thus a utility with much old plant and much debt issued when interest rates were low will have much lower costs for rate-making purposes than a similarly situated utility that recently added and financed a large new generating plant despite the fact that they may have the same marginal costs. Rates reflect the average historical cost of plant and equipment, average "embedded" interest rates on debt instruments, current nominal (in theory) costs of equity, and straight-line depreciation of the original cost of plant and equipment. Rates based on average historical costs may be below or above the true economic cost of providing additional electricity. Regulatory lag, of course, affects the actual relationship between prices and costs regardless of the way they are measured. Utilities with average historical costs (and prices) below marginal cost are reluctant to take on new loads at prices below what it really costs them to serve these loads.

89. Because of the accounting procedures used to determine rates, the addition of a capital-intensive nuclear unit can increase current rates for a utility dramatically compared to an adjacent utility that will not be adding plant to the rate base for a few years.

Clearly, shopping around for low regulated prices is not the same thing as shopping for power from the source with the lowest *economic* costs.

90. I use 90 percent for the following reason. About 80 percent of net generation for a typical IOU is associated with retail sales to its own customers; therefore, associated costs are subject to state juridiction. Of the remaining wholesale transactions, about half are associated with requirements contracts of the type that lead to price-squeeze charges. There is no reason to believe that prices for the remaining coordination transactions would be manipulated to implement the strategy. For simplicity I have merely treated these as though they were regulated by the states. Actually, retail *revenues* are probably a larger fraction of total revenues than their fraction of net generation, since they include distribution and customer costs.

91. Obviously, a large industrial customer making a location decision must be convinced that the low rates are not temporary and will not eventually be raised to a higher level than they would have been, but for the reduction in competition, to respond at all to the lower rates. On the other hand, such an eventual increase in prices is the only thing that will make the strategy profitable; thus a significant number of customers will have to be mistaken in order for predation to work.

92. In recent years several utilities have asked their state commissions to allow them to offer special discounts to some large industrial customers. Typically this has occurred in areas where economic activity was severely depressed and the utilities had excess capacity. These proposed rate reductions were to be temporary and were oriented toward helping firms in difficult economic circumstances maintain or increase production. They also reflect the fact that in the presence of excess capacity, short-run marginal cost is likely to be much less than posted rates. Allowing this kind of flexibility to reflect changing economic circumstances seems desirable. It would be unfortunate if such rate reductions got caught in the price-squeeze net.

93. My views on predatory pricing are discussed in Joskow and Klevorick, "A Framework for Analyzing Predatory Pricing Policy," *Yale Law Journal* 89, 2 (December 1979). Much of the literature on that subject is discussed in that article.

94. See *City of Groton* (1981) at 74,508 (5.5 months); and *Penn Power*, at 16,984 (11.5 months).

95. This is superficially related to the conjecture in the second part of the Averch-Johnson paper concerning the pricing of utility services when a regulated firm operates in both monopoly and competitive markets. To the best of my knowledge, this conjecture has never formally been proved. The mechanism suggested here is quite different. The Averch-Johnson conjecture is based on a static model and does not appear to rely on temporary price cuts.

96. I have not worked out exactly how this might occur; but it would appear that if regulators set rates based on a formula that establishes profits as the product of the allowed rate of return and the rate base, and the allowed rate of return is above the cost of capital, it will be profitable to integrate into retail markets and earn a supracompetitive return on the distribution assets. During the 1970s, when most of these cases arose, it was unlikely that the expected return on incremental investment was above the cost of capital.

There are, of course, numerous other "nonmonopoly" reasons when it might be in an IOUs interest and in consumers' interests for an IOU to take over a muni or coop distribution system. The IOU may be able to both supply and price distribution services more efficiently if it integrates forward, resulting in lower costs and prices on average and a rate structure that better reflects the cost of service. While the economies of vertical integration between the distribution level and the generation/transmission level appear to be modest, there may be economies of vertical integration at this level (see Joskow and Schmalensee for a discussion of vertical integration in this industry and other vertical contracting arrangements) that could be captured by acquisition. A larger IOU may be able to provide distribution services more economically than an individual muni (tax and interest rate subsidies aside) because it can take advantage of scale economies in maintenance, engineering, and procurement. An IOU may be able to revitalize a municipal system that has been allowed to deteriorate by a municipality. One has to look at the facts in each case. There should be no assumption that an interest in acquiring muni and coop distribution systems represents an intent to monopolize some imaginary retail markets where there is minimal competition to start with.

97. See *City of Groton* (1981), at 74,505.

98. See Joskow and Schmalensee (1983), chaps. 4–7.

99. See Joskow and Schmalensee (1983), part II.

10

Policymakers' Preferences for Alternative Allocations of the Broadcast Spectrum

Forrest Nelson and Roger Noll

A common task of regulatory agencies is to define and allocate among competing claimants rights to use a resource owned or controlled by the government. Rarely are regulators permitted to make such decisions solely on the basis of economic criteria; normally, the explicit, legislative purpose of the regulatory process is to take into account socially important values that might be ignored by private parties engaging in market transactions.

A prime example of this form of regulation is allocation of television channel assignments among cities by the Federal Communications Commission (FCC). The FCC manages the parts of the electromagnetic spectrum that are available for private, domestic use. Its responsibilities include setting aside frequencies that may be used for television stations and reserving rights to use these frequencies for specific geographic areas. After these assignments are made, the FCC proceeds to license a station; that is, it selects an entity from among competing applicants who will then be permitted to engage in television broadcasting.

In making television channel assignments, the FCC takes several factors into account: the likely economic viability of the station, the number of previous allocations to the same city, the mix of stations in the city (commercial versus noncommercial, VHF versus UHF), the technical problems associated with avoiding signal interference among stations. Precisely how these factors are taken into account and weighed against each other, however, has not been made explicit.

The question that motivated us in writing this chapter is whether channel-assignment decisions exhibit consistency with an articulable decision rule. There are several reasons for doubting that FCC allocation decisions are consistent and stable. First, because the noneconomic and nontechnical criteria are vaguely defined, they are susceptible to differing interpretations as well as different relative weightings, at different times and by different people. Second, the composition of the FCC and the relevant congressional oversight committees changes over time, reflecting political changes. This could be expected to have some affect on allocation decisions. Third, the FCC and its oversight committees are majority-rule institutions. In general, majority-rule voting does not produce equilibrium. More specifically, in the closely related case of license awards in comparative broadcast hearings, M. L. Spitzer has shown that FCC policies are susceptible to inconsistent decisions arising from the instability of majority rule.[1]

This chapter uses estimates of the structure of preferences of policy makers concerning alternative assignments of UHF television channels to simulate the allocations that would result from different procedures for aggregating decision makers' preferences. These simulations are compared with each other and with the present pattern of assignments to determine the degree to which the assignment process produces a consistent, stable outcome. The subjects whose behavior is examined here are six members of the FCC and nine members of the congressional committee that oversees the commission. The mechanism for revealing the preferences of each subject was an experiment in which subjects made choices among alternative channel assignments. Data collected from the experiments were fitted to theoretical stochastic models of qualitative choice to obtain estimates of assignment preferences as a function of the characteristics of candidate cities. These preference functions can be used for a number of purposes. In this chapter we focus on the pattern of allocations that emerges from a majority-rule institution comprising members having these estimated preference relationships, the differences between the two groups of policy makers (commissioners and members of Congress), and the consistency of the simulated results with historical allocation decisions.

The Channel-Assignment Problem

One of the principal responsibilities of the Federal Communications Commission is to define and allocate rights to use the electromagnetic spectrum for communications purposes. Since the early 1950s the FCC has reserved a large portion of the spectrum for television, and except for occasional tinkering at the margins, this element of spectrum allocation has been resolved. The next step, however, remains controversial: making channel assignments to particular cities. Because nearly all VHF channel assignments have been made and are being used, the major remaining task is to allocate the largely unused UHF spectrum, although the FCC is also in the process of squeezing in some additional low-power VHF channel assignments.

Exactly why the Congress wants the FCC to use an administrative process to allocate television stations among cities is a matter of some dispute. A definitive treatment of that issue is beyond the scope of this chapter. Suffice to say that the policy derives from the "local service doctrine," which holds that each community ought to have an equitable amount of locally controlled broadcasting outlets if the community is large enough to make local stations economically viable.[2]

The allocation problem faced by the FCC is to decide the maximum number of television stations that will be allowed to operate in each community. This task has three elements. The first is to determine which assignments are technically feasible in that they will not interfere with each other. The second element is to determine whether a particular station assignment is economically viable. In the mid-1970s, the FCC asked economists at the Rand Corporation to develop a model for estimating the future financial viability of UHF stations.[3] The resulting estimates of economic prospects could then be used to supplement the technical assignment model.

The third component of the allocation problem is to choose among the alternatives that are technically and economically feasible. One dimension that affects the choice, by virtue of the local service doctrine, is the pattern of existing allocations among communities. Presumably, the practical implication of the local service doctrine is to work toward equalization of viewing options across communities. Another dimension is the magnitude of the benefits from an assignment. This would tend to be an increasing function of the population served by a station, for two reasons: (1) for a given program, greater benefits are derived if more people watch it; and (2) the profit-maximizing strategy for a station, ceteris paribus, produces a positive relationship between program quality and potential audience. These two factors tend to work against the local-service doctrine because they lead to allocating more stations to larger cities than to smaller ones. Still another dimension of the problem is to decide what kind of station to form. The FCC usually decides at the channel-assignment stage whether a station will be commercial or noncommercial, although on a few occasions it has switched the status of an unclaimed assignment. Within each category it also decides indirectly the kind of programming that will be broadcast by virtue of the patterns of programming that develop as stations are added to a market. For example:

• The first three VHF commercial stations (or, with fewer than three commercial VHF stations, the first three commercial stations) will affiliate with a network.

• Technical contraints on VHF assignments make it unlikely any allocation will lead to a fourth commercial network.[4]

• Independent commercial VHF stations, because of signal-reception advantages, will outbid commercial UHF stations for the best programming not provided by the three major networks; thus the type and quality of programming on an additional UHF station depends on whether its independent competition is from VHFs or other UHFs.

• Second or third noncommercial assignments, because of the scarcity of programming available for them, will focus on providing reruns of programs from the national noncommercial network, very inexpensive, discussion-oriented local programs, and educational services.

With respect to commercial stations, access to television advertising by local merchants (in comparison with national and regional businesses) will be affected by the number and spectrum location of commercial outlets. An advantage of local UHF commercial independents in the eyes of the FCC is that they provide an inexpensive advertising outlet for local business which enables them to compete more effectively with larger firms.[5] Multiple stations also are thought to foster political competition in local affairs by increasing the number of independent points of view that can be given access to channels.

For these and other reasons, political decision-makers may have preferences among alternative channel allocations that would not be fully accounted for if allocation decisions were made solely on the basis of a station's economic performance. Most of these reasons are related to a few characteristics of markets that might be used as a basis for comparing their relative merits as recipients of a channel assignment. Among these characteristics are population, the number of stations already in the market, and the characteristics of the existing stations (VHF or UHF, commercial or noncommercial).

The Model and the Experiment

As noted, the purpose of the experiment was to gather information regarding allocation preferences. In this section we briefly summarize the model, the experiment, and the estimation procedures.

The most useful preference information is for a single individual and refers to the assignment of a single new station. The individual's perferred allocation can then be constructed from successive assignment of single stations; questions regarding allocation preferences of a group can be answered by considering methods of aggregating the individual preferences of group members. The first step, then, is specification of a theoretical model of qualitative choice behavior. The model we used is adapted from the random utility model developed by D. McFadden.[6]

The essential elements of this model are as follows. Let M be the number of markets to which television channels may be assigned, and let N be the number of categories of channels that can be placed in a market. Let A_{ti} be the vector of channel allocations by type to market i at time t, P_{ti} the population of market i at time t, and X_{ti} a vector-valued function of P_{ti} and A_{ti}. Write the vector of the P_{ti} values as P_t and of the A_{ti} assignments as A_t. Finally let Y_{tij} indicate whether the assignment at time t will be a channel of type j to market i, Y_t the vector of these indicators, and U_{tij} an unobserved random variable. A decision maker is assumed to assign each alternative an unobserved score, S_{tij}, which is determined by:

$$S_{tij} = \beta'_j X_{ti} + U_{tij}$$

and the logistic choice probabilities appear as

$$Pr(Y_t | P_t, A_t) = \prod_{i=1}^{M} \prod_{j=1}^{2} \left[\frac{\exp(\beta'_j X_{ti})}{\sum_{h'=1}^{M} \sum_{k'=1}^{2} \exp(\beta'_{k'} X_{th'})} \right]^{Y_{tij}}$$

The vectors β_1 and β_2 are the parameters to be estimated. The object of the experiment is to gather the data that make possible this estimation.

The general structure of the channel-assignment experiment is that it asks a subject to make a sequence of channel assignments among a group of cities that differ in population and initial assignment. The design of the experiment had to satisfy two highly binding design constraints: the statistical techniques employed required a large number of observations, and the experiment could take no more than a few minutes if cooperation was to be obtained from the highly placed government officials who were our subjects.

Although several forms of the experiment have been used, the following discussion describes the version used for the commissioners, members of Congress, and several high-level staff members from both groups. The earlier variants were applied to some staff and had different ranges of variation in independent variables and in the number of factors allowed to influence allocations. The final form of the experiment was based on experience gained from the earlier trials. The complete set of instructions to subjects and experimenters for the final version is available from the authors.

At the beginning of the experiment, a subject is confronted with an existing allocation to four cities. The subject is shown a game board which indicates the population of the area served by stations in each city and the number of stations already on the air in each of four categories: UHF and VHF stations of the commercial and noncommercial variety. The set of initial conditions used for different trials of the experiment is shown in table 10.1.[7] Having been shown the setup for trial 1a, the subject is told that in any city the first three VHF commercial allocations (or the first three commercial stations if there are fewer than three VHF commercial allocations) will be network affiliates; the rest of the commercial channels are independents. The experimenter then gives the subject four tokens representing VHF channels and a large number of UHF tokens. The subject is told to begin assigning additional channels among the four cities in order of the subject's assessment of the relative value of the alternatives. An allocation is made by placing a VHF or UHF token in one of the two station-type categories in one of the four cities.[8]

The subject allocates channels until one of two events occurs. If the subject believes no more channels serve a useful social purpose, the subject announces that the experiment is over. Otherwise, the subject is told that the experimenter will call the experiment to a halt in a few minutes, based on a random decision rule unknown to the subject. In practice, experimenters were told to stop the experiment after about twenty allocations or after about two minutes, whichever occurred first. The number of UHF tokens available to the subject was much larger than the maximum number of choices that could be made under this rule. The intent of the stop rule is to reinforce the instruction that each assignment is to be the best available alternative and not one element of an unordered set of several, essentially simultaneous assignments. Only in the former case would the set of assignments satisfy the characteristics of a random sample that are assumed in the theoretical model and the statistical procedures.[9] The number of times the experiment was run on each subject was made a variable. The experimenter was instructed to rerun the experiment enough times with varying

Table 10.1
Initial Conditions for Experiments

A. Initial allocations by frequency and type[a]

| | | Type | | | | | | | |
| | | Market A | | Market B | | Market C | | Market D | |
Trial #	Frequency	Comm.	Non-comm.	Comm.	Non-comm.	Comm.	Non-comm.	Comm.	Non-comm.
1a	VHF	2	1	2	0	2	0	1	0
	UHF	1	1	0	1	0	1	1	0
1b	VHF	2	1	1	0	2	1	2	0
	UHF	1	0	1	1	1	0	0	0
2a	VHF	1	1	2	1	2	1	2	1
	UHF	1	0	0	0	1	1	0	1
2b	VHF	2	1	2	1	2	1	2	1
	UHF	0	0	0	0	0	0	0	0
3a	VHF	1	0	0	0	1	1	2	0
	UHF	1	0	2	1	1	0	1	2
3b	VHF	3	1	3	0	3	0	3	2
	UHF	0	1	0	0	1	1	1	1
4a	VHF	1	1	2	1	1	1	1	1
	UHF	0	0	1	0	1	0	1	0
4b	VHF	2	0	3	0	3	0	2	1
	UHF	0	0	2	0	1	0	0	0

B. Population of markets[b]

Trial #	Market A	Market B	Market C	Market D
1a and 1b	5,000,000	1,500,000	400,000	100,000
2a and 2b	200,000	400,000	6,000,000	1,800,000
3a and 3b	1,200,000	75,000	500,000	4,500,000
4a and 4b	150,000	4,000,000	1,800,000	300,000

[a] Entries indicate the number of stations by frequency and type reassigned to each market at the beginning of the trial. "Comm." refers to a commercial assignment, and "noncomm." to a noncommercial channel.

[b] Entries are the population of the television market, normally somewhat larger than the metropolitan area in which a station is located. These figures appeared on the game board during the corresponding trial and were changed every second trial.The populations span almost the entire range of television markets, except that New York City and Los Angeles are not represented (both are much larger than any other television market). The remainder of the top ten markets range from three to eight million. Populations fall below 1 million at about the thirtieth ranked market. The hundredth largest market has a population of approximately 400,000; the one hundred fiftieth about 200,000; the two hundredth about 100,000. Thus each trial was constructed to have one city from the top ten, one from the next forty, one near the bottom of the top 100, and one from the remainder of markets, ranked 101 to the bottom, number 225.

initial conditions to generate at least fifty choices. Initial assignments among cities were changed when a run of the experiment was stopped and the next experiment begun; populations were changed after every other trial.

An important feature of the experiment is the absence of direct incentives to subjects. To pay subjects was impossible because they occupy positions in either the agency that would have paid the subjects or the congressional subcommittee that authorizes its budget. The problem in experimental design that this poses is that there is no reason to believe that the responses reveal true preferences. This should introduce no particular bias into the results, though it may make them essentially observations on random variables rather than the result of rational comparisons.

Two features of the experiment could counteract the tendency to give random, poorly considered answers. One is that subjects were told the truth about the purpose of the experiment, which is that the subject's responses may be used to make real allocations.[10] The second is that the experiment was designed to be enjoyable. This required creating an interesting task in an interesting setting and designing an experiment that is brief and fast-moving. To the extent that these elements succeed, the choices made by the subject should be more consistent.

Although the authors administered the experiment a few times, most of the data were collected by two staff members of the FCC who were assigned to the UHF Task Force. The authors trained the two staff members in experimental techniques and directed several experiments in the presence of one of them. For details of the experimental procedures, see our companion paper.[11]

Experimental subjects were selected in the following way. In 1978 all seven FCC commissioners and fifteen members of the House Subcommittee on Communications were asked to be subjects. One commissioner and six representatives refused. Included in the sample are commissioners Brown, Ferris, Fogarty, Lee, Quello, and White and Congressmen Brown, Gore, Mikluski, Moore, Moorhead, Moss, Skubitz, Stockman, and Van Deerlin.[12] All subjects were promised that the results of the experiment would be presented in such a way that their responses could not be matched to their names.

The data generated by an experiment on a single subject consist of (1) the initial conditions (population and allocation of stations in each of M

markets) for each trial, and (2) the sequence of new-frequency assignments in each trial. The current allocation in all markets on which each
new assignment is based can readily be calculated from the initial
allocation and the sequence of preceding assignments, which represent
increments to the allocation. Each subject participates in several trials
which have different intitial assignments and populations for the four
markets. If the data for all trials on one subject are combined, and if T is
the total number of new assignments made in all trials, then T observations $(t = 1, \ldots T)$ are collected on the variables defined above and on
each of the following:

CU_{ti} number of commercial UHF channel assignments in market i,

CV_{ti} number of commercial VHF channel assignments in market i,

NU_{ti} number of noncommercial UHF channel assignments in market i,

NV_{ti} number of noncommercial VHF channel assignments in market i.

$(i = 1, \ldots, M)$

To estimate, for each subject, the conditional logit model of choice
behavior described above, the vector A_{ti} is assumed to include the four
variables listed above. The Y_{tij} discriminate only between commercial
and noncommercial assignments, and not between UHF and VHF.[13]

The model that was fitted used the variables reported in table 10.2.
This set was chosen as the best for fitting the model to the data after
some experimentation with alternative specifications. To avoid the
potential danger of "overfitting" the data, nearly all the experimentation with alternative specifications used data from the pilot experiments. Moreover, the same model was applied to each subject, and
variables were added or deleted only if that change uniformly improved the fit across all pilot subjects. The result of the study was a
model that included nine variables and seventeen coefficients. The final
model was then fitted to the data obtained from the subjects of most
interest, commissioners, members of Congress and high-level FCC and
congressional staff members. Variables were eliminated from the model
at this stage to the extent possible without sacrificing predictive power.

Overall, the fit of the model for each subject is reasonably good.
Significance tests must be treated with some caution, given the small
sample sizes and the fact that the model was arrived at by some
searching over alternative specifications. The pseudo R^2s, computed as

Table 10.2
List of Exogenous Variables

X_1	Dummy—a constant term introduced to allow for gross preference differences between commercial and noncommercial assignments
X_2	#Com UHF—the number of commercial UHF stations (CU) currently allocated
X_3	#Com VHF—the number of commercial VHF stations (CV)
X_4	#Non-com—the number of noncommercial stations (NV + NU)
X_5	Pop/#Sta—population divided by total number of stations
X_6	Population—market population (P) (in millions)
X_7	Log pop—natural log of (population + 1)
X_8	Network—dummy variable for networks (1 if fewer than three commercial stations, 0 otherwise)

$1 - L(\hat{\beta})/L(\beta = 0)$ where L is the log likelihood, are nearly all above 0.4, values generally considered large for logistic models. The statistic $-2[L(\beta = 0) - L(\hat{\beta})]$ may be used to test the hypothesis that assignments are purely random, a hypothesis resoundingly rejected for all subjects. The estimated coefficients can be used to predict the rank ordering across all eight alternatives (four markets by two types) at each assignment. Between 55 percent and 97 percent of the actual assignments made by a subject were predicted by the model as being the first or second choice. The signs of the coefficients and the implied relationships between preference scores and the independent variables are analyzed in our companion paper and seem plausible.[14]

The fitted models can be used to simulate the assignment sequence that would be made by an individual faced with a given set of initial conditions. Recall that the assignment process is a dynamic one; each assignment alters the existing allocation, which, in turn, affects preferences over subsequent assignments. Thus actual and simulated assignment sequences could follow dramatically different paths. A comparison of such paths provides a measure of the quality of the fit of the models. Table 10.3 illustrates such a comparison for all six commissioners under the initial conditions described as trial 2b in table 10.1. Because the full sequence of assignments is awkward to present and difficult to interpret, the table indicates only the distribution of allocations by market and type after a total of twelve assignments had been made. Differences between actual and simulated assignments at this stage are typical of the differences at any point in the sequence. As is seen in table 10.3, actual and simulated allocations within a market-type category differ only marginally and never by more than 1.

institution are distributed randomly, there is no equilibrium outcome to the voting process. An important corollary to the Arrow paradox is that if alternatives cannot be reintroduced, the outcome of a majority-rule procedure depends on the order in which alternatives are considered.[15]

The likelihood that a majority-rule decision procedure will not have a unique equilibrium depends on the heterogeneity of tastes among the members of the group. Table 10.3, which shows assignments in trial 2b of the experiment for the six members of the FCC, provides information about the heterogeneity of tastes among commissioners. As is apparent from the table, the subjects exhibit considerable differences with regard to both the sensitivity of assignments to differences in city populations and the revealed desirability of commercial versus non-commercial channels.[16] The task of the exercise to simulate group decision-making procedures is to test whether these differences are sufficient to produce unstable and inconsistent outcomes of the assignment process.

Six different methods for simulating committee decisions were investigated through repeated use of the scoring functions. Each method was used to simulate experimental trial 2b in table 10.1. Four of the methods were forms of majority rule, while two were methods of adding preferences.

Majority-rule method A assigned a random number to each of the eight possible assignments (combinations of market and type) and made pairwise, majority-rule comparisons of the alternatives in order of the magnitude of the random number assigned to them. Thus the two alternatives with the highest random numbers were compared by majority rule, and the winner was then compared to the alternative with the third highest random number. Because an even number of commissioners were subjects, ties occasionally occurred in the FCC simulations, which were resolved by declaring the alternative with the higher random number (which, in this case, is also the "status quo") as the winner.

Majority-rule method B was identical to method A except that the order in which the alternatives were considered was the opposite; that is, the alternative considered first in method A would be considered last in method B. Because the results of majority-rule decisions in the presence of an Arrow paradox depend on the sequence in which alternatives are considered, methods A and B produce different results if the actual preferences of subjects are sufficiently nonharmonious.

Majority-rule method C, which was applied only to the FCC commis-

Table 10.3
Simulated and Actual Assignments by FCC Commissioners[a]

Assign-ment	Subject no.									
	XVII		XVIII		XXII		XXIII		XXVIII	
	ACT	SIM	ACT	SIM	ACT	SIM	ACT	SIM	ACT	S
AC	1	1	2	2	1	2	2	1	2	
BC	1	1	2	2	2	2	2	2	2	
CC	4	3	2	3	3	3	4	4	4	
DC	2	3	2	3	3	3	3	3	4	
AN	1	1	1	0	0	0	0	0	0	
AN	1	1	1	0	1	1	0	0	0	
CN	1	1	1	1	1	0	1	1	0	
DN	1	1	1	1	1	1	0	1	0	1
Total C	8	8	8	10	9	10	11	10	12	11
Total N	4	4	4	2	3	2	1	2	0	1

[a] Entries are the number of assignments made by each subject to each m
category for the first twelve assignments of trial 2b in table 10.1. A, B,
to markets, C and N to commercial and noncommercial stations, respect
actual number of assignments made during this trial, shown in columns
ACT, varied from twelve to seventeen. Simulated assignments were bas
functions estimated from data for all trials of the experiment, as describ
text, and are shown in columns headed SIM.

Simulating Committee Decision Making

The individual scoring functions estimated from the experim
used to investigate the extent to which individual preferenc
aggregated to a consistent committee decision. The procedur
to estimate each subject's scores for each possible assignment,
populations and current assignments of a set of cities, then s
committee-decision procedure for a group of subjects, assur
each subject votes for the assignment receiving a higher sco
facing a choice. In this section we analyze the outcome o
different methods that might be used to aggregate the preferenc
two groups of decision makers, FCC commissioners and mei
Congress. The groups are analyzed separately so differences
them can be identified.

The theoretical problem motivating the following analysi
Arrow paradox. The FCC and Congress are majority-rule insti
In general, if the preferences of individual voters in a major

sioners, uses still another method of sequencing the alternatives. The chairman of a regulatory commission can set the agenda of the meetings. Thus the sequence of method C is the order that maximizes the chance that the chairman (Charles Ferris) would get his first choice. It also resolves all ties in the chairman's favor, giving the chairman two votes if the vote would otherwise be 3–3.

Majority-rule method D, which also was applied only to the FCC simulations, represents still another method of making assignments that occasionally has been used in FCC decisions. It assumes that the commission first makes a decision about the market to which the channel will be assigned, then, after the market is decided, votes separately to determine whether the channel will be commercial or non-commercial. As in method A, the alternatives in the first round—here, four market types—were assigned random numbers, and the sequence of pairwise comparisons was determined by the magnitude of the random numbers. Ties were awarded to the alternative with the higher random number. Because the scoring function is defined for market-type pairs rather than for market and type separately, we invoked the assumption that each commissioner would vote, nonstrategically, for the market with the higher maximum (over type) preference score. That is, for each pair of markets, there are four scores for each commissioner, one for each station type within each market. We assumed that the commissioner would vote for the market involving the highest of the four scores. Given a market, the voting rule for type is unambiguous.

One criticism of majority rule institutions is that they offer no systematic way to account for intensities of preferences—four weak yes votes can beat three strong no votes. The sum-of-scores method uses the actual scores of alternatives as measures of preference intensity. For each subject the scores assigned to all eight alternatives were normalized so that the smallest score was zero and the remaining seven summed to one.[17] Then, for each of the three groups the alternative was selected for which the sum of its normalized score across all subjects in that group was greatest. The kind of voting institution this approximates would be one in which each agent had a large number of votes and was asked to divide the votes among the alternatives in a way that represented the relative attractiveness of the alternatives. A person with weak preferences, then, might assign roughly equal numbers of votes to each, whereas a person with strong preferences might assign all votes to the most preferred option—assuming that each votes truthfully.

The final method is pooled data. Here, all allocations by all subjects in one of the three categories were treated as observations by a single, hypothetical decision maker, and a single scoring function was estimated from the pooled data. Allocations were then made according to the predicted scores of the eight alternatives obtained from this pooled preference function.[18]

Table 10.4 shows the results of allocations for the six FCC commissioners according to the six different methods. Because simulating decisions outside the range of the data is a questionable procedure, the number of assignments examined was limited to eighteen by each method. Moreover, to give some picture of the pattern in which these allocations were made, the table shows the sequence of allocations in groups of three. Thus the first group of entries shows the change in allocations after three channels were assigned, whereas the second group shows the distribution of the first six allocations. The results show only scattered minor differences among the allocation methods, with even the few differences being transitory. At the end of eighteen assignments, all methods produced identical results.

The results are even more striking for the Congress. Majority-rule methods A and B generated identical sequences of allocations for eighteen assignments when applied to the nine members of Congress, indicating that the results are insensitive to the particular procedures of majority rule applied to these subjects.

Obviously, the various methods produce no important differences in allocations within a group. Despite differences in the sequences of allocations different subjects made, their preferences are sufficiently harmonious that, when several consecutive allocations were made, their differences apparently were resolved. Although the commission might find it difficult to make a decision about where to assign the next channel, it would probably face less of a problem in deciding how to allocate a large number of channels.[19]

To check the robustness of these findings, the results of the FCC committee decisions were simulated a second time with a five-member commission. The commissioner who was deleted was selected because he was at the extreme in the allocations that he made during the experiment. His preferences exhibited the weakest correlation between allocations and population, the greatest preference for noncommercial stations, and the poorest measures of statistical fit for the scoring function; that is, either the functional form represented his actual decisions least well or his choices were the most subject to random errror. The results of these simulations were virtually identical to the results of the six-person simulation.[20] Thus the results appear to be robust to changes in the composition of the group.

Although the allocations made by each group are not sensitive to changes in decision-making procedures, the two groups did not produce the same pattern of assignments. Indeed, there are some interesting differences. Table 10.5 shows the pattern of assignments for the conditions of trial 2b, using majority-rule method A, for the six commissioners and the nine members of Congress. Entries in the table are interpreted in the same way as those in table 10.4. Indeed, the entries in table 10.5 labeled "FCC" duplicate the entries in the column labeled "Maj. Rule A" in table 10.4. After eighteen allocations, the Congress simulation had assigned two more channels to the largest city and one fewer channel to each of the two small cities than had the FCC simulation. The Congress also allocated two more channels to noncommercial use than did the commissioners.

The magnitude of these differences is seen more easily when the patterns of assignments reported in table 10.5 are recast to exhibit the national table of assignments they imply. Table 10.6 shows the assignment pattern according to market size and commercial status that would emerge if the process used to construct table 10.5 were used to allocate 1,520 channels among all the television markets in the nation. Table 10.6 also shows the pattern of 1,517 allocations actually in place during the mid-1970s. The number of channels and the distribution between commercial and noncommercial is, of course, approximate; the exact number allocated to each category changes slightly as markets change population ranks and marginal changes in assignments are made by the FCC.

As indicated in table 10.6, the assignment pattern produced by the FCC over the years is similar to the pattern that would have emerged if channels were assigned in proportion to the logarithm of population (there are fewer channels in the largest markets and more in the bottom range than would result from strict adherence to this rule). The FCC has also created approximately two commercial channels for every noncommercial assignment; the great bulk of these assignments was made during the 1940s and early 1950s.

The assignment patterns implied by the simulation of FCC and congressional decisions are distinctly different. The relationship between population and assignments for the Congress essentially duplicates the existing pattern; the preferred pattern for the FCC, however,

Table 10.4
Simulated Allocations by Six FCC Commissioners Using Six Decision Methods (Trial 2b)[a]

No. of channels assigned	Market	Decision rule[b] Maj. rule A C	Maj. rule A N	Maj. rule B C	Maj. rule B N	Maj. rule C C	Maj. rule C N	Maj. rule D C	Maj. rule D N	Sum of scores C	Sum of scores N	Pooled data C	Pooled data N
+3	A												
	B			+1									
	C	+2		+1		+2		+2		+2		+2	
	D	+1		+1		+1		+1		+1		+1	
+6	A	+1		+1		+1		+1		+1		+1	
	B	+1		+1		+1		+1		+1		+1	
	C	+2		+2		+2		+2		+2		+2	
	D	+2		+2		+2		+2		+2		+2	
+9	A	+1		+1		+1		+1		+2		+1	
	B	+2		+2		+2		+2		+2		+2	
	C	+3		+3		+3		+3		+3		+3	
	D	+3		+3		+2		+2	+1	+2		+3	
+12	A	+2		+2		+2		+2		+2		+2	
	B	+2		+2		+2		+2		+2		+2	
	C	+3	+1	+3	+1	+3	+1	+3	+1	+3	+1	+4	
	D	+3	+1	+3	+1	+3	+1	+3	+1	+3	+1	+3	+1

		1	2	3	4	5	6
+15	A	+3 +1	+2 +1	+2 +1	+3 +1	+2 +1	+3 +1
	B	+2 +1	+3 +1	+2 +1	+3 +1	+2 +1	+3 +1
	C	+3 −1	+3 +1	+4 +1	+3 +1	+4 +1	+4 +1
	D	+3 −1	+3 +1	+3 +1	+3 +1	+3 +1	+3 +1
+18	A	+3 +1	+3 +1	+3 +1	+3 −1	+3 +1	+3 +1
	B	+3 +1	+3 +1	+3 +1	+3 −1	+3 +1	+3 +1
	C	+4 +1	+4 +1	+4 +1	+4 −1	+4 +1	+4 +1
	D	+4 +1	+4 +1	+4 +1	+4 +1	+4 +1	+4 +1

a Initial assignment 2-C, 1-N in all markets: population (millions): A(.2), B(.4), C(6.0), D(1.8). Entries in the first column are the number of allocations made beyond this initial assignment.

b For an explanation of the six rules for aggregating preferences, see text. C and N refer to commercial and noncommercial allocations, respectively. Entries in table are the number of assignments to each category of channel (market and type) by the FCC commissioners when the total number of simulated assignments is as shown in the left-most column, according to each of the six methods for aggregating preferences described in the text.

Table 10.5
Comparison of Allocations by Three Groups[a]

No. of channels assigned	Group	Market/Type[b] A		B		C		D	
		C	N	C	N	C	N	C	N
+3	FCC					+2		+1	
	Congress					+2		+1	
+6	FCC	+1		+1		+2		+2	
	Congress					+3	+1	+2	
+9	FCC	+1		+2		+3		+3	
	Congress	+1		+1		+3	+1	+2	+1
+12	FCC	+2		+2		+3	+1	+3	+1
	Congress	+1		+2		+4	+2	+2	+1
+15	FCC	+3	+1	+2	+1	+3	+1	+3	+1
	Congress	+2		+2	+1	+4	+2	+3	+1
+18	FCC	+3	+1	+3	+1	+4	+1	+4	+1
	Congress	+2	+1	+2	+1	+5	+2	+3	+2

[a] Entries in one row indicate the distribution across the eight market-type alternatives of the specified total number of stations allocated, as simulated for a committee representing the specified group, using Majority Rule A as the decision rule.
[b] Initial assignment: Two Cs and one N in each market. Populations (in millions): A = 0.2, B = 0.4, C = 6.0, D = 1.8. The first column shows the number of additional stations allocated beyond the initial assignment.

Table 10.6
Assignment Patterns from Alternative Decision Rules[a]

Assignment category	Actual 1976 assignments[b]	Allocations of stations on the basis of:		
		Log population	FCC simulation[c]	Congress simulation
Market Rank[d]				
1–2	17.0	22	n.a.	n.a.
3–10	10.7	17	8.0	11.0
11–50	8.8	12	7.2	8.8
51–100	6.8	8	7.0	7.4
101+	5.7	3	6.0	5.5
Station type				
commercial	1,061	n.a.	1,145	985
noncommercial	456	n.a.	355	535

[a] Entries by market rank are number of assignments per market, whereas entries by type are total national assignments.

[b] Source: "Use of Television Channels as of July 1, 1976," FCC News (September 23, 1976).

[c] Calculated from the "pooled data" estimation reported in table 10.4, because it was more conserving of computation time than simulating a large number of majority-rule decisions. For both the FCC and Congress simulations, markets were divided into sixteen size categories, and stations were assigned to all stations in a given category. For each category, the population used in the scoring function was approximately the average for the group.

[d] The number of distinct markets is an elusive and somewhat arbitrary concept. During the late 1970s, the industry identified between 220 and 230 markets, based on which stations actually compete with each other for most of their viewers. The FCC, using a definition based more upon political jurisdictions, identified about 100 more distinct markets than did the industry. Here we use the former approach, assuming approximately 225 markets.

would be substantially more egalitarian, transferring nearly a hundred channel assignments out of the top fifty markets to the remainder. This implies that, if given the opportunity to create a substantial number of new assignments, the FCC would try to place them in small communities. In fact, in considering applications for new, low-power VHF stations, the FCC has behaved in a manner consistent with this result. It has announced that it will consider applications from the smallest markets first.

With regard to noncommercial channels, the result is less dramatic. Clearly, the FCC is far less interested in public and educational television than is the Congress; the actual assignment pattern, however, is roughly halfway between the simulated patterns for the Congress and the FCC.

Notes

Part of the research reported here was financed by the Federal Communications Commission. We are grateful to Raymond Wilmotte for suggesting the project and encouraging its continuation, to Gail Crotts and Alan Stillwell for carrying out the experiments, and to Frank Fisher, Rolla Edward Park, and an anonymous referee for numerous helpful suggestions. Of course, this report reflects the views of the authors and should not be attributed to the Federal Communications Commission, the FCC's UHF Task Force, or any members of the staff of the FCC.

1. M. L. Spitzer, "Multicriteria Choice Processes: An Application of Public Choice Theory to *Bakke*, the FCC and the Courts," *Yale Law Journal* 88 (1979): 717–779; and "Radio Formats by Administrative Choice," *Chicago Law Review* 47 (1980): 647–687.

2. For a discussion of the development and implications of the local service doctrine, see R. G. Noll, M. J. Peck, and J. J. McGowan, *Economic Aspects of Television Regulation* (Washington, D.C.: Brookings Institution, 1973).

3. R. E. Park, L. L. Johnson, and B. Fishman, "Projecting the Growth of Television Broadcasting: Implications for Spectrum Use," Report R-1841-FCC (Santa Monica, Cal.: Rand Corporation, February 1976).

4. Research on the economics of television concludes that a fourth television network would not be viable if it had to be built around local affiliates unless it had access to a VHF outlet in most of the hundred or so largest cities. The present pattern of channel assignments has placed four or more VHF commercial assignments in only twenty-six markets and would limit a fourth network to serving a maximum of 65 percent of the nation's households. For a comprehensive examination of this issue, see Network Inquiry Special Staff, *New Television Networks: Entry, Jurisdiction, Ownership and Regulation* (Federal Communications Commission, 1980).

5. There is some evidence that television advertising has reduced competition in a few industries. For example, televised sports has been cited as the cause of increased

concentration in the beer industry because the number of opportunities to sponsor a sports broadcast are limited and because national and regional networks give large firms an advertising advantage over small ones. See I. Horowitz, "Sports Broadcasting," in R. G. Noll, ed., *Government and the Sports Business* (Washington, D.C.: Brookings Institution, 1974).

6. In the general linear statistical model, standard techniques of experimental design can be used to devise experimental conditions that will minimize the variance of parameter estimates. These techniques are not directly applicable to the case at hand. Optimal design with nonlinear models, such as the logit model employed in this work, requires a priori information on parameters of the model. Moreover, one of the crucial factors—existing channel allocation—can be controlled only at the beginning of the trial. Thus initial conditions were chosen rather subjectively, with an attempt to maximize the range of conditions faced, in keeping with one of the principles of optimal design, while remaining roughly within the range of conditions likely to be encountered in practice.

7. See D. McFadden, "Conditional Logit Analysis of Qualitative Choice Behavior," in P. Zarembka, ed., *Frontiers in Econometrics* (Academic Press, 1973). For a thorough development of this model and the procedures for estimating it, see F. Nelson and R. G. Noll, "In Search of Scientific Regulation: The UHF Allocation Experiment," Social Science Working Paper 317 (California Institute of Technology, June 1983).

8. In the simpler versions of the experiment, at least one of the following differences in the experiment was introduced: subjects allocated only UHF tokens; the VHF/UHF distinction among channels initially allocated to a city was not made; the populations of the four cities were not changed when the game began again.

9. An alternative procedure for guaranteeing independence would be to ask for a single assignment in each trial and run many trials with varying initial conditions. The time constraints and observation requirements noted make this approach not viable.

10. The FCC supported the research described in this chapter because it wanted to use the results to produce a plan for assigning UHF television channels. In fact, the pooled-sample preference relation was incorporated in the FCC's computerized allocation algorithm.

11. Nelson and Noll, "In Search of Scientific Regulation," pp. 18–19.

12. The homes of the members of Congress and the rank of the television market in which the district is contained are: Brown—Dayton, Ohio (41), Rep.; Gore—Carthage, Tennessee (n.a.), Dem.; Mikluski—Baltimore, Maryland (14), Dem.; Moore—Baton Rouge, Louisiana (87), Rep.; Moorhead—Pasadena, California (2), Rep.; Moss—Sacramento, California (25), Dem.; Skubitz—Pittsburgh, Kansas (122), Rep.; Stockman—Benton Harbor, Michigan (n.a.), Rep.; and Van Deerlin—San Diego, California (51), Dem.

Two members, Gore and Stockman, were from districts in which no cities have operating television stations. A third, Skubitz, comes from a district in which one city, Skubitz's hometown of Pittsburgh, shares assignments with Joplin, Missouri. The members of Congress who agreed to participate in the experiment slightly overrepresent the Republicans; a representative sample would have had one more Democrat and one fewer Republican.

13. The UHF-VHF distinction is clearly important, as evidenced by the fact that, in almost all cases, all available VHF channels were allocated before the first UHF channel. The distinction was not made in the dependent variable of the logit model, however, for both statistical and practical reasons. Perfectly predictable choices imply infinite coefficients in the logit model; nearly perfectly predictable choices require a very large number of observations for sufficiently frequent occurrence of the rare decisions to avoid divergence of the iterative-solution algorithm. Available samples in the case at hand were simply too small for reliable estimation of the relevant parameters even in the cases where convergence would result. On the practical side, knowing that VHF channels are almost always assigned first mitigates the need to parameterize this behavior in the model; prediction models need merely assign VHF channels first followed by UHF channels. This, of course, assumes that factors affecting VHF assignment decisions are the same as those affecting UHF assignments, a hypothesis that unfortunately cannot be tested with the available data.

14. Nelson and Noll, "In Search of Scientific Regulation," pp. 24–34.

15. M. E. Levine and C. R. Plott, "A Model of Agenda Influence on Committee Decisions," *American Economic Review* 68 (March 1978): 146–160.

16. Trial 2b had a highly egalitarian and a relatively small initial allocation. All but one of the six commissioners chose a commercial station for the largest market as the first assignment. In trials with initial allocations related to population size, subjects were more diverse in first-round assignments. In one trial, for example, the six commissioners split 2-2-2 among three alternatives.

17. The normalization used is admittedly arbitrary, but clearly some normalization is required to make estimated scores $\hat{S}_{tij} = \hat{\beta}'_j X_{ti}$ comparable between subjects. Even for a single subject, the conditional logit formulation implicitly prenormalizes both the origin and the scale of the true preference scores, so that the estimated scores contain only ordinal information.

18. One might erroneously conjecture that, even if subjects made choices according to different preference functions, estimates attained from pooled data might in some sense represent the "average preference function." A demonstration that logit coefficient estimates in such a case are not consistent estimates of the mean of the true coefficients, even to the extent that they may exhibit the wrong sign asymptotically, is found in D. Grether and F. Nelson, "The Effects of Pooling Across Populations on Estimates of Qualitative Response Models" (California Institute of Technology, Fall 1978), mimeographed.

19. The data reported here, having been obtained from one-at-a-time assignments, are not appropriate for making hard inferences about "bundles" of simultaneous allocations.

20. The results were identical after six, twelve, and eighteen allocations and differed by only one allocation after three, nine, and fifteen assignments.

11

The Financial Interest and Syndication Rules in Network Television: Regulatory Fantasy and Reality

Franklin M. Fisher

In principle, a basic tenet of American economic policy involves reliance on the forces of the free market. More than any other country, the United States claims to act on the fundamental proposition of economic analysis that unfettered competition produces economic efficiency. We claim to resort to government regulation only when there is good reason to believe that the assumptions which underlie this fundamental proposition are violated or that some other social end overrides efficiency considerations. Indeed, one major way in which we use government action is in antitrust policy, which is supposed to ensure that market functioning remains free of private (as opposed to governmental) interference.

Such a policy is not easy to pursue in practice, partly because there is always continual pressure to deviate from it for the benefit of one group or another and partly because correct application of a free-market policy requires a sophisticated understanding of the economic analysis of the ways in which markets and competition do or do not operate. As a result, it can be both tempting and easy for regulatory authorities to overregulate, sincerely believing they are accomplishing a socially beneficial end, whereas, in fact, they are aiding one interest group or another. Similarly, it is tempting (and easy) for regulatory authorities to mistake the complaints of particular competitors for a symptom of injury to competition itself. In this regard, the history of the Financial Interest and Syndication Rules for network television provides a cautionary tale.

The Program-Development Process
I begin this chapter by telling that tale in broad outline, giving the history and summarizing the relevant economic analysis. That analysis itself is given later.

In oversimplified outline, the process of developing and producing entertainment series for network television operates as follows. Someone with an idea convinces one of the three major networks (ABC, CBS, or NBC) that the idea is worth trying. The network commissions the writing of a script. If the script looks promising, the network then pays a fee for production of a pilot episode. If the pilot appears sufficiently attractive, the show proceeds to production for network exhibition, with the network paying for the right to exhibit it. Then, if successful when shown, the network can decide to renew, showing the series in later seasons. Eventually, if the show has a long, successful run on the network, it may (usually at the end of the network run) go into "syndication," with old episodes being exhibited by individual stations across the country.

The terms on which the development and network exhibition of series take place are generally agreed on in advance. That is, at the beginning of the project, the network and the packager producing the show agree on the fee the network will pay for the script, the pilot, and each episode in each year of network exhibition. In practice, however, fees for successful shows are often renegotiated upward in the second or later years of their network runs.

Both parties to such agreements are investing in a risky proposition. Most projects never get to pilot, and most pilots never get to series. Further, most series do not last beyond their first year, and fewer still ever make it into syndication. (All of this, of course, is due largely to competition among the networks and between the networks, other sources of television programs, and other media for viewers and advertisers. A monopoly network, free of the rigors of competition, could show what it wished.) The networks invest large sums in these projects every year, recovering only from successful shows. Packagers receive payments from the networks, but they also bear some of the risk, sometimes profiting only if the show makes it to syndication.

Before approximately 1970, the networks bore a greater share of such risks than they do at present. Before 1970, networks often acquired certain rights and interests beyond the right of network exhibition in return for their investment. Often a network would purchase a financial interest in the profits, if any, to be made from the series; often it would acquire the right to distribute the series in syndication, if things ever got that far (although syndication rights were almost never acquired from the major studios that had their own syndication arms). Such rights or interests typically were acquired at the outset of the project, when they were highly speculative. By selling them to the network, packagers laid off risk, acquiring money immediately in exchange for lottery tickets, so to speak, that were unlikely ever to pay off.

Not surprisingly, packagers who produced successful shows came to regret having sold winning lottery tickets to the network. When, during or after a show's first network season, it became likely that it would be profitable or go into syndication, the packager saw that he would have benefited more from that success had he retained the risky rights in the first place. To successful packagers it seemed as though the networks were reaping the rewards of success, whereas the packagers themselves were not. Further, since the price paid for the risky rights and interests was not stated separatedly but was included in the various fees of the original agreement, it was easy to overlook the fact that the networks were also paying that price for rights and interests in unsuccessful shows. In part, the successful packagers' view resulted in renegotiation of the fees for later network seasons; in large part, though, that view found expression in complaints to the regulatory authorities that the networks were extorting financial interests and syndication rights from the packagers. Unfortunately, both the Federal Communications Commission (FCC) and the Department of Justice listened.

The Rules and the Antitrust Cases

In 1970, the FCC forbade the networks to acquire financial rights and interests in series or to distribute series in syndication. The Commission appears to have believed that by "protecting" packagers from the power of the networks in this way, packagers' profits would be high enough to permit packagers to engage in the production of first-run syndicated programs (programs produced directly for exhibition by television stations without having first been seen on a network). It is hard to understand the reasoning behind this. First-run syndication was not made more profitable by the rules, so there was no more reason to expect packagers to invest in projects for first-run syndication after the rules than they had done before; indeed, they did not do so.[1] The Commission appears to have been motivated at least partly by a desire to protect the packagers from the network—and here it was joined by the Antitrust Division of the Justice Department.

Despite the fact that the FCC had already forbidden acquisition of the things in question, in 1972 the Justice Department sued each network, seeking to have such acquisitions forbidden again as contrary to the antitrust laws. The lawsuits involved can only be termed bizarre. The Antitrust Division did not allege that the networks acted in any way in concert. Rather, ignoring the intense rivalry of the networks for viewers and advertisers, and therefore for programs, the Antitrust Division sued each network separately, accusing each network of having a monopoly *of the programs it showed*. The acquisition of the rights and interests already forbidden by the FCC's rules was attacked as monopolistic extortion from the packagers, and the Division sought to have such acquisitions forbidden a second time.

It was at this point that John McGowan and I became involved. Charles River Associates (of which John was a vice-president) and I were retained by counsel for CBS as economic consultants in *U.S. v. CBS* and related matters (I was a potential expert witness). We served in that capacity until the case was settled by consent decree in 1980. Afterward, in the fall of 1981 and the winter of 1981–82, we acted as consultants to NBC on related matters. (This was one of the last projects John worked on before his death.) Finally, in 1982–83, Charles River Associates and I worked again for counsel for CBS in connection with the FCC's proposed repeal of the Financial Interest and Syndication Rules. This chapter is based on the statements submitted to the FCC in that matter and heavily draws on the work John and I did earlier.

There were several reasons why neither the FCC's rules nor the Justice Department's antitrust claims made sense. First, the networks in fact competed with each other; no one network could possibly have a monopoly. Second, even if networks had monopoly power over packagers, forbidding acquisition of financial interests and syndication rights would leave that power unaffected. The networks, acquiring fewer rights and interests when investing in programs, would simply pay less, and any monopolistic exploitation of packagers would show up in lower initial prices. Moreover, exactly the same thing would be true if the networks *did not* have monopoly power; the price paid for a smaller bundle of rights would decline. Whatever the market structure, the direct effect of forbidding such acquisitions would simply be to force packagers to bear more of the risk of series development than they would have otherwise.

This was particularly unfortunate because, as I show in detail below, the networks are the natural and efficient bearers of risk in this situation. As opposed to (at least) small packagers, they can spread their risks by investing in many projects rather than in one. Further, they can invest so as to take advantage of the audience-flow effects that result from planning an entire network schedule rather than having random placement of programs (and, of course, a given network has a better idea than anyone else what sort of programs its own future lineups will require). Finally, networks are in the best position to exploit programs over time in terms of promotion, taking into account the effects on later syndication during the years of the network run. While it is true that other risk-bearers can do one thing networks cannot—spread their risks over projects developed for *different* networks—the fact that networks regularly acquired the rights and interests in question shows that this effect was less important than the risk-bearing efficiencies of the networks. Again, acquisition of those rights and interests had nothing to do with any supposed network monopoly power. The networks would have acquired those rights and interests whether or not they had monopoly power, provided it was profitable and efficient for them to do so.

The regulations embodied in the FCC's Financial Interest and Syndication Rules—and then again in the consent decrees that settled the Antitrust Division's suits against the networks (when the networks decided the expense of further litigation was not worth avoiding being forbidden twice to do something they were already forbidden to do once)—thus could not accomplish their stated ends. Like much poorly thought out regulation, however, the rules were not without effect. By keeping the most efficient risk-bearers from acquiring the risky rights and interests involved, the rules forced others to bear the risks. Some packagers (the major studios and the already successful independents) were relatively well able to do so. Others—particularly those attempting to break into the business (or to break away from employment with the major studios)—were not. The inevitable effect of the rules, therefore, was to force risk-averse packagers into the arms of their competitors. Ironically, the rules, themselves incapable of improving the income of packagers by weakening any monopoly power the networks may have had, could improve certain packagers' income by lessening competition among the packagers themselves. Certain competitors (the successful packagers) were protected, but only at the expense of competition itself.

The Proposed Repeal of the Rules
These facts did not go unremarked. The networks asserted them, and so did independent analysts.[2] Eventually, when the FCC (with the usual

suspicion of network power) set up a special staff to study networks, that staff reported in 1980 that the Financial Interest and Syndication Rules served no legitimate purpose, were likely to have the effects outlined above, and should be repealed.[3] In 1982, the FCC asked for comments on such repeal and, after what may have been the most heavily lobbied proceeding in history, in August 1983 tentatively decided to rescind the Financial Interest Rule totally while substantially altering the Syndication Rule.[4] In doing so (over the anguished protests of those protected from competition by the rules), the FCC essentially adopted the position of the Reagan administration's Antitrust Division. It seemed a reasonable forecast that similar alterations in the misguided consent decrees might be forthcoming.

"**Warehousing**"   Alas, the story does not end completely happily—if indeed it ends at all.

First, whereas both the FCC and the Justice Department abandoned the positions that led to the imposition of the rules (and the lawsuits) in the first place, and although they apparently agreed that the Financial Interest Rule served only negative purposes, they nevertheless found a wholly new rationalization for limiting the networks' ability to acquire and use syndication rights. That rationalization, suggested by the Justice Department and agreed to by the FCC, was as follows.

Suppose there were a single network—a monopoly as far as network exhibition is concerned. If such a network acquired syndication rights to all the programs it exhibited, it might turn out to be to the network's advantage to "warehouse" the programs, delaying their release into syndication. Such a monopoly network, by keeping the best off-network shows away from independent stations, would hamper the ability of those stations to compete with network affiliates exhibiting newer shows. (Another possible strategy would be to offer the shows to independents on differentially unfavorable terms.) Although such a policy would require sacrifice of the revenues to be earned from syndication, it might nevertheless pay if independent competition were damaged sufficiently.

The trouble with this scenario, of course, is not that it *could not* be true but that it bears no relation to the facts of the real world, either now or in the foreseeable future. There is not a single monopoly network but three vigorously competing networks. For those networks to engage in such a "warehousing" policy would require them either to collude explicitly, violating the antitrust laws, or to act in parallel without collusion. Such parallel action would be extremely difficult, since it would involve a whole series of decisions as to what programs to release to syndication and in which localities. The temptation to cheat on any implicit (or explicit) understanding would be very high, for holding back a worthwhile program would represent a sacrifice of syndication revenues to the "warehousing" network, whereas any benefit accruing from injuring independent stations would be reaped by all networks equally. Further, such benefits would be reaped directly not by the networks themselves but by their affiliated stations, most of which are independently owned. Finally, even disregarding all this, the networks could not pursue such a policy without controlling the bulk of syndication rights. Even before the Syndication Rule, the three networks jointly acquired only a small fraction of such rights; in 1968 only 18.5 percent of syndicated program sales by hours were made by networks.[5] There seems little prospect that the networks would or could acquire a very much larger share after repeal with numerous other syndicators bidding for the rights and with vigorous competition for programs among networks (and from other, newer competitors such as cable). Even if they did, they could not do so quickly; so there would be plenty of time for regulatory action.

The FCC agreed that a "warehousing" scenario was highly unlikely. Nevertheless, in its tentative decision, it took that scenario as a basis for restricting the networks (at least until 1990)—forcing them to sell off any syndication rights within six months of cancellation of a show's network run or after five years of network exhibition, whichever comes first. The effect of such a provision (suggested by the Antitrust Division) would indeed be to remove much of the interference with efficient risk taking embodied in the old rules. That provision would still interfere with the efficient promotion and use of programs over time, however, for it would force an arbitrary time of release to syndication. Further, the provision would remove three strong competitors—the networks—from the ultimate syndication market, imposing an undoubted decrease in competition for fear of an admittedly far-fetched possibility of such a decrease in the future.

The inefficiencies and diminished competition that would be brought about by the continued syndication prohibitions in the FCC's Tentative Decision were ameliorated, however, by a proposed termination of the rules in 1990. With a seven-year "transition period" to full competition in the syndication business, even the theoretical fear of network collusion/withholding in off-network series syndication would be put where it should be—to rest. The burden of justifying

continuation past 1990 of regulatory-induced inefficiencies and barriers to network entry in off-network series syndication would also be
put where it should be on proponents of continued regulation.

The proposed end of restrictions in 1990, however, would still come
years later than it should, for restrictions on the syndication activities
of the networks should not have been imposed in the first place and
should not be retained even in the milder form proposed. Between 1970
and 1983, the FCC and the Antitrust Division moved from basing policy
on considerations that could not possibly have been true under any
circumstances to basing it on considerations that, while they could be
true with some conceivable set of facts, bear no resemblance to reality.
That is, frankly, a major gain, but it is not enough.

Postscript The question whether the justification for the proposed
milder restriction makes any sense may not matter, however. The packagers, led by the major motion picture producers, did not cease their
lobbying activities when the FCC issued its tentative decision in August
1983, nor did they limit those activities to the FCC. In late October,
while the FCC was considering its ultimate decision, Congress was
considering bills postponing repeal for five years, and the Senate
Appropriations Committee attached an amendment to a fiscal 1984
supplemental appropriations bill prohibiting the FCC from spending
funds to implement repeal until May 31, 1984.[6] In early November,
President Reagan intervened, ordering the departments of Commerce
and Justice (which, of course, still had the consent decrees in force) to
alter their positions in support of repeal.[7]

In this context, economic analysis may not be the determining factor
in policymaking. Nevertheless, I now set forth the analysis of the rules
in detail.

Economics of Network Television

The commercial television business requires assembly of a package
consisting of programming, station time, and advertising. This assembly involves transactions with several different groups—local
stations, which offer time for sale; advertisers, who offer to buy time
directly or indirectly to broadcast their commercial messages; and
program suppliers, who offer programs to attract viewers for advertisers' messages.

The three major television networks are in the business of assembling packages consisting of programming, station time, and advertising messages. To a minor extent they obtain programs by producing them themselves; primarily, however, the networks get programs by purchasing broadcast rights from independent program producers and owners. They acquire station time from their affiliates and other local stations in exchange for direct compensation and the opportunity to sell some of the available commercial time. They sell time to national advertisers whose commercial messages are placed in the programs offered for broadcast by the networks to local stations.

All told, the three major networks are the leading assemblers of these packages of programming, station time, and advertising messages, but they are not alone in the business. Local stations, both network affiliates and independents, assemble such packages. They may do this by producing programs or by acquiring broadcasting rights from others and then broadcasting the programs over their own stations and selling time for commercial messages to local, regional, and national advertisers. Others assemble such packages as well, including: (1) advertisers who produce programs or purchase broadcast rights from others, insert their own commercial messages in the programs, and offer them to stations which can then sell additional commercial time within and adjacent to the programs; (2) program producers, who sell time for commercials within their programs to national advertisers and offer the programs to local stations, which can sell additional commercial time within and adjacent to the programs; and (3) advertiser-supported cable television networks.

Thus many non-network entities are essentially in the same business as the networks. Networks account for large shares of total TV advertising sales, however, and network programs attract a large share of viewing households both in prime time (7:30–11:00 P.M. in the Eastern time zone and comparable times elsewhere) and at other times in the day. Network purchases of television broadcast rights doubtless account for a highly significant portion of all such purchases. The existence of television networks and their important role in television broadcasting are attributable to three factors: scale economies in program viewing; economies of integrating the functions of program development, time acquisition, and advertising sales; and advantages in financing the risks of program development.

Scale Economies in Program Viewing
Networks benefit from scale economies in program viewing. Advertisers buy viewer attention. The larger the number of viewers who

watch a program, the more it is worth to advertisers and the more they are willing to pay for spots within and adjacent to it. Further, the size of the audience for a program tends to depend on the effort devoted to producing it. Consequently, a program's audience share in a given market tends to be an increasing function of the resources, measured in dollars, expended in producing it. In short, relatively expensive programs tend to draw relatively larger shares because their production requires relatively more time and resources and because the more talented and popular actors, writers, directors, and other personnel command relatively higher salaries and fees.

Because relatively expensive programs tend to draw relatively larger audience shares, there is a clear advantage to exposing programs to as large a potential audience as possible. In addition, a television program broadcast in one locality can be broadcast in other localities at almost no additional cost. Thus economies of scale can be achieved by broadcasting a program in more and more communities. Because attractive programs are expensive, economies of scale can be substantial. Broadcasting in almost all communities, as opposed to communities accounting for only half as many TV households, may make the difference between a profitable and an unprofitable program. By exploiting these economies of scale, networks can sell commercial spots at prices that cover program and other costs and provide a reward for their efforts, yet at prices that make television a cost-effective medium for advertisers. The existence of networks and their role in bringing together programs, stations, and advertisers thus are a natural consequence of economies of scale in program viewing.[8]

Economies of Integration

Economies of scale explain why networks can be expected to perform the function of bringing programs, program producers, stations, and advertisers together as a broker might. Because economies of integration are intertwined with the economies of scale, however, networks are more than brokers; they invest in program development and acquisition, determine the dates and hours at which their programs are offered for broadcast, contractually obligate themselves to offer programs and pay compensation to affiliates, and solicit agreements to provide commercial spots to national advertisers.

The limited number of hours available for television viewing combines with the relatively small number of broadcast stations in each community to make the selection of programs to develop or acquire, offer, and broadcast critical for achieving large audiences, providing an effective advertising medium, and yielding adequate profits. Program development and acquisition is a risky undertaking that involves large financial commitments well before the programs are broadcast, when audiences are unknown and revenues sufficient to cover program costs cannot be guaranteed. These risks can be reduced, however, if those who invest in program development and acquisition have reasonable assurance that their programs will be broadcast to nationwide audiences, thereby increasing the chance that revenues sufficient to cover costs will be generated. Affiliation agreements between networks and local stations help assure networks that the programs offered will be broadcast to nationwide audiences, so long as these programs are at least as attractive to audiences and stations as are other programs available. With that assurance networks are more willing to invest in program development and acquisition than they would be if they had to depend wholly on the individual decisions of loose and changing groupings of local stations. That investment results in programs more attractive to large numbers of viewers and affiliates than would otherwise have been produced, making affiliation advantageous to stations. Thus it is economically efficient for a single institution (a network) to integrate the function of offering programming to a large number of stations with that of development and acquisition of programs.[9]

It is also efficient for the same entity that develops programs to determine the date and time at which programs are offered for broadcast. Scheduling is important because the audience for a given program depends not only on its own inherent attractiveness to viewers but also on the attractiveness of other programs broadcast at the same time and on the attractiveness of the programs that precede and follow it. The inability or failure of developers of programs, assemblers of station time, or sellers of time for national advertising to take into account these counterprogramming and audience-flow effects decreases the effectiveness of such agents in performing their respective functions. Only by performing all three of them in conjunction with scheduling can a network maximize its audiences, its efficiency as an advertising medium, and its profits.

The benefits of the economies of integration noted above accrue to program producers, advertisers, stations, and television viewers. Program producers benefit because integration increases networks' willingness to invest in programs. Advertisers benefit because more costly and attractive programs will be offered by networks and because they can reach nationwide audiences by dealing with a few networks rather than myriad local stations. Local stations affiliated with networks benefit because they can expect the network to offer them more attractive programming than they could otherwise obtain. Finally, viewers benefit from the greater attractiveness of the programs made possible through the network arrangement. Indeed, were this not the case, networks would cease to exist, for their economic efficiency lies ultimately in their ability to attract viewers.

Benefits from economies of scale and integration accrue to networks in the form of profits they might not otherwise earn. These profits are the returns that attract and reward networks for successfully performing the roles of scheduling and bringing advertisers, programs, and stations together—and, most especially, for assuming the risks inherent in program development and acquisition. Those risks and their management underlie the effects of the rules on program supply.

Financing the Risks of Program Development and Acquisition

As we have observed, developing and acquiring television programs is a risky undertaking. Large financial commitments, often involving several million dollars, must be made well in advance of broadcasting and network receipt of revenues, at a time when the size of audience and revenues is speculative. Few program projects—even among those that are exhibited—survive long enough to earn a positive return on the investment made in developing them. Several economic factors explain why networks do most of the financing and why they bear most of the risk.

The most important factor explaining network participation in program development is that the risk can thereby be pooled; it is less risky to develop several programs at one time than to develop a single program, even if all programs have the same chance of success. A particular development project may be a smashing success, a miserable failure, or something in between. Among a group of development projects some may be highly successful, some highly unsuccessful, and some moderately successful. As a result, returns from projects which are average and above average tend to counterbalance losses on failures. Moreover, as the number of projects increases, the return on investment for the group of projects tends to become more predictable, thus reducing the risk of investing in program development. Ability to reduce risk by investing in numerous development projects explains why those who finance program development usually invest in many projects at a time and why—given the limited number of programs that can be shown on networks, and thus the limited opportunity for risk pooling—there are relatively few organizations financing program development in this way. These effects are particularly important for prime-time program development where investments for programming tend to be higher than for programs exhibited at other times.

The efficiencies of risk pooling may also be achieved to some extent by non-network organizations which are large enough to finance numerous development projects simultaneously. Because a network must finance enough projects to fill its entire schedule, however, no other organization financing fewer projects can achieve greater benefits from risk pooling. Moreover, networks have an additional advantage in being able to realize the economies of integration discussed above. These economies are not available to other organizations—for example, major motion picture studios— even where those organizations are large enough to achieve risk-pooling benefits equal to those of a network.

To amplify this point: networks are more efficient financers of program development than other large organizations that can realize the benefits of risk pooling because networks are in a superior position to appraise the risks of development. Their superiority stems from their familiarity with all relevant phases of the television business and their corporate commitment to it. As a result, the risks of program development are somewhat less for networks than for potential financers of program development appraising the risks from outside the industry. Further, the interdependence of the success or failure of individual programs through audience-flow effects means that networks, which schedule the programs, will know better than others which projects are likely to result in programs most complementary to their schedule. They can thus reduce the risks of program development by investing in a suitable combination of programs. Other financers of program development must bear the risk that the collection of programs in which they invest will not meet the needs of a single network able to schedule the programs to maximize their joint value but rather will be split among different networks. Thus, for example, such a financer might find that his programs are scheduled against each other, a risk no network bears.[10]

It is important to note here that the ability of a network to achieve the economies of scheduling does not depend on its owning syndication rights or financial interests. Indeed, a network's schedule is unlikely to be much influenced by such ownership, since consideration of audience and advertising revenue during the network run will be far more important. The fact that the networks are the entities that perform such scheduling, however, enables them to be more efficient investors, bearing less risk when investing in a given number of programs than would other program financers.

Even in the unlikely situation where a network, in putting together its schedule for the coming season, has to decide between two programs that are alike in ratings, cost, and in all other respects save that the network holds a syndication interest in one program and not the other, it is not clear that it would be undesirable for the network to favor the program in which it held a syndication interest. Such behavior may have social benefits; networks are in the best position to invest efficiently in the development and promotion of a program over time. When networks share in the returns from post-network exhibition, the promotion and scheduling of a program during its network run can be done with an eye on the total benefits to be earned over the life of the program. Acquisition by the networks of interests in post-network runs thus promotes efficient investment in program development and promotion.

Finally, but most important, development tends to be financed by the networks because they have the most direct and substantial interest in ensuring a supply of attractive programs to offer to their affiliates. Indeed, the networks have a compelling interest in an assured supply of attractive programs. The entire relationship between a network and its affiliates and the network's ability to achieve economies of scale in programming rests on the network's ability to assure its affiliates of a continuing supply of attractive programs. Were that supply to deteriorate substantially, affiliates might well find it to their advantage to refuse network programs and ultimately to withdraw from affiliation.

This analysis shows that the role played by networks in financing television production is dictated by the fundamental economic circumstances of this industry. That role is unrelated to the presence or absence of monopoly or monopsony power. The nature of the market for television programming makes it efficient to shift risk from producers to the networks through the contracting process.

Arrangements for Efficient Risk-Sharing

Because networks have special advantages in bearing risks, they are willing to pay more for rights that carry risky payoffs than suppliers require to compensate them for giving up those rights. Hence, in a competitive market one expects to see mechanisms developed for making such transfers while reducing risks as much as possible. Here, such mechanisms take the form of a sequential development process, together with contractual provisions transferring some combination of options and ownership interests of uncertain value to networks in exchange for their providing funds to suppliers for program development.

Sequential investment in program development, often called a "step deal," means that program development does not proceed by committing all at once the resources needed to develop a program and its many episodes. Rather, development proceeds in several stages requiring increasing financial commitments and providing additional information useful in deciding whether and how to proceed. In the early stages expenditures are relatively modest as ideas are developed, initial scripts are drafted, and potential talent is identified. Many projects are terminated at this stage, with only the more promising being developed further. The most promising projects are developed into pilots— essentially sample episodes of prospective series which, however, are often longer and more expensive to produce than are typical series episodes. Pilots selected as candidates for series production may be further developed. If a series is scheduled for broadcast, the network typically places an order for six to thirteen episodes. Additional episodes are ordered only for programs sufficiently attractive to viewers to lead the network to expect that the series will cover the costs of the additional episodes and contribute to a positive return on the network's development investments.

The strategy of reducing risks by pooling development projects derives from the ability to offset losses on failed projects with gains from successful ones. Obviously, this strategy would not work if program producers could sell to other broadcasters the rights to successful programs whose development was financed by one network, or if they could raise license fees for successful programs so high that the developing network would not earn enough to provide a satisfactory return on its total development investment.

One way to preserve the advantages of risk pooling is for networks to develop programs themselves and thus own the broadcast rights outright. Indeed, networks have always done some program production, but it has not been their major mode of operation. Most programs, especially prime-time entertainment series, have been developed and produced by independent program producers under contract for individual programs to the television networks.[11] Most network-produced programs have been news, public affairs, or daytime programs. Risks on prime-time entertainment series have been absorbed by the networks through contractual provisions.

Contracts under which programs are developed and series episodes are supplied typically are negotiated early in the development process. The contracts may be quite informal and are often renegotiated. They provide for network payments of specified amounts at each stage, contingent upon the network's desire to proceed further, and include a schedule of license fees the network will pay for any episodes it orders. In addition, the network obtains exclusive rights to offer each episode for broadcast in the United States a limited number of times (typically twice). Although the network usually has a continuing option to proceed or to order new episodes, the option term is limited, and the contract specifies dates by which each network option must be exercised.[12] If the network chooses not to exercise an option, the contract lapses, and rights revert to the program producer. Although all contractual provisions vary from contract to contract and from network to network and additional terms may be included, the essential structure of these agreements provides to networks a geographically and temporally limited exclusive option to offer programs whose development they have financed. Without such options, networks would earn little or no return by financing program development and eventually would withdraw from that function.

Before the imposition of the Financial Interest and Syndication Rules, networks absorbed risk through additional contractual provisions granting them financial interests in certain non-network uses of programs in exchange for development financing. Those provisions absorbed risk because the rights sold to networks by suppliers represented investments that were profitable only if the program was successful. Attractive television programs produced for networks often earn revenues from a number of sources other than network exhibition; those revenues, however, are important only if the network run is successful and long enough.

The first source of this type of revenue is foreign syndication—revenues paid by broadcasters in foreign countries for rights to broadcast programs developed and produced by independent suppliers in the United States. Because U.S. networks acquire rights only for the United States, foreign syndication of a program can and does proceed simultaneously with broadcast of the program by stations in the United States. Another source of revenue is domestic off-network syndication, that is, the licensing for broadcast by local television stations, independent and affiliated, of programs previously offered by networks to local stations. Off-network syndication often occurs after new episodes of a series are no longer being offered by any of the three major television networks, but syndication can occur at any time the network does not have the exclusive right to offer the program. Still another source of revenue is merchandising—the sale of toys, clothes, and other goods associated with a program or its characters.

Before the rules were established, networks frequently participated in these non-network uses of programs, sometimes by obtaining the right to act as distributor or licensor of one or more rights to foreign syndication, domestic syndication, or merchandising and, more often, by sharing in profits from some of the non-network uses of programs.

The possibility of sharing revenues from non-network uses through these financial interests and syndication rights provided a mechanism for allocating risks between networks and program producers. To the extent that networks purchased financial interest or syndication rights, they assumed risks because potential syndication fees and non-network earnings were, if anything, even more speculative than the potential earnings of programs on the networks. Networks were willing (and better able than independent producers) to bear these risks because of their pooling ability and the economies of integration they enjoyed. Concomitantly, to the extent suppliers sold rights and financial interests to networks, they shed risk since they exchanged items of uncertain value for the value given in return by the network, that is greater fees and advances than would have been given had the rights not been sold. Further, to the extent that networks could anticipate participating in non-network earnings, both the prospective return to financing program development and network financing increased.

To absorb risk efficiently, networks or other financing entities must be able to reach agreements with program suppliers that reflect mutual desires. This means contracts for programs must be capable of transferring risk from suppliers with an interest in one or a few programs to networks with an interest in many. Otherwise networks could not pool risks, and suppliers could not reduce risks by transferring them to networks.

A logical way to transfer risk is for networks to make one or more early cash payments in partial return for the acquisition of rights whose value is uncertain and greater than zero only if the program succeeds. One way in which risk was transferred to a network before the Financial Interest and Syndication Rules was to sell it some combination of distribution rights, merchandising rights, and profit shares as part of the original deal under which the network agreed to pay for program development.

It must be emphasized that such exchange of distribution rights and profit shares for initial cash payments was in the interests of both networks and suppliers involved in a particular project. Networks, with the advantages of risk pooling and economies of integration, could afford to pay more for rights or profit shares than suppliers needed to compensate them for their valuation of the rights and interests given up and more than suppliers could get by selling those rights and interest to others who lacked the advantages of risk pooling and integration. Suppliers doubtless would have preferred to receive the same amount of financing *without* selling rights or profit shares, but competition among them prevented their doing so. Similarly, networks would have preferred to acquire rights or profit shares while paying less for program development than they actually did, but competition among networks for the network rights and among networks and others for distribution rights and profit shares prevented their doing so. The agreements reached reflected the networks' superior ability and willingness to assume risks and suppliers' desire to reduce them, as well as reflecting competition among networks and other distributors for rights, on the one hand, and competition among suppliers to sell broadcast and distribution rights, on the other.

The Issue of Monopsony
Despite the mutual benefits to be derived from selling profit-sharing and syndication rights to networks, some suppliers complained that they were forced to grant those rights and that they would have been willing to accept the greater risks involved in retaining the rights. Complaining suppliers, however, did not say they would be willing to accept both *more* risk *and* smaller network payments for program development; they said only that they preferred more to less, not that they would have been willing to accept less from networks in exchange for keeping the rights and options.[13]

The suppliers' real complaint may have been that they felt the total fees they received for the bundle of rights sold to networks were less than they would receive in a competitive market, rather than a specific complaint about the terms on which networks paid for program development. At least implicitly they seemed to believe that networks are too few and competition among them insufficiently vigorous.[14] Similarly, an important factor motivating the FCC's adoption of the Financial Interest and Syndication Rules was its perception that the three networks possessed monopsony power, that is, that the networks enjoyed market power as buyers in the program-supply market. If there is competition on the buyers' side of the program supply market, as well as on the sellers' side, surely the rules are unnecessary.

In fact, singly, the networks lack monopsony power; they compete vigorously among themselves for programming. Ultimately, networks compete among themselves for advertising revenues and with other suppliers of national advertising media, such as local television stations, radio stations, magazines, periodicals, and other media. Because successful competition for advertising depends on attracting large audiences, networks compete for the attention of viewers. The networks' need to attract viewers causes them to compete vigorously for the programming with which to do it. In addition, because networks cannot reach national audiences with the relatively few stations they own and operate, they must compete with other sources of programs to attract affiliates and induce them to broadcast the network-offered programs. This competition for programs and television exhibition rights has increased and will continue to increase as a result of new distribution technologies, for example, cable and pay television, multipoint distribution systems, and direct broadcast satellites.

Moreover, careful analysis demonstrates that even if the networks had monopsony power, the Financial Interest and Syndication Rules would have left that power unaffected. The contract between a network and a program supplier is a complex bundle of interrelated rights and terms. For example, price, option length, and exclusivity are important contractual terms in addition to whatever rights or financial interests the network might seek to acquire, at least prior to the rules. These terms can and do vary widely and from contract to contract. Because the rules created no more buyers and because they did not (and could not) regulate *every* contract term, they could not take away monopsony power even if it existed; the most they could do was to prevent its effects from being exercised in specific ways. If networks have significant monopsony power and can force program suppliers to accept lower than competitive prices, the rules do not change this characteristic of the market. Preventing a network from acquiring financial interests or syndication rights merely reduces the amount paid to a supplier, for the supposedly monopsonistic network will take into account the supplier's additional sources of income from selling to others rights the network can no longer acquire. In both a monopsonized and a competitive market, the rules lower the fees paid to packagers for network exhibition by an amount equivalent to the value of the rights that can no longer be transferred. (See the appendix to this chapter.)

Thus, whatever the state of competition for programs, ability to transfer some risks from program suppliers to financers of program development increases economic efficiency and is in the interest of financers and suppliers as a group, particularly new and potential entrants (although, as we shall see, they may not be in the interest of large, established suppliers). The Financial Interest and Syndication Rules impaired the ability of program suppliers to transfer risks to networks and thereby detracted from economic efficiency. They could not have limited monopsony power even had such power existed.

Effects of the Rules in the Marketplace for Syndicated Television Programming: "Warehousing"
By the time the repeal of the Financial Interest and Syndication Rules was under consideration in 1982–83, their inability to curb network power in the acquisition of program packages had been recognized. The regulatory authorities, however, raised a new issue: possible network power in the sale of off-network syndicated programs. In particular, the FCC and the Department of Justice were concerned that in the future networks might withhold some or all series from domestic syndication, delay entry of series into domestic syndication, or engage in other behavior calculated to make independent television stations less effective competitors of the network affiliates.

As we shall see, this concern was misplaced; indeed, the rules cause undesirable effects in the marketplace for syndicated television programming by eliminating the networks as competitors in that business. The rules do not permit ABC, CBS, and NBC to engage in the business of syndication, including syndication of motion pictures, in the United States. Depriving the buyers of syndicated programming of access to three additional sellers can only tend to keep prices higher than they otherwise would be. Keeping efficient, viable competitors out of a market cannot be an appropriate purpose of government regulation.

Those buyers of programming hurt by the rules are principally network-affiliated and independent television stations. Other firms buy syndicated programming as well, however. They include cable systems, "superstations" such as WTBS-TV in Atlanta, and emerging firms exploiting new technologies, such as direct-broadcast satellite.

The concern that elimination of the rules would damage rather than enhance competition is unfounded, for two reasons: (1) the networks lack the market power to make such behavior (referred to generally as "warehousing") effective strategy; and (2) even if they possessed such power, the networks lack the incentive to exercise it. First, in view of the vigorous competition among the networks and the competitive structure of the syndication business (which would be made even more competitive by the addition of three networks as sellers), warehousing would not be an effective method of hurting independent stations. For any advantage to be gained by withholding or delaying product or offering it to independent stations on discriminatory terms, the networks would, among themselves, have to control syndication of virtually all off-network programming of significant audience-attracting power, and all three networks would have to engage in collusion. These conditions were not satisfied before promulgation of the rules, and there is no evidence that warehousing occurred. Nor is there reason to believe that such conditions would exist or that warehousing would occur if the rules were repealed.

Before passage of the rules, the networks, either individually or collectively, were not dominant in syndication. In 1968 the three networks together had only 18.5 percent of syndicated program sales by hours.[15] There is no reason to suppose that networks would have a larger share if the rules were repealed. Such a share, even if held by a single network, patently would be insufficient to permit that network to damage independent stations through warehousing. Other programming would always be available from other sources to ensure that independent stations remained competitive with network affiliates. Thus, even if they colluded, networks could only injure themselves by foregoing syndication fees and engaging in warehousing; they could not effectively injure independent stations.

Moreover, collusion among networks is also required to make warehousing work. In the absence of collusion, a warehousing network would forego syndication fees without being able to prevent independent stations from access to the programs syndicated by its network rivals. There would be no benefit from this behavior unless the other networks were sure to engage in it as well. Yet the chances of collusion are too remote to justify the rules. Whatever else may have been said about the networks, it has never seriously been said that they collude; their competitive behavior is obvious and vigorous. Further, any collusive arrangement among the networks, short of a complete refusal to deal, would be almost impossible to police. The temptation to cheat would be strong, since significant additional revenue could be earned without losing the benefits of the conspiracy. Also, cheating would be difficult to detect, since the terms of the sales contracts are not public and the product is necessarily differentiated. How, for example, could one network be sure that another did not arrange the release of a particular program in a particular market earlier or on more favorable terms than collusion would dictate? Release can occur well before a program is actually shown, and contracts can involve rights to exhibition over several years. Further, the decision as to whether a particular program has been warehoused long enough is not one that lends itself to implicit or vague agreement.

The second reason why fears of network warehousing are unfounded is that it is difficult to imagine a situation in which a network would have an economic incentive to engage in program warehousing. It must be recognized that the beneficiaries of any injury to independent stations through warehousing would be the affiliates, which would gain some of the viewers the independents lose, and the other syndicators, including the other networks, who would sell their syndicated programs in substitution for warehoused product. The warehousing network would derive little direct benefit. To achieve an indirect benefit, the network would have to find a way to garner for itself some of the affiliates' increased profits. Whether and to what degree it could do that is speculative. Moreover, to the extent that independent stations were driven out, the bargaining power of the affiliates vis-à-vis the network would be increased, because the network would then lack alternative stations with which to affiliate. This would tend to shift profits to affiliates, not to the networks.[16] Therefore, it is practically inconceivable that a network would (even if it were able to collude with respect to syndicated programming) forego profits from syndication in hopes that it could somehow siphon off some of the affiliates' increased profits or earn greater advertising revenues by virtue of its affiliates' increased audiences.

An additional check on potential network warehousing behavior is the interest of non-network participants in the profits of syndicated programs. Although the holder of syndication rights decides when and where to sell and collects a fee for the sales, others typically are entitled to share the profits from syndication. The syndicator is thus under a fiduciary obligation to such participants to maximize the profits obtainable from exploitation. Warehousing would lead to disputes and lawsuits that warehousers would be likely to lose. It would also destroy the reputation of the network as a syndicator and make it difficult for the network to get programs to syndicate in the future or to get others to invest in programs it would syndicate.

Accordingly, concern over network warehousing in the syndication marketplace to the detriment of independent stations is unjustified. The possibility of its occurring surely is too speculative and remote to justify the loss of competition that the rules impose. Moreover, if the networks, which now have essentially no syndication rights, were ever to acquire a share of such rights so large as to make warehousing less speculative, there would be plenty of time for action.

Effects on Industry Groups and the Public of Disrupting Efficient Risk-Sharing

Whereas the possibility of an undesirable warehousing effect of repeal of the Financial Interest and Syndication Rules is speculative, the undesirable effects of retention are clear. The rules affect virtually all participants in the television industry and, of course, the viewing public. Among the firms affected are the networks, network competitors, major studios, independent program suppliers, potential new program suppliers, performing artists and other talent, affiliated television stations, independent television stations, and advertisers. The effect of the rules on each of these groups and on the viewing public is analyzed below. In reading that analysis it must be kept in mind that imposition of the rules in 1970 was only one factor affecting a changing industry. The analysis thus sets forth what the effects of the rules must have been relative to what would otherwise have happened, not relative to pre-rule history.

The reductions in the efficiency of risk bearing induced by the rules must be reflected in the amounts the networks are willing to pay for program development. The rules limit the value to the networks of the right to offer a program for network broadcast in the United States. Because entertainment programs are less valuable to networks, other factors being the same, than they were prior to the rules, the networks spend less on developing and acquiring such programs than would have been the case without the rules. The networks thus reduce payments for program development, license fees, and program promotion expenses below what they otherwise would be. The payments networks offer to independent suppliers of entertainment programs with a given level of attractiveness fall, and the network resources devoted to program development decline, other factors being the same.

Suppliers of programs, selling fewer rights to networks than before, thus receive lower payments because of the rules. They face the possibility of increased "deficit financing" where the "deficit" consists of production costs less *only* the network exhibition fee. The profits needed to induce suppliers to remain in the business must come from the returns they earn on the rights they now cannot sell to networks.[17] But those rights promise only a risky return. Because suppliers are less efficient risk bearers than are networks, those rights are worth less to them than they are to the networks (otherwise they would not have been sold), and suppliers are less willing to invest in making them pay off than networks would have been. Hence, overall investment in program development falls because of the rules, and programming attractiveness suffers, to the detriment of the viewing public (see the Appendix to this chapter).

Because the networks after the rules can share in the returns from risky ventures to a lesser extent than before the rules, they also have an incentive to alter their programming mix. They can be expected to acquire broadcast rights to fewer risky programs and to more less risky programs. For example, the networks can be expected to offer fewer entertainment series and to invest fewer resources in the entertainment series they do offer while offering more theatrical films and devoting more resources to movies made for television. In a competitive market, investment choices of this sort would be dictated by viewer preferences, free of interference from regulatory rules. The influence of the rules on programming choice thus skews the programming mix away from that which would have been dictated by viewers in the absence of the rules.

Further, because the rules apply only to the three existing commercial television networks and do not limit the rights other potential financers of program development and acquirers of entertainment programs may obtain, they place the networks at a distinct disadvantage in responding to increasing competition from alternative video distribution technologies, such as cable networks. Although the full effect of such competition lies in the future as such exhibitors increasingly move into financing their own first-run projects, it is plain that broadcast television networks have been hobbled in the competitive race by the rules; their competitors have not.

The rules have had differential effects on program suppliers. The rules relatively benefit the major studios, since, by virtue of their size, they are better able to absorb the risks of program development than are some of the independent producers with whom they compete. As a result, other factors being the same, one would expect an increase in the share of the major studios in the program-supply market and a decrease in the market share of smaller, independent producers.

In addition, after the rules, the major studios are the least expensive available source of risk capital for program development. Producers who want to shift some of the risk of program development, and who before the rules would have considered selling rights or interests to a network, are now largely limited to the major studios or perhaps other large distributors. Thus producers can expect to receive lower payments for the sale of profit-sharing and syndication rights. Because no other type of purchaser of the rights can bear risk as efficiently as the networks, the rights will be worth less to major studios or other large distributors than to the networks, and such purchasers will offer less for the rights. Thus the rules are likely to have particularly adverse effects on entrants and potential entrants into program supply. Because these firms tend to be small and to lack a track record, they are at a disadvantage relative to established program suppliers in obtaining funding for developing new programs. They develop few programs at once, so they are at a disadvantage as risk bearers relative to established firms, especially the major studios. As a result, entry into program supply becomes more difficult, established firms are less likely to be displaced, and concentration among program suppliers increases relative to what would have happened without the rules.

More specifically, without the option of obtaining development funding from the networks, program suppliers can either turn to other sources of funding, finance program development themselves, or use both methods of financing. Whatever their choice, they end up with higher costs or less revenue than in the absence of the rules. Since non-network firms are less efficient than the networks in absorbing the risks of program development and acquisition, any specified rights to syndication distribution and profit sharing are worth less to them than to the networks, and they will offer the supplier less compensation for the rights than the networks would have offered.

On the other hand, to the extent that the suppliers finance program development themselves, their costs rise because they, too, are less efficient at risk bearing than are the networks. Whether the supplier funds program development from retained earnings, the sale of new equity, or borrowing, stockholders or creditors will demand a premium that reflects the greater risks borne by the supplier. Thus the costs of all suppliers following this financing strategy rise, but the costs of new, smaller suppliers rise disproportionately more than the costs of the larger, established suppliers, leading to a reduced rate of entry and an increase in concentration among program suppliers.

It is important to note in this regard that existing program suppliers (especially the major ones) may feel that the rules benefit them. Even though decreasing the available options for development funding can directly benefit no supplier, it will hurt small suppliers or potential entrants more than larger, established suppliers. Therefore, even though any particular established supplier would prefer to shift *his* risk to the networks, established suppliers as a group may be better off if *no* supplier can do so and potential entrants are hampered. By adopting the Financial Interest and Syndication Rules, the FCC may have facilitated a cartel arrangement which suppliers could not have brought about themselves and which prevents or hampers new suppliers from joining (and competing with) the club.

It is not at all clear, however, that the gains to the larger established program suppliers from the rules will persist. If the program-supply industry was competitive before the rules, and the rules do not fundamentally alter its competitive structure, any profits above the competitive level created by the rules will attract new firms to the industry, and entry will continue until profits fall to a competitive level. On the other hand, if the program-supply industry was not competitive before the rules, or if the rules, by increasing concentration or impeding entry, fundamentally change the structure of the industry, higher profits may continue even in the long run. If the rules increase long-run profits, it will be because the commission, through its regulations, created market power or facilitated its exercise.

The effects of the rules on performing artists, writers, and other talent are closely tied to their effects on the viewing public. Thus the effects on the two parties can be discussed together. The rules induce a change in the programming mix of the networks. Because the networks cannot earn as much from their programming investments as before, they invest less in programming and move resources away from more innovative (hence, riskier) programming to less risky, tried-and-true types of programming. The networks offer fewer entertainment series and more sports events and movies, both theatrical films and movies made for television. They do so, even though a successful entertainment series will attract larger audiences than successful movies, because the risks associated with entertainment series are greater. The new mix of programs, however, is not simply a market response dictated by viewers but is induced by a change in the allocation of risk caused by regulatory intervention in the marketplace.

These changes in risk and program mix have implications as well for performing artists, writers, and other talent. Demand for their services declines as the networks invest less in programming. In addition, as part of their risk-reducing strategy, the networks will tend to favor programs with performing artists and writers who have a proven track record. Rewards to "stars" thus increase relative to rewards to less well known talent. Just as in the case of the effects of the rules on program suppliers, in the long run fewer actors and writers will have the opportunity to develop a professional reputation. The result contributes to less diversity in programming than otherwise would be dictated by viewers.

Viewers, therefore, see less diverse and less innovative programming on network television than would occur in the absence of the rules. Indeed, that effect may carry over into non-network television, especially cable, by making it unnecessary to compete with networks in innovative programming If such new sources of programming as cable press their advantage over the restricted networks by acquiring relatively innovative first-run programs, viewers desiring such programs will find that they are available only at the price of a subscription fee rather than on free network television.

The Financial Interest and Syndication Rules have effects on television stations, both affiliated and independent. Because affiliated stations receive less attractive programs from the networks, their entertainment series tend to fall in popularity relative to the programs viewers can watch on independent stations, cable systems, or other media. A decline in the audience size of prime-time entertainment series lowers potential advertising revenues and the value of network affiliation. The corresponding improvement in the relative position of independent stations is only a short-run phenomenon, however. Over time, the stock of programs broadcast by independent stations turns over, and the less attractive programs produced after the advent of the rules make up a larger portion of their broadcasts. In the long run, both affiliated and independent stations tend to lose market share to other media and earn a lower level of revenue and profits.[18]

Finally, the rules have an effect on advertisers. As network programming attracts smaller audiences as a result of the rules, advertisers will find that network television is a relatively less cost-effective means of reaching potential customers and will reallocate their expenditures to other media. Moreover, even if the rates for network advertising fall to reflect smaller audience size, advertisers cannot be fully recompensed because, with smaller audiences, they lose some of the benefits from utilizing the otherwise most effective medium.

Thus the rules disrupt efficient market operation and risk sharing. They cannot limit network power, and they are, if anything, anticompetitive through their elimination of the networks as sources of financing to packagers (especially new packagers) and sources of syndicated programs to stations. The retention even of the limited form of the rules proposed by the FCC in 1983 can be justified only from the point of view of private rather than public interest.

Appendix

This appendix demonstrates three propositions concerning the Financial Interest and Syndication Rules. The first is that the rules, by restricting the rights that can be sold to networks, have the effect of lowering the total equilibrium price paid by the networks for television programming, ceteris paribus. The second proposition is that the rules also lower the attractiveness to viewing audiences of television programming produced and sold to the networks. The third proposition is that the rules skew the choice of program types in favor of less risky or less innovative programs. The analysis assumes that networks compete for programs.

In analyzing the effects of the Financial Interest and Syndication Rules on the price and attractiveness of television programming, it is important to bear in mind that the transaction between a network and a program supplier involves a package comprising a bundle of rights in the program, including a set of property rights related to its network exhibition and, prior to the rules, sometimes to its syndication or other secondary uses. Because the rules essentially restrict the set of property rights the networks may acquire to those involving network exhibition, a package of programming available to the networks after adoption of the rules is inferior to one available before the rules, even if the program components of the two packages are of the same quality or audience attractiveness.

Hence, when I say that the rules necessarily lower the price paid by networks for programming, I mean the *total* price. In fact, the amount of money paid for the bundle of rights which the rules still permit networks to acquire goes up, making programming more costly. However, that money price does not go up sufficiently to offset the fact that certain rights are no longer being sold. The total money actually paid by networks goes down—but only because networks get less for what they pay. The price paid by networks for the rights they still get goes up.

I shall analyze the effects of the rules on three variables. The first variable is the price the networks pay for the packages of programming they acquire. Second is the level of attractiveness to audiences of the programs the networks acquire. Third is the cost to the networks of acquiring a program with a given level of attractiveness to viewing audiences.

It is important to realize that "attractiveness" as used here is defined as the attractiveness of a program to viewing audiences. Related to this, in the demonstration below, the "quantity" of programming is to be thought of not as measured in numbers of programs but as measured in total audience—in short, "attractiveness."

To evaluate the effects of the rules on the prices networks pay to suppliers and on the level of program attractiveness to audiences, consider D_0D_0 and S_0S_0, the demand and supply curves for program attractiveness prior to adoption of the Financial Interest and Syndication Rules (see figure 11.1). It is simplest to think of these curves as relating to a single program. The supply curve slopes upward because generally it takes more inputs to make a program more attractive. Essentially, the demand curve is the networks' demand for viewer attention—"attractiveness." The equilibrium price and attractiveness, P_0 and Q_0, respectively, are determined by the intersection of D_0D_0 and S_0S_0.

Before the rules, independent producers were free to sell various financial or distribution rights related to syndication to the networks, along with the network exhibition rights. The rules essentially forbid the sale of such non-network financial or distribution rights to a network. This prohibition tends to shift both demand and supply

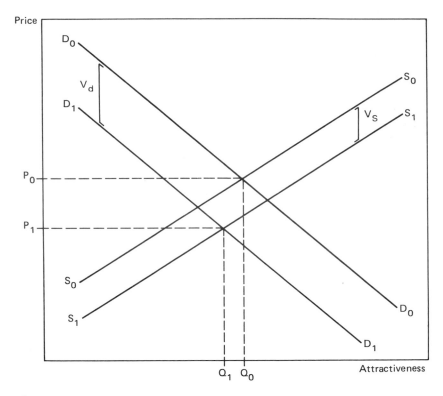

Figure 11.1
Supply and Demand of Programming Attractiveness

curves. The demand curve shifts down by the amount of the value of
the syndication-related rights to the networks, V_d. That is, because the
networks now receive a smaller bundle of rights when they acquire
television programming, they are willing to pay less. The post-rule
demand curve is labeled $D_1 D_1$.

The supply curve also shifts down—here, by the amount V_s—the
value of the financial interests to the independent producers who now
retain those rights. In other words, the producers now retain more of
the rights and as a result are willing to accept a lower price from the
networks. The new supply curve is labeled $S_1 S_1$.

Because both supply and demand curves have shifted downward, it
is clear that the new (post-rule) equilibrium price, P_1, must lie below
the old (pre-rule) equilibrium, P_0. What happens to the equilibrium
attractiveness depends on the relative shifts in demand and supply

curves. Downward shifts in the demand curve tend to reduce attractiveness, ceteris paribus, whereas downward shifts in supply increase attractiveness, ceteris paribus. Figure 11.1 shows a decrease in equilibrium attractiveness from Q_0 to Q_1. This decrease occurs because the figure was drawn so that the downward shift in the supply curve, V_s, was smaller then the downward shift in the demand curve, V_d. This result is not an accident. The assumption that the demand curve shifts by more than the supply curve (i.e., $V_d > V_s$) reflects the fact that the networks can absorb the risk associated with the non-network financial interests more efficiently than program suppliers. That is, rights to off-network syndication and profit sharing are more valuable to the networks than to the suppliers.

To prove that the equilibrium price and attractiveness of television programming will fall under the Financial Interest and Syndication Rules, under the assumption that financial interests are more valuable to the network than to the independent producers, consider the following.

Let $q^d = D(P + a)$

$q^s = S(P + b)$

where q^d and q^s are, respectively, the program attractiveness demanded and supplied, $D(.)$ and $S(.)$ are the demand and supply functions, P is program price, and a and b are shift terms. The shift term a is equal to 0 before the rules and equal to V_d when the rules are in effect, since the price which calls forth a given level of quality demanded must fall by V_d after adoption of the rules. The shift term b is equal to 0 before the rules and equal to V_s once the rules are in effect. Define $K = V_s/V_d$. Because the networks are better equipped than the program suppliers to handle the risk associated with financial interests and syndication rights, $0 < K < 1$.

In equilibrium, the attractiveness demanded will equal the attractiveness supplied. That is:

$$D(P + a) = S(P + b) = S(P + Ka)$$

both before and after the rules. Differentiating this expression totally with respect to a yields:

$$D'\left(\frac{dP}{da} + 1\right) = S'\left(\frac{dP}{da} + K\right)$$

Rearranging terms gives:

$$\frac{dP}{da}(S' - D') = -KS' + D'$$

$$\frac{dP}{da} = \frac{-KS' + D'}{S' - D'} < 0$$

The derivative of P with respect to a is negative, since K is positive, S' is positive, and D' is negative, making the numerator of this expression negative and the denominator positive. This implies that price will fall as fewer financial interests can be transacted.

As noted above, the equilibrium attractiveness, q, is determined by the intersection of the supply and demand curves. That is,

$$q = D(P + a) = S(P + Ka)$$

both before and after the rules. Differentiating totally with respect to a yields:

$$\frac{dq}{da} = D'\left(\frac{dP}{da} + 1\right) = S'\left(\frac{dP}{da} + K\right)$$

Substituting the expression for $\dfrac{dP}{da}$ and rearranging terms gives.

$$\frac{dq}{da} = D' + \frac{D' - KS'}{S' - D'}D'$$

$$\frac{dq}{da} = \frac{S'D'(1 - K)}{S' - D'} < 0$$

Thus, in equilibrium, the attractiveness to audiences of television programming declines as the fraction of syndication-related rights that cannot be transacted increases.

There is another way to think about this. The analysis so far indicates that, with the Financial Interest and Syndication Rules, networks offer smaller total payments to program suppliers because the programs offered to the networks are now worth less to them. That is, the networks spend less to obtain a set of property rights that are more restricted than they were previously able to negotiate. Although the networks are paying less and receiving programming of lesser attractiveness to audiences, it is important to realize that the cost of the rights actually conveyed for programming of a *given* level of audience attractiveness has *increased*.

To the extent suppliers are not as efficient as the networks in bearing risk, syndication rights and financial interests are worth less to program suppliers than they would be to the networks in the absence of the rules. Hence, program suppliers must choose between receiving lower total payments for the full set of property rights in their programs from the network and a distributor together and retaining the syndication rights themselves but at an increased exposure to risk. Smaller payments for syndication-related rights must be offset by higher payments for network exhibition rights if the program suppliers are to recover their full costs, including a competitive return on their investment. If the program suppliers instead choose to retain syndication-related rights, they will demand a risk premium for their greater exposure to risk. With either outcome, the networks must pay a higher price for the level of programming quality they obtain.

In diagrammatic terms, think in terms of the supply curve not for the production of programming in attractiveness units, as in figure 11.1, but for the supply of that programming for the network run *only*. That supply curve represents what the suppliers will accept for conveying the rights to the network run and can be thought of as the total they will accept for producing the programs less the value to them of non-network uses. Because the rules prohibit sales of non-network rights to the customers who value them most, their effect is to reduce the value of such rights and, hence, shift upward the supply curve for the network run. This produces an increase in the price networks must pay for the rights they can still get for programs of given attractiveness; naturally, it causes a decline in the amount of attractiveness they are willing to buy.

The full set of price effects can be illustrated by an analogy. Suppose a customer of a clothing store is accustomed to buying suits with two pairs of pants, although the store also sells suits with one pair of pants. One day he finds that the store is selling only suits with one pair of pants. The customer pays less for the suits he buys but obtains only one pair of pants. In fact, he finds that the suits with one pair of pants cost more than they did previously, although not as much as did suits with two pairs of pants. It is true that the customer is paying less for his suits, but only because he is now getting one pair of pants instead of two. He pays more than he would have earlier for a suit with one pair of pants.

So far, the analysis relates to the supply of and demand for attractiveness for a given program. That means the demand curves are drawn with the prices of other programs constant. The analysis applies to all programs, however; hence, the other prices will change. Clearly, the prices that will be most affected are those for programs in which financial interests and syndication rights are most important. These are the riskier, more innovative programs. Thus the price of those programs (for the rights actually acquired under the rules) will go up relative to the price of less risky programs. The price of theatrical movies, for example, will not be directly affected. The result of this change in relative prices will be to shift network demands away from risky or innovative programs toward less risky, less innovative programs, even though, on average, viewers would prefer the mix of programs that would occur without the rules.

Notes

As explained below, this paper is taken from my statements submitted to the Federal Communications Commission on behalf of CBS, Inc. in BC Docket No. 82–345 ("In the Matter of Amendment of 47CFR §73.658(j) (l) (i) and (ii), the Syndication and Financial Interest Rules"). Over our many years of involvement with these subjects, John McGowan and I spoke with and received comments from a large number of people, and it is not possible to thank them all here. Particular thanks, however, go to John Appel, William Baumol, David Blank, David Boies, Robert Bolick, Steven Edwards, Paul Joskow, Stephen Kalos, George Vradenburg III, Robert Larner, Donald Prutzman, Paul Saunders, and especially Robert S. Rifkind. As usual, errors are mine, not theirs.

1. Production for first-run syndication did increase, but this was largely due to the concurrent adoption of the Prime Time Access Rule, which effectively limited networks and off-network syndication by network affiliates to the last three hours of prime time. The gap was largely filled with game shows rather than shows of "network quality," such programs as the popular "Muppet Show" being rare exceptions.

2. See, for example, Stanley Besen and Ronald Soligo, "The Regulation of Television Program Production and Distribution: Some Preliminary Thoughts, "mimeographed (copy placed in Network Inquiry Docket, 21049); Robert Crandall, "FCC Regulation, Monopsony, and Network Television Program Costs," *Bell Journal of Economics and Management Science* 3 (Autumn 1972), pp. 483–508; also "The Economic Effect of Television-Network Program 'Ownership'," *Journal of Law and Economics* 14 (October 1971), pp. 385–412; Bruce Owen, Jack Beebe, and Willard Manning, *Television Economics* (Lexington, Mass.: Lexington Books, 1974).

3. Network Inquiry Special Staff of the Federal Communications Commission, *Final Report on New Television Networks: Entry, Jurisdiction, Ownership, and Regulation* (1980), vols. I and II (cited below as "Staff Report"); *Recommendations of the Network Inquiry Special Staff to the Federal Communications Commission* (December 1980).

4. FCC BC Docket No. 82-345, "Tentative Decision and Request for Further Comments," August 4, 1983.

5. Staff Report, vol. II, p. 578.

6. See "Reagan Upstages the Networks in Syndication," *Business Week* (November 7, 1983), pp. 51–52.

7. "The President's Priorities," *New York Times* (November 7, 1983), p. A22.

8. Direct economies achievable by spreading high program costs over large potential audiences probably do not explain why each of the three television networks has roughly 200 affiliates rather than some much smaller number. The 200 largest TV markets contain more than 99 percent of the TV homes, and the top 100 contain approximately 85 percent. The additional saving in cost per viewer obtainable by expansion into the 50 or 100 least populous markets is probably small and may not compensate for the costs of interconnection, together with payments to the affiliates at the level made to affiliates in larger markets. Stations in smaller markets, however, desire to affiliate with a network because of the benefits of affiliation to them rather than because of the economies they provide to the network. A network reaps most of the economies of scale from spreading expensive programs by having affiliates in the largest 100 to 150 markets. At that point there is considerable advantage to stations in the smallest 50 to 100 markets from affiliating with a network and gaining the right to broadcast highly attractive programs. These smaller stations may even be willing to affiliate on terms that require them to absorb some or all the costs of interconnection and accept lower rates of network compensation. See Staff Report, vol. II, p. 115.

9. Note, however, that these efficiencies result in programs with mass appeal. Such programs, which may display depressing similarities, generally are not uplifting and educational. In this chapter, program "quality" and "attractiveness" are judged by audience size. This is not, of course, the only possible criterion.

10. The fact that non-network entities can spread risks over different networks, thus insuring themselves against the collapse of a given network's entire schedule, does not appear important.

11. Network production of entertainment programs for prime-time broadcast is now severely restricted by the terms of consent decrees signed in or before 1980 by the networks as a result of the antitrust cases brought by the Department of Justice.

12. These option terms are also limited by the consent decrees.

13. Cf. Staff Report, vol. I, p. 508. In addition, as discussed below, major suppliers (and, perhaps, even all established suppliers) might prefer that *no one*, especially not their competition, be able to transfer such rights. Established suppliers have this preference not because it is in the interest of any one supplier to be himself barred from transferring rights but because existing suppliers, better able to bear risk than are new ones, gain an advantage over new and potential suppliers if no one can shift risk. That advantage, by reducing the competition they face, can outweigh the disadvantage to existing suppliers of being prevented themselves from shifting risk.
by themselves being prevented from shifting risk.

14. In other contexts, suppliers have complained that competition among the networks is too vigorous, as manifested by a tendency for networks to cancel series that do not demonstrate success after the broadcast of the first few episodes.

15. Staff Report, vol. II, p. 578.

16. One potential benefit would be larger network advertising revenues if warehousing were to increase the audiences of the networks' affiliates at the expense of independent stations during times when network programs are broadcast. It should be kept in mind, however, that the network affiliates would not attract the entire potential audience of the independent. Only some fraction of that audience would turn to the network's affiliate in the absence of the warehoused program. Others would watch programs on other stations, and still others would not turn on their television sets. In addition, as a practical matter, independent stations tend to use off-network series most heavily at times when network service is not offered.

A warehousing network might also derive direct benefit in the five markets in which it owns and operates stations. Such local markets, however, are among those in which independent stations are most numerous and strongest and off-network syndicated programs are most valuable. Thus, the syndication profits that would have to be foregone to gain any additional profits for the station owned and operated by the network would be large. In addition, most of the benefits from keeping programs from independent stations would accrue to the other two network stations, which, with a few exceptions, are also owned and operated by their networks in the pertinent markets. Thus, most of any possible benefit from warehousing in owned and operated station markets would accrue not to the warehousing network, but to its rivals.

17. Suppliers may attempt to get around this by shifting risk to the networks in other ways, for example, by longer option terms. Options, however, were limited in 1980 by the consent decrees; in any event, if longer options were an efficient way of transferring risk, they would have been sold before the rules.

18. The rules may have worked to make entry into television broadcasting more difficult. To the extent that new independent stations rely on off-network syndicated products for their programming fare, in the long run they will find fewer off-network syndicated programs available as the networks reduce the number of entertainment series they offer for broadcast.

12

Borrowing from Peter to Pay Paul: More on Departures of Price from Marginal Cost

Almarin Phillips and Gary L. Roberts

Much of the current support for deregulation of various industries is based on the view that the price structure in those industries is grossly inefficient. Instances where regulators encourage—or, at least, permit—prices to be set below marginal cost are often assumed to provide evidence of regulatorily induced resource misallocation. Further, prices set by incumbent firms at levels below marginal cost are seen as an instrument designed to inhibit entry by potential competitors.

Following Ramsey (1927) and others,[1] this chapter examines the structure of optimal profit-constrained prices for demand-interrelated products. In contrast to previous analyses, however, we focus on the conditions under which the prices of some products are optimally set below marginal production cost. Allowance is made for the potential existence of consumption externalities within the regulated set. Even apart from these externalities, interrelations among demand functions generally yield deviations from the "inverse elasticity rule" of Baumol and Bradford (1970) and, indeed, the possible appearance of rates that are below the marginal cost of producing the services to which they pertain. The admission of externalities in consumption leads to further efficiency reasons for setting rates below marginal cost.

Our argument is straightforward. The optimal pricing rules are presented in the next section. These rules acquire an especially simple structure, provided there are no income effects within the regulated sector. The next section illustrates the results for the special case in which there are two regulated commodities. We note the possible policy implications in the last section.

General Rule for Optimal Pricing

We assume that community preferences are consistent with the existence of a "representative consumer" and are given by the indirect utility function

$$V(P, I) \tag{1}$$

where $P = (p_1, \ldots, p_n)$ is the vector of prices and I is income. The properties of this function ensure that demands for products $x_1, \ldots, x_n$ can be determined as functions of prices and income by the equation

$$x_i(P, I) = -\frac{\partial V}{\partial P_i} \bigg/ \frac{\partial V}{\partial I} \quad \text{for } i = 1, n. \tag{2}$$

Products are partitioned into two groups: the regulated set $(x_1, \ldots, x_m)$ and the unregulated set $(x_{m+1}, \ldots, x_n)$. Prices $(p_{m+1}, \ldots, p_n)$ and income I are assumed to be exogenously determined and are unaffected by the prices in the regulated set $(p_1, \ldots, p_m)$.

Social welfare is defined by the function

$$W(P, I) \tag{3}$$

and is related to consumer preferences by the marginal conditions

$$\frac{\partial W}{\partial P_i} = e_i \cdot \frac{\partial V}{\partial p_i} \tag{4}$$

for $i = 1, m$;

with

$$\frac{\partial W}{\partial p_i} = \frac{\partial V}{\partial p_i}$$

for $i = m + 1, n$

and

$$\frac{\partial W}{\partial I} = \frac{\partial V}{\partial I}.$$

The factor e_i is incorporated to reflect the possible divergence of social and private value for individual price changes within the regulated product set.[2] Positive externalities are associated with values $e_i > 1$, negative externalities with values $0 < e_i < 1$.

The planning problem is to choose prices $p_1, \ldots, p_m$ to maximize equation (3), subject to the revenue requirement

$$\sum_{i=1}^{m} p_i \cdot x_i = C(x_1, \ldots, x_m); \tag{5}$$

where the quantities $(x_1, \ldots, x_m)$ are determined by equation (2) and the cost function, C is defined in terms of the exogenously given numeraire.

The first-order conditions for this constrained maximization problem are given by

$$\frac{\partial W}{\partial p_i} + \gamma \left[\sum_{k=1}^{m} p_k \cdot \frac{\partial x_k}{\partial p_i} + x_i - \sum_{k=1}^{m} \frac{\partial C}{\partial x_k} \cdot \frac{\partial x_k}{\partial p_i} \right] = 0, \tag{6}$$

for $i = 1, m$,

where γ is the "shadow price" associated with the revenue requirement (5). Equations (2) and (6) can be used to rewrite these optimization conditions:

$$\sum_{k-1}^{m} (p_k - \frac{\partial C}{\partial x_k}) \cdot \frac{\partial x_k}{\partial p_i} = \lambda_i \cdot x_i \tag{7}$$

for $i - 1, m$,

where

$$\lambda_i = -(\gamma - \frac{\partial V}{\partial I} \cdot e_i)/\gamma.$$

If $e_i = 1$ for all $i = 1, m$ (implying there are no system externalities), equation (7) simplifies to the more familiar formulation,

$$\sum_{k-1}^{m} (p_k - \frac{\partial C}{\partial x_k}) \cdot \frac{\partial x_k}{\partial p_i} = \lambda \cdot x_i \tag{8}$$

for $i = 1, m$,

where

$$\lambda = -(\gamma - \frac{\partial V}{\partial I})/\gamma < 0.$$

The purpose of our analysis is to identify demand conditions that yield optimal prices below marginal production cost for some subset of the products in the regulated set. To simplify this task, attention is restricted to the special case in which demand for each of the regulated goods is independent of income level. This assumption underlies much of the existing, partial equilibrium analysis of optimal commodity pricing and provides a good approximation when the regulated set comprises a small portion of total consumer expenditure.[3] Furthermore, the additional structure imposed on the optimal pricing conditions (7) by the absence of income effects simplifies and clarifies their general structure.

The system of demand functions defined by equation (2) yields a "substitution matrix":

$$S = \begin{bmatrix} S_{11} -----S_{1n} \\ \vdots \qquad \vdots \\ S_{n1} -----S_{nn} \end{bmatrix} \tag{9}$$

with

$$S_{ij} = \frac{\partial x_i}{\partial p_j} + \frac{\partial x_i}{\partial I} \cdot x_j$$

for $i, j = 1, n$.

This matrix is symmetric and negative semi-definite. It follows immediately that if $\partial x_i/\partial I = 0$ for all products in the regulated set, the ordinary demand derivatives necessarily satisfy

$$\frac{\partial x_i}{\partial p_j} = \frac{\partial x_j}{\partial p_i} \tag{10}$$

for $i, j = 1, m$.

In addition, the $m \times m$ matrix defined by these derivatives is then negative semi-definite.

The symmetry conditions (10) can be used to rewrite the optimal pricing conditions (7) in the form

$$\sum_{k=1}^{m} \left(p_k - \frac{\partial C}{\partial x_k} \right) \cdot \frac{\partial x_i}{\partial p_k} = \lambda_i \cdot x_i \tag{11}$$

for $i = 1, m$.

Using matrix notation, this system of equations becomes

$$A \cdot T = \lambda \cdot X, \tag{12}$$

where A is the symmetric, negative semi-definite matrix of demand derivatives $\partial x_i/\partial p_j$, T is the vector of optimal "mark-ups" $p_i - \partial C/\partial x_i$, λ is the diagonal matric of externality augmented shadow prices λ_i, and X is the non-negative vector of demands. Prices of some commodities are optimally set below marginal production cost whenever solution vector T has some negative components. In the next section, demand con-

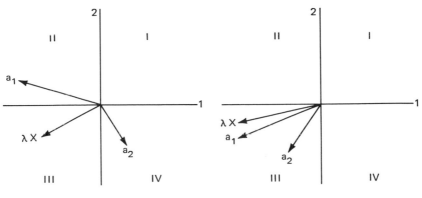

Figure 12.1   Figure 12.2

ditions yielding this result are examined for the simple two-product case.

A Two-Commodity Illustration

With two products in the regulated set, the optimal prices are determined by the matrix equation,

$$
\begin{bmatrix} \dfrac{\partial x_1}{\partial p_1} & \dfrac{\partial x_1}{\partial p_2} \\ \dfrac{\partial x_2}{\partial p_1} & \dfrac{\partial x_2}{\partial p_2} \end{bmatrix} \begin{bmatrix} p_1 & \dfrac{\partial C}{\partial x_1} \\ p_2 - \dfrac{\partial C}{\partial x_2} \end{bmatrix} = \begin{bmatrix} \lambda_1 & 0 \\ 0 & \lambda_2 \end{bmatrix} \begin{bmatrix} x_1 \\ x_2 \end{bmatrix}
\tag{13}
$$

A geometric representation of this equation is given in figure 12.1, where the columns of A are denoted a_1 and a_2, respectively, and RHS is labeled λX. If there are no externalities (so that $\lambda_1 = \lambda_2 < 0$), vector λX necessarily lies in quadrant III. Vectors a_1 and a_2 are constrained only by the requirement that $A = [a_1, a_2]$ is symmetric and negative semi-definite.[4]

The optimality of setting one of the two regulated prices below marginal cost depends on the location of vector λX relative to the cone generated by a_1 and a_2. In figure 12.1, λX lies inside this cone; thus the prices of both commodities exceed their marginal production cost. Generally, if there are no positive externalities, substitutability between the two commodities is sufficient to ensure that both optimal prices exceed marginal cost.

Figure 12.2 shows a demand configuration yielding an optimal price below marginal cost for commodity 2. The precise requirement is given by

$$\frac{\partial x_2}{\partial p_1} \cdot \frac{1}{\lambda_2 x_2} < \frac{\partial x_1}{\partial p_1} \cdot \frac{1}{\lambda_1 x_1} < 0, \tag{14}$$

with

$$\frac{\partial x_2}{\partial p_2} \cdot \frac{\partial x_1}{\partial p_1} > \frac{\partial x_1}{\partial p_2} \cdot \frac{\partial x_2}{\partial p_1}. \tag{15}$$

For $\lambda_1 = \lambda_2$, (14) and (15) can be combined to obtain

$$\frac{p_1 \cdot x_1}{p_2 \cdot x_2} \cdot \frac{\partial x_2}{\partial p_2} \cdot \frac{p_2}{x_2} < \frac{\partial x_2}{\partial p_1} \cdot \frac{p_1}{x_2} < \frac{\partial x_1}{\partial p_1} \cdot \frac{p_1}{x_1} < 0. \tag{16}$$

The logic of this example is straightforward. With no externalities, equation (11) calls for prices to be set such that the proportional reduction in demand is equalized across all commodities in the regulated set. If demand for product 1 is sufficiently greater than demand for product 2 (and the two products are complementary), increasing the price of product 1 yields a proportional reduction in the demand for product 2 which is greater than that of product 1. The price of product 2 must be lowered to counteract this relatively large cross-price effect.

The conditions under which the optimal p_2 is below marginal cost are somewhat restrictive. Nevertheless, it is easy to identify situations in which these conditions are likely to hold, particularly when the demand for x_2 is small relative to the demand for the complementary product x_1. The effect of externalities on the optimal prices is obvious. From equation (8), a value of $e_2 > 1$ will, other things being equal, tend to lower the optimal p_2 and, because of the operation of the budget constraint, raise the optimal p_1. In addition, the optimal p_2 is more likely to be below marginal cost the stronger (weaker) the cross (own) price effect.[5]

Concluding Observations

Although the possibility of regulatorily efficient—or, indeed, profit-maximizing—prices set below marginal cost has been recognized in theory for many years, this possibility has not received the attention it deserves. Further, there appears to have been much greater recognition of the possibility that optimal prices will fall below marginal cost due to externalities than because of demand interrelationships. We suspect that the latter are quite important in many regulated markets, particularly when one price relates to something like access to several services and other prices relate to the rate of use for those services.[6]

Without wishing to overstate the relevance of our purely theoretical findings to the "real world," a few additional observations are in order. First, in the absence of external subsidies, efficient pricing by a regulated, multiproduct monopoly requires that the regulated firm be permitted to capture internally—that is, for it to realize by itself—the gains and losses in revenues and the costs occasioned by demand interdependencies among the regulated products. If this is not the case, the regulated firm cannot satisfy the revenue constraint (5) in an efficient manner. Divestiture of a single regulated firm into several firms will cause efficiency losses if no market or non-market method for pooling revenues is available.

Second, since the existence of either demand interdependencies or externalities may result in some optimally regulated prices being below those that would obtain with neither of these conditions present—and, since a concommitant of this is the likelihood of higher prices for the other regulated products—complicated problems of sustainability arise. Although sustainable prices may well exist for some conditions of nonzero cross elasticities, they need not exist for all cross-elasticity configurations. The same is true with respect to externalities. It is clear from theory that the fact of successful entry into one or more of the markets occupied by an incumbent regulated firm is not conclusive evidence of either the absence of natural monopoly cost conditions or inefficient pricing. As Faulhaber (1975) and others have shown, regulation-imposed entry barriers may be necessary to maintain efficient prices when demands are interdependent or when externalities exist.

Finally, because efficient pricing with or without any $e_i > 1$ may include some prices that are less than marginal cost, a simple marginal-cost test such as the single product Areeda-Turner (1975) rule is not sufficient for assessing entry-preventative predation on the part of the regulated firm. As shown by Ordover-Willig (1981), a price-floor rule can be fashioned to take demand interdependencies into account. The rule uses what has been called the "burden test" and examines changes in contributions to profits and overhead costs, with cross demand effects included. Interestingly, however, the conceptually simpler Baumol (1979) "quasi-permanence" test would still be applicable. The regulated firm could, and should, permanently keep some prices below marginal cost where cross-demand conditions or externalities so require.

Notes

Numerous helpful comments were made by readers of an earlier draft of this chapter, prepared by the senior author. Comments by an anonymous referee led to a substantial recasting of the first version and the inclusion of Gary L. Roberts as co-author. If rank did, indeed, have its privileges, the senior author would be tempted to lay blame for remaining errors on his junior. Roberts, however, denies the existence of privilege; we share the blame for shortcomings.

1. For references, see Atkinson and Stiglitz (1980).

2. Our admittedly "loose" incorporation of consumption externalities follows Rohlfs (1979). A formally superior method of incorporation is provided by Sandmo (1975).

3. See Willig (1976).

4. For any specific choice of utility index, there will obviously be a relationship between A and X. There is no general a priori restriction on the potential configurations, however. Numerical examples yielding at least one optimal price below marginal cost are easily constructed. Let $x_1 = 300 - 2p_1 - p_2$ and $x_2 = 150 - 2p_2 - p_1$ represent demand conditions in the region where prices and quantities are nonnegative, and set $C(x_1, x_2) = 9,150 + 10x_1 + 10x_2$. The appropriate prices are then given by $p_1 = 80$, $p_2 = 5$.

5. The same may be true of profit-maximizing prices for unregulated, multiproduct firms. Tying arrangements, of course, usually involve goods with complementary cross-demand relations and may entail a price for the tying product that is below marginal cost. See Burstein (1960). Even without formal tying arrangements, sellers induce buyers to trade with them by utilizing demand interrelationships. For example, gambling casinos entice patrons through use of low-priced transportation, lodging, and food. Presumably, this practice increases the demand for gambling—where price seems to exceed marginal cost. Less notoriously, stores in a shopping mall may jointly provide free parking—that is, an access price below marginal cost—to encourage customers to visit the mall.

6. The earlier version of this chapter used telecommunications as a reference. The market conditions assumed in that version depicted x_2 as being roughly related to access to the system and x_1 as being use of the system. This is not a realistic view of the demands for telecommunications services, however; demand for access is clearly derived from the consumer surplus attaching to the use of linear prices for toll services. This relationship means that the two demands are complementary. Contrary to the conditions shown here, it also means that correct analysis must be in the context of two-part tariffs. Roberts includes in his forthcoming doctoral dissertation a formal, two-part tariff version of the pricing rules given here.

References

Areeda, P., and D. Turner (1975). "Predatory Pricing and Related Practices under Section 2 of the Sherman Act." *Harvard Law Review* 88 (3), 697.

Atkinson, A. B., and J. E. Stiglitz (1980). *Lectures on Public Economics*. McGraw-Hill, New York.

Baumol, W. J. (1979). "Quasi-Permanence of Price Reductions: A Policy for Prevention of Predatory Pricing." *Yale Law Journal* 89 (1), 1–26.

Baumol, W. J., and D. F. Bradford (1970). "Optimal Departures from Marginal Cost Pricing." *American Economic Review* 60 (3), 265–283.

Burstein, M. L. (1960). "The Economics of Tie-In Sales." *Review of Economics and Statistics* 42 (1), 68–73.

Faulhaber, G. R. (1975). "Cross-Subsidization: Pricing in Public Enterprises." *American Economics Review* 65 (5), 966–977.

Ordover, J. A., and R. D. Willig (1981). "An Economic Definition of Predation: Pricing and Product Innovation." *Yale Law Journal* 91 (1), 8–53.

Rohlfs, J. (1979). "Economically Efficient Bell System Pricing." Bell Laboratories Economic Discussion Paper No. 138.

Sandmo, A. (1975). "Optimal Taxation in the Presence of Externalities." *Swedish Journal of Economics*, 77, 86–98.

Willig, R. D. (1976). "Consumer Surplus Without Apology." *American Economic Review* 66 (4), 589–597

Contributors

M. A. Adelman is Professor of Economics, Massachusetts Institute of Technology

Roy T. Englert, Jr. is an associate in the law firm of Wilmer, Cutler & Pickering, Washington, D.C.

Franklin M. Fisher is Professor of Economics, Massachusetts Institute of Technology

George A. Hay is Professor of Law and Economics, Cornell University

Paul L. Joskow is Professor of Economics, MIT

William J. Kolasky, Jr. is a partner in the law firm of Wilmer, Cutler & Pickering, Washington, D.C.

Robin C. Landis is an associate in the law firm of Cravath, Swaine & Moore, New York

John J. McGowan was Vice President of Charles River Associates, Boston

James W. McKie is Professor of Economics, The University of Texas at Austin

Forrest Nelson is Associate Professor of Economics, University of Iowa

Roger Noll is Professor of Economics, Stanford University

J. A. Ordover is Professor of Economics, New York University and Adjunct Professor of Law, Columbia University Law School

Almarin Phillips is Hower Professor of Public Policy and Professor of Economics and Law, University of Pennsylvania

Phillip A. Proger is a partner in the law firm of Baker & Hostetler, Washington, D.C. and Adjunct Professor of Law at the Georgetown University Law Center

Robert J. Reynolds is Senior Economist, ICF Incorporated

Gary L. Roberts is on the staff of the Federal Trade Commission

Ronald S. Rolfe is a partner in the law firm of Cravath, Swaine & Moore, New York

Bruce E. Stangle is a principal in Analysis Group, Inc., Cambridge, Massachusetts

A. O. Sykes is an associate in the law firm of Arnold & Porter, Washington, D.C.

R. D. Willig is Professor of Economics and Public Affairs, Princeton University

Index

Acquisition bans, and Hart-Scott-Rodino
　Act, 71
Adelman, Morris A., ix, 101–110
Anticompetitive behavior:
　analysis of, 133–141
　as barrier to entry, 134–136
　criteria for, 133–136
　incentives for, 118–124
　injunctions and, 51–52
　mergers as incentive for, 121–123
　nonprice, 115–129
　price discrimination as incentive for,
　　119–121
　pricing rigidities as incentive for, 121–123
　rate-of-return regulation as incentive for,
　　123–124
　specific practices of, 136–141
　　cancellation penalties, 139–140
　　integration of function, 138
　　long term leases, 139–140
　　"premature" announcement of new
　　　products, 140–141
　　tying, 136–138
　tactics of, 115
Antitrust policy:
　antitrust laws, and promotion of efficiency,
　　204–213
　in petroleum industry, 15–42
　profits-concentration relationship
　　and, 2
　White House Task Force on (1969), 2
Areeda, P., 134, 305

Bain, Joe S., 2, 6, 135
Barrier(s) to entry:
　and anticompetitive behavior, 134–136
　defined, 134–135, 145–146 n
　reentry, defined, 129 n
Baumol, W. J., 299, 305
Baxter, William F., 50, 59, 71
Bothwell, James L., 102

Bradford, D. F., 299
Bradley, Joseph F., 56
Broadcast industry, allocation of spectrum in,
　241–260
　experimental procedure for, 244–251
　mathematical model for, 245
　problems of, 242–245
　simulation of committee decision making in,
　　251–260
Broadcast industry, network television. (See
　also Financial Interest and Syndication
　Rules for Network Television)
　antitrust cases and, 265–270
　economics of, 270–290
　economies of integration in, 272–274
　financial risks of program development in,
　　274–276
　financial risk-sharing, 276–280
　monopsony in, 280–282
　program development process in, 263–265
　scale economics in, 271–272
　"warehousing" in, 268–270, 282–285
Brozen, Yale, 2

Capacity, excess, 19–20
Cities Service Company ("Cities"), 16–42
　and production of gasoline, 33–42
　and production of kerojet, 18–33
City of Mishawaka, 199–204, 219, 220
Clayton Act, and anticompetitive mergers,
　51–52
Competition:
　fringe area, 212–213
　paradigm of, 1
　in petroleum industry, 15–42
　and profits, 160
　retail, 209–212
Complementarity, supply, 86
Conduct (marketing) orders, 70–71
Coops (cooperative facilities), 177 (See also
　Electric power industry)

Cost(s):
  marginal, 299–306
  supply curves and, 155–158
Cross-elasticity, of supply, 98 n

Demand substitution (of kerojet for other
    fuels), 27–30
Demsetz, H., 3
Divestiture:
  and anticompetitive mergers, 51
  post-merger, efficacy of, 52–56
Dixon, Paul Rand, 57

Electric power industry:
  application of antitrust laws and, 182–185
  coops (cooperative facilities) in, 177
  effects of price-squeeze litigation on,
    223–227
  federal power systems in, 177
  franchises in, 205–209
  fringe area competition in, 212–213
  intentional price squeeze and, 213–222
  IOUs (privately owned utilities) in, 175–176
  munis (municipal utilities in), 176–177
  "pancaking" and rate increases in, 195
  policies in, 173–227
  price-squeeze doctrine and, 185–220
  Public Utility Holding Company Act of 1935
    and, 183
  Public Utility Regulatory Policy Act of 1978
    and, 179
  regulation of, 175–182
  retail competition in, 209–212
  retail sales in, 175
  Robinson Patman Act and, 183
  Rural Electrification Act (REA) of 1936 and,
    177
  scope of, 175
  Sherman Act and, 183
  structure of, 175–182
  unintentional price squeeze and, 222–223
  wholesale transactions in, 175
Elzinga, Kenneth, 52, 70
Elzinga Study, of post-merger divestiture,
    52–53
Englert, Roy T., Jr., ix, **49–72**
Entrenchment, 8
Entry: (*See also* Barrier(s) to entry)
  of kerojet, 19
  potential, 6–8
Evans, David S., vii

Federal Communications Commission (FCC),
    responsibilities of, 242–245
Federal Energy Regulatory Commission
    (FERC): (*See also* Electric power industry)
  price-squeeze test of, 194

and regulation of IOUs, 179, 180–182
Federal Power Act: (*See also* Electric power
    industry)
  and allocation of hydroelectric power, 178
  and IOUs, 180
Federal Trade Commission Act, 51–52
Financial Interest and Syndication Rules for
    Network Television, 263–296 (*See also*
    Broadcast industry, network television)
  equation for effects of on price equilibrium,
    293–294
  and programming attractiveness, 291–296
  and programming price, 291–296
  proposed repeal of, 267–268
  retention of, 285–290
Fisher, Franklin M., vii–xii, 3, 4, 133–134,
    153–170, **263–296**, 266, 305
"fix it first" rule, 59
FPC v Conway, 188, 189–192, 197
Franchise(s):
  and electric power industry, 205–209
  and supply curves, 155–158
Franchise(s), exclusive, 153–170
  and costs, 157, 158–168
  and negative externalities in distribution,
    157, 158–168
  competitive dealers versus full integration
    and, 158–162
  competitive dealers versus monopoly dealer
    and, 162–166
  real differences among firms and, 156–157
  rising input prices and, 157
FTC v Exxon Corporation, 70
Function, integration of, 138

Gasoline:
  Cities Service Company and, 33–42
  Gulf Oil Corporation and, 33–42
  marketing of, 33–35
  measurement of market shares of, 34, 35
Greenwood, Joen E., vii, **133–134**
Guidelines of the Department of Justice for
    Mergers (1968), 1, 8–9
Guidelines of the Department of Justice for
    Mergers (1982), 15, 16, 41–42, 72, 86
Gulf Oil Corporation ("Gulf"), 16–42
  and gasoline, 33–42
  and kerojet, 18–33

Hand, Learned, 141–142
Hart-Scott-Rodino Antitrust Improvements
    Act (1976), 49
  and acquisition bans, 71
  passage of, 57
Hay, George, vii, ix, **15–42**
Herfindahl-Hirschman Index (HHI), 16
  calculation of, 43 n

Hold-separate decree, 69–70

Injunctions, and anticompetitive mergers, 51–52
Integration, vertical, 4–6 (*See also* Franchise(s), exclusive)
and entry barriers, 5
and foreclosure, 5, 6
and integrated entry, 5
and Task Force on Productivity and Competition, 6
International Salt Company v United States, 50
IOUs (privately owned utilities): (*See also* Electric power industry)
Federal Energy Regulatory Commission (FERC) and, 179, 180–182
Federal Power Act and, 180
Public Utility Regulatory Policy Act of 1978 and, 179
regulation of, 178–182
Robinson Patman Act and, 183
Sherman Act and, 183

Joskow, Paul L., x, 173–227

Kauper, Thomas F., 56, 57
Keeler, Theodore E., 102
Kerojet:
Caribbean imports of, 30–32
and Cities Service Company, 18–33
demand substitution of by airlines, 27–30
entry of, 19
excess capacity of, 19–20
and Gulf Oil Corporation, 18–33
market-share calculations of, 18–19
"overflying" and supply of, 28, 29
"recapture" and supply of, 29
supply flexibility of, 19
supply substitution of, 21–24
"tankering" of, 28
Kolasky, William J., ix, 49–72
Kwoka, John, 3

Landis, Robin C., x, 131–143
Lerner index, equation for, 109
Long-term leases, and anticompetition, 139–140

McGowan, John J., vii–ix, 1–11, 3, 4, 59–60, 133–134, 266
McKie, James W., ix, 85–97
Mann, Michael, 2
Market conduct, Sherman Act and, 131–143
Market, geographic:
analysis of, 35, 38, 39, 40
and the petroleum industry, 24–27
Market performance, and conduct, 1

Market share:
defined, 101
and profitability, 101–110
Marketing (conduct) orders, 70–71
Merger(s), 1–11 (*See also* Merger(s), anticompetitive)
acquisition bans and, 71–72
divestiture and, 51
economic principles of, 1
as efficiency enhancers, 8–9, 59–60
as incentive for anticompetition, 121–123
policy, 10, 11
profits-concentration relationship and, 2–4
Merger(s), anticompetitive 49–72
Clayton Act and, 51–52
conduct (marketing) orders and, 70–71
guidelines for relief for, 60–72
hold-separate order and, 69–70
injunctions and, 51–52
premerger notification and, 56–58
rescission and, 69
restructuring of, 58–59, 61–69
Yale Study of, 53–55
Merger Guidelines of the Department of Justice for 1968, 1, 8–9
Merger Guidelines of the Department of Justice for 1982, 15, 16, 41–42, 72, 86
Monopsony, in broadcast industry, 280–282
Mueller, Willard F., 57
Munis (municipal utilities), 176–177 (*See also* Electric power industry)

Nelson, Forrest, x–xi, 241–260
Nixon, Richard M., and Task Force on Productivity and Competition, 6
Noll, Roger, vii, x–xi, 241–260

Oil, crude, refinement of, 17, 18
Ordover, J. A., x, 115–129, 303
Otter Tail Power Company v United States, 199, 201
"Overflying," 28, 29

PAD (Petroleum Administration for Defense) Districts, 17
"Pancaking," and rate increases, 195
Peck, Merton J., vii
Penalties, cancellation, 139–140
Perry, Martin K., 187
Petroleum Administration for Defense (PAD) Districts, 17
Petroleum industry: (*See also* Cities Service Company; Gasoline; Gulf Oil Corporation; Kerojet)
antitrust policies in, 15–42
competition in, 15–42
Pfunder, Malcolm, 53

Phillips, Almarin, xi, **299–306**
Plaine, Daniel, 53
Premerger notification, and anticompetitive
  mergers, 56–58
Price(s), optimal:
 general rule for, 299–304
 two-commodity case for, 303–304
Price discrimination, 119–121
Price rigidities, 121–123
Price squeeze(s):
 doctrine of, 188, 189–192, 197
 economics of, 116–117
 in electric power industry, 185–220
 intentional, 213–222
 as monopolizing device, 186
 unintentional, 222–223
Price-squeeze test, 194
Profits:
 competition and, 160
 monopoly and, 162
Profits-concentration relationship, 1–4
Profitability:
 equation for, 101
 and market share, 101–110
Proger, Phillip A., ix, **49–72**
Public Utility Holding Company Act of 1935,
  183
Public Utility Regulatory Policy Act of 1978,
  179

Rate-of-return regulation, 123–124
Ravenscraft, David, 3, 102
"Recapture," 29
Reciprocity, 7, 8
Refining, of crude oil, 17, 18
Rescission, 69
Restructuring, 61–63
Reynolds, Robert J., ix, **15–42**
Roberts, Gary L., xi, 299, 306
Robinson Patman Act, 183
Rodino, Peter W., Jr., 57
Rolfe, Ronald, S., x, **131–143**
Rural Electrification Act (REA) of 1936, 177

Scherer, F. M., 39–40, 102
Schmalensee, Richard, 109
Shepherd, William G., 102
Sherman Act:
 and electric power industry, 183
 and market conduct, 131–143
SIC (*see* Standard Industrial Classification)
Solomon, Ezra, 3
Standard Industrial Classification (SIC), 85,
  87–97
 and antitrust suits, 90–96
 basis of classification of, 87–89
 and constrained *de novo* entry, 90–91

description of, 96–97
 and substitutions, 92–95
Stangle, Bruce E., ix, **101–110**
Stauffer, Thomas R., 3
Stigler, George J., 2, 40, 135
Supply:
 complementarity of, 86
 cross-elasticity of, 98 n
 flexibility of (kerojet), 19
 inferior source of, 118–119
 substitution of, 21–24, 86
Supply curves, franchises and, 155–158
Sykes, A. O., x, **115–129**
Sylos-Labini, Paolo, 6

"Tankering," 28
Television (*see* Broadcast industry)
Tennessee Valley Authority (TVA), 177
Turner, D., 134, 305
Tying, 136–138
 defined, 147 n

*United States v Aluminum Company of
  America*, x, 132, 141, 186–188, 193, 218
United States v CBS, 266
*United States v E. I. du Pont de Nemours and
  Company*, 51
*United States v United Shoe Machinery
  Corporation*, 139

von Weizsacker, C. C., 134–135

Wallich, Henry C., vii
"Warehousing" of television programs,
  268–270, 282–285
Weiss, Leonard W., 9, 101, 102
White House Task Force on Antitrust Policy
  (1969), 2
Whittemore, Anne Marie, 53
Williamson, Oliver E., 9
Willig, R. D., x, **115–129**, 305

Yale Study of anticompetitive mergers, 53–55